THE "NEW WOMAN" REVISED

THE "NEW WOMAN" REVISED

PAINTING AND GENDER POLITICS ON
FOURTEENTH STREET

ELLEN WILEY TODD

UNIVERSITY OF CALIFORNIA PRESS

BERKELEY   LOS ANGELES   OXFORD

University of California Press
Berkeley and Los Angeles, California

University of California Press, Ltd.
Oxford, England
© 1993 by
The Regents of the University of California

Library of Congress Cataloging-in-Publication Data

Todd, Ellen Wiley.
    The "new woman" revised : painting and gender politics on
fourteenth street / Ellen Wiley Todd.
        p. cm.
    Includes bibliographical references and index.
    ISBN 0-520-07471-8 (cloth : alk. paper)
        1. Feminism and art—New York (N.Y.)—Catalogs. 2. Art, American—
New York (N.Y.)—Catalogs. 3. Art, Modern—20th century—New York
(N.Y.)—Catalogs. I. Title.
    N72.F45T6 1993
    757'.4'0974710904—dc20

                                                    91-44292

The publisher gratefully acknowledges the contribution provided by the Art Book
Endowment Fund of the Associates of the University of California Press, which is
supported by a major gift from the Ahmanson Foundation.

Publication of this book has been aided by a grant from the Millard Meiss
Publication Fund of the College Art Association of America.

Printed in the United States of America
9 8 7 6 5 4 3 2 1

FOR MARTIN

CONTENTS

ACKNOWLEDGMENTS

When my niece Karen Todd wrote a biographical sketch of me for her eighth-grade English class, she contrasted her impatient nature to my deliberate one: "she takes life the way she eats crab: she does the work first, then delicately picks at the cleaned meat." Witnessing at the time my total absorption in full-time teaching and dissertation writing, she marveled at what she perceived as my ability to sustain a high degree of deferred gratification. Throughout this project, composing acknowledgments has been, like savoring cleaned crab, a great source of pleasurable anticipation. It marks a point of closure and the moment when I can finally commit to print sentences that, in spite of a lengthy mental gestation, convey all too inadequately my gratitude to those whose support made this book possible. I can only hope that the individuals mentioned here can move beyond the limiting convention of names in acknowledgments to recall the moments of collegial interaction, intellectual exchange and collaboration, and friendship that sustain all our scholarly endeavors—and which have been mine in abundance.

A fellowship from the Smithsonian Institution, a grant from the Samuel H. Kress Foundation, and a summer stipend from George Mason University contributed to the research and writing of the book. Judith Zilczer at the Hirshhorn Museum and Sculpture Garden, Virginia Mecklenberg and Lois Fink at the National Museum of American Art, and Garnett McCoy and the staff at the Archives of American Art provided invaluable guidance during my fellowship. In 1987, I was invited to take part in a summer institute on "Theory and Interpretation in the Visual Arts" sponsored by the National Endowment for the Humanities. All the participants in our lively group challenged me to rethink the theoretical framework of the book, especially Shelly Errington, Kathryn Fruhan, Ludmilla Jordanova, Janet Kaplan, Linda Nochlin, and Irit Rogoff. I am enormously grateful to Michael Ann Holly and Keith Moxey for including me in the institute and for their ongoing engagement with the project. I would also like to thank the Millard Meiss Publication Fund of the College Art Association of America for awarding a subsidy to support the production of this book.

Private collectors who opened their homes so that I might view paintings and museums and galleries that have allowed me to view and research individual works are acknowledged in the list of illustrations. Special thanks are due to the staff members at the Forum Gallery, the Midtown Payson Galleries, and the Zabriskie Gallery; to Toni Powers at Dodge Color Photo, Inc.; and to Anita Duquette at the Whitney Museum of American Art for her help in locating obscure photographs. I am indebted to Sheila Levine and Stephanie Fay at the University of California Press: Sheila's commitment to the manuscript and her unwavering calm during my anxious moments have been invaluable—and her friendship one of the rewards of this process. Stephanie scrutinized the manuscript at every level, expertly sharpening my wandering prose. My colleagues in the Art and Art History Department at George Mason University never failed to understand my immersion in the writing and editing of the manuscript and the complexities of production.

Over the years, at conferences and informal gatherings, I have benefited from numerous interchanges with friends and colleagues in Art History, American Studies, and Women's Studies. For their contributions and encouragement I thank Denise Albanese, Nancy Anderson, Brandon Brame Fortune, Marilyn Cohen, Diane Dillon, Marianne Doezema, Estelle Freedman, Jim Herbert, Helen Langa, Suzanne Lewis, David Lubin, Michael Marlais, Elizabeth Milroy, Wendy Owens, Kathy Peiss, Phyllis Rosenszweig, Roy Rosenszweig, Sally Stein, Susan Sterling, Claire Tieder, Amy Vandersall, Alan Wallach, Tom Willette, and Rebecca Zurier. Insightful comments from Patricia Hills, Patricia Mathews, Whitney Chadwick, and Roland Marchand helped me to rework the manuscript in its later stages.

Two scholars in American Art History changed the course of my own academic life. At a crucial turning point in graduate school, Elizabeth Johns urged me to trust my instinct and study American Art. She welcomed me into her graduate study group at the University of Maryland, making it possible for me to continue exploring a new field; thanks to her I have never looked back. In all areas of academic endeavor, Wanda Corn continues to be a shining example. No matter what the demands of her own scholarly, professional, or teaching activities, she patiently unraveled numerous dissertation drafts, interrogated my assumptions, and helped me reshape the project—tasks performed with her keen awareness of the always present but seldom obvious relation between the person and the project. I cannot imagine how this book could have been written without her.

Not all debts are scholarly ones. Through twenty years of friendship, Janet Martin never lost faith in me. Doreen and Harold Zisla and Ilene Birge saw me through difficult personal times with unmeasurable love and generosity. As kind and forgiving roommates at various stages of the process Cindy Meyers-Seifer, Gail Sonnemann, and Denise Albanese deserve special thanks. Suzanne Kinser continues to inspire me with her own devotion to writing. Cathy Popkin's well-developed sense of the insignificant, coupled with her ironic wit, has transformed scholarly despair into wry amusement on many occasions. Joan Stevenson, my regular partner for two years of memorable Monday lunches, helped me launch this, and other of life's projects. Closer to home, Beverly Hitchins and Gail Walker have boosted my spirits with many happy evenings.

This book was written during a 1989–90 leave of absence, which I spent in Columbia, South Carolina. There I reap the one benefit of a commuting relationship—a second home with wonderful friends and colleagues. The scholars on Hagood Avenue produced three manuscripts that year, thanks in part to excellent communal meals, calming postprandial dog walks, and spontaneous philosophical conversations. Ferdy Schoeman was always close at hand, expressing thoughtful interest in my work, and he and Sara Schecter Schoeman gave unforgettable meaning to neighborhood life. I am grateful to Joan Gero and Lee Jane Kaufman for our spirited feminist lunches. I would also like to thank Stephen Loring, David Whiteman, Brad Collins, R. I. G. Hughes, Alfred and Angela Nordmann, and Davis Baird. Finally there was Linda Weingarten. Over afternoon teas at the end of our respective workdays, Linda and I savored the pleasures of women's space and time. Her intuitive wisdom, her joy at friendship's adventure, and her courage delighted and motivated me in ways I may never fully understand, but will never forget.

There can be no greater satisfaction than combining close friendship with scholarly and personal interests. I share this special configuration with four women who, with rich and abundant insights, have patiently read and commented on virtually every word of this project in its various permutations. At George Mason University, Sheila ffolliott has been the ideal colleague, helping me read the old masters and think about feminist art history. Barbara Melosh has been a thoughtful and skillful guide to the cultural history of the Depression. Our suppertime readings in literature, film, and feminist theory, not to mention her own work on New Deal public art, contributed enormously to my rethinking the manuscript and to the quality of my life. Though academic geography has placed us at great distances from one another, Melissa Dabakis and Cécile Whiting have been my most challenging critics and my greatest sources of inspiration. I cannot possibly convey in a sentence what a decade of intellectual collaboration and companionship has meant. I can only hope that since they sometimes know what I am feeling before I do myself they will understand the fullness of my gratitude when I thank them for the gift of their friendship.

I am fortunate to have the encouragement of a wonderful family, whose history and customs are woven through this book in ways that continue to surprise me. My grandmother Frances Ellen Wiley Hofman, who marked her one-hundredth birthday shortly before her death two years ago, was my first new woman. Determined and fiercely independent, she was a business executive, devoted to her family, a dedicated consumer of every conceivable new technology, and clear about women's proper roles—everthing imaginable but the priesthood and the presidency. Though she might have quibbled with some of my assessments, I know she would have been pleased. My parents, Jan and Rocky Gray, gave me a New York home for lengthy stretches of research, well after they thought the nest was empty, and enthusiastically followed exhibitions and publications to learn about my artists. Their love and support made the book possible long before it began.

My sister, Sarah Todd, has cheered this book from afar, contributing her fine artist's eye to the analysis of pictures and her excellent photography to all stages of the project. I thank her for her gift of unconditional sisterly affection, for her intelligent perspective, and for sharing her wise and whimsical daughter, Frances Garretson, with me.

I can never properly thank Bill, Eva, and Karen Todd for all that they have so unselfishly given me—from the years of family walks and Sunday dinners to the unspoken understanding of all my choices. As senior family academic, Bill has been both my adviser and friend, rejoicing with me at every milestone. Early on he provided a model of integrity for a scholar-teacher's life and offered sage counsel. If I cannot repay his many gifts, I look forward to presenting this book, hoping it will be worthy of standing alongside his own contributions on the family bookshelf. Finally, watching Karen become a young woman of grace and intellect has been deeply satisfying; I would remind her that she too continues to be a "significant person" in my life.

True to Karen's characterization, I have saved the best for last. Martin Donougho has been my wise and gentle companion for the last five years, patiently enduring the pleasures and pitfalls of book production. He gave me a room of my own for writing, deployed his philosophical acumen to tighten my arguments, reanimated my drooping spirits with another brisk walk—accompanied by lively discussions from his storehouse of cultural knowledge—and has generously followed baseball rather more than I do cricket. My life is immeasurably enriched by his presence. So that he might know how much his love has meant, I dedicate this book to him.

E. W. T.
Washington, D.C.
May 1992

ILLUSTRATIONS

MAPS

PLATES
Following page 78

INTRODUCTION

But there *is* no single all-embracing theory of the subject and social relations in history, and women gain nothing from indulging the humanist desire for one. We have to work with different frameworks in the full knowledge of their incompatibility, testing them against each other, reading through them the historical material that can itself throw light on their usefulness.

LISA TICKNER,
"Feminism, Art History, and Sexual Difference"

Between the world wars, four New York City painters from a group later called the Fourteenth Street School added new female types to American Scene painting and produced a distinctive iconography of American womanhood. Taking their subject matter from the Union Square–Fourteenth Street district where they rented studios, the urban realists Kenneth Hayes Miller (1876–1952), Reginald Marsh (1898–1954), Raphael Soyer (1899–1987), and Isabel Bishop (1902–1988) portrayed the neighborhood's women as shoppers, office workers, and salesgirls. Known as the poor man's Fifth Avenue, the Fourteenth Street neighborhood housed bargain clothing stores, movie theaters, small offices, banks, and insurance companies as well as the headquarters of numerous radical organizations and publications. These institutions answered consumers' needs and provided jobs or community and political networks for the ethnically diverse population that converged on the district from New York's Lower East Side.

Shoppers and working women were almost unprecedented in American art. Why do they appear at this time? Most obviously because they were everywhere in the Fourteenth Street neighborhood and thus were logical subjects for artists dedicated to American Scene realism—the depiction of modern society as it appeared in their immediate environment. Furthermore, although modern buying and selling patterns had been introduced as early as the 1880s, they finally consolidated only in the 1920s. In the interwar period, with increased mass production, widely available products, and a vastly expanded advertising industry, Americans themselves became conscious of consumption as central to their way of life.[1] Novels, government tracts, social science monographs, and articles by social commentators, educators, and activists "documented and dissected, celebrated and abominated the new culture of consumption."[2] As "household managers" (a phrase advertisers coined to glamorize the American housewife) women were the primary consumers.

They also staffed the enormous bargain emporiums and small specialty stores that surrounded Union Square, and they served as secretaries in the banks and insurance and utility companies.[3] Nationwide, the clerical worker and saleswoman were well established in the labor force. Businesses had increased their use of office machines and had developed bureaucracies that required efficient secretarial workers, and the garment and retail industries had expanded. Between 1890 and 1920 the number of women typists, stenographers, and salespeople grew from 171,000 to 2 million, and among working women the percentage employed in the clerical and sales fields rose from 5.3 to 25.6.[4] By 1930 one out of every five working women in the country held a clerical job, and in New York City the ratio was nearly one out of every three.[5]

In these shoppers and workers the artists found female types who exemplified the New Woman in her public role. Since the end of the nineteenth century the phrase "New Woman" had been the focal point for an ideological discourse on gender difference and the changing social order. Numerous forms of representation—including art, literature, cartoons, cinema, and advertising—shaped this discourse, interpreting and constructing the social relationship between the sexes—"constructing" because sexual identity is neither biologically determined nor fixed, but rather made and remade under historical circumstances. Works by the Fourteenth Street School, which participated fully in this discourse, can be read as part of the process by which the feminine was constructed at the time.

This book examines how four artists developed pictorial strategies that embody changing ideologies of gender during the interwar period. Each painter self-consciously merged features of the contemporary scene with old master conventions: Miller and Bishop adopted images of women from classical sculpture and from Renaissance and baroque portraiture for their subjects; Soyer took images of female workers from nineteenth-century genre painting; and Marsh borrowed sexual stereotypes from contemporary advertising and cinema and placed them in settings that hark back to historical, mythological, or religious subjects. The artists' strategy served several purposes. First, it ennobled the "common man," celebrating the democratic ideals of average Americans during the Depression. Furthermore, it legitimated American painting by placing it within the canon of Western European art. A home-grown American realism that was also part of an established tradition functioned as an antidote to encroaching European modernism. By the end of the 1920s American art critics who despised the work of Picasso and Matisse were calling for a new American renaissance; the urban scene painting of the Fourteenth Street School answered the call. Finally, in conflating artistic traditions and the contemporary scene, the paintings addressed the issue of female types, one not necessarily discussed by the institutional practitioners of American art. The paintings can thus be situated in the larger discourse on new womanhood and shown to embody dominant ideologies of gender, occupation, and class.

Commentators observing the bourgeois woman's growing engagement with educational, political, and occupational pursuits outside the home began by the 1890s to characterize her as the "New Woman," an independent person with a public role. Successive generations of women and men from various political and social perspectives invoked the phrase in analyzing and celebrating the changing behavior of modern women—or in abhorring and condemning it. Although new womanhood was primarily a middle-class discourse, the phrase "New Woman" eventually encompassed many meanings, accumulated class-specific stereotypes, and, as Carroll Smith-Rosenberg has argued, challenged existing gender relations and the distribution of power.[6]

Different ideals of new womanhood came to reflect the accomplishments and the preoccupations of different generations of women. Around the turn of the century, for example, the New Woman had a college education, campaigned for the vote, became a social worker in the spirit of Progressive Era reform, and frequently remained single. By the teens, the emergence of a modern discourse on feminism and debates about sexuality sharpened discussions about the New Woman. After enfranchisement and into the Depression, women and men shied away from the collective demands of feminist political reform in favor of an individualized feminism. The period was one of accommodation between older and newer models of femininity as well as one of divisiveness among feminists, who debated notions of equality versus difference and woman-centered versus heterosexual ideals.[7] The New Woman of the 1920s and 1930s was a moderate sort, hoping to capitalize on new job possibilities and to make herself attractive with the mass-produced products of the clothing and cosmetics industries. Unlike many of her older feminist sisters, she was unwilling to sacrifice the dream of a newly fashionable companionate marriage for a career. This revised New Woman of the 1920s chose feminized activities. At home, she focused on consumption; if she worked, she sought either a clerical or a retail sales position.

The Fourteenth Street School's representations of women both participate in the larger discourse on new womanhood and, for the most part, affirm traditional ideologies of domesticity, heterosexuality, femininity, and motherhood. None of the images, however, can be definitively linked to a single unifying conception of womanhood, or to a particular constituency of feminist viewers. Moreover, despite the effects of combining contemporary and old master conventions, many of the paintings enact or expose incipient contradictions in the positions designated for women in the consumer culture and at work. Through iconography and style—space, figure composition, color, and light—and through nuances in the painterly surface, the works often question what is imaged and reveal shifts or tensions embedded in the social fabric.

Any discussion of new womanhood and its representations must emphasize the historical and ideological complexity of both.[8] At any given historical moment new womanhood encompasses contradictory discourses on gender difference related to sexuality, motherhood, work, the family, feminism, femininity, and masculinity—to name only the most obvious. New womanhood is thus one site of the continuous production, definition, and redefinition of women's roles and women's behavior. It is where various political and power-related interests intersect. The phrase "new womanhood" can be shown to reproduce or challenge dominant ideologies, depending on when, how, by whom, and in whose interests the term is used and to what ends. Neither the "new" nor the "woman" of this construct is a fixed term. Analyzing new womanhood involves determining whether the new woman is continuous with earlier and more traditional conceptions of woman, or how the notion "woman" at a given moment is understood in relation to the notion "man."[9]

All these considerations shape my study, the questions it raises, its methods of analysis, and my own position as a viewer and interpreter of the paintings. They grow out of recent concerns in feminist art history and, more generally, the relation between feminist theory and women's history. To think about new womanhood (a socially constructed and historically shifting category of woman) and its representations (produced by historically situated makers under specific historical circumstances and shaping our perceptions of social reality) is to ask what notions of sexual difference and gender relations are played out in these paintings, how that process is being accomplished, and to what effect.

To address these questions, I interpret the paintings as both historically embedded and characterized by intertextuality, understanding the two conditions as intertwined. I am using *intertextuality* here as Lisa Tickner does, conceiving of the work of art as a text rather than a discrete object of value. This visual text as such loses its boundaries and becomes a site where meanings are "constantly circulated and exchanged among other texts [i.e. paintings, writings] and between other sites in the social formation [i.e. new womanhood]."[10] This project involves combining potentially contradictory (though not irreconcilable) insights from poststructuralism, Marxism, and feminism. I share the concerns of materialist feminists who want both to understand language as a source of meaning and the locus of human subjectivity and to grasp the historically specific experience (the social, economic, political, and institutional practices and habits) of individuals who produce or view or inhabit a particular set of representations—in this project, the artists, the subjects of the images, and the viewing audience. I will shuttle in different chapters between the paintings, the artists, and the viewer—both then and now—and their particular engagement with the ideological discourse of new womanhood.

Chapters 1–3 provide a historical and methodological framework for readings of individual works by the four artists considered in Chapters 4–7. Chapter 1, "The 'New Woman' Revised," examines visual and verbal representations of new womanhood from the 1890s to the Depression in light of the situation in which the New Woman arose, brought into the public arena by technology and industry, her life reshaped by institutional and political changes. In this initial chapter I take up the multiple senses I attach to my title. The New Woman has been revised—"real" women experienced the world in new ways as a result of historically changed circumstances in the twenties and thirties. The paintings express these historical changes, in part by altering turn-of-the-century conventions of urban realism or figurative painting. At the same time, the discourse of new womanhood is under continuous revision, negotiation, and contestation through a variety of representational/textual practices. Finally, I am re-viewing both the historically situated new women (and men) and the discourse of new womanhood through my own contemporary lens.

In this chapter and throughout my study I interpret paintings as visual texts with fluid boundaries, open and connected to other visual and verbal representations that carry the rhetoric of new womanhood. I use the term *language* (with special emphasis on pictorial language) as the historian Joan Scott broadly defines it: "any meaning-constituting system—strictly verbal or other—through which meaning is constructed and cultural practices organized."[11] Language becomes the starting point for understanding how social relations are conceived and how they work. Although certain poststructuralists claim that language (and hence texts) have no single fixed meaning, the premise that "all the world's a text" suggests that there can be no understanding of individual texts. Meanings (of new womanhood, for example) are endlessly deferred or totally relativized. I argue instead that there is a range of possible meanings within which a text can be understood. Texts acquire meanings within specific interpretive communities at any given historical moment, and meanings change as those communities shift and bring new understanding to the cultural codes by which the texts are structured.[12] Images of women in the Fourteenth Street School paintings elicited different responses from contemporary male and female viewers; as part of a later interpretive community of feminist art historians, I ask how the various components of these artists' pictorial language came to signify a range of largely conventional and acceptable notions of womanhood within a larger discourse on the New Woman.

Michel Foucault's concept of discourse is useful in answering questions about the role of language and the structure of institutions in constituting meaning. Joan Scott, examining poststructuralist theory for feminism, points out that discourse is neither language, text, nor image but rather a "historically, socially, and institutionally specific structure of statements, terms, categories and beliefs." Meanings are contested within "discursive fields of force" whose power resides in claims to knowledge—claims that are themselves embodied in writing, in professional organizations, and in social relationships. Since discourse is expressed in organizations and institutions as well as in words (or images), these also function as documents to be read. Art schools and art history, for example, are institutions supporting the discourses of art; the institutionalized discourse of advertising and home economics contributed powerfully to the social construction of womanhood. Finally, Scott points out that discursive fields "overlap, influence, and compete with one another," appealing to their respective (apparent) objective and (hence) unquestionable truths for authority and legitimation.[13]

Foucault's concept of discourse and discursive field makes it possible to show how seemingly different texts or arguments share the same assumptions. Thus, as part of showing how new womanhood is constructed in the paintings, this study will also ask how such representations work within or against other constructions of new womanhood in other texts, other discursive fields, and other levels of ideological practice.[14] These images have been constructed within the discursive field of art—one that includes texts on art criticism and theory, artists' biographies, and the practices of educational institutions and museums. But the New Woman as shopper and worker has also been constituted within other historically specific texts. I set these texts against one another to show how the pictures embody contemporary attitudes and perceptions about women's lives, reinforcing or, occasionally, challenging dominant patriarchal assumptions.

Chapter 2 introduces artists whose lives are neither well known nor fully chronicled and draws on interpretive material ranging from my own interviews with Soyer, Bishop, and surviving friends of the artists to archival, biographical, and critical sources. It contrasts the artists' family and class backgrounds, gender identities, the time and place in which each came of age, and the artistic and social spaces within which they produced their images of the Fourteenth Street neighborhood and its New Women.

I use poststructuralist accounts of subjectivity to frame discussions of the artist in relation to his or her work and the rewriting of art-historical biography.[15] Especially useful are those accounts that insist on both the historical nature of gendered subjectivity in relation to concrete habits, practices, and discourses and the notion of a general subject continuously individuating itself by constructing an identity and understanding itself and the world from various potentially contradictory subject positions. Such accounts allow for some agency on the part of artists and viewers without losing hold of the ways in which both are constructed in language, discourse, and ideology. In other words, the subject cannot construct itself but can choose (from an available set of representations) how it is to be constructed.

These premises are crucial to feminists who wish to "diminish the centrality" of the artist as the humanist subject—the sole originator of meaning and knowledge—

by focusing on the historical conditions of the artist's practice.[16] Chapter 2 discusses the particular and often contradictory ways in which the artists' identities and experiences were shaped or challenged by new womanhood and suggests how various institutional practices and art theoretical or critical discourse helped to mold the critically successful figurative strategies the artists used to give the ideology of new womanhood prominent visual representation.

Chapter 3 combines an account of neighborhood history with a discussion of Fourteenth Street–Union Square imagery by other contemporary artists; it also analyzes how the debates about art and politics inflected these representations. I have studied newspapers, periodicals, and guidebooks to reconstruct both the course of events around Union Square and contemporary perceptions of the neighborhood's diverse population. I place the paintings of the four artists among the range of representations of the district, showing that the artists' strategies, with few exceptions, are mainstream and middle-class. I ask how they alternately confront and circumvent the ethnic and class diversity of the area through composition or the selection of subjects. Only Miller among the four artists never portrayed the unemployed men who frequented Union Square Park during the Depression. All four artists, however, unlike their social realist contemporaries, avoided depicting the radical demonstrations that occurred in the district, concentrating instead on the daily life of the neighborhood, especially the activities of women.

Paintings by the four artists construct different kinds of new women and different features of new womanhood. Each artist envisioned a distinct female type that includes some aspect of mainstream new womanhood. In Chapters 4–7—two on shoppers and two on working women—I examine these images of new women in the context of women's domestic lives, a flourishing consumer culture, women's labor, and the feminist movement in the interwar years. For example, the models of womanhood in Miller's and Marsh's different images of Fourteenth Street shoppers have little to do with independence, economic self-sufficiency, or gender equality—values espoused by radical feminists between the wars. In Chapter 4 I present Miller's matronly shopper as a stable nurturing figure contained by carefully constructed settings and modeled on classical and Venetian Renaissance prototypes. She resembles the new stereotype of the professionalized homemaker promulgated by business and by moderate feminists who wanted to accommodate the liberation of the enfranchised woman to her ongoing role as homemaker.

In Chapter 5, I demonstrate that Marsh's voluptuous shopper, placed in settings that recall old master paintings, resembles the popular Siren of thirties movies and advertisements. Although she embodies the glamour and sexual liberation of the new woman, she is a lower-class figure, constructed for the sexual pleasure of the masculine viewer. Marsh's paintings suggest uncertainty about whether women were liberated by consumer choice or seduced by the media to transform themselves into visual and sexual commodities. In some works they tower above men who appear helpless at their beauty; in others they are de-individualized types, trapped in dense shopping crowds.

Raphael Soyer and Isabel Bishop portrayed two distinctive types of wage-earning women. In Chapter 6, I show how Soyer's image of shopgirls begins to subvert prevailing middle-class conceptions of women's roles. Poses and gestures convey the wearying effects of working life that lower-class retail saleswomen on Fourteenth Street were said to experience. They are the only Fourteenth Street images in which women directly confront the viewer. Using Degas as his prototype, Soyer in the 1930s resurrected the historical stereotype of the exploited shopgirl that contrasts with the 1920s model of the department store saleswoman portrayed by Miller, whose model of middle-class success more closely fit the discourse of new womanhood.

In Chapter 7 I relate Bishop's images of youthful office workers to issues of sexual difference, including the problem of spectatorship addressed by the artist as a New Woman representing new womanhood. Bishop reinterpreted Rembrandt to create unsexualized close-ups of office workers, alone or in intimate conversation; atmospheric pastel color and light mask the dramatically changing conditions of the clerical worker's job. Bishop's paintings present women as models of individual achievement—the ideal new woman described by job counselors and employers in the constricted job market at the end of the Depression.

In the chapters on the four artists, I place the Fourteenth Street works in each artist's oeuvre of the twenties and thirties. In addition, I explore the relationship of these works to other artists' paintings of women and men, to media images, and to political cartoons. I draw on women's history and psychological and sociological studies from the twenties and thirties. Shopping guides, fashion magazines, the advertising industry, and career advice literature for women chart the changes in what was deemed appropriate "womanly" appearance and behavior. I look at a variety of representational discourses about the New Woman with the aim of showing how they may inhabit the same ideological sphere.

As an art historian feminist viewer of these paintings I have revised my own position as I located contradictions in the material itself and encountered changing explanations of art, society, and women's history in the 1920s and 1930s. American art historiography itself presented several contradictions. First, depending on the focus of the study and the works selected, scholars place the artists into one of several categories of 1920s and 1930s realism. All four are understood broadly as painters of the American Scene who observed contemporary life without displaying an overt political attitude. I have adopted this understanding, qualifying it, however, to make a place for the nuances of the period's own critical voices. As early as 1934 Marsh was proclaimed the urban counterpart to America's regionalist triumvirate, Thomas Hart Benton, John Steuart Curry, and Grant Wood.[17] By contrast, those who locate a critical edge in certain works by Marsh and Soyer place them among the social realists who wanted art to take an activist stance for social betterment. Those who see a studio practice at the core of Soyer's art-making activities de-politicize his works and place him, along with Miller and Bishop, in the tradition of the studio picture painters.[18] Finally, especially since the 1930s, apologists for modern abstraction, with its attendant claims of universalism, have dismissed the four artists' works as academic, uncritical, and sentimental.[19]

Such inconsistency suggests the complexity of each artist's vision, the failure of totalizing categories, and the need to examine individual works in their particular historical configuration. It also suggests a need to highlight the centrality of debates about the relationship between art and society in this period without losing sight of art as in some way constitutive of both "social" and "political" ideologies—in this study, of ideologies of gender. In the Depression, artists and critics alike called for greater social responsibility on the part of the artist. Demands for an intelligible pictorial language (some form of realism) that would portray the local and specific habits of life for the average American viewer became the order of the day. Artists on the Left in the early years of the decade took the demand for realism further, arguing for an art made by a community of worker-artists that made the plight of the proletariat visible. By mid-decade, government programs for the arts embraced the more centrist ideology of American Scene realism and gave the artist a public role as decorator of the nation's government buildings. On post office walls across the land, artists, who for the first time were given a major public role in picturing the nation's past and future, celebrated the virtues of democracy in monumental images of urban and rural life as well as life within the American family.[20]

In portraying the daily life of average Americans, the works I discuss here share certain aims with the public art programs. At the same time, however, they are easel paintings, made in the private space of the studio for a bourgeois audience that went to galleries and museums and purchased works for private consumption. Moreover, the artists who made them held different positions with respect to the prevailing gender system and class structure and, as a result, were interpreted variously according to the ideology of American Scene painting: one woman (Bishop) and three men; one Russian Jewish immigrant (Soyer) and three middle- to upper-middle-class artists born in different generations.

I wanted at first to reclaim these images of Fourteenth Street women for a historical account of an era when the marriage of culture and politics gave men and women at all levels of society a more equal stake in American life. But such an explanation came quickly to seem unworkable, not only because of the pictorial presentation of these subjects but because of the period itself. Whether seen as the time when the welfare state began or as a time when a more conservative version of industrial capitalism was maintained, the interwar years produced great social upheaval; but this upheaval, unlike that in other progressive eras, was accompanied by no major feminist reform.[21] In chronicling the period, feminist historians have cited as evidence of the demise of feminism the defeat of the first Equal Rights Amendment (E.R.A.); a vociferous back-to-the-home movement; and, in the Depression, government-sanctioned campaigns against married women workers. At this time, nonetheless, more women worked in government administration than at any other period in American history; in the art world, more women artists found employment on government projects. My interpretation of interwar feminism follows that of Nancy Cott in *The Grounding of Modern Feminism,* which charts the diffusion of the women's movement after suffrage into a multiplicity of organizations, voices, and conflicts. In the 1920s the feminist movement did not end; there was a shift to a modern feminism, in which tensions between modernity and tradition, equality and difference are always in flux.[22]

In developing an interpretive model for the Fourteenth Street School paintings, I am drawn back to the works themselves. Their pictorial language simultaneously accommodates and conflicts with the feminisms and gender ideologies of the interwar period. Because I see the works as sites of contradictory discourses on new womanhood, I use a model of analysis that allows me to encompass the contradictions and to see history as a process of transformation rather than as a totalizing triumph or failure on the part of one group over another. Even as gender relations were negotiated and changed during the period, power remained unequally apportioned. The images must be analyzed with that inequality always in mind.

One final note about my discussion of these paintings. My primary concern here is not to reassess the position of these artists in American art history, or to evaluate their aesthetic achievements. All four artists were well known in their day, and most art histories treat them as among the important urban realists of the period. This is a feminist project whose goal is not the recovery of lost women artists but rather an engagement with what Mary Poovey calls a "historicized demystifying practice" whose goal is to "chart more accurately the multiple determinants that figure in any individual's social position and [relative] power and oppression."[23] Thus my task is not to make Isabel Bishop as good an artist as the men. Nor do I want to mine the paintings for some kind of pure feminist content, condemning those that fail to meet my criteria. The aesthetic and feminist standards to which these paintings are held are themselves socially and historically constructed. My concern is to understand how the conventions of visual representation work within a historical constellation of events, material practices, and ideas to construct the unequal relations of power that are part of the ideologies of gender in the interwar period. To do this is come to a provisional understanding of the historical relations of gender. From that may follow some understanding of ourselves and the possibilities for change.

CHAPTER ONE

THE "NEW WOMAN" REVISED

Here she comes, running, out of prison and off pedestal; chains off, crown off, halo off, just a live woman.

CHARLOTTE PERKINS GILMAN,
"Is Feminism Really So Dreadful?"

Who was the "New Woman?" What roles did popular culture or high art image making assume in the production and dissemination of different ideals of new womanhood? How did viewers understand such images in relation to women's changing experiences at work, at leisure, and in interpersonal relations? How are representations of new womanhood beginning in the 1890s pertinent to the Fourteenth Street images of women by four artists in the 1920s and 1930s? Historical and methodological considerations justify a broad introduction to the discourse of new womanhood. First, even though historians chart a perceptible shift to a post-franchise model of new womanhood more overtly "feminine" and individualized, ideological connections with earlier models remain. Because representational conventions and typologies of womanhood keep both the continuities and the changes in play in the Fourteenth Street works, it is important to chart them. In different ways, for example, Marsh and Soyer in the 1930s draw from John Sloan's turn-of-the-century depictions of working-class femininity. At the same time, each artist's interpretation can be situated in 1930s representational and historical contexts related to art, women, leisure, and work. Second, the artists themselves lived through the generations of new womanhood. They forged new identities, viewed with new eyes, and modified representational practices in light of shifting discourses on realist art and new womanhood. Finally, in these historical discussions of new womanhood I put into practice the kind of intertextual and historically grounded readings I use in subsequent chapters. These readings clarify the relationships between ideas manifested in images and other forms of representation. They also provide a wider context for gendered interpretations of paintings by taking into account a variety of historically situated, classed, and gendered viewers.

For both earlier commentators and present-day historians, the phrase "New Woman" conjures up dozens of images, verbal characterizations, and notable exemplars. At the end of the nineteenth century it stood for the middle- to upper-middle-class woman's evolutionary progress toward modernity and, in particular, her movement from the home to the public sphere. Women born between the late 1850s and 1900 made up the first two generations of new women. As Carroll Smith-Rosenberg has pointed out, bourgeois matrons bequeathed to their daughters the women's institutions—social and literary clubs, reform and suffrage groups—that demonstrated new possibilities for women outside the home. Thanks to the establishment of women's colleges, these young women received a higher education in the 1870s and 1880s and pursued careers as teachers, social reformers, health experts, writers, artists, and physicians in the years up to the First World War. These women, like their mothers, adhered to the values of community service rooted in small-town America and concentrated their efforts on social justice, world peace, and remedying the ills of industrializing cities.[1]

In such activities and in their campaigns for suffrage many first-generation new women retained ideals of female virtue and nurturance from earlier decades, making a place for themselves in the political arena as the nation's caretakers, its guardians of spiritual resources. Some, like Charlotte Perkins Gilman, attempted dramatic reforms of middle-class social conventions, campaigning for more communal and cooperative domestic services to free working women from home and child care. Others, like Margaret Sanger, addressed issues of reproductive rights and explored changing attitudes toward female sexuality. Unlike their mothers, many college-educated new women postponed marriage indefinitely. Instead, they established strong networks among women (some of which included lifelong same-sex intimate relationships) in the educational institutions and settlement houses that gave them their new occupations. Whether they renounced marriage because of a single-minded determination to carry on the world's work or from a longstanding perception that a career was incompatible with marriage and motherhood, many in the first generation preserved the nineteenth century's strong tradition of female bonding, but now from a position of economic independence outside matrimony. Whatever their exact position, these new women questioned marital norms and prevailing notions of gender difference and sought different social and sexual relations with men.[2]

While some middle-class new women at the turn of the century bypassed marriage for careers and woman-centered social and political activities, young immigrant women expanded the traditional boundaries of permissible heterosexual interaction. By day these women provided a frequently exploited pool of unskilled labor for factories, department stores, and offices, laboring, sharing meals, and traveling alongside men, with whom they chatted and flirted. By night many abandoned their cramped tenements as well as constricting Old World models of court-ship. Unchaperoned, they found release from the monotony of daily wage labor in new forms of commercialized leisure. Brightly lit dance halls, amusement parks, nickelodeons, and later movie houses opened up to them a stimulating, often erotic, world of pleasure. New dances demanded sensuous bodily movement or physical closeness. Darkened theaters encouraged kissing and petting. Mechanized rides at Coney Island flung couples together or exposed women's bodies to eager male bystanders.[3]

The appearance and behavior of these working-class women suggest that new womanhood crossed class, ethnic, and gender boundaries and show how in the multivalent discourse of new womanhood ideologies and practices of gender dif-ference were negotiated, political power and personal autonomy demanded, and the larger social order contested by men and women. An immigrant woman at the turn of the century was rarely called a New Woman by literate commentators. Indeed, as Kathy Peiss points out, some of the settlement-house reformers who trained lower-class women in the genteel ways of the middle class were among those most dismayed by the ability of some lower-class women to subvert that training. The reformers deplored the threat of mechanized leisure to the urban cultural land-scape of the bourgeoisie. And they were puzzled by those working-class women who continued, by and large, to choose the heterosexual world of commercial plea-sures over the female-centered community of the neighborhood settlement house. In a number of instances, working-class women reshaped middle-class reformers' ideas of leisure and women-centered activities by pressuring them to stage mixed-sex dances and parties at neighborhood community centers. In this way the new immigrant women played their part in weakening the borders between male and female spheres, foreshadowing the ideology of heterosexual interaction that would come to dominate postwar gender relations.[4]

Many second-generation middle-class new women, like their working-class sis-ters, repudiated nineteenth-century bourgeois sexual conventions. These women were fully at home in urban culture. Beginning about 1910, with this second gen-eration, *feminism* entered the lexicon of new womanhood, often becoming syn-onymous with it. As a term, *feminism* came into use at a time when nineteenth-century terminology—the "woman movement," "woman's rights," or the "cause of woman"—began to sound outdated. In its early stages, as Nancy Cott has dem-onstrated, feminism emerged from the ideological Left. Its tenets were articulated by a vocal minority of women among those intellectuals and activists embroiled in the cultural, social, and political rebellion centered in Greenwich Village. Though most early feminists were women from bourgeois backgrounds entering professions newly opened to them, they were sympathetic to socialism and often paired the two isms as the foundation of social change. On the one hand, they found parallels between socialism's analysis of the oppressed classes and claims for women. On the other hand, they identified the trade union woman as a source of strength and a model of economic independence.[5]

Though dependent on the ongoing women's movement in general and the suffrage movement in particular, feminism in the teens took a more radical stance than either, thereby altering and expanding the agendas of these movements. Furthermore, though its strongest adherents remained a small minority, radical feminism developed during the only decade when women's suffrage coalesced into a mass movement. Cott explains how women forged alliances across class, race, and educational lines as they shared the suffrage platform and experimented with political activism. Feminists questioned the dominant claim made by suffragists that a woman's moral superiority would improve political life. They substituted for this domestic, duty-bound ideal of femininity a notion of women as humans fully equal to men. The Feminist new woman of the teens had as a goal "the emancipation of woman both as a human-being and as a sex-being."[6] More preoccupied with self-development than self-sacrifice, the feminist made independent choices in career, politics, relationships, and individual style. This growing concern with individualism arose in a context of group consciousness, however. In 1912, for example, twenty-five Village women, headed by Marie Jenny Howe, established Heterodoxy, a group whose organization and ideals expressed the central paradox of feminism—women's desire to be individuals without losing their collective political and social identity.[7]

Those who attached *feminism* to "new womanhood" in a positive sense glossed the latter term as a reinvigorated demand for economic independence, equal rights, and, above all, sexual liberation. As feminists had abandoned moral superiority in the name of equality, they asserted parallel male and female erotic drives. A woman would make her equal claim to passionate sexual fulfillment in the context of an intimate and mutually supportive heterosexual (though not necessarily marital) bond. Feminists accepting this guideline in the teens valued heterosexual relationships more than any group in the women's movement before them; many also valued friendships with women, and their ranks included a number of lesbian couples. Still others fought respectability from the ranks of the birth-control movement, linking sex oppression to class oppression. Finally, while women like Olive Shreiner championed women's sexual nature as equal to men's, others, like the popular Swedish feminist Ellen Key, celebrated eroticism from a position of difference. For Key, a woman openly expressing her sexuality manifested her sacred and superior maternal role.[8]

Feminism and feminist New Women in the teens sustained a series of paradoxes that would disperse into patterns of conflict, accommodation, and revision in the 1920s. Women claimed to be both like men and different from them. They demanded to be understood as economically independent individuals in a collective sisterhood. Under the unifying banner of suffrage (though many suffragists spurned both radical demands for economic independence and sex rights) feminists for a brief interval made this sequence of contradictions coherent.[9]

From the end of the nineteenth century through the teens an extraordinary range of pictorial and verbal texts embodied the historical changes as well as the debates about women's roles encompassed by new womanhood. Easily read images, most featuring women as types, were produced through technological advances in the printing industry. Such images, in posters, magazine and newspaper advertisements, and department store displays, became part of the popular visual culture. Whether turn-of-the-century images of women were produced for mass consumption or for an elite patronage, they used a variety of conventions to chronicle, advocate, or contain social change.

Within a decade after the term "New Woman" first appeared in contemporary journals, the coolly elegant Gibson girl began her twenty-year reign as America's most popular visual type (Fig. 1.1), first in *Life* magazine, then in every imaginable artifact of American material culture. Doulton porcelain, commemorative spoons, umbrella stands, matchboxes and whisk-broom holders bore her figure. Thanks to pyrography, the decorative hobby of the day, enthusiasts burned her image into every available leather and wooden surface. For the male bachelor's apartment interior decorators marketed wallpaper with a repeat pattern of four Gibson girl faces. Commentators puzzled over her appeal, and in her heyday one of them named the types: the beauty, the athletic girl, the sentimental girl, the girl with a mind of her own, the ambitious girl, and—the universal favorite among men—the charmer. Of her creator, Charles Dana Gibson, Homer Fort wrote

> His pen has caught the true inspiration and he embodies in one composite picture the vivacity, the independence and hauteur, the condescending amiability, the grace and the catholic spirit of the daughter of this great Republic. You like his women, whether in a magazine or in life and you instantly know she is neither English, French or German. Instinctively you say: "This is the American woman."[10]

For some, the Gibson girl synthesized the best of Anglo-American traits to that time; for others, her stature and self-possession took on a larger meaning as emblems of America's international accomplishments and conquests.[11]

For many women the Gibson girl also exemplified prewar new woman's self-assured independence. Arguing that she brought together and represented the positive changes for women that had occurred during the nineteenth century, Charlotte Perkins Gilman contrasted her in 1898 with the average American woman: she was "braver, stronger, more healthful and skillful and able and free, more human in all ways."[12] In an often-cited article of 1901, the writer Caroline Ticknor dramatized the startling newness of the New Woman in an imaginary encounter between the Gibson girl and her predecessor, the "steel-engraving lady." The latter—a corseted

1.1 Charles Dana Gibson, "One
Difficulty of the Game: Keeping
Your Eye on the Ball," from
Americans, 1900.

1.2 A steel-engraving lady. Division of
Costume, National Museum of
American History, Harry T. Peters
Collection, Smithsonian Institution.

fragile beauty—was a product of antebellum fashion lithographs (Fig. 1.2). In Ticknor's scenario, she sits at her embroidery frame, tending hearth and home and awaiting Reginald, the man who adores his "lady love" and places fair womanhood on a pedestal. The statuesque Gibson girl, dressed in a shorter skirt and comfortable walking shoes, and tanned from exercise in the sun, has dropped in on the steel-engraving lady before meeting her male companion on the golf course. The Gibson girl instructs her fair-skinned predecessor in the ways of modern womanhood:

We have done away with all the over-sensitiveness and overwhelming modesty in which you are enveloped. . . . When a man approaches, we do not tremble and droop our eyelids, or gaze adoringly while he lays down the law. We meet him on a ground of perfect fellowship, and converse freely on every topic. . . . Whether he *likes* it or not makes little difference; *he* is no longer the one whose pleasure is to be consulted. The question now is, not "What does man like?" but "What does woman prefer?" That is the keynote of modern thought. You see, I've had a liberal education. I can do everything my brothers do; and do it rather better, I fancy. I am an athlete and a college graduate, with a wide universal outlook. My point of view is free from narrow influences, and quite outside of the home boundaries.[13]

The Gibson girl goes on to assure her astonished companion that she plans to enter a profession, and to "purify the world of politics." Home is now an insufficient vocation, and a woman's duty is to make the most of her talents and be self-supporting. " 'Heaven helps her who helps herself' suits the 'new woman,' " the Gibson girl proclaimed. "This is a utilitarian age. We cannot sit down to be admired; we must be 'up and doing'; we must leave 'footprints in the sand of time.' "[14] After listening to her modern guest, the steel-engraving lady concluded the conversation by contrasting the goals of her education with those of the Gibson girl, and by expressing regret for the passing of an ideal of genteel womanhood.

The theory of my education . . . was designed to fit me for my home; yours is calculated to unfit you for yours. You are equipped for contact with the outside world, for competition with your brothers in business; my training merely taught me to make my brother's home a place which he should find a source of pleasure and inspiration. I was taught grace of motion, drilled in a school of manners, made to enter a room properly, and told how to sit gracefully, to modulate my voice, to preside at the table with fitting dignity. In place of your higher education, I had my music and languages and my embroidery frame. I was persuaded there was no worthier ambition than to bring life and joy and beauty into a household, no duty higher than that I owed my parents. Your public aspirations, your independent views, your discontent, are something I cannot understand.[15]

Ticknor heightens the differences between the two women through a series of oppositions that exaggerate the Gibson girl as a model of change. She links the ideology of new womanhood with historically specific ideals—equality, for example—that are usually assumed to have a fixed meaning. In this text, to be equal is to be permitted an education and a turn on the playing field, but not a place in the political process. Turn-of-the-century women made the Gibson girl a symbol of their campaigns for equality, two of the principal quests being exercise and dress reform.[16] Ticknor made women's adoption of "mannish" behavior and dress the precondition for equality.

Like many successful cultural stereotypes, the Gibson girl could be manipulated and interpreted in a variety of ways. Ticknor's text, which is unillustrated, actually makes her more of a reform figure than the visual image was intended to be; neither the Gibson girl nor her creator, Charles Dana Gibson, was a radical figure. Gibson mistrusted organized feminism, fearing it would make women too masculine. He deplored the extreme tactics of radical suffragists and, until his own wife served as a Democratic committeewoman, had reservations about women's political role.

In one particularly telling cartoon, Gibson showed his Gibson girl being notified of her election as sheriff by a group of homely female politicians while her husband and children look on, dismayed. In another, "A Suffragette's Husband," Gibson portrays the anti-feminist caricature of the New Woman as a battle-ax (1911; Fig. 1.3), her bulk compromising his frail masculinity as they sit at the breakfast table. Though Gibson enjoyed the Gibson girl's athleticism and frequently portrayed her bicycling or golfing (usually with a male companion), her movements remained graceful and her creator refused to clothe her in trousers. Though she looked independent, she was only occasionally portrayed as a working woman, and then only as a nurse or secretary, not as a reformer in a settlement house—a position often held by educated new women. Her cool aristocratic demeanor was modeled on that of women in New York's high society, which Gibson himself frequented, and her aloofness preserved a Victorian ideal of chastity and gentility.[17]

In his survey of Gibson girl iconography, Robert Koch observed that Gibson was a romantic, primarily concerned with love and marriage and their effects on women of his class. He campaigned vigorously against the marriage of beautiful wealthy women to aging European aristocrats. At the same time, he presented courtship "as a matter of mutual respect and admiration," predicting the companionate ideal of subsequent decades.[18] The Gibson girl was a figure of accommodation. She mirrored the aspirations of many young women who wanted both possibilities and limits. As Fairfax Downey wrote in his sometimes patronizing account of the Gibson girl in 1936, "Little girls everywhere, who relinquished the ambition to be President to little boys and who did not then even hope to be Madam Secretaries in the Cabinet, did determine to be Gibson Girls when they grew up."[19] Because she assumed an independent air without radically challenging patriarchal assumptions, the Gibson girl became the most visible and acceptable symbol of new womanhood at the turn of the century.

1.3   Charles Dana Gibson, "A Suffragette's Husband," from *Other People,* 1911.

Even as the Gibson girl became a popular icon, American painters found ways to portray the modern ideal without violating the conventions for depicting women in high art. The most fashionable portrait painter of the day, John Singer Sargent, was praised for a bravura painting technique that captured the elegant costumes, sparkling jewelry, and sumptuous settings of his high-society subjects. Many of Sargent's portraits of women, for all their animation, mark off a separate and unchanging world of Gilded Age wealth and privilege.

Thanks to a chance set of circumstances, Sargent's portrait of Mr. and Mrs. I. N. Phelps Stokes strikes a thoroughly modern and slightly unconventional note (Fig. 1.4). In a portrait intended as a wedding gift from her prominent New York banker husband, Edith Stokes was to have been seated in a green evening dress with her Great Dane beside her. After four sittings, Sargent saw her one morning fresh from a tennis game, dressed in a mannish blue serge jacket, a shirtwaist, and a full white skirt that permitted freedom of movement. The artist immediately wanted to paint her as she was and asked her to pose to reveal her stature.[20] Edith Stokes stands confidently, facing the viewer and smiling. Her brightly lit figure, its costume delineated by broad angular slabs of paint that belie accepted notions of femininity, fills

1.4 John Singer Sargent, *Mr. and Mrs.
I. N. Phelps Stokes,* 1897. Oil on
canvas, 84¼″ × 39¾″. The
Metropolitan Museum of Art.

the foreground, partially blocking that of her bearded husband in the shadows to
her right. Originally, she was to have stood with her hand resting on the head of
her Great Dane; after three sittings, Sargent substituted the figure of her husband
and the straw hat.[21]

Since the strikingly modern aspects of this painting—costume, pose, and placement of figures—are still worked through accepted conventions of turn-of-the-
century portraiture for elite patrons, the painting remains situated within the mod-

erate discourse of new womanhood. The smiling figure of Mrs. Stokes is more like the aristocratic Gibson girl, as girl athlete and charmer, than like the demanding suffragist. Though we know the figure of her husband was added later, his closed stance contrasts with her expansive one; as she is depicted, she dominates the relationship, taking center stage and demanding for herself the larger share of the viewer's attention. The composition thus constructs a prominent position for a female viewer, a secondary one for the male viewer. At the same time, however, the figure of Edith Stokes necessarily remains a primary object of the male viewer's gaze. Moreover, her husband reported that Sargent himself was most pleased not with the figure of Edith herself but with the spiral stroke with which he represented the enormous engagement ring on her left hand—a sign of the male patron's proprietary rights and financial power over his wife.[22] Evidence that the painting's representational strategies negotiated the controversial issues of new womanhood is provided by one account of critical responses to the portrait that suggests anxiety about unleashing modern woman's sexuality—anxiety that increased in some quarters with even the smallest sign that women were moving away from nineteenth-century norms of genteel behavior:

> The Stokes portrait, accomplished by the collision of accidents, has been credited with a social probity melodious to modern ears. Mrs. Stokes held her straw hat where the great dane ought to have been, at the very point in her husband's anatomy where spirited critics have been moved to assert she is desexing him.[23]

Arguments against the new woman's moving into the public realm—through work, higher education and a professional career, women's reform movements, the suffrage campaign, and feminism or through new forms of commercialized leisure—signaled a profound cultural change: the erosion of separate spheres. Since the 1830s, with the emergence of industrialized capitalism, bourgeois and elite culture had defined separate spheres of activity for men and women. This governing Victorian ideal placed women at home as self-sacrificing guardians of the family and as good mothers preserving traditional values while men left for the public world of work, to do battle in the marketplace. The figure of Edith Stokes with her husband in an undifferentiated setting suggests those boundaries were deteriorating.

By contrast, visual reinforcement of the ideology of separate spheres appears in paintings of the middle- to upper-middle-class domestic interior popularized by the Boston school painters at the turn of the century. Influenced by Vermeer's light-filled, geometrically ordered interiors, painters like Edmund Tarbell, Frank Benson, Joseph Rodefer De Camp, Philip Leslie Hale, and Joseph Paxton produced images of sweet, quiet women reading, having tea, crocheting, or sitting with their children. Whether shown absorbed in reverie or in quiet tasks, all remain undisturbed by encroachments from the world of work. Edmund Tarbell's *Girl Crocheting* is typical (1905; Fig. 1.5), combining the color and softness of Impressionism with academic drawing and a composition dictated by the works of the old masters, one of which appears in the work. The stern papal figure of Velázquez's Innocent X presides over the woman bathed in idealizing light. As in many of these works, the woman's position is carefully circumscribed by the geometry of the composition and by such props as the gateleg table that closes off the pictorial space from viewers. Alternatively, she is contained by the fluid volume of a large interior space that is opposed to the light of the unlimited world outside.[24] If one were to choose from the art of the period images that epitomize the competing values articulated by Caroline Ticknor's 1901 piece on the steel-engraving lady and the Gibson girl, Tarbell's *Girl Crocheting* and Sargent's painting of Mr. and Mrs. Phelps Stokes would come close to the mark.

Although women in interiors were not a subject unique to Boston and its painters, this genre had a particular cultural resonance in a city whose upper-middle-class population included a surplus of single educated and publicly active women pursuing professions and campaigning for suffrage alongside a powerful anti-suffragist contingent in the women's movement. In her study of the Boston school, Bernice Kramer Leader argues that these works, made by a highly successful group of painters for Boston Brahmin patrons, can be read ideologically as anti-feminist.[25] Leader, who attributes anti-suffrage sentiments only to those painters and patrons known to be actively engaged in the anti-suffrage movement, claims that all these artists can be understood as traditionalists regarding woman's sphere. Many of the prominent men who purchased paintings by the Boston school not only belonged to the most conservative social, religious, and political constituencies in Boston but also worked to preserve the past through membership in genealogical and historical societies, support of cultural institutions, and the purchase of paintings that upheld their values. Men who believed they had the most to lose from the erosion of separate spheres and the concomitant realignment of social and political hierarchies seem to have been among the most avid collectors of images of passive and dutiful women safely ensconced at home. The artists who painted these images espoused similar values. Artists and patrons together fashioned an ideal woman representing values they wished to preserve, a pictorial substitute for the publicly active women around them.[26]

In Boston, male and female suffragists and anti-suffragists alike used the ideology of separate spheres in their arguments. Suffragists revised the notion of woman's sphere, emphasizing woman's natural moral superiority in purifying the political arena. Anti-suffragists took a narrower view, arguing that woman's laudable characteristics resulted from her continued position in the home. Entry into the world of politics would not only rob her of her natural attributes but, in so doing, would prove "disastrous to harmonious social order."[27] For anti-suffragist male viewers the painted image might have functioned both as a substitute for an ideal of wom-

1.5 Edmund Tarbell, *Girl Crocheting,* 1905. Oil on canvas, 30″ × 25″. Canajoharie Library and Art Gallery, Canajoharie, New York.

anhood that was slowly eroding and as a subtly coded message to discourage female viewers from entering the public arena. For the like-minded wives, sisters, and daughters of the works' patrons and painters there was an ideal to preserve. Female suffragists may have read such an image as an ideal to renovate. Many new women wanted less to reverse established gender hierarchies than to accommodate values rapidly coming into conflict in a modern world. Thus the paintings may have been constitutive in different ways for the male and female viewer. The popularity of these works among an elite audience gives evidence of the continuing importance of the ideology of separate spheres—albeit under revision—among a powerful social constituency comprising both men and women.

Even if they construct viewing positions for both sexes, the portraits and domestic genre paintings of the Boston school were painted by male painters for male patrons. Many women artists in turn-of-the-century Boston, however, achieved critical acclaim and professional success in the mainstream academic circles frequented by the Boston school. Having trained seriously in art, usually with Tarbell or Benson, they made their reputations and gained financial independence chiefly through portrait commissions; in their pursuit of art as a profession rather than an avocation, these women artists began to challenge the stereotype of the lady painter and made a place for themselves among professional new women. Some of their most revealing works, especially in light of the shifting discourse of new womanhood, were their self-portraits. Conventionally, artists have used this genre to fashion an artistic identity or to augment social or professional status. Some self-portraits by turn-of-the-century women conveyed their changing status as women artists; others interrogated the artists' identity as women in ways that at times exaggerated and at times obliterated prevailing notions of female difference.[28]

By 1909, when she turned forty, Marie Danforth Page was a highly successful portraitist who worked out of the studio she had established in her Back Bay home in 1896, when she married the research bacteriologist and physician Calvin Gates Page.[29] In 1909 she painted two self-portraits. In the first, she gazes forthrightly at the viewer, a fashionable modern woman preparing to go out, adjusting the large ties of her broad-brimmed hat under her chin. The same year, she painted an elaborate portrait of her husband that included another self-portrait (Fig. 1.6). Her most ambitious work to that date, it bears the imprint of both her Boston training and the influence of Velázquez. Calvin Page is a serious seated figure painted in the blacks, browns, and grays conventionally used in male portraits. In a large framed mirror behind him is a shadowy full-length reflection of the artist. She wears a long smock, holds her palette, and stands before a canvas bearing the image of her neighbor's four-year-old son, Malcolm Stone, whose portrait she was painting at the time. This child's reflected image, aligned along a vertical axis directly above the likeness of Page and similarly posed, suggests a generational relationship.[30]

Lacking written evidence of Marie Danforth Page's intentions, we can ask about the effects of her compositional conceit in light of ideologies of gender and competing discourses of new womanhood in turn-of-the-century Boston. Trevor Fairbrother's account of her reflection—she is a "hovering angelic form" presiding over the "anxious presence" of her husband[31]—is altogether in line with the ideology of separate spheres that envisioned separate roles and social spaces for women and men. Dr. Page is the material presence, situated in the world of work and rendered in solid masses of paint. His wife, depicted in loose diaphanous strokes with flickering highlights creating a corona around her head, floats in a separate, superior, and spiritualized realm, almost like an idea he carries in his head. The child's image gives the most precise embodiment of her sphere, shining out far more prominently than any other part of the reflection. Together, the presences suggest familial harmony.

Although this interpretation gains credibility in the context of Danforth's Boston training with Benson and Tarbell and her own social position, the painting also problematizes the ideology of separate spheres. The painting asserts the presence of the professional artist, standing with her palette next to the product of her craft. The child is not hers, and her (painted) husband gazes on an image of a working woman artist. The artist's reflection can thus be read as that of the female slowly emerging from the shadows (as well as contained by them), a gradual rather than an abrupt process. She presents her own image, not alone and self-confident, as in her other self-portrait, where she envisioned herself as a woman of fashion, but in

1.6 Marie Danforth Page, *Calvin Gates Page*, 1909. Oil on canvas, 41¹/₂″ × 24¹/₂″. Private collection.

conjunction with that of her husband. At the same time, her reflection in the mirror tells us that she makes both her own image and that of her husband the subject of her constituting gaze.

Where Page's reflection seems to signal a tentative embarkation into a new world, *A Motion Picture*, Margaret Foster Richardson's unprecedented self-portrait, captures the sense of unfettered possibility inscribed in the new woman by her most optimistic and progressive advocates (1912; Fig. 1.7). Painted when the artist was thirty-one, the portrait shows her ready for work, moving toward the light, paintbrushes in hand. Rather than fashioning herself according to some ideal of domestic beauty (for which she had ready models in the work of her Bostonian teachers Joseph De Camp and Edmund Tarbell and in her own early images of domestic interiors), she effaces many of the contemporary markers of femininity. The freeflowing lavender-gray smock she wears and her severe white collar with a masculine tie make the body androgynous. In contrast to more elaborate Gibson girl coifs, the artist's hair is drawn back in quick practical fashion, and she wears eyeglasses. A full-size figure who fills the otherwise empty frame, she strides, turning her eager face toward the viewer without slowing her progress. It is as if Richardson has

1.7 Margaret Foster Richardson, *A Motion Picture* (self-portrait), 1912. Oil on canvas, 40³/₈″ × 23¹/₈″. The Pennsylvania Academy of the Fine Arts, Philadelphia.

provided a visual image for Charlotte Perkins Gilman's description of a feminist— a woman freed from the trappings of Victorian femininity and the ideology of women's sphere.³²

The visual language of these portraits and self-portraits reads both with and against the grain of competing ideals lodged in the discourse of new womanhood. Such readings suggest how language is both an empowering and a constraining device, dependent on the gender and class of producing and viewing subjects. The paintings by Sargent, Page, and Richardson capture the positive spirit of new womanhood in its early decades—its vitality and health, its self-assured professionalism. But even as this new identity is conferred through altered conventions of pose, gesture, costume, and activity, little else disturbs the conventions of large-scale academic portraiture and self-portraiture at the turn of the century. Settings remain fashionable or simply unspecific. The subjects themselves conform to the middle- to upper-middle-class ideal of new womanhood. These paintings and others like them accommodated themselves to an already permissible discourse of new womanhood that opened social spaces to women without reversing traditional hierarchies of gender.

These paintings also embodied the so-called genteel tradition that sought, in the words of William Dean Howells, to portray "the more smiling aspects of life, which are the more American and [to] seek the universal in the individual rather than the social interests."[33] In much of the high art and the popular culture of the period, idealized or spiritual women functioned as both bearers and signifiers of the genteel tradition. Female allegorical figures in murals and on public monuments of the Gilded Age personified timeless values of Truth, Justice, and Beauty. In domestic interior imagery women preserved the spiritual serenity of the home from encroachments by the world. Portrait images provided standards of middle- to upper-middle-class decorum. By the turn of the century, even as Boston school paintings in the genteel mode reached the apex of their popularity, critics began not only to fault them for their academic conventions but to devalue them in a hierarchy where the masculine was superior to the feminine. Charles Caffin, reviewing American paintings at the 1900 Paris Exposition, found them overly pretty and "lacking in marrow." Instead of trying to convince, the paintings sought not to offend, offering "irreproachable table-manners" rather than "salient self-expression."[34]

Whereas Caffin's readers might infer from his distinction between "manners and self-expression" an opposition between masculine and feminine in the genteel tradition, George Santayana made it explicit. His purpose in "The Genteel Tradition in American Philosophy" was to demonstrate the difference between authentic (male) experience and artificial (female) decorum; more broadly, he sought to link progress and modernity with the masculine, regression and tradition with the feminine.

> The truth is that . . . one-half of the American mind, that not occupied intensely in practical affairs, has remained, I will not say high-and-dry, but slightly becalmed; it has floated gently in the back-water, while, alongside, in invention and industry and social organisation, the other half of the mind was leaping down a sort of Niagara Rapids. This division may be found symbolized in American architecture: a neat reproduction of the colonial mansion . . . stands beside the sky-scraper. The American Will inhabits the sky-scraper; the American Intellect inhabits the colonial mansion. The one is the sphere of the American man; the other, at least predominantly, of the American woman. The one is all aggressive enterprise; the other is all genteel tradition.[35]

Insistence on the feminine attributes of genteel culture served both to re-fix gender boundaries against the incursions of new women and to devalue the activities of professional women in the social and cultural spheres. Important challenges to what many critics and commentators saw as a bourgeois "feminization" of American culture arose in the naturalist fiction of authors like Theodore Dreiser and Upton Sinclair and in the art of the Ashcan school realists—precursors of the Fourteenth Street School artists. As Rebecca Zurier has shown in her work on the Ashcan school and on *The Masses,* painters like Robert Henri, John Sloan, George Luks, and George Bellows gained their reportorial outlook from their experience as newspaper artists. They earned their reputations as artistic "revolutionaries" by abandoning academic subject matter, turning instead to life among the working classes on the Lower East Side. Guided by their teacher, Robert Henri, Ashcan school artists came to believe that the character of America's immigrant and working-class population was more authentic than that of the middle and upper-middle class. Forced to confront the crowded conditions of urban life head-on, this population experienced work and leisure unmediated by bourgeois niceties of behavior—what Henri and others would have called the burden of bourgeois social conventions. From the artists' middle-class vantage point working-class life was richer, more exciting and varied. To capture its directness and vitality, the artists rejected academic painting, whose careful drawing, polished surfaces, and finished contours became metaphors for the artifice of bourgeois life itself. Instead they painted directly on the canvas with rapid strokes, charged with emotion, that were meant to express the sense of life in the raw these artists felt as witnesses to a new, fundamentally different, American life.[36]

At times the artists revealed their own middle-class predisposition to view their subjects as the exotic other, or to make the working poor heroic while ignoring the daily grind of their lives. As realists sympathetic to or active in socialist politics, the Ashcan painters portrayed specific incidents and actual sites, living among their subjects as the Fourteenth Street School artists would do a generation later. Many worked in Greenwich Village; Sloan found much of his material near his home-studio in the heart of the Tenderloin, the most notorious center for vice and prostitution in turn-of-the-century New York. Through this reportorial practice and direct style of painting they showed that a democratic and pluralistic society comprised a population beyond the genteel middle class.[37]

Encouraged by Henri, who counseled each, "Be a man first, be an artist later," a number of male artists associated with the Ashcan circle repudiated the genteel feminized artist type of the late nineteenth century.[38] The sometimes tough, sometimes athletic behavior of artists like Henri or Luks, who adopted an aggressive, hard-drinking stance and staged boxing pantomimes to *épater les bourgeois,* or George Bellows, who portrayed violent boxing matches, reveals a broader middle-class cultural anxiety about masculinity and femininity.[39] Celebrated by President

Theodore Roosevelt, who became its major exemplar, the cult of the strenuous life became enormously popular at the turn of the century. Its advocates promoted outdoor activity in general: healthy new women, for example, favored bicycling and golf. Middle-class men looked to boxing, football, and baseball to make themselves tougher and more competitive—indeed more efficient—in modern industrial society. Those who advanced strenuosity and athletic pursuits argued that they would reinvigorate the "delicate indoor genteel race" and prepare men for leadership in the modern world.[40] For the artists, athletic endeavors and an energetic, spontaneous approach to painting served to refute gentility on the one hand and reassert masculinity on the other.

Among the Ashcan painters, John Sloan became the primary chronicler of the youthful working-class new women who inhabited the tenements, labored in the shops and factories, and spent their leisure time in the dance halls, parks, and movie houses. His portrayal of these women as cheerful rather than downtrodden can be linked to the genteel tradition's preoccupation with distancing women from commerce and politics. Though a socialist, contributing drawings and cartoons regularly to *The Masses,* Sloan insisted that paintings be lighthearted, humorous, or sympathetic in their commentary. His own paintings, he said, simply documented his "interest in humanity, at play, at work, the everyday life of city and country."[41] Had Sloan chosen to depict, for example, working-class men at work, his paintings might have become embroiled in issues of labor and class conflict, thereby violating both his own and the art establishment's injunction against painting as propaganda. Women, as Patricia Hills has pointed out, were the perfect subject, especially women at leisure. They allowed Sloan to locate a revitalizing spirit in the working classes—indeed to present the issue of class in high art—without violating institutionalized mythologies about women.[42] Paradoxically, however, even as Sloan deferred to the genteel tradition, he expanded the acceptable subject matter and representational practices for depicting class and gender in high art.

Sloan's images encompass a wider range of social spaces and activities of working-class new womanhood than had previously been represented in American easel painting; in many of these works women are emotionally and physically active, even raucous. Frankly, yet discreetly and even ambiguously, many of Sloan's paintings also expressed the open sensuousness of working-class new women's leisure pastimes. In this way the artist made visible—even celebrated—one of the most controversial aspects of new womanhood: sexuality. Furthermore, he employed narrative strategies in some works that allowed him to play with the sometimes euphemistic or ambiguous responses of middle-class commentators to these women. The commercialized world of leisure and the male-female relationships practiced within it generated a large body of commentary on working-class sexual morality at the turn of the century. As boundaries blurred between middle-class public and private spheres in industrializing cities, class distinctions broke down as well. The

1.8   John Sloan, *Sunday Afternoon in Union Square*, 1912. Oil on canvas, 26¼″ × 32¼″.
Bowdoin College Museum of Art, Brunswick, Maine.

middle class struggled to contain the new sexual practices, fearing they would
destroy middle-class social institutions, particularly that of procreative sexuality in
marriage.[43] Finally, one can argue that some of what we read in Sloan's images may
arise not only from his observations of working-class women but also from what
he learned about sexual attitudes and expectations from his intellectual peers,
including the radical feminists of Greenwich Village. In other words, representations of sensuous working-class women were not only the exotic Other but also
sites for the production of a freer sexual ideal advocated by one group of new
women.

Sunday Afternoon in Union Square expresses many of these ambiguities (Fig
1.8). Executed in May 1912, the painting shows two eye-catching young women
strolling through the park.[44] Both wear showy versions of contemporary dress that
reveal their figures; the one to the left is heavily made up, with reddened lips and
rouged cheeks. The artist gives both women artificial gestures, carefully choreo-
graphed to attract attention. They walk in perfect tandem, placing their bowed and

pointed shoes before them like chorus girls. One cocks her arm, tilting a bright pink parasol so that it frames her plumed hat. The other extends her arm, swinging her purse from the end of a finger. Sloan has positioned this arm so that it bisects the body of the man directly behind her while the purse seems to trail seductively down his leg. Behind this man, who raises his hand to his mouth in an ambiguous gesture of amusement or embarrassed speculation, another pauses to watch the women. Several other city types are arranged on park benches, a number of them responding directly to the central players. Two girls, in white dresses and hats, follow the main figures with their gaze; one whispers from behind her hand. An older gentleman leans toward them, perhaps eavesdropping on their commentary.

Because of its composition, which places the central figures in front of a group of observers they have just passed, and the elaborate narrative staged through poses and gestures, the painting asks, just who are these young women, or, more to the point, what kind of young women are they? They might be prostitutes taking a Sunday walk. In the teens the Union Square district bordered one of the major neighborhoods for prostitution and served as a site of solicitation. The women's costumes and flirtatious gestures add another clue. Heavy makeup, extravagantly large hats, and the soft purse dangling prominently from the end of a string were professional trademarks.[45] In this scenario, the girls seated at the left and the woman in her shirtwaist at the far right can be read as genteel foils to the strolling women, the standing men as voyeurs or potential clients. Sloan on several occasions just prior to beginning this painting referred directly to prostitution in his graphic work, and he depicted well-known sites of prostitution in several paintings.[46]

For solid middle- to upper-middle-class reform-minded viewers with a sketchy knowledge of New York neighborhoods and social life, female behavior was either respectable or promiscuous. In the opening pages of his novel *Sister Carrie,* Theodore Dreiser spelled out the precariousness of female virtue and the clear choice available to women entering the city, where a young girl either "falls into saving hands and becomes better, or she rapidly assumes the cosmopolitan standard of virtue and becomes worse. Of an intermediate balance, under the circumstances, there is no possibility."[47] Given the dread of prostitution expressed in contemporary journals, middle- to upper-middle-class viewers accustomed to seeing women represented in genteel domestic surroundings might well find solicitation and, as critics argued about Sloan's work in general, vulgarity in this scene.

While allowing for such a reading, the painting engages a broader and somewhat more complex understanding of working women's sexuality. Some young working women, who wanted to participate in the public world of pleasure, freely adopted and often mixed modes of dress from high society and the subculture of prostitution. In "putting on style," as Kathy Peiss has demonstrated, these young women could at once signal their aspirations to a higher social station and reveal their desire for greater independence and sexual expressiveness, manifested by displays of conspicuous behavior. Other working-class women saved to buy colorful clothes, affirming their progress toward a better life or their entry into American culture by buying a new outfit.[48]

Virtually all working-class women were poorly paid. Immigrant daughters living at home were expected to turn over their paycheck to the family, in return for which they might receive a tiny allowance for clothing or transportation. Women who lived independently or shared quarters with friends eked out an existence, often skipping meals to buy new clothing or pay for commercialized entertainment. While some young women became prostitutes to make ends meet, others used different tactics to negotiate the new social spaces where sexuality and commercialized leisure intersected. A number practiced "treating," offering a date or a steady boyfriend a range of sexual favors, from kissing to intercourse, in exchange for an evening at the dance hall or at Coney Island. Such women were called charity girls, to distinguish them from regular, or even occasional, prostitutes who exchanged sex for money. Many women accepted the risks of treating—the threat to whatever respectability they wished to maintain—to gain access to a world of pleasures that gave them a sense of autonomy and freedom lacking in their working lives.[49]

Viewed in this light, the narrative in Sloan's *Sunday Afternoon in Union Square* plays with notions of female desirability and respectability. Furthermore, by posing observers behind the central figures, the painting constructs a range of viewer-subject positions apart from those of the gaping male viewer and the disapproving upper-middle-class academically schooled patron. For example, a female working-class viewer of Sloan's painting, sympathetic to women seeking ways to meet men outside the home, might identify with the two girls seated on the left. Rather than condemn the central figures for conspicuous behavior, she might admire them for their colorful finery and their skilled flirtation. She might see them as figures to emulate—as new women entering public leisure spaces and carving out a heterosocial sphere that emphasized greater sexual autonomy and personal freedom.[50]

The flip side of this viewing pleasure *and* identification on the part of one class of contemporary female spectator is that the central players are also set up as beautiful objects of a primarily voyeuristic male gaze. Even as Sloan examined the way these working women negotiated their social and cultural identities with a degree of independence, he was taking a reportorial delight in the beauty of his strikingly clad female subjects. Consequently they are subject, like virtually all women in representation, to a powerful "regime of looking" that reinstates historically specific relationships of "sexual power and subordination."[51] Here the kind of female independence represented was predicated on the assumption of men's economic superiority—women depended on them for treating. Institutions of leisure were operated by entrepreneurial males according to that assumption. There was, in short, a double edge to this emerging sexual autonomy; if working women were more independent, they were nonetheless kept in economically subservient positions.[52]

1.9   John Sloan, *Sunday, Women Drying Their Hair,* 1912. Oil on canvas, 26″ × 32″. Addison
Gallery of American Art, Phillips Academy, Andover, Massachusetts.

Though his paintings were criticized and rejected by academic juries, in them
Sloan redefined and extended the social spaces within which women could be represented in high art. His paintings of lower-class women also encompass a range
of possible settings and experiences. In *Sunday, Women Drying Their Hair* Sloan
captured an altogether different moment in these women's lives (1912; Fig. 1.9).
For virtually the entire turn-of-the-century working class, the six-day work week
was the norm, with Sunday the only day of leisure. Some used the day for excur-
sions; others caught up on domestic chores and prepared for the next work week.
Leisure remained unstructured, occurring at spontaneous moments during the day.
Sloan's painting documents such a moment. It shows three young women on a
tenement rooftop, the only sunny place among the crowded city buildings. There
they hang out their laundry and chat while letting the sun dry their hair.

For all its apparent innocence, this scene combines signs of class and sexuality
to mark these as working-class new women, who flout virtually every sign of Victorian gentility. Their youth and their appearance together would have suggested
to contemporary viewers and even casual readers of muckraking literature that they

shared an apartment, living without any traditional guardian of female virtue. In a semi-public setting, seen from a slightly elevated viewpoint, the women, framed by vertical smokestacks so that it seems as if we and others can observe from neighboring tenements, display themselves unselfconsciously in ways more appropriate to the privacy of the bedroom. One woman arches her back and stretches up to catch the sun. Another elevates her bare arm like a nude model and lets her shoes fall off, exposing her bare feet. A third, clad only in what appears to be an untied shirtwaist or chemise and slip, shakes out her unbound hair. The artist modified poses from contemporary studio painting or photography to achieve his casual effect. Apart from depicting working-class women as more openly sensuous—the sketchy, spontaneous brushwork emphasizes both the roughness of the surroundings and the animation of the subjects—the paintings show that the working-class new woman's vitality was also a positive sign of her independence. With the exception of *Sixth Avenue and Thirtieth Street,* few of Sloan's portrayals of working-class women can be associated with the poor-worker-as-victim literature produced by reform-minded social workers of the Progressive Era.

Sloan's paintings represent competing notions of gender and class at the turn of the century. Informed by his interactions with Greenwich Village feminists—from Max and Crystal Eastman to Emma Goldman—Sloan made paintings that confront the spaces of working women's lives and in so doing challenge the ideal of separate spheres and blur the boundaries of public and private life. Middle- and working-class new women sought realms of personal autonomy—through work, leisure, and a revolution in notions of sexual expression and sexual satisfaction within marriage. In taking on these issues through the images of exuberant working women, often in amusing situations, Sloan borrowed a device from turn-of-the-century movies, which used humor to make fun of and hence blunt feminist claims for equality. Like many moviemakers, who worked for a largely working-class audience, Sloan celebrated the spunk of women who could make their way through the demanding, occasionally terrifying, urban world. But these women found their pleasures in a heterosocial environment of commercialized leisure—not in feminist utopias or in woman-centered campaigns for reform. In this way the paintings incorporated the Progressive Era's liberal ideals of new womanhood without undermining patriarchal cultural norms.[53]

Around World War I, as the Gibson girl became obsolete, the designation new woman evoked a range of types that cut across class and occupational boundaries and signified a variety of social, sexual, and political practices. The new woman could be seen as a tough spinster feminist, a fast-dancing flapper, a free-love Greenwich Village bohemian, an avid careerist, a working mother, or a charity girl.[54] All these types, however, exemplified women's increasing engagement with social spaces that were public, urban, and modern.

Even if members of all classes and ethnic backgrounds resisted the most radical implications of feminism's specific campaigns for equality, communal domesticity, free love, and the right to the ballot, many accepted the broader ideals and typologies of new womanhood. In "The Unrest of Modern Woman," for example, Susanne Wilcox made a clear-cut distinction between a "conspicuous minority of restless, ambitious, half-educated, hobby-riding women" and the "submerged majority of sober, duty-loving women," all "secretly dissatisfied with the *role* of mere housewife" and eager to participate with men in the "game of life."[55]

Although this middle range of positive responses to the New Woman continued to be varied and selective according to the different institutional and ideological backgrounds of commentators, two common threads remained. One attributed new womanhood to forces of social rather than biological evolution and stressed woman's human nature. A second claimed the moral attribute as the primary one of womanhood. "The new woman is the old woman under new conditions," wrote Louise Connoly in 1913. She is new in "accidentals" rather than "essentials," and her "advance" results from changes in education, "labor saving inventions," new notions of physical development and efficiency, and an increasing claim of the individual against class privilege resulting from "a great wave of democracy."[56] The greatest enticement for women to move to the public sphere was the demand for a dutiful citizenship in the new morally self-conscious body politic. Two months after Connoly's piece appeared, Norman Hapgood reiterated her arguments in an editorial for *Harper's Weekly,* claiming that the new woman's place in the world would generate higher intellectual and moral standards.

> The Feminist Movement, properly understood, is merely the moral movement in human evolution. It is merely the substitution of modes of thought based on present conditions of industry and education for modes of thought which were built up under a system of constant warfare and general ignorance. The movement of women toward contributions to the world's ethical progress is just as resistless as the march of general education or the movement of industries out of the home into the factories. . . . The publication that undertakes to express progress can no more leave this movement out of account than it can ignore labor, or the relation of government to wealth, or scientific agriculture or public schools.[57]

In spite of such attempts to link new womanhood with social improvement or the moral attributes of femininity, not everyone felt kindly toward the new woman. Antagonism was grounded in middle- and upper-middle-class anxieties about social and political change. Domestic interiors by turn-of-the-century Boston school painters quietly reified the dutiful, submissive, hearthbound ideal of womanhood even as historical evidence suggested the new woman was moving away from the home. A more virulent strain of anti–new woman rhetoric spoke of biological rather than social evolution, employing the more misogynistic notions of Darwinian evolutionary theory to argue that women were undifferentiated beings, ranked with children or savages beneath fully evolved rational men, who were predestined to rule the world. In the grand scheme, women by nature could lay claim only to specific sexual and reproductive functions; they were meant to serve as passive helpmeets to men in their own quest for preeminence in the world. If a woman strayed from her course, she threatened the natural social order.

As Bram Dijkstra has shown in *Idols of Perversity,* this most extreme version of anti–new woman sentiment found international expression in academic and literary painting around the turn of the century. In America these works were widely known, thanks to their exhibition and subsequent circulation through reproduction in periodicals. They were also more popular than paintings by Ashcan school realists, whose depictions of exuberant working-class women marked a distinct shift in what many wanted to see as the natural order. Dijkstra shows how paintings that depicted women as allegorical figures or as subjects in mythological, medieval, or biblical narratives belonged to a scientific and literary discourse that waged a war on women on "the battlefield of words and images."[58] Dijkstra also argues that the most vehement anti-woman strain categorized women according to a powerful dualism as either virgins or whores, self-sacrificing angels or consuming, lustful demons. At first the more passive types—submissive, childlike, often weightless "collapsing women"—were equated with the "angel" of the Victorian home. Somewhat later in the century a fascination arose with the angel's opposite, the vampire, the prostitute, the murderous Judith or the power-depleting Delilah. Kenneth Hayes Miller's teacher, Kenyon Cox, portrayed another popular evil woman in his two-panel depiction of Lilith consorting with a serpent above the Temptation and Expulsion (1892; Fig. 1.10). Eve's wicked predecessor in the Garden of Eden embodied all the powerfully negative forces attributed to the serpent demon. Such representations of women marked them as feminist predators, robbing worthy men of their place in the world. Whether fragile or feline, however, each typology degraded women, expressing anxiety about changing distributions of social and economic power increasingly signaled by the new woman.

In chronicling visual manifestations of the battle between the sexes at the turn of the century, Dijkstra examines various forms of late nineteenth-century academic painting against intellectual conditions that continued to influence early twentieth-century ideas about sex as well as race and class. Confronted by massive waves of immigrants beginning around 1880, many well-to-do, conservative native-born Americans worried that racially inferior strains from eastern and southern Europe would pollute the pure Anglo-Saxon American. Commentators anxiously noted the diminishing birthrate in the native-born middle-class population (still the most strongly perceived locus of new womanhood). Claiming that women had an obligation to "preserve the race," they cautioned them against pursuing a career or public service at the expense of a family.

1.10   Kenyon Cox, *Lilith*, c. 1892. Present location unknown.

Pictorially, especially in popular graphic imagery related to the anti-suffrage campaign, the angry evil feminist was often pitted against the benign mother or the "angel," negating compromise positions with iconography and physiognomy suggesting such opposites as good and evil, beautiful and ugly and the corresponding categories of civilized and rational against bestial and disordered. Tom Fleming's "Home or Street Corner for Woman? Vote No on Woman Suffrage" features two roundels (1915; Fig. 1.11), one with the Renaissance Madonna's successor, the serene mother with her cheek pressed against her child's, the other with a shrieking feminist, teeth bared, eyes rolled upward in satanic agony, and hair in Medusa-like disarray (a reference to her rejection of childbearing). The two roundels contrast

1.11 *Top:* Tom Fleming, "The Home or Street Corner for Woman? Vote No on Woman Suffrage," 1915. Lithograph, 18″ × 30″. Rare Books and Manuscripts Division, The New York Public Library, Astor, Lenox and Tilden Foundations.

1.12 *Above:* Rodney Thomson, "Militants," *Life,* March 27, 1913.

1.13 John Sloan, undated. Illustration for Mary Alden Hopkins, "Women March," *Collier's*, May 18, 1912. Crayon, ink, and pencil on white paper, 8½″ × 11″. The University of Michigan Museum of Art.

social rectitude with social disorder—both the responsibility of woman. Rodney Thomson's "Militants," an illustration for *Life* magazine, uses physiognomic categories to describe the militant Feminist (1913; Fig. 1.12). In row one, "As They Are," Thomson shows the militant as a hag with masculinized features; one of the major arguments against feminism and new womanhood centered on women's unsexing themselves or becoming masculine. In row two, "As They Think They Are," the feminists are beautiful heroines, saints and angels—this row could also be captioned "As Men Would Like Them to Be." The highest form of life is both the most beautiful and the most recognizably feminine. In row three, "As They Appear to the Police and Shopkeepers," the bestial nature of the militant emerges as she grows horns and pointed ears and again bares her teeth.

In contrast to these works, John Sloan's pro-suffrage drawings, published in Mary Alden Hopkins's 1912 article "Women March," provide a middle ground ignored in the anti-suffrage images. The drawing of four women marching retains the image of the suffragist as a mature woman, past the bloom of youth (Fig. 1.13). Sloan's women are proud and determined as they march in step, but their faces and

1.14   John Sloan, "Hooray, Hooray for Mother," 1912. Illustration for Mary Alden
       Hopkins, "Women March," *Collier's*, May 18, 1912. Ink and charcoal with
       traces of gouache on paper. Collection of Gary M. and Brenda H. Ruttenberg.

poses are pleasant and nonthreatening. This drawing's pendant, "Hooray, Hooray
for Mother," depicts a distinguished and enthusiastic father with three children
cheering as their (unseen) mother marches for the vote (Fig. 1.14). Here, mother
and father (the feminine and the masculine) exchange spheres, contributing to both
the private and the political, without compromising either category (compare this
drawing with Fig. 1.3, Gibson's anti-feminist cartoon of the overbearing wife opposite her emasculated husband).[59]

Although Sloan's two drawings portray traditional roles for women, together
they enact the contradictory premises of women's rights advocates—and of the
modern feminist movement—that coalesced in the suffrage campaign in the teens.
As Carrie Chapman Catt proclaimed in "Why Women Want to Vote" in 1915, the
vote was both a right of women as persons, equal to men, and their duty as women,
different from men.[60] Women needed equality so that they might express their differences; their contributions as a group would help in areas that were more properly
theirs—for example, government regulation of housing and factory working con-

ditions and community betterment. Furthermore, with the twentieth-century shift to an urban industrial environment populated by dozens of ethnic groups, voting came to express not just individual but also group interests. In such a climate, the suffrage platform temporarily balanced women's diverse interests with the individual woman's access to the vote. Nancy Cott summarizes this balance: " 'Sameness' and 'difference' arguments, 'equal rights' and 'special contributions' arguments, 'justice' and 'expediency' arguments existed side by side," forging a balance that was neither "accommodationist" nor "conservative" but "encompassed the broadest spectrum of ideas and participants in the history of the movement."[61] With this coalition in 1920, women achieved the vote.

For most historians enfranchisement has marked the end of an era in feminism, a great divide in women's history. Commentators writing about the interwar decades focus on the political results of the franchise, the economic gains and losses of women in the work force, and the effects of both on women and the family, the implications of the "revolution in manners and morals" for women's emotional and sexual behavior and the new culture of consumption. Depending on their own historical vantage point, and to some extent their gender, writers since the late 1920s have claimed virtually everything and nothing for women, seeing them as either "struggling victims" or "active participants" in American history. In characterizing this historiography between 1920 and 1970, Estelle Freedman shows how writers alternately argued "that the vote was not used, that it had brought equality; that women became men's equals in the world of work, that they had remained in traditionally feminine occupations; that the sexual revolution had changed women's lives, that the revolution was more a literary than an actual occurrence."[62]

In considering these contradictions, Nancy Cott has looked at feminist intents in the "context of the conditions for or against their accomplishment." For her the 1920s were the end, not of feminism, but only of the suffrage campaign. "We should recognize the surrounding decades as a period of crisis and transition. The modern feminist agenda—to enable female individuals with several loyalties to say 'we' and to achieve sexual equality while making room for sexual difference between women and men—was shaped then." Part of that struggle consisted then, as now, in finding "language, organization, and goals" that express and help to maintain "functional ambiguity" rather than "debilitating tension" in the central paradox of the modern women's situation—her simultaneous equality with and difference from men.[63]

By the late 1920s there was a fresh outpouring of literature and commentary on the feminist New Woman; new womanhood was elided with or became a substitute for feminism, as demonstrated in the title of one of the more important published debates, "Feminism: Views for and against: A Symposium on the New Woman." *Current History* magazine dedicated its October 1927 issue to the debate, arguing,

"There is perhaps no aspect of present day social history more controversial in character or more delicate in its implications than that of the new status of woman."[64] A substantial body of this literature combined conservative social analyses with anti-feminist assumptions in theorizing about the New Woman's happiness in relation to societal health. Deeply concerned with her air of self-sufficiency (linked to her economic independence), the escalating divorce rate, and the decline of patriarchal authority, some writers argued that women were becoming too masculine, others that both the economy and the culture were overfeminized.[65] In either case, writers offered solutions that would re-fix the masculine and the feminine in more distinct, hence more traditional, categories while still allowing for something like "progress." Harriet Abbott's "Newest New Woman," as "the most modern" feminist, born at the very moment of the franchise, would place rights, freedom, suffrage, intelligence, and selfhood in the service of all the traditional obligations of women's sphere—self-sacrifice in "service to her family, her neighbors, her nation and her God."[66]

Abbott's credo typifies a shift in emphasis from the late 1920s through the first years of the Depression, when the literature on the woman question increased at the same time that a once quieter, though never absent, voice from the earlier decades of reform began to reassert itself. Some commentators argued that feminism was outmoded, having served its purpose of bringing women out of their separate sphere into the modern world; others, fearing feminism's futuristic or utopian projection of a genderless world, countered by invoking the importance of the family to social cohesion.[67]

In 1927, the writer Dorothy Bromley made the New Woman the quintessential figure of accommodation in this minefield of representations. Like Caroline Ticknor, the apologist for the Gibson girl, Bromley used the rhetoric of opposition to contrast two recent types: Like Ticknor, she staged a changing of the guard, pitting the angry feminist of the immediate prewar years against the New Woman of the post-franchise decade, the "Feminist—new style." In choosing the term *feminist,* Bromley acknowledged that the latest New Woman profited from her prewar sisters' struggles to gain the franchise. At the same time, however, Bromley wanted to rid "the average male" of the idea that the new woman was a "sterile intellectual" who cared only about "expressing herself—home and children be damned." For Bromley, "old-style feminism" suggested "either the old school of fighting feminists who wore flat heels and had very little feminine charm, or the current species who antagonize men with their constant clamor about maiden names, equal rights, woman's place in the world, and many another cause . . . *ad infinitum.*"[68]

To do away with the idea of the New Woman as "fighting feminist," Bromley formulated a credo for the new woman in her twenties and thirties. This "truly modern woman" was well dressed, fond of men, and interested in a full life that included pursuits outside the home as well as marriage and children. She valued her career for its creative outlets and for the economic self-sufficiency it provided. She cared about men and women as individuals but not women en masse, believing that as a collective entity women were frequently narrow, strident, and petty. She believed in being chic, and preferred "to keep the intonations of her voice and the quality of her gestures purely feminine, as nature intended them to be."[69] While conceding that the passionate premarital affair was permissible in the new climate of greater sexual freedom, she maintained a belief in monogamy and the marital bond. Within her "companionate" marriage, however, the new feminist demanded greater freedom, honesty, and intimacy.

Bromley sharpened distinctions between feminists who had worked together to gain the vote and women who now turned away from collective goals to concentrate on individual fulfillment. Bromley's old-style feminist lacked charm, denied the special qualities of her sex, and abandoned her "natural" roles of wife and mother. In Bromley's text the Gibson girl's looser, more tailored dress and assertive behavior— once positive signs of greater equality—become negative by association with the exaggerated stereotype of an immediate postwar feminist. Bromley has reinstated the "grace of motion" and vocal modulations of Caroline Ticknor's steel-engraving lady in her new-style feminist, whose voice and gestures were those intended by "nature." Charlotte Perkins Gilman's earlier characterization of the Gibson girl as "stronger," "braver," more "healthful," and more able sounds like the description of a healthy male soldier; the turn-of-the-century new woman who had fought for suffrage and had claimed a place in the political world had needed to develop a range of "masculine" skills. Once the battle was won, however, she could return to the home front and recultivate previously neglected attributes of womanhood. This is not to say that Bromley's new-style feminist is like Ticknor's steel-engraving lady. Bromley's new woman accepts woman's right to work and participate in the democratic process and is interested in self-fulfillment rather than selfless devotion to an ideal of duty and submissiveness. Her new woman, nonetheless, is continuous with a heterosexual ideal that privileges wifehood, motherhood, and feminine charm over a strong woman-centered community that might threaten the patriarchal order.

Another writer, Lillian Symes, who like Bromley distanced herself from the "unpowdered, pioneer suffragette generation" of "braver, grimmer, and more fanatical feminists . . . who had to make the famous choice between 'marriage and career,' " distinguished herself and her peers from another new woman, the "postwar, spike-heeled, over-rouged flapper of today."[70] Condemned by some as representing the demise of femininity and its moral dignity—especially as the gawky figure contrasted with the Gibson girl in *Life* magazine (Fig. 1.15)—for others she symbolized what the franchise really granted: sexual "liberation." Symes argued that the flapper failed to understand the deeper social and political implications of the prewar women's movement.

1896   1926

Thirty Years of "Progress"!

1.15 "Thirty Years of Progress,"
      drawing for *Life* magazine
      featuring the Gibson girl of 1896
      and the Held flapper of 1926.

We grew up before post-war disillusionment engulfed the youth of the land and created futilitarian literature, gin parties, and jazz babies. If in those younger days we believed didactically in our right to smoke and drink, we considered over-indulgence in either "rather sloppy" if not anti-social. If we talked about free love and if a few even practiced it "as a matter of principle," we should have been thoroughly revolted by the promiscuous pawing and petting permitted by so many technically virtuous young women today. . . . Promiscuity was the one thing worse than marriage without love. We were idealists, you see, in our quaint way, and we took ourselves rather seriously. . . . From Olive Schreiner, Ellen Key, and Charlotte Perkins Gilman came our phraseology. . . . If all this makes us sound like prigs, I can assure you we were not. We made ourselves as attractive as we knew how to be, we were particular about our clothes, and few of us ever "sat out dances."[71]

The new, accommodating, feminist was aptly represented in the frontispiece to *Current History*'s symposium on the New Woman (Fig. 1.16). This figure could be comfortably situated between the Gibson girl and the flapper. Youthful, she wears contemporary fashions, having traded in her flat heels for high ones. She has not yet bobbed her hair—it is drawn back neatly from her attractive but not heavily made up face. Her stance is firm, but stable rather than aggressive. Attributes of

1.16 "The New Woman Emerging out of the Past," frontispiece for "A Symposium on the New Woman," *Current History* 27 (October 1927).

past and present accomplishments surround her: a pen, a globe, and books suggest her education and her literary production; a lyre and mask her cultural preoccupations; a T-square, an architectural plan, and scientific instruments her recent professional pursuits. Women's past and present roles are represented in a tapestry: wife-mother, spinner, pioneer woman, and turn-of-the-century athlete. Old and new remain inseparable.

In Bromley's and Symes's attempts to moderate the discourse of new womanhood one can locate both a credo for what some Greenwich Village radicals in 1920 called post-feminism and defenses against what Symes later called the new masculinism.[72] The new man, according to Symes, was ambivalent about modern women, a "gentleman who expects you to assume half the financial obligations and all the domestic ones."[73] In a world with diminishing job opportunities and increasing economic demands on the consumer a man felt a loss of both his ability to be the sole provider and his competitive edge against the new woman. Under these circumstances, he thinks back "wistfully" to his mother's time, when the position of woman did not need to be examined. Many male writers in the late 1920s and early 1930s argued that competition and public life undermined women's nature. Henry R. Carey concluded in a 1928 critique of rising divorce rates that "the quickest way to kill divorce is to restore to all loyal husbands . . . that natural authority which is theirs anyway the moment anything goes wrong. . . . it is surely a pity to destroy a family because the wife, who would not tolerate effeminacy in a man, insists on masculine activities for herself."[74]

Symes claimed that many of the diatribes against modern womanhood came from intellectuals, men "in a position to express what they feel." A writer herself, Symes felt that her male peers found it difficult to adjust to the industrial civilization that had helped to create public roles for women. "Creative" men, hypersensitive and unstable, had a "fairly large proportion of the so-called feminine qualities." Instead of "making peace with this happy combination, [they] are constantly at war within themselves." Symes noted furthermore that women have competed most effectively with men in the arts, causing men to feel a loss of love and of power. She concluded that the struggle between love and power was common throughout history, but because "man has acquired the habits of superiority and because that superiority is now being challenged, he is suffering more than woman from the ravages of this conflict. If it is ever resolved, the new masculinism will go the way of the old feminism."[75] Symes's analysis points to an anxiety about masculinity in the artistic and intellectual community that recalls the debates about gentility versus masculinity at the turn of the century.

Symes's and Bromley's articles were written as the Fourteenth Street School artists were producing some of their early representations of women shoppers and workers. Bromley's, in particular, deserves a closer look in light of the relation between these representations and her new-style feminist. Although *anti-feminist* is not a 1920s or 1930s term, the historian Lois Banner has used it to label Bromley's new composite because it describes a woman more concerned with individual goals than collective reform. Rayna Rapp and Ellen Ross suggest a less dramatic opposition, arguing that "lifestyle" feminism supplanted "activist" feminism as the new consumer culture co-opted feminist issues and a feminist rhetoric.[76] This shift transpired partly in response to a widely held belief perpetuated by popular historians, businessmen, politicians, and the media that women had achieved liberation. Having done so, women were more inclined to seek self-fulfillment through consumption (with the flapper and the homemaker becoming the principle targets for advertisers), through a new job, and through the family than to continue crusades for women's rights. Furthermore, those who resented the franchise claimed that in gaining rights, women had lost privileges like leisure and self-indulgence and the right not to work. In 1930, a woman who chronicled the aspirations of young college graduates wrote about yet another new woman:

> Here they are, all fresh and educated and ready to be good wives and mothers. And bent on being feminine, first and foremost, with a strong bias toward being supported. They have heard a lot about women's work and women's working, and some of them have experienced both. They know all about woman's place in the world of finance

and commerce and industry. . . . They see their elders fighting time and tide to hold their places in a world which is, say what you will, largely run by men, and they think it's poor policy. The younger women are going to fight for the privilege of being supported, coddled, courted and cherished. They consider feminism an artificial word.[77]

Finally, many commentators in the late 1920s accepted women's right to work but insisted that women not combine a career with marriage.[78] Their discussions were fueled by a concern for the future "wholeness" of the American family. They reassigned traditional roles to women, claiming that women who worked outside the home could improve family life through consumption. Benjamin Andrews wrote in 1929, "The world in which the typical family lives is the world built for it by the woman who spends."[79]

Within these generally conservative and individualistic trends of the 1920s, sales and clerical jobs, like those of the women imaged in Fourteenth Street School paintings, offered the new woman socially acceptable and desirable opportunities. By the post-franchise decade, almost 90 percent of retail sales positions were held by females, and the jobs had been stereotyped as woman's work since shortly after the war.[80] In these jobs, women served others and behaved in ways that did nothing to alter traditional womanly roles. Moreover, since young unmarried women most often filled these jobs, they were perceived as temporary positions, to end at marriage. Although the Depression and attendant job scarcity helped to solidify the growing public belief that a woman's proper place was at home, sex-stereotyped sales and clerical positions posed no threat to either the beleaguered male work force or traditional patterns of male and female behavior. Consequently, this kind of work continued to remain acceptable throughout the Depression.

The shift from political engagement to self-involvement through consumption, family life, and economic independence and the belief that certain jobs were more appropriate for women than for men was also touched by and at the same time reflected the central political debate in the post-franchise women's movement, over protective labor legislation for women. This debate divided those feminists who argued for gender difference from those who wanted gender equality.[81] The first camp included the majority of middle-class feminist reformers, trade unionists, and other advocates for working-class women who continued to believe in women's separate and special attributes—their moral superiority and nurturing capabilities—as mothers and childbearers. They argued that wage-earning women needed better hours and working conditions to preserve and protect their physical stamina for motherhood. These moderate feminists also argued that women workers were both poorly organized and overburdened with the responsibilities of work and motherhood; protective laws would win them the conditions men gained for themselves in trade and labor unions. Women in this group worked for legislation to preserve culturally sanctioned roles that signified for them an important achievement in the quest for political power.[82]

In the other camp (led by Alice Paul's National Woman's Party—the NWP), more militant feminists demanded nothing less than full equality. These largely upper-class and professional women submitted a draft of the first Equal Rights Amendment to Congress in 1923. They discounted all claims for women's biological inferiority and moral separateness, arguing further that protective labor legislation should be based on occupation rather than sex to maintain the principle of equality for all. Women could not be protected by separate laws and still be considered equal to men.[83] Moderate feminists, unwilling to risk legislative gains they had already made and seeing no legislative lobbying by the NWP on behalf of both sexes, accused the NWP of making class-based legislation for the bourgeoisie. They banded together against the smaller and more radical group and helped defeat the Equal Rights Amendment in 1923.

Members of the NWP, perceiving self-interest strictly in gender terms, believed that all women shared a sense of oppression as women. They also saw women as strong equal producers alongside men rather than as dependent wives and mothers in need of special protection. Their abstract sense of women's unity, expressed in the language of liberal individualism, and their single-minded devotion to equal rights blinded them to the diverse experiences of women from other classes and ethnic backgrounds. Furthermore, the political climate of the 1920s—after the Bolshevik Revolution and the Red scare and the general return to "normalcy" under Harding—contributed to divisions within the feminist movement. In particular, it marginalized the Left, splitting the socialist and feminist coalition that had been so important in the teens by branding elements of it anti-American and anti-family. Within the NWP, equal rights became the single issue as class consciousness became the centerpiece of Communist party doctrine.[84]

For all but the most radical feminists, the continuity of nineteenth-century thinking on women's separate sphere modified feminist thought during this period and served to reinforce a status quo based on the deeply held assumption that gained the day with the demise of the Equal Rights Amendment. Even though economic and social forces drew women into the public world of work and politics, women's natural roles were still those of wife and mother. Within the broader discursive framework of new womanhood I call this long-standing and essentially middle-class belief the ideology of woman's proper place.

Living in neighborhoods where modern womanhood took shape, the four artists of the Fourteenth Street School were fully enmeshed in debates about it. Around Union Square they found their female subjects in occupations that were implicated in the same debates, though in different ways. From art schools and art periodicals and in museums they discovered pictorial strategies that allowed them to join contemporary exchanges on the experience of modern womanhood. The interactions of each artist with these different facets of social and cultural life are the subject of the following chapter.

CHAPTER TWO

THE ARTISTS

The entire Fourteenth Street group was motivated by an interest in the picturesque, in spectacle, in action, and in local color. If there was criticism, it was only by implication. On the whole, they were more interested in the excitement of urban life.

MILTON W. BROWN, 1955

The problem of writing an artist's biography lies at the heart of Alison Lurie's 1988 novel *The Truth about Lorin Jones*. Polly Alter, an art historian and feminist employed by a New York museum, has recently mounted her first exhibition, Three American Women. The show generates such a strong critical and financial interest in the overlooked work of one of these women, Lorin Jones, that Polly receives a grant to write her biography. The story Polly determines to tell, based on her initial research into Lorin's life for the exhibition, is that of a shy, fragile woman, manipulated by men, even driven toward the self-destructive behavior that caused her early death. Lorin's husband, an older and highly esteemed art critic, had kept her from contact with the art world; her cagey dealer, who believed there was no such thing as a great woman artist, had barred her from the decision-making process in the exhibition of her work; her feckless young lover, an irresponsible poet, had run with her to Key West, then abandoned her in the days of her final illness. Polly, encouraged by a circle of supportive feminist friends, will breathe new life into her beautiful and gifted subject, transforming her from victim to heroine.

When she finishes her research, much of which consists of interviews with Lorin's relatives, friends, and associates, Polly is confused and feels "her subject splitting into multiple, discontinuous identities."[1] Polly also realizes that the shape of her account will determine her own future; to write the book from the perspective of Lorin's dealer and former husband (portraying Lorin as a "neurotic genius") would mean presenting them in a generous light. This approach would guarantee the book good reviews and assure her acceptance in established (male) art circles. To follow her original plan would gain her the praise of feminist critics but harm the professional connections she had already cultivated.

Polly comes to understand (though not in these terms) that along with Lorin, each of her informants is a divided, inconsistent classed and gendered subject with a correspondingly different take on Lorin's life, and on one another. Beyond the consensus that Lorin was beautiful and talented, Polly finds little agreement. If all informants tell the truth, there is no one truth about Lorin Jones; there are only various stories. Polly also senses the shifts in her own version of Lorin. Different Lorins emerge not just with the imposition of other views but with her changing reactions to events in her own life and their parallels or divergences from those of Lorin's life. Her own identity and Lorin's are "subjectivities in process."

Faced with portraying Lorin Jones as either "innocent victim" or "neurotic unfaithful, ungrateful genius," Polly rejects both choices as "all lies" and decides to tell instead "the whole confusing contradictory truth," even if it means producing a narrative that will be "unfocused" and "inconsistent."[2] Though Polly realizes that Lorin's life has moved through a number of contradictory subject positions, represented in part by the narratives of her informants, she still believes that she can arrive, through multiplicity, at something like the truth. In fact, Polly will add yet another, perhaps fuller, account to the chain of stories (texts), but it too will become the subject of another interpretation.

Although I have not confronted the extreme contradictions of this fictional narrative, I use Polly's dilemma to problematize my own "biographical" account of four contradictory subjects. I discuss the four artists individually and in relation to one another—chronicling the "road to Fourteenth Street," where they found the common subject matter that gave them their name. I want to show how their lives, beliefs, and activities were bound up in a process of social change; personal artistic development cannot exist outside of historical processes, institutions, or ideologies. Although all the artists shared subjects and a commitment to painting the contemporary scene by drawing on the art of the past, each pursued that commitment from within a particular constellation of experiences, some shared, some not. They arrived at Fourteenth Street via different paths; differences of generation, class, gender, social life, education, and politics make for different patterns of interaction in their lives and art. Miller, a generation older than the other three artists, was a close friend and teacher of Marsh's and Bishop's. Soyer was a Russian Jewish immigrant whereas the other three were native-born and middle to upper-middle class. Bishop worked as a woman artist among the men. In the early thirties, Soyer joined the Communist John Reed Club while Miller, the most politically conservative of the group, found fault with leftist activities; Bishop and Marsh could be characterized as New Deal liberals, though neither became a political activist during the Depression.

The problem of individual versus group identity looms large, especially since the designation Fourteenth Street School was initially general and fundamentally ahistorical. Coined by John Baur in 1951, during the early days of the New York school and formalist criticism, the name referred to certain formal categories of style. Baur described the Fourteenth Street School artists as romantic realists working in either a hard or a soft manner. They rediscovered "the poetry of the city and its poor," thereby continuing the revolution in subject matter initiated a generation earlier by the Ashcan school realists.[3] Though Milton Brown's brief 1955 analysis looks at how the group's training and influence make them a "school," "Fourteenth Street realism" remains a general term describing the urban version of American Scene painting and its best-known practitioners.[4] I retain the name here because it is familiar and convenient and because it designates a historically specific and symbolic social environment in which women imaged by these artists became major players.[5]

A second problem of group biography has to do with unequal evidence and its relation to artistic production. Accounts of individual artists cannot treat their lives and work as parallel; large bodies of archival material offer valuable insights but also leave large lacunae, as do monographs and exhibition catalogs. Critical response, depending on the fate of each artist's reputation, has been quantitatively as well as qualitatively mixed. Gallery records exist for Bishop and Marsh in the 1930s but are more difficult to locate for Soyer. Miller left a large personal correspondence in which he records what he read and discusses his artistic philosophy, but he destroyed much of his early work. Marsh obsessively documented his comings and goings and his working habits in daily diaries. Biographers, though reticent about his personal life, have often focused on his personality and the psychological motivations underlying his art. Miller and Marsh died in the early fifties, when the interest in 1930s realism was at a standstill and before the recording of oral histories became a standard research technique. Like Miller, Bishop destroyed much of her early work (though some photographic records remain), but she talked at length about her art and her experiences as a female artist in interviews, especially after her first retrospective exhibition in 1974. Soyer destroyed his diaries from the 1930s and showed his works at several galleries, none of which kept records that survive. With the renewed interest in realism and the relation between art and politics in the seventies, Soyer, like Bishop, has been the subject of many interviews, including my own. He has also written four accounts of his travels and experiences, including that of being an artist.

A third problem (the one most closely related to Polly's dilemma) has to do with the "teller of the tale" and the uses to which the evidence is put. In accounts of their own work (statements about intention), artists determine how the work will be seen and read and how their lives will be understood—they create themselves. Such texts—whether personal interviews, autobiographical narratives, or biographies—are produced under different conditions, function according to their own conventions, and should be understood as both evidence and interpretation. As such they need to be historicized and weighed alongside other accounts rather than privileged as the most accurate statement of the work's meaning. The four members of the group spoke in different ways about their intentions: Miller believed that form was more important than subject, Marsh wanted to re-create the grand manner in his art, Bishop was concerned with the aesthetic problem of how to create movement, and Soyer claimed that he only painted what he saw and tried to make a picturesque arrangement. Many of their statements focused on the making of art or on the need to belong to part of a larger artistic tradition. Although all acknowledged the need to make contemporary life their primary subject, they rarely spoke about their attitudes toward shopping or working women in the Depression.

Artists' statements (and the concerns of their interrogators) may change over time to reflect a shift in critical interest (their own or that of a period) or a change in the market for their work. When I first interviewed Raphael Soyer, for example, his replies to my questions were almost verbatim transcriptions of his earlier writings in which he told anecdotes about his life and work that expressed his artistic values and his vision of the artist's social role. By the early eighties, however, Soyer was enlarging earlier accounts of the Depression to include a nostalgic invocation of the art world of the 1930s. In particular, he cited the struggles for political freedom (the fight against Fascism) and social betterment among an egalitarian community of artists. His understated critique of "blue chips in art" and artists as "celebrities" in the early eighties needs to be seen as part of a larger challenge by intellectuals on the Left to the values of the art world and the effects of Reaganomics.[6]

Biographers' narrative styles, artistic values, and subject positions can resemble or differ radically from those of the artists they discuss. Lloyd Goodrich, for example, who wrote monographs on Miller, Marsh, and Soyer, was Marsh's closest childhood friend. He studied with and wrote the first extended account of Miller, in 1930, and produced a substantial volume on Soyer in 1972. Goodrich followed a chronological model of development from the artists' youth to maturity. Based on his own frequent interactions with his subjects, his descriptive accounts deal with the artists' processes and concern themselves with artistic motivations and intentions. Although he was willing to discuss their general psychological makeup when I interviewed him, Goodrich was exceptionally discreet about their personal lives.[7]

To avoid a reductive biographical analysis of the works as direct transcriptions of individual artists' experiences, I emphasize the social and historical circumstances of making and viewing art, an approach that revises conventional critical assumptions of the artist as solitary creator. Each of the four artists was a historically located producer, painting in a New York City studio on Fourteenth Street according to the general dictates of American Scene painting and figurative composition in the twenties and thirties. Each worked through and was supported by an emerging network of art institutions in the interwar decades—galleries, museums, art schools, and social or political organizations supported them even as their works affirmed the artistic values of those institutions that sought to reconcile modernity and tradition. Moreover, a critical discourse explained, and continues to explain, how they worked and how their pictures are to be read. Finally, the four artists of the Fourteenth Street School were very much part of the world in which the discourses on new womanhood took shape. Whether in their personal lives or friendships, in their intellectual preoccupations, or in their artistic surroundings, they experienced the social changes and the social conflict brought about by changing gender roles and shifting notions of class. Such changes involved families, the world of work, and the institutions that helped to form their painting practices, not to mention the entire range of determining structures outside the artists' control. The artists (to quote Griselda Pollock) are themselves subjects "articulated through the visual and literary codes of [their] culture and inscribing across them both [their] particular history and the larger social patterns of which all subjects are an effect."[8]

In the four accounts that follow, I will touch on individual lives and social interactions that illuminate the artists' representations of new womanhood, considering the bearing of these elements on the meaning of the paintings in individual chapters on female types. The artists came to negotiate a middle ground in both their personal lives and artistic strategies by the late 1920s, when all began to paint the contemporary scene. To varying degrees they embraced the social changes of their time, but most did so without radically altering established gender roles.

KENNETH HAYES MILLER

Although Kenneth Hayes Miller was the most conservative in social and political outlook of the four artists I discuss, he spent his childhood in an environment that challenged many of the social and sexual underpinnings of Victorian America. Miller was born in 1876 to Annie Elizabeth Kelly and George Miller, who lived in the Oneida community, one of the more successful and long-lived of the nineteenth-century utopian experiments (1848–1879). Within the settlement, founded by John Humphrey Noyes (Miller's granduncle by marriage),[9] Oneidans, like the Shakers and the Mormons, combined a religious quest for spiritual perfection with a desire to alter monogamy and the nuclear family.[10] They did so, as Louis Kern has explained, through communal sexuality, complex marriage, and a eugenic experiment called stirpiculture. To separate the joyous amative component from the unwanted propagative result of sexual intercourse, Oneidan males, counseled by their leader Noyes, developed a system of male continence by which the male completely withheld ejaculation, permitting his female partner orgasm without fear of conception. This system of *coitus reservatus* was a version of the nineteenth-century spermatic economy doctrine, which held that the loss of seminal fluid would debilitate male vitality, in its most extreme form causing complete mental and physical deterioration. Whereas the usual solution was abstinence, the system of male continence permitted frequent sexual encounters in a community where free love (understood not as promiscuity but as a belief that love rather than marriage should determine sexual relations) was both central and sacred. It also allowed the male to develop and subsequently practice an extreme form of sexual self-control that demonstrated male perfection.[11]

Behind the system of complex marriage lay the assumption that the most unselfish love was one that subordinated individual desire and romantic feeling to the communal good. Hence, all men and women in the community were married to one another. Men could request sex from any woman in the settlement, and although a woman could refuse, she was not permitted to initiate any such encounter. Sexual pairings came under community surveillance, which took the form of regular mutual-criticism sessions. In 1867, as the ranks of single or widowed women grew and as the system of male continence proved an effective method of birth control, Oneidans instituted the eugenic experiment known as stirpiculture. Community leaders (principally Noyes himself) either selected or approved couples for childbearing.[12] The healthiest women mated with men who best exemplified perfectionist ideals to produce offspring who would improve the race or, at a more mundane level, fill a need within the community. It is said, for example, that Miller's parents were designated to produce a badly needed carpenter.[13]

George Miller and Annie Kelly, like many second-generation Oneidans, grew dissatisfied with complex marriage; couples designated for reproduction often forged romantic attachments. Community efforts to rechannel these bonds and to negate maternal connections by placing children in communal nurseries met with increasing resistance both inside and outside the community. In 1879 these pressures sent Noyes into exile near Niagara Falls; community members who moved to the Oneida suburb of Kenwood restored monogamous marriage among themselves. Miller's parents, who married and had another child, Violet, in 1882, followed Noyes and spent several years in the Niagara settlement before returning to Kenwood. George Miller worked for the various business ventures attached to the community, the most successful of which was Oneida Silver. During his son's adolescence, he managed the silver company's New York office. Kenneth attended the Horace Mann School, and in the 1890s took classes at the Art Students League, where he studied with the academic artists Kenyon Cox and H. Siddons Mowbray. Until World War I he maintained close ties with Kenwood, corresponding regularly with a cousin and friend and visiting his mother there during the summer. Miller established his residence in New York, where his attempts to earn a livelihood as an illustrator proved unsuccessful. He began earning a steady income as an art teacher, first at William Merritt Chase's New York School for Art (from 1899 until 1911, when it closed) and then at the Art Students League.[14] Miller's first wife, Irma

Ferry—whom he married in 1898—came from Kenwood, although she had never been part of the original community. She and Miller divorced in 1911, and Miller married Helen Pendleton,* a young art student with whom he had an apparently happy, if not always monogamous, marriage.[15]

Despite the radicalism of the Oneidans' separation of reproductive demands from the pleasure of sex, the community's social and sexual ideologies continued to reflect both the sexual tensions and the patriarchal structures of late nineteenth-century bourgeois society. Louis Kern shows how community practice was designed to effect social order. Women in the settlement received respect without any accompanying alterations in material circumstances or roles. They held positions of authority in community kitchens and nurseries, and although they attended mutual-criticism sessions, male leaders made all policy decisions. Oneida doctrine held that women were in need of control. In contrast to the Victorian cult of true womanhood, which granted women moral superiority for chastening the sexually uncontrolled male, the Oneidan philosophy reversed the charge. Women were selfish and sexually licentious; their nature was grounded in base physicality. Male love was noble and unselfish. Male continence, a demonstration of greater self-control, not only signified male superiority but also protected the spiritual male from entrapment by female sexuality. In this ideology women became objectified goods, controlled by the male, who maintained his power over them by reserving his semen.[16]

Conditioned by a biblical claim that man was above woman in all things and by a notion of biological difference that prescribed separate roles for men and women, most Oneida women accepted the doctrine of male superiority. Their rebellion in the late 1870s was shaped less by a demand for equal rights than by a desire to return to traditional monogamy and a family organization rooted in the ideology of separate spheres. This assertion of women's natural superiority within the family, conjoined with a belief in women's natural submissiveness and duty, challenged the values of Oneida and eventually undermined the all-encompassing yet precarious structures of social control.[17]

Over the years Miller's intellectual response to the Oneida ideology was part rejection, part accommodation. The artist's belief in certain Oneidan ideals was not simply an extension of Oneidan values but the integration of Oneida's principles of sexual radicalism (and its attendant conflicts) into a particular segment of the larger New York intellectual milieu. Throughout the teens Miller lived near Green-

---

*Although I refer to all four artists by their surnames, when I discuss the male artists with their wives, all of whom took their husbands' names, I have sacrificed absolute consistency, attempting to balance one preference, for an egalitarian practice (i.e. Kenneth Hayes Miller and Helen Pendleton Miller), with another, for a straightforward style (i.e. Kenneth and Helen Miller). In a few instances I retain a male artist's surname alongside his wife's first name (i.e. Miller and Helen). While this may not be fully satisfying, it avoids making the marriage sound like a law practice (i.e. Miller and Miller).

wich Village, where many of the most radical new woman gathered, in company with male writers, social reformers, and literary figures, to articulate new forms of feminism, modern love, and socialism. One component of their sexual discourse focused on separating reproductive concerns from sexual pleasure—also a central concern in the Oneida community. At the same time, however, writers began to express what Ellen Kay Trimberger has defined as the desire "to combine mutual sexual fulfillment with interpersonal intimacy."[18] Under the influence of the European writers Edward Carpenter and Ellen Key (an advocate of shared passion and friendship whose *Love and Marriage* Miller read avidly), Village intellectuals challenged the ideal of separate spheres. Where nineteenth-century feminists wanted to create more equal marriages by deemphasizing passion (and hence reproduction), thereby freeing women to enter the public sphere, their twentieth-century Village counterparts campaigned for birth control and advocated a psychological and sexual intimacy that would make men and women fully equal. Women would share men's public roles while males would share the domestic sphere.[19]

In its most radical formulation this ideal of psychological and sexual intimacy and equality was short-lived, its fullest articulation, acceptance, and practice limited to the teens. By the 1920s it had become generalized as the middle-class ideal of companionate marriage. The intellectuals, many of them male, who continued to support the notion of sexual intimacy did so now in the context of marriage and family rather than a love relationship. Furthermore, in the less politically progressive climate of the postwar years a greater level of intimacy became possible as women refocused their energies, empathizing with men from the domestic sphere. The companionate ideal accommodated sexual intimacy without recognizing ideals of equality.[20]

Like other middle-class intellectuals of his generation who had migrated to New York, Miller experimented with social and political radicalism in the teens. In 1916 he voted for the Socialist candidate Eugene Debs and marched with his suffragist wife Helen for "votes for women." His circle of literary acquaintances included Theodore Dreiser, a close friend whose social realist novels were singled out by Randolph Bourne in his *New Republic* book reviews for their direct and honest treatment of American life and sexual mores. Miller admired Van Wyck Brooks, Sherwood Anderson, and the literary and music critic Paul Rosenfeld, an avowed cultural nationalist, who proclaimed Miller an important *modern* American painter—along with Albert Ryder, Marsden Hartley, Georgia O'Keeffe, Arthur Dove, and Alfred Stieglitz—in his 1924 publication *Port of New York*. Though Miller never mentions meeting Max Eastman, the artist was particularly interested in his literary criticism; Eastman was the editor of the radical *New Masses* whose political activism included his organizing a men's committee to support suffrage. Finally, during this period Miller embarked on a systematic study of the works of Freud. Although he wanted principally to understand the relation between the unconscious and creativity, he also professed an interest in Freud's insights into femininity and human sexuality.[21]

Miller's activities and interests also conformed to a generational pattern: short-lived political radicalism succeeded by conservatism in the twenties and thirties. Furthermore, his marriage made conventional demands on his wife while permitting him both greater independence and control. Miller supported the family primarily through teaching at the Art Students League. Although Helen Miller was also a practicing artist, she assumed all traditional familial duties, especially following the birth of their only daughter, Louise, in 1914. Throughout the teens, Miller and Helen seemed to have a close and intellectually stimulating relationship; they read literature to one another in the evenings, went out with friends, and became deeply interested in Freudian psychology.[22] When Miller moved to his Fourteenth Street studio in 1923, the dynamics of the marriage changed. Armed with a new knowledge of Freud, the Millers evolved a more open, though still committed, relationship. During the week, Helen and Louise remained at the family home a short distance from the studio, where Miller lived during the week, returning home on the weekends. Around this time, Miller began a succession of liaisons with female art students. Helen and the current mistress presided over the weekly Wednesday afternoon teas Miller held in his studio for more than a decade.[23]

Students and close friends who came to the teas have noted contradictions in Miller's personality and behavior. He was by many accounts a stern and exacting teacher, who imparted a wealth of knowledge to students but exerted a strong control over their production. Most considered him a deliberate and disciplined (if not talented) artist. They described his approach to painting and to life as intellectual and ascetic; one student called him an "uptight New Englander"—a reference, perhaps, to the Oneida ideal of male self-control.[24] Alexander Brook, another student, once told Raphael Soyer, "When Miller is finished criticizing a painting of yours, you feel like pushing your foot through it."[25] He was also described as sensitive and vulnerable to criticism—and as a man who possessed a deeply romantic and sensuous side.[26]

Throughout the twenties and thirties, Miller continued to express great affection for Helen and Louise in notes penned from his studio.[27] His correspondence with his mother—herself a fiercely independent yet loving woman—conveyed the devotion of a dutiful son. Although Miller's sexual behavior typified that of urban intellectuals in the teens and 1920s, his letters reveal that he continued to hold deeply conventional attitudes about women's separate roles. On more than one occasion, for example, Miller professed his inability to care for himself without Helen's nurturing skills. He often told his mother that Helen would have to explain Louise's progress since he had been too preoccupied with work to notice. At Christmas in 1915 he wrote, "I know you are hungry for news of Louise, what new words she has learned and new ways. I can't recall. Helen will not fail you in these topics I am sure."[28] Clearly he considered Helen's maternal responsibilities more significant than his paternal ones, more a part of her natural sphere of activity. Miller expressed great admiration for Helen's painting and accepted a woman's need to have outside interests. "Helen wants to get into some kind of practical work as Louise gets older," Miller wrote to his cousin Rhoda Dunn. "The business of being merely a wife and mother is too deadening for always."[29] By "practical" he seems to have meant the feminized occupation of clerical work; several years later he expressed delight with Helen's progress in typing. In spite of Miller's concessions to modern womanhood, however, their companionate marriage centered around his own activities as teacher and artist, their emotional life around his needs, which he controlled. Helen's role was that of wife and mother first and artist last.[30]

Miller's social and sexual behavior must be interpreted in light of his experiences both in the Oneida community and in Greenwich Village during the teens and twenties. He accepted the greater sexual freedom espoused in both communities, and he believed in human perfectionism and in male superiority as the means to social control. At the same time, his parents' accounts of Oneida's repressive measures made him suspicious of certain forms of radical social and political change. Studio liaisons notwithstanding, he clung to the ideal of companionate marriage. Then in the early 1930s, when he was close to sixty and when many younger artists joined the political Left, Miller expressed his deep reservations about all revolutionary activities. He rejected his own experience of what he called communism (Oneidan communism had aspirations very different from those of the intellectual Left of the thirties), arguing that individual rather than communal values must remain at the heart of the American political system.[31]

REGINALD MARSH

Some of Miller's values would be passed along to one of his more admiring protégés, Reginald Marsh. Although Marsh also came to Greenwich Village in the early 1920s, he arrived via a route different from Miller's. Furthermore, he experienced New York and the Village through the eyes of a postwar generation of youthful artists and writers, not, like Miller, as a member of a generation that came of age in the 1890s, participated in the Armory Show, and advocated suffrage. Miller came from a solidly middle-class background; Marsh's inherited wealth, upper-middle-class background, education, and marriage gave him ready access to the established art world.

Marsh's early biography resembles the romantic narrative of the artist-to-be. He was born in Paris in 1898 over the Café du Dôme, a well-known gathering place for artists. As a small child he was sickly and passed quiet hours reading and sketching. Both parents were artists, supported by income inherited from Marsh's paternal grandfather, who had made a fortune in the Chicago stockyards. Marsh's father,

Fred Dana Marsh, exhibited at the Paris Salon and made his reputation painting portraits in the then popular style of John Singer Sargent. In 1902, when he was only thirty-one, the National Academy of Design elected Fred Marsh an associate member. He went on to execute several mural commissions and finally painted men working on the construction of New York's early skyscrapers.[32] Lloyd Goodrich, Marsh's early biographer and childhood friend, characterized Fred Marsh as a man of too many talents who never realized his potential as a painter. Disillusioned with his career, he turned to amateur inventing and architectural projects. And he discouraged his son from becoming a professional artist.[33] By contrast, Marsh's mother, Alice Randall, enthusiastically supported her son's career choice. Alice had received her training from the academic artist Frank Vincent DuMond in the early 1890s and went on to become a painter of miniatures.

The Marsh family returned to America when Reginald was about four and settled in Nutley, New Jersey, then populated by many artists and writers. Marsh's childhood and adolescence were typical for his social class and background, with private schools and summer vacations in the fashionable seaside retreat at Sakonnet, Rhode Island. Marsh spent his junior year of high school at Riverview Military Academy in Poughkeepsie, New York, followed by senior year at the prestigious Lawrenceville Preparatory School. In the fall of 1916 he entered Yale University, where he decided to major in art.[34]

Yale educated him in the tradition of high European culture—literary classics and, in art, the Renaissance masters. Studio training at the university remained fully academic,[35] but Marsh found a release from the regimentation in illustrating a variety of popular subjects for the Yale *Record*, a humor magazine. Campus colleagues appreciated his depictions of muscle men, locomotives, pretty girls, and Yale social events so much that by his senior year the editor of the *Record*, William Benton, took the unprecedented step of paying Marsh fifty dollars per month for drawings to be used in the magazine after Marsh's graduation. Finally, university life also introduced Marsh to the fast-paced life of contemporary privileged youth he would pursue further in Greenwich Village. He took part in all the pleasures— alcohol, girls, and dancing parties—of American social customs and gender relations in the postwar world.

Marsh arrived in New York with his sights initially set on newspaper and magazine illustration rather than painting. In a short time he established himself as a free-lance illustrator, accepting assignments that gave him much of his subsequent New York subject matter and working for publications targeted to vastly different audiences. From 1922 to 1925, the popular new tabloid the *Daily News* employed Marsh to sketch and write critiques for their vaudeville column. Frank Crowninshield from the high-style magazine *Vanity Fair* sent Marsh on his first of many trips to Coney Island. For the new *New Yorker*, Marsh drew sketches to illustrate theater and film reviews and created portraits of well-known figures for the magazine's Profile section. He also entered the world of theater as a set designer; in 1923 he worked with Robert Edmond Jones of the Provincetown Playhouse on sets for a revival of the play *Fashion; or, Life in New York*. Even when Marsh took up painting, he continued to illustrate, working for periodicals as varied as *Fortune* and *Life* and, for a short period in the early 1930s, for the radical publication, the *New Masses*.

Marsh developed his attachment to Greenwich Village bohemia during the early twenties, as the prewar generation gave way to the postwar generation. Although he numbered some of America's foremost realist writers among his friends and acquaintances—among them John Dos Passos and Theodore Dreiser—Marsh arrived just after the most radical women's rights activity, labor unrest, anti-war activism, and artistic experimentation had either subsided or taken a more moderate course. Many progressive writers and artists associated with *The Masses* had left the Village for Europe, for the New York suburbs (Floyd Dell, Max Eastman, and Boardman Robinson, the contemporary cartoonist Marsh most admired, made Croton-on-Hudson a suburban bohemia), or the Southwest (Mabel Dodge Luhan and, at least part-time, John Sloan). A number became more conservative in their outlook. Floyd Dell, the arch supporter of feminism and free love in the teens, advocated monogamous marriage and stable sexual relationships by the 1920s—a revised new womanhood.[36] Many felt that the Village had lost its sense of serious artistic purpose and had turned into a haven of commercialism, tourism, and pseudo-bohemianism. Speakeasies attracted outsiders and rents climbed (prompting a number of artists to look to Fourteenth Street for cheaper studios). In *Exile's Return*, Malcolm Cowley distinguished the individualism of his own apolitical "lost" generation of the 1920s from the collaborative socialism of earlier intellectuals: " 'They' [the earlier group] had been rebels: they wanted to change the world, be leaders in the fight for justice and art, help to create a society in which individuals could express themselves. 'We' were convinced at the time that society could never be changed by an effort of the will."[37] The distinction Cowley made is like that between prewar activist feminism and post-franchise individualized feminism.

Throughout the twenties Marsh gave full attention to advancing his career. He filled his time with schooling and educational travel and took advantage of exhibition opportunities and illustration assignments. He must have decided to study painting almost immediately after coming to New York because he took painting classes from John Sloan and Kenneth Hayes Miller during the 1921–22 season at the Art Students League. Marsh's "conversion" to painting and his increasing respect for the old masters began seriously with a six-month European trip to Paris, London, and Florence beginning in December 1925, followed by more study with Miller. By the end of the decade, Miller and Marsh had forged a close personal friendship along with what would be a lifelong student-teacher bond. Marsh would later claim that he showed Miller everything he made. In turn, Miller encouraged Marsh not to forsake the working-class urban subject matter and sketchy illustrator's style he had learned from Sloan but rather to integrate his love for the old masters with his more inclusive reportorial approach.[38]

Marsh's decision to become a painter and his respect for the canonical works of old master painting cannot be considered surprising given a family background rooted in the American academy and a Yale education that emphasized the heritage of Western European thought and culture. In 1923 he married Betty Burroughs, a fellow student at the Art Students League, whose father, Bryson Burroughs, had been curator of painting at the Metropolitan Museum of Art since 1907. Throughout their marriage, which ended in divorce in 1933, Marsh and Betty resided in the Burroughs family home in Flushing. This environment continued his early connection to the world of art and fueled his desire to extend the tradition of high European art to the American scene.[39]

Betty ultimately found that Marsh, despite his family's wealth and his ties to the conservative art world, behaved in ways that made her feel rootless and kept the two of them from settling into the family life she eventually desired.[40] Though biographers and close friends described him as a shy and gentle intellectual who read Shakespeare, Dante, and Proust, Marsh was frequently rough edged, his interactions abrupt. Edward Laning characterized him as a Jimmy Cagney gangster type, a "tough dead-end kid" who spoke out of the side of his mouth.[41] Social interactions were not always smooth, though Marsh's detailed diaries from 1929 through the 1930s show that he led an active social life. Close friends, like Miller, Bishop, and Laning, another pupil of Miller's who also painted Fourteenth Street subjects in the early 1930s, made their way to the Burroughs family home on Sundays. Marsh had regular lunch, dinner, and movie engagements, and frequently attended art openings. In fact, the diaries describe a frenetic pace of working and socializing combined with an emerging pattern of success that left little room for family life. Even when Marsh inherited an estate of close to $100,000 on his grandfather's death in 1928, he chose to remain in the Burroughs family enclave rather than move to a new home. In 1928 he supplemented the Flushing workplace with his first Fourteenth Street studio, at 21 East Fourteenth Street. By this time he had been an established illustrator for seven years, was fully committed to his study of painting, and had expanded his work into printmaking (etching and lithography) and watercolor (a medium that brought him his first one-man shows). The new studio location gave Marsh, who was seldom without a sketch pad, direct access to neighborhood subjects that would occupy him for the next several years—the burlesque houses, the young women on Fourteenth Street subway platforms, and, by the early 1930s, the neighborhood's unemployed men. Moreover, his new studio was only a few doors away from Miller, Bishop, and Laning. In this way, he strengthened already close personal and artistic ties.

Marsh's growing success, his additional studio space on Fourteenth Street, and changing expectations for family life on his wife's part brought out differences that culminated in divorce. The ten-year marriage records many of the tensions of the shifting practices and discourses attached to new womanhood in the interwar years. Betty Burroughs had been an archetypal urban flapper in the early 1920s—bright, well-to-do, and, like her future husband, caught up in the fast pace of postwar city life.[42] Her letters to Marsh, many written from Ogunquit, Maine, where she summered with friends, urged him to come up to parties. Her prose is punctuated with contemporary slang. She often referred to Marsh as "you Old Thing," and she signed her letters "s'long." Several early letters project a certain level-headed cool:

> Say, young feller me lad, you worry your Auntie when you write her affectionate letters. It ain' that she minds your being affectionate (Lord knows, you do it at your own risk) but she suspects such sentiments to be subject to change without notice to the public. In other words I don't respect the impulses of a moment. . . . Be sure of constancy before expressing affection. Not that anyone can avoid pain in these matters of the heart—but perhaps the amount can be reduced by a little judicious forethought. I think my heart is the consistency of cold pea soup. Anyhow, it is not to be allowed to get the jump on me without the full approval of my head. I don't believe in the one love of a lifetime stuff but on the other hand, falling in love is too serious a matter to indulge in unless you are banking on it lasting a reasonably long time.[43]

Betty's prose makes the strong declaration of independence required of the 1920s flapper. In another letter to Marsh, dated July 19, 1923, Betty chastised him for being too dependent on her, asserting her independence but also revealing an anxiety typical of the period: that there might be too great a reversal in traditional gender roles. Ultimately, she calls on Marsh to go his own way, to "conceal" some of his need for her:

> Your first letter gave me a horrid sick feeling. You said something about being a barnacle—cleaving to me as to a rock. . . . But seriously, ye Gods, Reg, there is an awful grain of truth in it and I won't face life with you on my skirt tails—Life my child is a rocky road at best and with an inert drag behind—Please assure me that you will go your own gait—a good swift, clear-headed pace—and may even be able to give me a hand up over bad spots. What a sensitive soul you are. There are things I want to ignore (like your feeling of dependence on my energy) but you feel them and haven't the wit to conceal.[44]

While Marsh was in Reno in the winter of 1933 awaiting their divorce, he received several letters from Betty that suggest how changing definitions of independence, dependence, and the sexual freedom permissible in a companionate marriage all entered into their decision to part. Betty, who had wanted a child, gave birth to a son, Caleb, in July 1932; early in 1934 Marsh gave the child over for adoption to the man Betty married.[45] Marsh's career had blossomed more rapidly than Betty's, and he became more preoccupied with his own work and grew apart from her. Betty, who ten years earlier had cautioned Marsh about his dependence, now spoke of her own need for an "absorbing, exclusive love," one she believed her new husband would be able to give her.

Following his divorce Marsh returned to New York, where he engaged in a ten-month flurry of social activity before marrying the painter Felicia Meyer in January 1934. His diary entries for 1933 suggest that he floundered during this year between marriages: they were garbled and cryptic, the writing often sloppy and illegible where before it had been neat. (Since childhood, Marsh had kept careful journals in which he recorded all social activities and everything from the weather to the number of paintings, watercolors, and etchings he did in a month.) Moreover, the content of the entries shows changes in his life. His earlier work patterns—painting by day, working on prints in the evening—seem more erratic. He dined out almost every night or, with the repeal of prohibition, met friends for cocktails. Occasionally he noted his hangovers.[46] During this period Marsh devoted less energy to painting, more to cartoons and etchings. Marilyn Cohen has suggested that although the Depression accounted for Marsh's expanding his subject matter to include images of unemployed men, events in his own life during 1933 also contributed to the proliferation of scenes showing drunken vagrants and Bowery derelicts.[47] In an entry for November 25 Marsh first mentions Felicia Meyer, his future wife. After their initial lunch date, they were together nearly every day for lunch, dinner, and dances. Marsh went to her family's vacation home in Dorset, Vermont, for Christmas, and they were married the following month. At that time they moved down the street from the apartment Marsh had occupied since his divorce (at 11 East Twelfth Street) to 4 East Twelfth Street. For the rest of his life, Marsh's studio would never be more than two blocks from his apartment, which housed his etching press.[48]

Marsh's life without a partner—to judge from his diaries and accounts by friends—lacked structure. In 1934 Marsh resumed his regular working habits; he became enormously productive again and made some of his best work. His own desire for structured work time emerges in affectionate triweekly correspondence with his new wife, Felicia (whom he called Timmy), the following summer. (Like Betty, Felicia left New York for New England in the summer to paint landscapes.)[49]

To a greater extent than is apparent with any of the other artists, biographers and interpreters of Marsh's life have deployed psychoanalytic categories to describe his personality and his art in terms of generational tensions and gender conflict. Marilyn Cohen, whose interpretation of the self-referential side of Marsh's art will be taken up more fully in Chapter 5, argues that the repetition of subjects and themes has as much to do with his psyche as with his wish to chronicle the urban scene.[50] Both Lloyd Goodrich and Edward Laning focus on Marsh's extreme competitiveness, connecting it to his need to affirm his masculinity. It is revealed in Marsh's childhood diaries, where he gauged his self-worth according to his athletic achievements.[51] Lloyd Goodrich explained that Marsh "always tried desperately to act like a perfectly normal boy interested chiefly in sports and fights." He was interested, in other words, in asserting his masculinity against the more genteel pursuit of art as practiced at home by both parents.[52]

His competitiveness continued into his adulthood. Laning recounts two events that reveal Marsh's continuing need to assert his virility:

> One night, it must have been about 1933, I went to dinner with Reg and Jacob Burck (then the cartoonist for the *Daily Worker*), and after dinner we went back to Reg's place. He was then living alone, between marriages. In his top floor apartment on Twelfth Street he had installed his etching press. When we entered, he looked at the press and said to us, "John Curry was here this afternoon. He put his shoulder under that press and lifted it off the floor!" Reg took off his jacket and lunged at the press. He struggled until the sweat poured from his forehead. He couldn't budge it. Some years later on a government art assignment during the Second World War, his ship crossed the Equator and he was "hazed." He was blindfolded and required to "walk the plank." Reg didn't merely jump as he was commanded to do. Instead, he posed on the board and dived into the empty canvas tank—and broke his arm.[53]

As time went on, Marsh's intense competitiveness channeled itself into his artistic production, over which he maintained strict control. Never without a sketchbook, he drew and painted by day and kept track of the number of evenings he etched every month and the number of sketching trips he made to Coney Island. Determined to excel in every medium—as an illustrator, cartoonist, painter, muralist, and printmaker—he produced an extraordinary quantity of work, some of poor quality because of his experimentation. He also wanted to be involved in all aspects of the art world. He served on the Art Students League board and eventually taught year-round, even though he was financially independent. His artistic activity, fueled by a desire for success, was also, as Marilyn Cohen has argued, driven by a need to prove himself "as a man."

A number of Marsh's friends, among them Raphael Soyer, suggested that his competitiveness contributed to his early death. Soyer, who depicted Marsh at work in the early 1940s with an etching plate in his hands, recalled that Marsh's "prodigious" energies made it impossible for him to pose unoccupied for what was to have been a more straightforward portrait.[54] Laning, somewhat cynical himself about American cultural stereotypes of masculinity, characterized Marsh as the victim of the Hemingway syndrome:[55]

> Like all the American boys, Marsh was overreaching himself. Like Fitzgerald, Pollock and Hemingway, he killed himself. Or something in our culture goaded him, and them, beyond human endurance, and *we* killed them. Miller always told us "know your limitations," but this is the lesson that the American Boy, even the most studious, never learns.[56]

According to Laning, Marsh's tough exterior was a facade for a vulnerable, shy, and gentle person who competed to win the approval of those on whom he was dependent. Marsh confessed his deep insecurity to Raphael Soyer when he told his fellow artist that he was undergoing psychoanalysis. He confided to Soyer that every time his mother had left him for even a short period of time, he had feared she would never return.[57] Marsh evidently longed for his father's approval, rarely forthcoming in a relationship Laning has described as "strained and difficult." An academic painter, Fred Dana Marsh was unable to accept Marsh's energetic and fundamentally unacademic style. Marsh's late 1920s representations of working men building skyscrapers and his interest in mural painting may have been attempts to please his father by repeating his themes or to compete with his father's own earlier successes. Marsh's family, concerned about his preoccupation with illustration and lower-class subjects, may have encouraged him to work with Miller, the most academically schooled and tradition-minded teacher at the league. Ironically, Miller encouraged Marsh to retain the most sexual, and hence "improper," side of his art. According to Laning, Marsh's subsequent dependence on Miller occurred in part from a need for a substitute father figure.[58]

However personal Marsh's need to affirm his masculinity may have been, it was also cultural. During Marsh's boyhood the reinvigoration of middle-class manhood was envisioned as an antidote to the loss of personal autonomy accompanying the shift from an individually controlled home-based economy to a consumption-oriented industrial one. Masculine vigor would make American commerce more competitive. As for the artist, the rough masculine type admired by Robert Henri and some of his followers would counter the notion of the artist as a feminized type, operating at the periphery of American culture, as Marsh's parents did by the teens. As Marsh came to artistic maturity in the 1930s, he witnessed the greatest challenge to date to the long-standing link between masculinity and work as millions of men lost their jobs. Though never in financial danger, Marsh used work as a means to personal autonomy, a reaffirmation of his masculinity, and, with that, an affirmation of the centrality of the (male) artist in American society.

ISABEL BISHOP

Based on her professional successes and personal life, the values she espoused, and her ability to negotiate the more open but still male-dominated art world of the 1920s and 1930s, Isabel Bishop's position as a second-generation New Woman is secure. Described by all who knew her as dignified, articulate, and diligent about work, yet modest and ladylike in demeanor, Bishop seems to have achieved that delicate balance between femininity and self-sufficiency that characterized the revised New Woman. Like Marsh, Bishop came from an upper-middle-class background. Her family valued education, encouraged her to become financially autonomous, and gave her the means to achieve her goal. At the same time, by virtue of her circumstances and her sex, her situation in relation to the prevailing ideologies of gender and class was different from that of Miller and Marsh. Reviewing her life in the 1920s and 1930s from the vantage point of the 1970s and 1980s, Bishop noted the contradictory position she occupied as a woman artist. Even where she avoided interpreting her experiences and choices in feminist terms, her narrative discloses points of discomfort and contradiction as she moved through an established gender system.

Bishop's parents were descended from old, prosperous, and highly educated East Coast mercantile families.[59] Sometime in the 1880s they founded a preparatory school in Princeton; Bishop's father was a scholar of Greek and Latin, her mother an aspiring writer. By the time Bishop was born, in 1902, the youngest of five children by thirteen years, her parents had abandoned their dream of running the school. With the birth of the first of two sets of twins, her mother was overwhelmed by the combination of childcare and administrative responsibilities. Her parents suffered a number of disappointments during Bishop's youth. After giving up their school, they moved to Cincinnati (Bishop's birthplace), where her father worked first as a teacher and then as principal of the Walnut Hills School. When Bishop was about a year old, they moved to Detroit, where her father accepted a poorly paid job in a high school, teaching Greek and Latin; later he became principal. Just as she graduated from high school at age fifteen, he was fired for administrative incompetence, a charge Bishop remembered as trumped up to make her father a scapegoat.[60]

Throughout her childhood, Bishop's parents depended on the financial generosity of James Bishop Ford, her father's wealthy cousin. When her father lost his Detroit job, Ford found him a position, complete with residence, in a military academy that he had endowed. Earlier, his help had made it possible for the family to maintain living standards barely above genteel poverty. For a time in Detroit they lived in a marginal working-class neighborhood adjacent to a wealthier one. Bishop recalled learning about class divisions at an early age when her parents ordered her not to play with neighborhood children who were "different."

Throughout Bishop's childhood and adolescence, class anxiety and gender difference assumed the various forms typical of the period. Bishop's mother, an early feminist, worked for women's suffrage and urged her daughters toward the independence that had been unavailable to her once she started her family. Bishop was a late arrival to the household; her mother once told her that she often felt more like a grandmother than a mother. Bishop's college-age sisters assumed parental roles when home on vacation, prescribing her dress according to gender codes.

> They would go off to college and when they came home they'd pick up their interest in me, like a parent. . . . One of my sisters had me in Eton collars and tunics; then she went off and another came home and disapproved of those dull clothes and put me in some fancy little things. Everyone was trying to do something to me, except my mother. She was indifferent.[61]

To avoid housework and childcare, Anna Bishop turned to her pet project—a translation of Dante that she undertook after teaching herself Italian. Though Bishop later understood the restricting demands placed on her mother by the conventions of middle-class life, she often felt alone during her childhood, ambivalent about the distance her mother placed between them. Her father, more sympathetic to her, perhaps because he saw himself as something of an outcast, took her on as his "special interest." Although she loved and respected him, Bishop "hated" the division of her family into camps; her father openly placed her and himself in opposition to her mother and her siblings.[62]

Bishop's art education began at age twelve, when her parents enrolled her in a Saturday morning life drawing class at Detroit's John Wicker Art School. Given her age and a substantially restrained upbringing, her first encounter with the heavy-set female nude was a shock, but it gave her a headstart in what was usually considered more advanced training. When Bishop graduated from high school, at age sixteen (just after her father lost the Detroit job), she was sent off on her own to New York. There she became one of a number of proper young ladies studying illustration at the School of Applied Design for Women and living at the Misses Wilde's boarding house on the Upper East Side. Her parents wanted her to earn her own income, and an occupation in the graphic arts, with training acquired in a relatively protected environment, seemed the safest route. Bishop thus entered New York under very different circumstances and within different social spaces from Marsh, the twenty-year-old Yale graduate.

Within two years Bishop had grown dissatisfied with her training and her restricted environment. Even though she had been able to move directly into the life drawing class at the School of Applied Design for Women, the school itself failed to meet her needs. In the summer of 1919 she went to Woodstock, the popular artists' colony, to take a life course taught through the Art Students League. In 1920 she decided to abandon graphic arts and move toward a career in painting. James Bishop Ford, her father's cousin, who had already supported her early schooling, agreed to extend her monthly stipend so she could concentrate on her education; he would remain Bishop's patron for well over a decade.[63]

Bishop left the Misses Wilde and moved to the Village with two other women. In her first season at the league, she capitalized on the loose structure that allowed students to sign up for different classes every month. Her enrollment card records a smorgasbord: life classes with Miller; painting with the academic artist DuMond; advanced modernism in Max Weber's course on late cubism; and lectures by Robert Henri. Weber was highly critical of her work and, not surprisingly, the eighteen-year-old Bishop felt intimidated. From Henri she recalled learning the value of experimentation. She was "fascinated" by Henri but "frightened" and "too scared to put out anything for criticism."[64] By the end of the year, Bishop had found her mentor. During the entire 1921–22 league season she studied life drawing and painting exclusively with Miller. The following season, 1922–23, while living on Eleventh Street in Greenwich Village, she added an afternoon studio with Miller. There she would have begun her friendship with Reginald Marsh, who was taking his second round of Miller courses. That summer she met and studied briefly with Guy Pène du Bois.

The years 1923 to 1926 were difficult for Bishop, both personally and artistically—in part because of new possibilities for women: "It was a time of freedom for women to do what they wanted to do, but freedom can be intimidating."[65] She moved to 21 Perry Street in the Village and set up a studio at 15 East Eighth Street, determined to be an artist. But she had difficulty managing all aspects of her life:

> I went out to be an artist. I painted little brown pictures that were too dark but they weren't invalid. I can still bear to look at them today but I couldn't stand the isolation. I was desperate. I thought of just disappearing, just dropping out of the world. I thought of suicide, of becoming an alcoholic (although I never went to bars). Then it occurred to me that I should go back to the League so that I would be with my peers. I then would have some part of my day structured because I found I was sitting up all night and sleeping during the day. I was a disorganized person.[66]

During these three years, Bishop spent only four months in Art Students League classes. With the encouragement of Pène du Bois, she exhibited three small works in two Whitney Studio Club shows. Then, at twenty-four, she made three attempts to commit suicide over an unsuccessful love affair.[67] By that time, Bishop was desperate for both colleagues and a more structured existence. She moved her studio–living quarters to 9 West Fourteenth Street, a second-story space opposite the entrance to Hearn's department store and a block away from Miller. She returned to the league as a "graduate" student, and for the next five seasons, through May 1931, spent all or part of the school year studying with Miller. By that time, Miller had begun teaching his mural-painting class, which featured advanced study in Renaissance formal principles. That summer, after she completed her studies, Bishop, Miller, and Laning sailed to Europe to study old master painting in Paris, London, and Madrid museums. Bishop embarked on another European tour in the summer of 1933, accompanied by Miller and Marsh.[68]

Bishop's apprenticeship—both her formal training and the time she spent preparing a body of work for exhibition—was a long one. For the rest of her life her methods of working would be painstaking and slow, her output small. Some of her first earnings came through portraiture. A home for the aged in Peekskill hired her to paint portraits from photographs, and she recalled that either in 1930 or 1931 she felt proud to pay income tax for the first time. In 1932 Alan Gruskin, a young Harvard graduate enthusiastic about American art, invited Bishop to be one of thirty artists to join his new venture, a cooperative gallery in Manhattan. For the sum of five dollars per month, artists could participate in a continuing group exhibit and also have one-person shows. Bishop joined in 1932 and in 1933 held her first solo exhibition featuring seventeen works including still lifes, a self-portrait, small Union Square panoramas, and even two golf scenes. In three more one-person exhibitions (in 1935, 1936, and 1939), group shows, and national exhibitions she showed her genre paintings of young working women. Museums began to purchase her works, and she began to receive awards and increasingly positive reviews.[69]

In the summer of 1934, when she was thirty-two, Bishop married Dr. Harold Wolff, a neurologist who worked at New York Hospital and later became well known for his work on such diverse topics as brainwashing and headache pain. At the time of her marriage she moved her studio from Fourteenth Street to 857 Union Square West (overlooking the public speakers' platform at the north end of the square), where she would remain until 1984. In interviews with Helen Yglesias shortly before her death Bishop discussed both the implications of her choosing to marry and the circumstances of her marriage,[70] suggesting how her choices were economically and socially different from those made by her male artist friends. Her comments also open up issues of influence for male and female artists in general and for Bishop herself in particular.

Bishop claimed to have married Harold Wolff out of "desperation" to extend the conditions she had established over the years as essential to her life—uninterrupted time and financial support for the single-minded pursuit of her art. By 1934 she was in the process of breaking away from two important systems of support, both male. After nearly fourteen years she could no longer rely on her father's wealthy cousin, and, having signed a contract with Midtown Galleries, she felt even more keenly her commitment to being a professional artist.[71] At the same time, Bishop was re-evaluating her aesthetic allegiance to Kenneth Hayes Miller, her long-time friend and mentor. This re-evaluation was complicated by Miller's anti-individualistic aesthetic pronouncements in the mural-painting class and by her responses to that teaching as a woman student in the late 1920s in a male-female teacher-student relationship.

In his teaching Miller expressed the belief that modern French painters like Picasso and Matisse sacrificed an important social function of art—the communication of an idea about contemporary life—to create paintings that embodied only an immediately recognizable artistic personality. To counteract this tendency, he argued that the art of mural painting should be collaborative and anonymous. Miller never suggested that all artists work together to produce a single mural; for him collaboration meant that everyone should work from similar principles of Renaissance composition to de-emphasize individual style.

Bishop was particularly susceptible to these ideas. When she returned to the league to study in 1926, it was with a clean slate; unlike Marsh, for example, she had not already worked for several years as an illustrator or made trips abroad to study art. She had not adopted a particular subject or a method of working. Furthermore, as a woman, she had long been subject to the instructional and prescriptive content of male discourse. She was, as she described it later, much more willing than other students to accept Miller's doctrines, as a result of which she produced a number of works in the five-year period 1928–33 that were immediately recognizable to critics and friends as those of a Miller student (see Figs. 2.2 and 3.7). When she came to understand how Miller's values might be holding her back, she began to work more consciously to develop her own painting technique and subject matter.[72] As the economic, social, and intellectual circumstances of Bishop's life and career shifted, "marriage resolved the desperate difficulties. So, you see, I felt I had no other choice."[73]

By the 1930s already powerful prescriptions against the combination of marriage and career for middle- to upper-middle-class women escalated. Based on her observations of both her mother's thwarted career, with its effects on her childhood, and her few women friends' struggles to balance traditional wifely duties with artistic aspirations, Bishop's fears of marriage seemed well grounded. As she recalled it later, in an acute summary of the modern New Woman's dilemma, the marriage of her close artist friend Katherine Schmidt to her fellow artist Yasuo Kuniyoshi embodied the conditions she hoped to avoid.

> Yasuo Kuniyoshi's first wife was a close friend, Katherine Schmidt, a very distinguished artist. She was very young when they married. She tried to do everything. They lived in Brooklyn Heights. She came into Manhattan every day to work in the lunchroom of the Art Students League. Katherine kept a meticulous house and did the rounds of the dealers with her husband's work, Kuniyoshi's work. All that while painting some of her own best pictures. I didn't know that I could function like that.[74]

After fifteen years of maturing into a serious professional artist, Bishop had experienced enough of the artistic community to know that her long searching process of production, not to mention her temperament, required quiet, uninterrupted hours in a studio separate from her domestic environment. Harold Wolff enthusiastically supported her endeavor in a way that was atypical for a male of his generation, profession, and character. Formal and unyielding, Wolff was evidently feared by students and colleagues for his obsessive and uncompromising demands for perfection even in insignificant details. His authoritarian hand operated on the home front as well. Friends recalled dinner parties orchestrated and presided over by Wolff, who distributed cards that listed times for each event (including the hour for departure), intervals of silence for music, and topics of conversation. On such occasions, Bishop graciously played the part of docile spouse. For the first fifteen years of their marriage, Wolff's mother lived with them. She provided some childcare when their son, Remson, was born in 1940; her presence, as Bishop characterized it, was both "helpful" and "difficult."[75]

Bishop's life encompassed a series of inconsistencies, and she was obliged to occupy or negotiate contradictory subject positions. She possessed all the old-fashioned attributes of a gracious lady—she was quiet spoken, generous, and conciliatory to a fault.[76] At the same time, she was professionally ambitious and as fully committed to her work as her male artist friends and her husband. To achieve her goals—many of them predicated on an economic and social independence that the culture neither sanctioned nor made easy for women to attain—she had to tread a precarious path between independence and dependence on men in positions more powerful than her own (her father, her wealthy relative, Miller, and finally her husband). Bishop claimed that her relentless pursuit of her career rather than marriage kept her second cousin James Bishop Ford interested in maintaining her stipend; he would not have continued to support a man for such a long time. Her husband, who was passionate about music and art, was proud of her accomplishments but also undoubtedly impressed with the correspondence of her rigorous six-day work routine to his own. In exchange for what may have been his overwhelming exactness in domestic affairs, Bishop gained his respect for her professional needs. "We left the house together every morning," she remembered. "He went on to his work and I went to my studio. There was never any question about it."[77]

Their union was a version of the modern companionate marriage, forged out of mutual respect rather than romantic love and, perhaps on Bishop's part, out of economic and cultural necessity: women married. A revealing letter from Reginald Marsh to his wife Felicia, dated August 9, 1934, conveys the precipitousness with which Bishop married once her decision was made and the way the marriage from its inception was fully integrated with her working life:

> Guess what—Isabel walked into my studio at about two o'clock today, started looking around as usual, and with a sudden shy exclamation uttered a most astonishing—"I just got married half an hour ago." What, what, wonderful [indistinguishable word] congratulations, let's have a drink? "no, no, I am going back to my studio to get to painting—painted all morning, suddenly decided to get married at noon." Well, who's the man—husband? Dr Wolfe, you met him at our [i.e., Marsh and Felicia's] house this winter.[78]

Bishop's early career in institutional situations was similar to that of her male counterparts. In fact, at an early age she left woman-centered instructional and living situations to compete on her own in established centers for making and exhibiting art. When she confronted decisions complicated by her status as a woman painter, she never looked to woman-centered organizations for support. Her choice of individual over collective achievement was not only the dominant model in the culture at large but also one given official sanction by important female critics in the art world itself. In separate reviews on the occasion of the fourth annual exhibition of the New York Society of Women Artists in February 1929, the critics Margaret Breuning of the *New York Evening Post* and Helen Appleton Read of the *Brooklyn Eagle* condemned the society, not for the quality of the work shown, but for its very existence. Breuning asked:

Where are the organizations of artists that these ladies, now exhibiting, wish to join and cannot because of their sex? What galleries are closed to them as women? Why should the New York Society of Women Artists, however admirable their exhibition may be, exist, except as a confession that its members do not wish to compete with their masculine confreres, but desire the immunity of feminine fragility to be extended to them.

Evidently under this aegis they desire that their work shall not be judged with impartiality, but with chivalry and the tacit watchword of the Old South. "Gentlemen, remember that she is a lady." . . . But why should young women who pride themselves on being modern revert to the doubtful protection of outworn procedure and band themselves together in this clinging vine sort of attitude?[79]

Read echoed Breuning's sentiments: "The issue at stake is, Why have a women's organization at all? The time has passed when women need to band themselves together in order to break down the prejudice against the possibility of feminine accomplishment in art."[80]

The powerful perception in the discourse of revised new womanhood that women had achieved equality with men thanks to the franchise blinded both Breuning and Read to the inegalitarian conditions of the art world and the art market, not to mention sanctions against married women following careers. Moreover, both writers accepted the companionate ideal promoted by social scientists and psychologists, who labeled "female-centered sociability as deviant."[81] To operate successfully, these critics seemed to claim, one needed to participate in the "normal" art world of male-female relationships. Like Bishop, who never joined these groups, women and men alike agreed that individual accomplishment was a matter of individual responsibility. Whether or not Bishop was fully conscious of her choices, at the time, she either found, or was fortunate enough to have presented to her, a way to proceed in the art world as a woman making art perceived worthy of being judged alongside that of her male peers.[82]

RAPHAEL SOYER

Although Bishop's position in the contradictory discourse of mainstream new womanhood complicated her personal life and career, thanks to outside support she had educational opportunities that brought her to the center of the art world by the 1930s. Moreover, she could move in circles with artists of her own social, educational, and class background, many of them involved in organizing institutions of support for artists throughout this period. Unlike Bishop, who would always be marginalized by a gender system that placed women outside the normalized model of male artistic achievement, Raphael Soyer was marginalized by socio-economic conditions, immigrant status, and personal circumstances that initially denied him the educational and social opportunities that placed Marsh and Bishop at the center of the art world. At the same time, however, Soyer's intellectual environment and cultural tradition made him sympathetic to exploring artistic conventions compatible with those adopted by other members of the Fourteenth Street School. By the 1930s, because of his background and his imagery, Soyer came to exemplify the successful American immigrant artist.

The biographical narrative of Raphael Soyer and his twin brother, Moses, contains many of the same tropes of the artist's childhood as that of Reginald Marsh. Raphael was the sickly twin who almost died at birth; both his parents were "artistic," and they encouraged their children to draw (three of the six children—Moses, Raphael, and their younger brother Isaac would become professional artists). Just as Marsh found his subjects in the popular culture of his childhood, Raphael Soyer became a "confirmed realist" with a desire to "paint people" after watching one of his father's students do a drawing from life.[83] But Soyer's circumstances were dramatically different. He and his twin, Moses, were the oldest of six children, born in 1899 in the small Jewish community of Borisoglebsk, Russia. Raphael's father, Abraham, was a scholar and teacher, "employed by the fifty or so aristocratic Jewish families to teach their children Hebrew."[84]

Although the family was poor, Abraham's position as a scholar, rather than an artisan or factory worker, gave them status in the community and later in America.[85] It also gave them access to literature and art. By the time they had been admitted to the local gymnasium at age twelve, they had read much of the Russian literature in their father's study, including works by Dostoyevski, Chekhov, and Tolstoy; in Russian translation they devoured Dickens, Thackeray, and their favorite American novels, *Tom Sawyer*, *Uncle Tom's Cabin*, and *The Prince and the Pauper*. Their parents decorated their living space with works by their own hands and postcard reproductions of Russian works and old master paintings; in particular, their father introduced them to Rembrandt, Raphael, and Michelangelo.[86]

Their early life also had a political dimension. Raphael recalled being taken to Zionist meetings with the other older siblings, Moses, Fannie (a year and half younger than the twins), and Isaac. The Soyer home also served as a congenial meeting place for young Jewish intellectuals. By the autumn of 1912, however, these gatherings aroused the suspicion of czarist authorities. The governor of the province refused to renew Abraham Soyer's residence permit, making the Soyers victims of the widespread oppression of Jews that escalated after the failure of the 1905 revolution. Within the month, the entire Soyer family made their way to Liverpool and then Philadelphia, their passage paid for by a Philadelphia relative. They were part of the last wave of Eastern European Jews who immigrated to America. (Between 1881 and 1914 approximately one-third of the population immigrated.) Several months after arriving, according to Raphael, Abraham Soyer found work in New York, writing for commercial Yiddish publications and teaching Hebrew.[87]

It is difficult to characterize the impact of the immigrant experience on Soyer's family. They arrived in America after two generations of immigrants had settled in New York, and they chose to live in a small Bronx community rather than at the center of immigrant life, the Lower East Side. The father's income was small, and the older children eventually followed the immigrant pattern of living at home and bolstering family earnings with part-time work. Yet neither the mother nor Soyer's sisters worked the long hours in factories or sweatshops typical of tenement families. By the early teens, the family's quarters were large enough for the mother to designate one room as the brothers' art studio. Typically, life in the New World was far more difficult on parents than on children, and the Soyer family was no exception. Raphael recalled his father being at times "childishly uncompromising, unable to cope with the inconsistencies of his world" and "the turbulent inner life of our bewildered mother." She was frustrated by the "void in her own intellectual growth, the realization of which made her alternately angry and melancholy."[88] Both the elder Soyers, like many immigrants of their generation, would have been confused by a range of customs and social practices at odds with those they had brought with them from Russia. For both parents, change was undoubtedly difficult.

The twins, as the oldest children, also faced a number of difficulties. By the time they arrived in America, Raphael and Moses were better educated and more sophisticated than most American children their age. Unlike their younger siblings, who quickly learned English, they clung to their Russian and consequently were placed with grade school children much younger than themselves. Finding this experience both frustrating and humiliating, they dropped out of Morris High School in 1916—the same year Marsh entered Yale. Although their decision disappointed their parents, who had dreamed of sending their children to college, the family needed the twins' income. A middle-class notion of adolescence as an extended childhood, a period of education and leisure, was foreign to the immigrant family's sense of financial obligation. In an aside on his adolescence Soyer recalled his inexperience and his naive social behavior but stated, "I don't remember myself ever having been young in years."[89]

For Raphael, the years from 1914 to the late 1920s were occupied by part-time work, an artistic education pieced together at a variety of institutions, and hours spent in the back room of his apartment practicing his drawing and painting. He worked first as an errand boy for four dollars per week, then as a general utility boy for a clothing factory for seven dollars per week. In 1914 he and Moses learned about free evening classes at the Cooper Union, where they could draw from life; to be able to take part in them, he tended a newspaper stand from five in the morning to three in the afternoon. In the fall of 1918, when the twins entered day classes at the National Academy of Design, Raphael found a night job within walking distance of the academy, as a soda jerk. Until the spring of 1922, he studied on and off with the artists George Maynard and Charles Curran, elder statesmen at the academy who taught students in the style of Sargent and Whistler, still the most fashionable American painters in conservative circles.[90]

The academy must have shocked the nineteen-year-old Soyer, who, apart from one childhood trip to Moscow to see Russian painting and regular Sunday walks to the Metropolitan Museum with his brothers, had had little exposure to art in museums and was unfamiliar with the contemporary art scene. On the one hand, the academy was the most conservative of all the American art schools—and the bastion of the genteel tradition. Patrons of its annual exhibitions, an elite social community from which the immigrant Soyer would have been excluded, sought to preserve the artistic status quo. When Soyer entered his first life class, he felt "as overwhelmed by the work of the students as Gogol's hick, Vacula, was when he came to Moscow."[91] On the other hand, a group of younger students wanted to challenge the academy's teachings and its canon by introducing more contemporary art theory and by looking at post-impressionist painters, then considered modern—chiefly Cézanne. Though Soyer felt too shy to even speak to the students with whom he shared classes—among them immigrants like Ben Shahn, the future art historian Meyer Schapiro, and Paul Cadmus—it was the beginning of his education in contemporary American art.

Shortly after the Soyer twins began to study at the academy, they decided it was unwise for them to study and paint together because of their closeness in attitude and interests. Raphael stayed at the academy, and Moses moved to the Educational Alliance, a cultural center on the Lower East Side founded for the children of immigrants. Even with this separation, Moses continued to play an important role in Raphael's education, owing in large measure to his more gregarious temperament and perhaps to the similarity between the social milieu of the Educational Alliance and their own social milieu. Moses, who made friends easily and brought people home to family gatherings, seemed to become assimilated into American life more quickly than Raphael.

Moses was also instrumental in introducing his brother to other kinds of art. Sometime in the early 1920s, Moses attended a Sunday afternoon drawing session at the Ferrar Art Club where Robert Henri gave critiques to participating students. On one occasion, Henri faulted Moses's drawing for its superficial characteristics and its lack of "volume" and "significant form"—modernist terms from Roger Fry, new to Moses, that had been introduced into the American critical and instructional lexicon in the years after the Armory Show. Henri gave Moses copies of the radical publication the *Liberator* to study, pointing in particular to its images of lower-class women and children drawn by Daumier. Moses shared these, along with drawings by Sloan, Henri, Robert Minor, and George Luks, with both Raphael and Isaac:

What impressed us most was the up-to-dateness, the contemporary spirit of the content of the pictures. These artists dealt with everyday common people and with their humble hard lives at home and in the shops. There were also pictures of strikes, police brutality, child labor and so forth. We also liked the frank, biased attitude of the artists. They were not afraid to moralize. They were kind to the poor and dealt cruelly with the rich.[92]

Although Moses recollected their first exposure to contemporary urban realism from the vantage of the Depression, when artists on the Left sought just such an approach, the introduction was nonetheless important—Raphael claimed that it made him question what he was learning at the academy. By the early 1920s he had learned of the Art Students League, in particular its radicalism and its modernism as taught by teachers like Weber, Bellows, and Sloan. It was, as he recalled, "livelier, freer, noisier, and less orderly" than the academy. Though Soyer wanted to attend league classes, the monthly fee of fourteen dollars seemed prohibitive. Fortunately, an uncle who took an interest in his work gave him enough money for three months of instruction. From January through March 1923, when both Bishop and Marsh were enrolled in Miller's life classes, Soyer decided to study with Guy Pène du Bois.[93]

In choosing a teacher, Soyer avoided the two men whom he believed to be the most popular instructors at the league. The first, George Luks, conducted painting demonstrations with "too much of a display" for the reticent Soyer. The second, Kenneth Hayes Miller, "long nosed and grim visaged" but with a "kind smile," presented a different problem. Soyer disliked Miller's work—later he claimed that the gestures "didn't feel right"—and was concerned about the degree of influence Miller continued to have on his students, who remained friends long after they finished studying with him. By contrast, Soyer appreciated du Bois's work, his unassuming personality, and his unobtrusive method of teaching. After studying with du Bois, Soyer began to paint a series of Bronx and Lower East Side street scenes and small canvases featuring family events, friends, and models.[94]

To this point, except for his schooling, Soyer had made few friends outside his family and the immigrant community. He later characterized the period from the late teens to the mid-twenties as one of deep personal alienation, describing himself as the "shyest, the most inward, non-communicative character, almost to the point of being retarded."[95] In 1926, however, when Moses received a traveling scholarship, married, and left for two years in Europe, Soyer began gradually to emerge from his deep reserve and found ways to exhibit his art. Through a sequence of incidents, Soyer was drawn into the museum and gallery circles, already frequented by Miller, Marsh, and Bishop, that made up the institutional mainstream for contemporary American Scene realism and figurative painting.

Soyer initially exhibited a small Bronx street scene in the annual nonjuried Salons of America exhibition in 1926. Alexander Brook, a onetime student of Miller's and a highly regarded figure painter, was working as a talent scout for Juliana Force, the director of the Whitney Studio Club. Brook saw and liked Soyer's work, no doubt because, like his own, it drew heavily on the stylistic mannerisms of the French painter Jules Pascin, which were influential in figure painting of the late 1920s. The two artists met and the naturally outgoing Brook helped the painfully shy Soyer to sell that canvas and several other small pieces. Brook next brought Soyer to the Whitney Studio Club, where he met some of the regular members in sketch classes—Peggy Bacon (Brook's wife at that time), Marsh, Katherine Schmidt, Yasuo Kuniyoshi, and Adolph Dehn, the cartoonist, another student of Miller's. Beginning in 1928, when the club became the Whitney Studio Galleries, Soyer exhibited there and received financial support. Whenever he finished a painting, he would take it to Juliana Force. She would ask Soyer how much he wanted for it; he would ask between one and two hundred dollars, depending on its complexity, and she would pay. As Soyer recalled, "I went home and told my mother that now I felt like a real artist, people were paying good money for my pictures."[96]

At the Whitney Studio Club Soyer also became reacquainted with du Bois who, along with Brook, encouraged Soyer to take his work to the Daniel Gallery. This gallery was a logical choice for Soyer. From 1913, when it opened, to 1932, when it became a casualty of the Depression, Charles Daniel was one of the few New York dealers to represent contemporary American art and to support young artists.[97] After looking at Soyer's *Dancing Lesson*, a small canvas depicting Soyer's sister Rebecca (Rebbie) teaching Moses to dance in the company of family members, Charles Daniel told Soyer that if he produced eleven more works, he would give him a one-man show. The artist complied, and a year later, in April 1929, Daniel mounted Soyer's first exhibit. Several works sold, and Soyer received positive reviews. He stopped working at part-time jobs and took a succession of Lower East Side studios. In 1931 he married Rebecca Letz, whom he had known for several years as his sister Fannie's school friend, and took his first studio in the West Fourteenth Street district. For the next five years the Soyers led a somewhat peripatetic existence, moving frequently between apartments on West Fourteenth Street and in the West Village. Soyer explained that since landlords would often give a month's free rent to a new tenant, and since they owned only a few household goods, they moved often. In 1938, when he rented a studio at One Union Square, down the hall from Marsh's, the family moved to the Upper West Side, near Columbia University.[98]

Rebecca Soyer taught primary school for much of her adult life, even during the Depression, at a time when married women teachers frequently lost their jobs to men who were out of other work. Her regular income contributed substantially to the couple's well-being and allowed them occasionally to help out less fortunate artist friends.[99] Rebecca was also politically active. Along with Soyer's artist friend Nicolai Cikovsky, she encouraged Soyer to attend his first meetings at the Communist-run John Reed Club for Artists and Writers in late 1929. There, Soyer joined the Communist party and participated in many of the most important political events of the 1930s; he helped to produce collective political satires and club murals, he taught painting, and he demonstrated with fellow artists against the destruction of Diego Rivera's Rockefeller Center mural. By mid-decade he had become a member of the Artists' Union, and he joined the committee that organized the first American Artists' Congress in February 1936.[100]

With his reticence in meeting people, Soyer as a young man had few close women acquaintances. Because Rebecca Letz was Fannie's friend, she entered the family social circle, where Soyer felt most at ease. She also typified the immigrant women Soyer knew, aspiring educators and professionals who placed a high value on intellectual achievement. The encouragement of such achievement had long been part of a household routine by which Soyer's parents fostered competitive ambition among the children, scrutinizing drawings by the three brothers, praising those they judged the best. Soyer's youngest brother, Isaac, and his sister Rebecca both became teachers. Fannie, the older of the two girls and only a year and a half younger than the twins, attended college and became a psychoanalyst. Soyer described her as the most gifted of the children, with an "understanding and perception of human relations beyond the grasp of her brothers."[101]

Elizabeth Ewen looks at how immigrant mothers and daughters in different ethnic groups struggled to bridge the gap between Old and New World models of social interaction and gender conflict. Some of her distinctions, when placed alongside Soyer's recollections of family life, suggest how Soyer himself may have understood and negotiated class and gender ideologies. In immigrant families work was the norm for daughters. In the most patriarchal Jewish families, where boys were considered more important than girls, parents sacrificed the education of daughters for the sake of the sons. In the Soyer family, education and professional training were important for both sexes.[102] In the 1920s as the Soyer children made friends, found their own occupations, and became American citizens, the patriarchal quality of their family life was replaced by self-involvement. Soyer's mother encouraged her daughters to follow the new opportunities available to women in America, even if she could not.

Though he would not necessarily have recognized the middle-class ideology of new womanhood, Soyer knew young women in the immigrant community who adopted it. They pursued the professions that opened most easily for women—in education and the social sciences—seemingly without experiencing the middle-class conflict about combining marriage and career. As Soyer explained it, he did not grow up around "aristocratic" women, and since so many immigrant women contributed to the family income at an early age, it was "perfectly natural" for women to expect to work. Soyer, however, could not recall knowing any of the women who later became subjects in his paintings: those who worked in factories, retail stores, or offices—the most common workplaces for immigrant women. Nor did Soyer associate with women and men who engaged in the new forms of commercialized leisure. Soyer's models throughout the Depression, actively employed or not, came almost exclusively from the world of culture. Several were actresses or poets, and a number were dancers whom he met through Moses's wife, herself a dancer. Still others were art students or the wives of other artists—Walter Quirt's wife posed for drawings and a lithograph. Though Soyer characterized a number of his early models as "pre-flower children" or "hippies," he described only one of the women—a model named Kathleen—as a true "radical."[103] Fundamentally, Soyer's community was composed largely of intellectuals and professionals.

For all the presence of a revised new womanhood, there were places within the radical artistic community frequented by the Soyers from which women were largely excluded and where feminism played a diminished role. Although Rebecca Soyer urged Raphael to join the John Reed Club and was herself an active member, the club at times made women feel unwelcome. One of the first times he attended a meeting, Soyer invited the model he had been working with to join him. She was the only woman present, and after several pointed "amused and questioning" glances from the men conducting the meeting she became self-conscious and departed.[104] When women did participate in club events, they concerned themselves with the club's agenda, which was not a feminist one. Soyer, for example, recalled Rebecca's involvement with the Scottsboro case and with issues of male unemployment, but nothing related to women or women's work. He did not remember hearing about or reading the Communist party publication *Working Woman*, produced between 1929 and 1935 to report on the militant strike activities of women and blacks. The exclusion of women from club activities and the omission by the Left of any systematic account of women's experience in class struggle was part of a wider failure of the Left in the 1920s and 1930s.[105] The division between feminism and socialism was also symptomatic of both the conflict and stagnation within the post-franchise women's movement. As Barbara Melosh has demonstrated, the liberal agenda of the New Deal was the only major progressive program in America up to that time unaccompanied by feminist reform.[106]

Throughout the Depression Soyer lived a double existence with respect to the art world—half on the political Left, half at the center. He was soon well known and sought after as a teacher. The John Reed Club asked him to teach on the strength of a positive review by Henry McBride shortly after his first show at the Daniel Gallery.[107] In 1933, shortly after his third one-man show, the Art Students League overhauled its staff; Marsh was elected vice-president and several new instructors were hired, including Soyer, Brook, and Kuniyoshi. Soyer taught during the entire 1933–34 season and sporadically from 1935 to 1942. When he needed money, he would take on a teaching assignment; when he did not, he would stop teaching. Between Raphael's income from periodic teaching and from painting and

Rebecca's income from teaching, the couple achieved a measure of financial stability during the Depression.[108]

Soyer's art generated substantial interest. In 1932 the artist received the Kohnstamm Prize for his painting *The Subway* at the Chicago Art Institute's annual exhibit. In 1933 the Metropolitan Museum purchased his *Girl in a White Blouse*; by the end of the following year a total of nine canvases had been purchased by nationally known museums.[109] After the Daniel Gallery went under, Soyer showed once at L'Elan Gallery in 1932 and then began to make the rounds looking for another gallery. Valentine Dudensing of the Valentine Gallery gave Soyer five hundred dollars for the first four paintings he brought into the gallery and then exhibited his work in five one-man shows between 1933 and 1938.[110] After a joint exhibition with Peggy Bacon at the Rehn Gallery, where Marsh, Miller, and Edward Hopper showed regularly, Soyer received a visit from Pegeen Sullivan of the Associated American Artists Gallery—a new organization that Soyer later characterized as the first of the "plush, commercial" galleries. To persuade Soyer to join, Sullivan told him that the gallery had already signed up the highly publicized Regionalist triumvirate of Benton, Curry, and Wood, thereby assuring the gallery's prestige. She also promised that the gallery would take over payment of his studio rent. For Soyer, the latter argument proved persuasive.[111] By the early 1940s Carl Zigrosser wrote of the Soyer brothers:

> These immigrants from a foreign land have contributed to the melting pot, have given richly of their store of feeling and compassion, of their skill and sensitiveness to beauty. The father's prophecy regarding his sons has come true: they are citizens of this great Republic and they contribute their talents and strength to its growth.[112]

Raphael Soyer had become a true American artist.

THE AMERICAN SCENE

How did the four artists interact socially and politically with one another, and how did each confront the possibilities for making art? To put the question differently, what were the broader social and institutional conditions and the critical discourses through which they produced their work? In the 1920s and 1930s the Fourteenth Street School artists entered the mainstream of American art and eventually held important positions in it. The notion of a mainstream entails the recognition of a broad institutionally sanctioned consensus about the most important art of a period. By consensus, an urban, figurative version of American Scene realism was included in this art. Mainstream art in turn identifies, legitimates, and propagates intellectual ideas, values, and ideologies; it may reveal through images how the contemporary world functions or how certain groups perceive the world.[113] Works by the Fourteenth Street School artists raise broad questions about the relation between art and society as well as art and politics. For example, do the representations of urban women in these works legitimate or interrogate the discourse of new womanhood as it came to be understood in the interwar decades?

Artists who work within a mainstream do so in complicated ways, sometimes adopting its conventions and values, at other times rebelling against them. It is often difficult to unravel an artist's conscious and strategically planned negotiations with a mainstream from those that are unconscious and somehow "naturalized." Moreover, even as it constitutes itself, an artistic mainstream is always in flux or being redefined with respect to opposing systems it excludes. At the same time, the mainstream may find ways to incorporate some of those very exclusions into a new rhetoric, thereby blurring the boundaries it strives to maintain. Artists in the mainstream gain both individual recognition and social power thanks to validation by other institutional systems of power, whether informational and intellectual (critics, gallery owners, museum curators, and art teachers) or economic (museums, galleries, and, in the 1930s, federal patronage).

The Fourteenth Street School artists were part of a larger group of figurative American Scene painters—artists like Hopper or Pène du Bois—who entered the mainstream in the 1920s. They continued many of the progressive views of the Ashcan painters from the first decade of the century and set themselves against two opposing factions in the art world. Like John Sloan and Robert Henri, they continued to challenge the conservative National Academy of Design—with its rigid exhibition policies, artistic practices, and elite subjects. They also resisted the radical experimentation in abstract forms and deeply personal content of artists whose styles derived from advanced European modernism—like Weber, for example—and whose patrons were Alfred Stieglitz and Walter Arensberg, among others. Fundamentally, these urban realists and their allies were representational artists who embraced American subjects and followed American traditions of realism as established by Thomas Eakins and carried on in the work of the Ashcan school.

As part of their realist program, these artists were also deeply committed to depicting the figure. Although there was no single figurative style or subject, there was a strong figurative tradition in both European and American art of the 1920s that led artists to paint studio pictures (Bernard Karfiol, Alexander Brook, Yasuo Kuniyoshi), portraits (Eugene Speicher), and genre scenes (Glenn Coleman). The Fourteenth Street School artists placed their figures in urban settings; their American scenes constituted a form of genre painting that focused on the lives of average Americans in everyday city situations without attempting to make overt criticisms of their subjects' environment or circumstances.[114] Finally, they dedicated themselves to the old masters.[115] In their work all but Soyer, who looked to Degas and other nineteenth-century precedents, borrowed from what they considered to be an accepted canon of great art extending back through the Renaissance. And in many cases they made their stylistic and iconographic references to their sources direct and recognizable.

The artists of the Fourteenth Street School were not merely practitioners of a figurative tradition of American Scene realism; they were an integral part of a powerful network of influence that helped to promote and disseminate that tradition. Both the Art Students League and the Whitney Studio Club validated figurative realism in its various manifestations, patronized and publicized the Fourteenth Street School artists, and helped to launch their careers. In the 1920s a majority of the instructors at the Art Students League, where all the artists studied and eventually taught, gave instruction in figurative art. Miller was joined by artists like Guy Pène du Bois (a onetime Miller and Henri student), who taught Soyer and advised Bishop; by John Sloan, with whom Marsh and Edward Laning studied for a time; and by George Bellows, Robert Henri, Walt Kuhn, and Thomas Hart Benton, to name but a few. In the 1930s, all the Fourteenth Street School artists taught at the league themselves. Its institutional structure allowed students to change teachers monthly, giving them a chance to sample a variety of figurative approaches.[116]

For young artists, Gertrude Vanderbilt Whitney's various Whitney institutions provided major patronage and in many cases economic support. Prior to the founding of the Whitney Museum of American Art in 1930, Whitney created congenial places for artists' exhibits, sketch classes, and social activities: the Whitney Studio (1914–27), the Whitney Studio Club (1918–28), and the Whitney Studio Galleries (1928–30).[117] In 1927 the art critic Forbes Watson, who preferred both the art and the climate of the Whitney institutions to Alfred Stieglitz's 291, claimed that the Whitney Studio Club "has probably done more than any other single institution to bring to the notice of the public the creative younger artists."[118] Raphael Soyer, who benefited from Whitney patronage and financial support, described the club as the "main gateway to an art career." Alexander Brook called the Whitney organizations a "steppingstone for the artists to gain recognition from critics and dealers. . . . Introductory exhibitions [were] specifically limited to those who did not have an outlet for their work."[119]

In addition to receiving patronage, the Fourteenth Street School artists perpetuated the tradition of figurative realism through their own activities. Gertrude Whitney named Kenneth Hayes Miller and a group of his students who had studied together at the league—Peggy Bacon, Alexander Brook, Louis Bouché, Katherine Schmidt, Reginald Marsh, and Henry Schnakenberg—charter members of the Whitney Studio Club. In 1923, when the club moved to a Greenwich Village house next door to the Whitney Studio, Juliana Force, Mrs. Whitney's major assistant, hired Alexander Brook as assistant director, talent scout, and organizer of exhibitions.[120] Bacon, Schmidt, and her husband, Yasuo Kuniyoshi—also a Miller student—along with Guy Pène du Bois continued to act as advisors to Mrs. Whitney, recommending artists with views sympathetic to their own. Raphael Soyer's introduction to the

Whitney Studio group provides a case study in the workings of Whitney patronage.

In addition to study at the league and patronage from the Whitney organizations, artists practicing figurative realism found support and information in *The Arts*, the most important new publication for independent-minded American artists.[121] Founded by Hamilton Easter Field (who in 1922 also established the Salons of America, where Soyer first exhibited), *The Arts* from 1920 to 1931 embodied many of the progressive and liberal values promulgated by Mrs. Whitney. She in turn provided "financial and moral support" to the magazine from 1923 to 1930.[122] Broad-minded in its tastes, the magazine set out "to devote its pages entirely to significant works of the present and past that are in tune with the grand tradition of all time. As a record of what is happening today it is the most complete and uncompromising and therefore the most reliable."[123] With Hamilton Easter Field's death, the editorship passed to Forbes Watson, who promised to uphold the values of its founder. In the first of his monthly editorials he steered a moderate course: "[*The Arts*] will be a mouthpiece for neither the radical nor the conservative exclusively, but for art quite regardless of tags. . . . It does not intend to wave the flag, but quite frankly it does intend to stand with the American artist against timidity and snobbery."[124] The magazine's staff included critics who waged war with academic institutions still entrenched in the 1920s but stopped short of fully advocating abstract art.

Like Mrs. Whitney, *The Arts* sought out and publicized new talent. One of its regular columns, entitled Young America, as early as 1923 featured the recent Yale graduate Reginald Marsh as an ambitious realist artist, ready to paint "America's grand subject."[125] This chatty piece was written by Alan Burroughs, son of the curator of painting at the Metropolitan Museum and Marsh's brother-in-law. Lloyd Goodrich also wrote for the magazine and later became an editor.[126] In 1930, he published his book on Kenneth Hayes Miller through the Arts Publishing Corporation. The book was actually subsidized by Isabel Bishop, who felt Miller deserved more recognition. She approached Goodrich, who was sympathetic to Miller's ideas, having studied painting with him in the teens at the league, and all parties agreed to the proposal. Shortly thereafter, Alan Burroughs wrote another short monograph on Miller for the Whitney Museum's American Artists Series.[127]

Miller and his students Marsh, Bishop, and Laning were close friends, particularly from about 1927 to 1934. During this period they were all involved with the league and the Whitney organizations; after 1934 they saw one another less frequently. By then Marsh and Bishop had new families, all the artists showed their works at different galleries, and each had become involved with additional projects outside the league and what was by then the Whitney Museum.

In the earlier years they had been part of a larger group, a "Miller gang," as Marsh referred to it in his diaries, that included artists like Brook and Bacon, Kuniyoshi and Schmidt, and a variety of Miller's older students from the teens and

1920s. These artists socialized regularly. On the weekends they went to meals at the Burroughs family home in Flushing. They met in neighborhood restaurants and bowled together for a time in the early 1930s.[128] Miller held his weekly Wednesday afternoon teas for all his students, past and present. Many of them were financially comfortable thanks to their families (Marsh, Bishop, and Laning) or to a combination of teaching and artistic success. (In 1931 Miller made enough from the sale of his works to take a year off from teaching at the league; Laning took over his class.)[129] Most came from middle- to upper-middle-class families that had been in America for several generations, and all were tied by professional association and friendship (and in Marsh's case marriage) to established institutions and publications in the art world. Marsh gained additional opportunities thanks to a network of Yale men who occasionally paved the way to artistic projects. William Benton, the advertising mogul who later became president of Encyclopaedia Britannica and a senator, was a devoted friend and regular patron. The editor and publisher Henry Luce gave Marsh illustration assignments for *Life* magazine.[130]

Soyer was a partial exception to this pattern, with his Russian Jewish immigrant's background and his social and financial history. Obliged to work at a series of menial jobs to make ends meet, he had neither the time nor the means to socialize or attend bowling parties. He made many of his contacts either through his twin brother, Moses, or at the John Reed Club. His first contact with the "Miller gang" came through Alexander Brook, whose support awed Soyer since he perceived Brook to be the "darling" of the American art scene in the late 1920s. Though he considered Brook a "wonderful, exuberant, and talented man and a good friend," the two men never socialized.[131] Instead, Soyer forged friendships limited to the space of the artist's studio. He posed for Brook, shared models, and, beginning in the 1930s, painted numerous portraits of his fellow artists, Marsh among them. The studio neutralized class and status distinctions that Soyer seemed to associate with the Miller group among the Whitney artists.[132] Despite being at the margins of their circle, Soyer knew their work through publications and exhibitions and respected it. He in turn received praise for his work from all quarters of the artistic and critical mainstream.[133]

In mainstream American art during the 1920s the critical terms characterizing the works of these artists, drawing them into American Scene painting, were continually being qualified. One anonymous reviewer of a 1927–28 traveling show mounted by the Whitney Studio Club struggled to place a number of Whitney painters; finally he described them as "intensely contemporary, but not radical, representing the conservative element of the left wing in American art."[134] The description was apt for this particular moment, one that signaled the beginning of a shift in the perception, criticism, and marketing of American art. Earlier in the wake of the 1913 Armory Show one group of critics, dealers, and artists generated interest in both post-impressionist painting and the formalist European theories of modernism by which these works came to be understood. After World War I, in both literary and artistic circles, the cultural nationalist critics called for an indigenous modernism. Then, beginning around 1927, critics who discovered artists like Hopper and Charles Burchfield began to favor an uncritical "realist" art that was non-European in both content and style ("intensely contemporary, representing the conservative element of the left wing"). Finally, in the wake of the stock market crash, critics like Thomas Craven, the chauvinist exemplar of American Scene criticism, became openly hostile to European modernism; Craven faulted dealers who continued to sell what critics deemed inferior European art at the expense of American work. European modernism, critics like Craven argued, had run its course. Its formalist theories had served an educational purpose by showing artists new techniques. But now, especially in the disorienting times of the Depression, it was up to American artists to return to socially meaningful art that communicated important American values to a wide audience. Magazines like the *Art Digest*, the *American Magazine of Art*, and *Creative Art* proselytized the growing American Scene movement, which called for realism over abstraction and the depiction of everyday American subjects.[135] Reginald Marsh, in a rare statement—a 1933 essay on Edward Laning for *Creative Art*—adopted the rhetoric used by some of the nationalistic critics and verified the importance of the American Scene.

> He [Laning] is singing *The Sidewalks of New York* to the tune of the Italian Renaissance—the national anthem of Fourteenth Street. Young enough, luckily, to have escaped the spell-binding attractions of bewitching boudoir painters of the "since Cézanne" regiments, or the National Academy banalities, or the aerial Stieglitz acrobats, he has, by virtue of the "pernicious" Miller influence, studied the more mature methods of the great schools, which beg to show us that, after all, there is a world of real people, both male and female—flesh, blood, elbows, facial expression, unbroken necks—a world that has more in it than rubber clouds, hors-d'oeuvres, cockeyed tables, splintery napkins, jittery Africans, one-sided women, and blandishing dealers who can hypnotize rich Americans into seeing purple paradises in picture puzzles.[136]

Because paintings by the Fourteenth Street School encompassed several generations of American art theory and practice, they exemplify the complex shifts and contradictions in the discourse of American Scene realism. While their works depict average women and men in the contemporary environment and combine old master traditions with American sources, there were two fundamentally different versions of what we might call Fourteenth Street realism. Kenneth Hayes Miller forged a classical realism with a related pedagogy in the 1920s and continued to practice it, with certain modifications, in the 1930s. This style manifested itself in early panoramas of Union Square by Bishop and Laning, produced at the end of the decade and during the first years of the Depression. Reginald Marsh and Raphael Soyer practiced an updated version of turn-of-the-century Ashcan school realism. These two styles, and hence the representations of women, read differently from a 1930s and a late twentieth-century vantage point, and it is worthwhile to understand some of the contradictory implications.

In both his teaching and his painting, Miller embraced the academic view that all art should recall the great Western tradition by appropriating conventions from early works rather than by imitating nature.[137] Miller had come to artistic maturity in the 1890s and adopted the canon of old master painters taught him by his instructors Kenyon Cox and H. Siddons Mowbray. With few exceptions, they favored Italian Renaissance artists like Raphael, Michelangelo, and the Venetians Titian, Giorgione, and Veronese. Miller also professed admiration for Rubens, Rembrandt, Delacroix, Ingres, and, among more recent painters, Renoir.[138] These painters provided the direct prototypes for Miller's Fourteenth Street shoppers.

To make his classsicizing realism contemporary, however, Miller grafted a modernist rhetoric onto this essentially academic pedagogy. Although he saw himself as a painter of contemporary subjects rather than a modernist (a term he used narrowly, to describe European artists like Picasso and Matisse), he and other figure painters of his generation borrowed ideas, artistic models, and the rhetoric of early formalist critics like Bernard Berenson, Roger Fry, and Clive Bell to bring a more cautious strain of modernism to their figurative work. For these critics, and eventually for Miller, the term *modernism* no longer defined a simple art-for-art's-sake philosophy but centered instead on the creation of solid, "plastic," and "significant" form and a coherent design dependent solely on the internal structural logic of the painting.[139] The figure remained crucial, but both the subject and the expression of an emotional attitude toward that subject were secondary to the creation of form. Because figure paintings by Renoir and Cézanne were seen to continue the old master tradition both by restoring a structure and solidity lacking in the art of the impressionists and by concentrating on form independent of subject, these artists became models for Miller. Armed with formalist values, Miller looked more closely at Renoir's paintings. For Miller, Renoir's late work became the source through which he could enter the canon as a contemporary old master. Miller also reconsidered his Renaissance predecessors afresh and claimed, "What makes the old masters great is the rightness of their abstract design."[140]

A survey of Union Square paintings by Miller, Laning, and Bishop makes it clear that right design meant simple, legible, and geometrically balanced compositions filled with carefully modeled, weighty figures. The orientation of these nearly symmetrical paintings is usually frontal, and figures appear as if on a stage. In paintings of full-bodied shoppers, Miller frequently orchestrated the design around repeated volumetric curves and countercurves, using rounded hats and furs to echo the shape of the female form, or matching a mannequin with a shopper. Such shapes would be held in place by stabilizing verticals and horizontals, often in the form of columns or the frames of store windows; see, for example, *Sidewalk Merchant* (c. 1940; Fig.

2.1 Kenneth Hayes Miller, *Sidewalk Merchant,* c. 1940 (revision of *In Fourteenth Street,* 1932). Oil on plywood, 36″ × 45⅝″. The University of Texas at Austin, Archer M. Huntington Art Gallery.

2.1 and Plate 1). In *Dante and Virgil in Union Square,* Isabel Bishop scrupulously divided and subdivided her panoramic composition into zones, each containing a separate unit of her subject (Fig. 2.2). Laning used color to help structure his self-consciously formalized designs. In *Fourteenth Street* (Fig. 2.3), the pinks, blues, and reds in the limited Sienese-derived palette are placed at equidistant intervals to create an even rhythm of figures moving across the picture plane.[141] In all these works, because of the order and simplicity of the composition and the legibility of the design, the viewer is made aware of the formal qualities. The demonstration of a studied design was one of the major aesthetic aims of the classical strain of Fourteenth Street realism.

Miller's pedagogy and practice can be read as a historical palimpsest, beginning around the time of the Armory Show (where Miller exhibited four paintings in the American section), with each "layer" corresponding to a particular historical moment and satisfying a variety of sometimes contradictory critical voices. Those

2.2　*Top*: Isabel Bishop, *Dante and Virgil in Union Square*, c. 1932. Oil on canvas, 27″ × 52″. Delaware Art Museum, Wilmington.

2.3　*Above*: Edward Laning, *Fourteenth Street*, 1931. Tempera on canvas, 30″ × 40″. Collection of Whitney Museum of American Art, New York.

1. Kenneth Hayes Miller, *Sidewalk Merchant*, c. 1940 (revision of *In Fourteenth Street*, 1932). Oil on plywood, 36″ × 45⅝″. The University of Texas at Austin, Archer M. Huntington Art Gallery.

2. Kenneth Hayes Miller, *Department Store Shoppers*, 1930. Oil on canvas, 24″ × 17¹/₈″. Hirshhorn Museum and Sculpture Garden, Smithsonian Institution.

3.   Reginald Marsh, *In Fourteenth Street,* 1934. Egg tempera on composition board, $35^{7}/_{8}''\times 39^{3}/_{4}''$.
Collection, The Museum of Modern Art, New York.

4. Reginald Marsh, *Show Window,* 1934. Egg tempera on board, 42″ × 34″.
The Saint Louis Art Museum.

5. Raphael Soyer, *Window Shoppers*, 1938. Oil on canvas, 36″ × 24″.
New Jersey State Museum, Trenton.

6. Raphael Soyer, *Shop Girls,* 1936. Oil on canvas, 30″ × 40″. Collection of Babette B. Newburger.

7.   Isabel Bishop, *Tidying Up,* c. 1938. Oil on canvas, 15″ × 11¹/₂″. Indianapolis Museum of Art.

8. Isabel Bishop, *At the Noon Hour,* 1939. Tempera and pencil on composition board, 25″ × 18″. Museum of Fine Arts, Springfield, Massachusetts.

who cautiously advocated modernism after the Armory Show adopted the evolutionary model of the show's organizers, who emphasized modernism's links to the past and its adherence to unchanging principles of design rather than its radical newness. In "Evolution, Not Revolution in Art," for example, the critic Christian Brinton stressed the concomitant need in art for progress and respect for tradition—values Miller promulgated in naming canonical works and in supporting unchanging formal values.[142] By the 1920s, critics seeking an indigenous base for art broadened the meaning of modernism to include both abstract and representational works featuring contemporary American subjects portrayed according to accepted formal standards. Staunch advocates of modernism, like the critic Paul Rosenfeld, praised Miller's art. Then, in 1929, the curators of Nineteen Living American Painters at the new Museum of Modern Art chose Miller's work for exhibition. In making their selection, they overlooked Miller's academicism and emphasized the modernist credentials of his classical realism.[143]

Another group of critics who favored representational American art but whose anti-European and anti-modern views grew stronger with the Depression, often reiterated the artist's responsibility to the public. Their ideas were initially given currency by well-known conservative turn-of-the-century academic critics. Miller's teacher Kenyon Cox and the critic Frank Jewett Mather disdained what they believed was an excessive individualism in modern abstraction, which kept the public from understanding art. Mather argued that the artist must heighten his sensitivity to the public and must make art according to accepted codes and conventions. In short, the artist must work in a recognizable academic or old master tradition.[144] In all his teaching, but especially in his mural-painting classes beginning in 1927, Miller similarly argued for legibility and against artistic individualism; indeed, personal expression in art should give way to form. In this way Miller linked modernism to an anti-modern justification for representational American art.

In favoring form over individual response to subject matter, Miller opposed the central tenet of Ashcan school realism preached by Robert Henri and inherited and practiced by Reginald Marsh and Raphael Soyer. Marsh's and Soyer's updated Ashcan school realism also approached the contemporary scene through an old master tradition. Having been trained in the 1920s, these artists, like Miller, concerned themselves with pictorial order and coherent design as major goals of making art.[145] But their work was linked to the emotional "Art for Life's sake" vision of Ashcan painters like Sloan and Henri as much as to the academicism of American Renaissance painters like Cox.[146] Marsh and Soyer were less theoretical in their approach and worked more often from models than from a series of formal principles.[147] Their concern to respond as individuals to contemporary life made them less dependent on the self-consciously applied formalism favored by Miller, Bishop, and Laning. Their position on the twin heritage of "formalism" and "emotionalism" approximated that of Forbes Watson, who favored a balance between the intellectual and the emotional (with the latter more important). An admirer of

Henri, Watson stressed the importance of the artist's connection and response to life over a response to art. At the same time, he argued that the response must be made through an interpretation of form, color, and design that would demonstrate the artist's reinterpretation of tradition.[148]

Within this configuration of ideals and attitudes, Marsh and Soyer looked to different old master sources and developed different styles of painting, especially in the Fourteenth Street images of the 1930s. Marsh, who had been trained as an illustrator, like his Ashcan predecessors, depicted American city life, seeking to capture the vibrancy and the energetic pace of its rhythms. To infuse his crowded street scenes with movement, he looked more to Michelangelo and Rubens than to Raphael.[149] He exaggerated movement by personalizing Rubens's drawing style; using tempera with a draftsman's touch, he created intricate patterns of choppy strokes overlaying patchy areas of thinly applied color. He used tempera to achieve effects different from those usually sought by artists working in this unspontaneous and craftsmanlike medium, associated with the anonymous treatment of Renaissance panel paintings. Painting quickly, he achieved a sketchiness of style that recalled the looseness and painterly surface of the Ashcan painters.

Soyer, unlike Marsh and the other Fourteenth Street realists, made close-up studies of individual moods and feelings, drawing from American and European painters of psychological portraits like Eakins and Degas. Critics frequently described his work as naturalistic. He developed a compositional format that brought the subject close to the viewer, placing ranks of city dwellers or individual sitters in shallow spaces close to the picture plane to fill virtually the entire composition. He chose casual poses and haphazard arrangements of figures, and he applied his paint with a blurred softness different from Marsh's harsher sketchiness. Using stylistic conventions that recall Degas, Soyer scrutinized the ennui of city dwellers or the barrenness of the urban scene during the Depression.

Many of these stylistic distinctions appear in works produced during the early years of the Depression. In 1932, for example, Miller and Marsh both painted images of Fourteenth Street shoppers outside Fourteenth Street stores (Figs. 2.1 [Plate 1] and 2.4). Like Miller, Marsh adopted a planimetric composition and worked with crowds of human figures. But there the similarity ended. Where Miller's image is calm, ordered, and lucid—his matrons all the same, his forms clearly demarcated by heavy contours, his illumination even—Marsh's crowd is all confusion. Dozens of women and men of all shapes, sizes, and ethnic types are packed together on a shallow sidewalk, awaiting the sale boldly advertised in the signage. These figures are in constant, even violent, motion, filled with baroque exuberance. In the foreground, one young woman leaps off the sidewalk like an Olympic javelin thrower. The entire picture is made even more active through Marsh's jittery calligraphic line and his patchy chiaroscuro. And his palette, in imitation of old master paintings, is primarily golden browns and grays, with only small areas of brighter

2.4 Reginald Marsh, *Fourteenth Street*, 1932. Tempera. Present location unknown.

color. Though Marsh's energetic scene is harsher in style and more confusing in composition than John Sloan's earlier paintings of everyday street life in lower Manhattan, it recalls these works and resembles Sloan's later images of Fourteenth Street's Tammany Hall and Olympic Burlesque (Fig. 2.5).

Soyer's naturalism contrasts with Bishop's classicism in the two painters' neighborhood panoramas, *Fourteenth Street* (1935; Fig. 2.6) and *Dante and Virgil in Union Square* (Fig. 2.2). In *Fourteenth Street* Soyer captured a segment of the street under construction, a view out his studio window.[150] The street and the building site with its tiny workers, dilapidated shed, and littered timbers recedes on an angle, in an arrangement less symmetrical than Bishop's carefully measured planimetric design. Thanks to Soyer's painterly brushstroke and darker palette, the buildings seem dingy and the overall facade of the street remains unharmonious. Streaks of paint suggest the contours of buildings silhouetted against the sky but do not delineate the heroic skyline usually associated with Manhattan that Bishop's work celebrates. The white building adjacent to the construction site bears an unsightly scar where the lower stories of windows have been blocked off. Soyer seems unafraid to show both change and decay. His image suggests a city in constant transition rather than one that has been momentarily stilled and flooded with sparkling light to mark its prosperity.

Both versions of Fourteenth Street realism can be understood as part of the figurative version of American Scene painting. The classical realism of Miller and his students Bishop and Laning in their early work was characteristic of and formed

2.5 John Sloan, *The Wigwam, Old Tammany Hall*, 1934. Oil on compressed board, 30″ × 25″. The Metropolitan Museum of Art.

by artistic and critical values in the 1920s, an era of relative prosperity and normalcy. The clear ordered expression of these painters generalized the participants rather than focusing on their individual humanity. It was a style admirably suited to embody the kinds of business values promoted by Fourteenth Street's commercial advocates in the 1920s and Miller's celebration of the matronly shopper.

2.6   Raphael Soyer, *Fourteenth Street*, c. 1935. Oil on canvas, 19¹/₈″ × 27¹/₈″. Collection of Leo S. Ullman, New York.

Reginald Marsh and Raphael Soyer developed styles that were energetic or emotional rather than classicizing; these painters were more inclusive than Miller and Bishop in their portrayal of Fourteenth Street subject matter. Though both retained conventions from the figurative traditions they learned in the 1920s at the Art Students League, their Fourteenth Street–Union Square paintings were formed by the increased social awareness, concern, and anxiety of the 1930s more than the idealized optimism of the 1920s. To the extent that their art, unlike that of the social realists, offers no overt challenge to the economic or social order, Marsh and Soyer remain within the American Scene tradition. But because their images of Fourteenth Street capture either its tawdry quarters, its unemployed men, or its radical constituencies, these artists engage the darker, more anxious, and finally more socially involved side of that tradition. As a consequence, whereas Miller's, Bishop's, and Laning's images unequivocally celebrate life in Union Square, Marsh's and Soyer's images do not. Instead, their paintings capture ambiguities and inconsistencies in the Fourteenth Street milieu as it was perceived in the twenties and thirties. That neighborhood and its representations are the subject of the following chapter.

CHAPTER THREE

THE NEIGHBORHOOD

In my estimation Union Square, while a facet of the American scene, is not
typically American at all. A visitor from the South, the Middle-west or the
Pacific coast, is struck by the foreignness of the section at the very first glance.
    But in its flavor, its pushing, unconscious brutality, its search for bargains
even at the fracture of a limb, its busy shoppers on one side of the street and aim-
less, floating crowds on the other side, there is something American to the core.
    Against this strident, viciously competitive background, I have thrown the
figures of my novel. . . .

ALBERT HALPER on his novel *Union Square*

The competing discourses encompassed by American Scene painting—on art, artists, politics, and gender—have to some extent overshadowed the issue of new
womanhood in art. But it is in often contradictory images and texts that the ideals
of womanhood were constituted, though seldom explicitly. I turn in this chapter
from new womanhood and the circumstances of artists' lives to the social, cultural,
and political stage on which representations of new womanhood took shape: Fourteenth Street.

    In the early years of the Depression, New York's Union Square–Fourteenth Street
neighborhood was a subject for artists and writers of all political persuasions. But
that had not always been the case. In March 1933, just after the release of his
Literary Guild selection novel *Union Square*, Albert Halper expressed surprise that
no one had written an extended work about this neighborhood.[1] He based the novel
on his experiences living and working there, making the book a study of what he
perceived to be the neighborhood's character and types. For Halper, as for the
Fourteenth Street artists, whose realism was concerned with the constantly shifting
texture of contemporary life, the square and its occupants became the signs of the
dramatic social, economic, and cultural upheaval of the interwar period.

    In large panoramas of neighborhood crowds or in paintings and prints of neigh-
borhood types, these artists represented urban America in transition. Kenneth
Hayes Miller, Reginald Marsh, Raphael Soyer, Isabel Bishop, and their colleague

Edward Laning joined the artists, illustrators, authors, and journalists who observed the environment and its human drama. Some took an optimistic and progressive stance, focusing on the neighborhood's partial rejuvenation during the twenties. Miller, Bishop, and Laning, for example, defined the neighborhood as a crowded but prosperous center for banking, commerce, and retail trade inhabited by middle-class shoppers and office workers. Others, less celebratory, featured the tawdry shopping and loud entertainment attractions along East Fourteenth Street. Reginald Marsh focused on the ethnicity of Lower East Side residents—immigrants and working-class Americans—who came to the district for its cheap mass-produced goods and amusements. The south side of the square, more than the others, seemed to epitomize the district and the troubling social issues related to mass culture between the wars. Finally, with the onset of the Depression, still others examined the neighborhood's half-century role as the center and symbol of American radicalism. Although some of the most politically minded artists and writers depicted specific debates, rallies, and instances of police brutality, others, like Soyer and Marsh, looked with more general sympathy on the working-class women and unemployed men whose plight in the 1930s became a topic of the discourse on art and politics.

The Fourteenth Street artists cultivated all these elements of the district. They frequently heightened the impact of their imagery by superimposing an old master tradition that idealized, romanticized, or exaggerated their subjects. Though neither politically radical nor conservative in their artistic outlook—at least as they and their critics understood those terms vis-à-vis the ideology of American Scene painting—they nonetheless produced representations of a neighborhood whose very activities symbolized the most politically charged issues of the day. Through artistic strategies that alternately selected, transformed, and evaded features of the neighborhood, the artists inscribed gender, class, and ethnic difference in images of work, unemployment, leisure, and consumption. As a result, their pictures of shopping and working women as well as those of other neighborhood subjects demonstrate a range of socially engaged responses, from optimism to ambivalence to veiled interrogation of the social order. Ultimately, their complex pictorial strategies captured the multivalent textures of Union Square in the 1930s:

> The place was a polyglot of nationalities, a clash of ideologies, a roar of violent and chaotic action; in its honest and genuine concern for betterment it had always been American to the core. . . . Union Square is the past forever being overthrown; the future being forever coaxed into existence. It is the vortex of change; it is America in transition.[2]

In the early 1920s, the Union Square neighborhood was acquiring a new commercial look after two decades as one of the most depressed districts in New York. Union Square had been an upscale residential, cultural, and commercial center during the second half of the nineteenth century. From 1854, when the Academy of Music opened on the south side of East Fourteenth Street, to 1883, when the Metropolitan Opera opened on Times Square, Union Square gave New York its opera. Irving Place Theater and Tony Pastor's, on the north side of Fourteenth Street opposite the music academy, provided New Yorkers with good theater. Both Tiffany's jewelry store and Brentano's bookstore catered to an elite clientele from their first stores on Union Square West.[3] Some of the best of the new department stores in the 1870s moved to the vicinity of Union Square. Hearn's was founded on West Fourteenth Street in 1879 and remained in the block between Fifth and Sixth avenues through the Depression. Macy's had its original store adjacent to Hearn's until 1901, when it moved to Thirty-fourth Street. From 1877 to 1906, B. Altman and Company set major trends in women's fashions from its store on the west side of Sixth Avenue at Eighteenth Street, two short blocks from the square.[4] When Fourteenth Street's popularity as a fashionable shopping district began to diminish in the late nineteenth century, most of the stores followed their elegant patrons to the newer residential areas further uptown.

By about 1900 the centers of commerce had moved uptown or downtown, and virtually all the residences in the district had been replaced by office or commercial structures in the eclectic architectural styles of the American Renaissance period (Fig. 3.1). While the district maintained its general character as an entertainment and shopping center, the upscale entertainment of Fourteenth Street between Third Avenue and Union Square gave way to the diversions of mass culture. One elderly district resident later recalled the shift:

> During the last several decades of its existence, the Irving Place [Theater] deteriorated from Ibsen and Shakespeare to second-class vaudeville shows, to third-class motion pictures, and finally to fourth-class Burlesque, with hearty emphasis on the Strip Tease Department, until the local constabulary closed the place.[5]

As the district declined, real estate values plummeted, and many of the surviving neighborhood residences and abandoned offices were transformed into garment sweatshops. Close to both a cheap source of labor on the Lower East Side and the garment district to the north, it became the center for workers in the needle trades.[6]

Shortly after World War I, developers began to renovate the neighborhood. New businesses settled in and the district took on the appearance of an energetic and prosperous commercial center. This image, though based on new development, was initially fashioned in the pages of New York newspapers. There, local business leaders celebrated the renewal of Union Square and Fourteenth Street, and, in a spirit of Babbitt-like boosterism, eagerly paraded its advantages over those of other neighborhoods. In a climate of postwar prosperity they created a bright new look for the district that reflected American material prosperity and progress, an optimism that lingered into the first years of the Depression. Within this context

3.1 Berenice Abbott, Union Square West, nos. 31–41, October 26, 1938. Photograph. Federal Art Project, "Changing New York." Museum of the City of New York.

of promotional rhetoric the contemporary classicism of Miller's, Bishop's, and Edward Laning's neighborhood panoramas supported the upbeat vision.

In 1926 members of the Fourteenth Street Association of business leaders collaborated on a major article for the Sunday *New York Times* summarizing their views of the district and their hopes for its prosperity. Clarkson Cowl, president of Hearn's department store, spoke of Fourteenth Street's comeback as inevitable.[7] C. Stanley Mitchell, a bank president, emphasized the financial stability of "business and real estate, credit and asset." He pointed to the principal advantages of the district for business—its central New York location, its unusual transit and traffic facilities, and its proximity to a "most attractive" residential area.[8] Union Square was in the heart of town and Fourteenth Street was the longest east–west thoroughfare in Manhattan. During the building boom of the 1920s, scores of new apartment houses were erected in Greenwich Village, just south of the square, and Fourteenth Street retailers, who had always known that New York's retail trade would follow residential development, expressed delight at this new trend.[9]

Transit remained a controversial issue for businesses in the metropolitan area. Union Square had a long history of traffic congestion extending back to the 1890s, when trolley lines were first installed. W. A. Rogers's 1897 illustration for *Harper's Weekly* titled " 'Dead Man's Curve'—New York's Most Dangerous Crossing" shows the double curve at the corner of Broadway and Fourteenth Street, around which the trolleys raced (Fig. 3.2). In spite of police guards, the trolleys regularly claimed victims among those unaccustomed to the speed and attendant danger of modern electrified transportation. Marsh updated this theme in a 1940s Chinese ink and watercolor called *Dead Man's Curve* or *Dangerous Curves*, in which exuberant young girls, startled by a large truck blocking their path, move to get out of the way (Fig. 3.3). The image carries a double entendre related to Marsh's fascination with sexually provocative—even dangerous—women. Dead Man's Curve now threatens those who, like the leering occupants of the truck, can be distracted in traffic by a display of curvaceous beauty.[10] The perils of Union Square traffic persisted into the Depression.

Proper transit was crucial to making Fourteenth Street an attractive retail and business district. As a result, the Fourteenth Street Association, headed by its president, H. Prescott Beach, quoted endless statistics relating retail commercial success to the growing number of people using new subway and bus routes. Beach urged a recalcitrant New York transit system to finish those subway lines that transported shoppers to Manhattan from other boroughs. Merchants also supported such projects as an interurban bus terminal to alleviate some of central Manhattan's bus and motorcar traffic and a tunnel under the Hudson River to transport shoppers from New Jersey.[11] Finally, in 1931 the Fourteenth Street Association helped to win the debate to keep the Sixth Avenue elevated in place until 1938, when the completed Sixth Avenue subway line took over its route.

In all these debates neighborhood merchants contended with several related issues. First, they wanted to ensure that as many shoppers and workers as possible could make their way to the neighborhood with ease. For Hearn's president, Clarkson Cowl,

> the strategic key to successful development of any centre, whether it be for merchandising or housing or manufacturing, is "you can get there" with collegiate emphasis on the word "get." Youth emphasizes the fact that it has no time to waste but . . . neither the businessman nor any other has time to waste in this present civilization.[12]

Along with efficient transit, business leaders wanted merchants and neighborhood associations citywide to impose order on the increasing chaos of both vehicular and pedestrian traffic. Finally, they placed a high value on the pleasantness of the environment and the need to scale down the crowded cityscape. Clarkson Cowl equated "the great stores of New York" with "what the country store is to the village; there

3.2 *Left:* W. A. Rogers, " 'Dead
Man's Curve'—New York's
Most Dangerous Crossing."
Illustration for *Harper's
Weekly,* March 27, 1897.

3.3 *Below:* Reginald Marsh, *Dead
Man's Curve,* or *Dangerous
Curves,* 1940. Chinese ink and
watercolor, 26″ × 39″.
Memphis Brooks Museum of
Art.

comes to be the feeling of friendly helping and exchange [that] serves to bring the people and serve the community interest."[13] Another neighborhood merchant, impressively named Washington Irving Lincoln Adams, claimed that the "Americanization" of the foreign-born fostered community solidarity more readily in old-fashioned neighborhoods like Fourteenth Street where some feeling of community already existed.[14]

Using pictorial strategies derived from Miller's contemporary classical realism, Bishop and Laning produced a number of works that embody these ideals of communal harmony. Both artists painted images of neighborhood crowds, expanding on Miller's image of the single or paired shopper. Bishop's *Dante and Virgil in Union Square* (Fig. 2.2) and Laning's *Fourteenth Street* (Fig. 2.3) adopt small-scale formats related to larger Renaissance murals: a frieze of figures extends across the foreground, parallel to the picture plane. The frieze is broken into small groups of shoppers, businessmen, families, and workers—those deemed most important to the well-being of the American economy and its social order. Members of these groups interact cordially and democratically.

Pictorially, the businesses and transit structures of the district organize the movement and the lives of the participants. In Laning's *Fourteenth Street* a massive compositional ellipse created by the elevated railway in the middle ground and the crowd of figures in the foreground sets up a clockwise movement that figuratively moves the shoppers and workers through a regulated daily cycle of work and consumption. In Bishop's *Dante and Virgil in Union Square* the buildings tower above the crowd, helping to direct them along the major pathways of commerce. As I have already noted, an insistent feeling of repose and stability in these works emerges from the arrangement of the whole along carefully measured horizontals and verticals. In *Dante and Virgil in Union Square*, the composition is divided vertically like a triptych, with two panels of equal size flanking a larger central panel. In this central panel, architecturally undifferentiated buildings form a neutral foil for the dark silhouette of the equestrian monument of George Washington. Rising above the crowd at the exact center of the composition, this commanding Father of the Country becomes the counterpart of Christ in Majesty in a religious triptych, ruling over commerce and the souls of its practitioners.[15] In this painting and others the crowd is cast as a universalized community of urban dwellers: middle-class white adult shoppers or workers and their children. In the words of the neighborhood merchant Adams, everyone has been "Americanized."[16]

Although neither Bishop nor Laning intended these small works as murals, they were painted with Miller for the mural class at the Art Students League and resemble miniature murals in conception, subject, and decorative intent; Bishop designed *Dante and Virgil in Union Square* as an overmantle painting. Miller began to offer his mural course in 1927, just as mural painting came to be heralded as the ideal medium for creating a nationwide renaissance in art. By the early 1930s, when

Bishop and Laning produced these works, the rhetoric of advocacy surrounding mural painting was part of the increasingly nationalistic discourse of the American scene movement that would fuel the government art projects of the decade.

Inspiration for making murals to celebrate the American experience lay close at hand; the Mexican muralists Diego Rivera (whose controversial Rockefeller Center mural sparked one of the decade's most important debates about artists, patrons, and politics) and José Orozco lived and worked in New York and proclaimed the importance of making murals accessible to a broad public. Between 1930 and 1932 Thomas Hart Benton executed two mural cycles that generated substantial and, by the late 1930s, controversial press. *America Today*, his 1930 mural cycle painted for the New School for Social Research on West Twelfth Street, featured both regional and urban mass culture; Lloyd Goodrich praised its "restless vitality" and its Americanism. Critics who believed that the artist's best subject was his own environment commended the topicality of Benton's murals. For these critics mural art at its best was anti-elite, communicating the positive aspects of urban and rural culture to the average American through the eyes of an artist who could take an "objective" view of the subject.[17] At its worst, for other critics, mural painting was flamboyantly partisan and unable to deal with the large-scale technical problems of wall decoration. Murals by American Painters and Photographers, the opening show for the Museum of Modern Art in 1932, was faulted for precisely these reasons. Eager to jump on the mural bandwagon, the museum gave artists with little prior experience six weeks to produce sketches and a large-scale panel; but even the disapproving critics recognized the importance of the museum's effort for the production of American murals.[18]

In his own teaching Miller again sought a middle ground. His mural course became a practicum in both the forms and values that later characterized the government's programs. Miller took accepted Renaissance mural masters as his example: Giotto, Masaccio, Piero della Francesca, Veronese, and Rubens, to name those cited by Forbes Watson in his historical essay "Perspective on American Murals," written to document art made for the government projects in the 1930s. Miller then urged his students to substitute inspired scenes of contemporary American life for earlier images of the deeds of heroic patrons. Miller shared the belief of the writer who argued that the mural painter had a unique opportunity for "public service":

> His task is to search the inarticulate soul of a people for those universal characteristics which make and sustain its greatness. His job is to give faith-inspiring form to these qualities, whether through historical, contemporary, or symbolical figures. The day of meaningless ladies styled Truth, Justice, Virtue, and so forth, is over. Equally unpalatable as public fare are personal convictions based on a merely personal view of life, and, at the opposite pole, the parade of art for art's sake esthetics. The strong, harmonious images which reveal our nobler qualities will strike a responsive chord in the public breast.[19]

In their classically composed friezes of Fourteenth Street figures, their generalized individuals, and their homogeneous community, Laning and Bishop took a more distanced and detached view of the square and fashioned a harmonious, even ennobling, vision of everyday commercial life. In both form and subject their miniature murals suggest an economic system whose responsible members together will create a productive society. In the early days of the Depression their image would have either projected an optimistic future or recorded (nostalgically) the immediate past for a viewer who valued American material progress.[20]

The sense of order and community that pervaded the rhetoric of Fourteenth Street businessmen, and the imposition of a classical order on Union Square paintings by Miller, Laning, and Bishop were a response to—perhaps even an attempt to control—a neighborhood undergoing extraordinarily rapid change in the 1920s. An article on building activity around the square opened with the statement, "Probably nowhere else in town is there such a concentration of building as is going on around Union Square at the present time"; it demonstrated that the activity was, in the first six months of 1928, higher than for the first six months of 1927 in all of Manhattan.[21] By late September 1929 businessmen were anticipating enormous changes in property values. They were also beginning to accept the lower-class entertainment offerings of East Fourteenth Street as both inevitable and profitable.[22] As early as 1926, they had anticipated the latest form of popular entertainment by constructing the New Academy of Music across from the old.

> The New Academy will accommodate 5,000. It will be devoted exclusively to high-class screen productions interwoven with stage attractions. A pipe organ is being installed at a cost of $60,000 containing the full instrumentation of a symphony orchestra and also that of a jazz combination. . . . Mr. Fox's confidence in the future of the block is demonstrated by the large investment which the Fox Theatres Corporation has made in the latest addition to its chain of theatres.[23]

Because the artists witnessed neighborhood growth, it is worth taking a brief tour around the square with the aid of descriptions, maps, and photographs to chart some of the more important changes.

By 1930 the Union Square district housed six banks. Most occupied imposing classically styled turn-of-the-century buildings that lent an aura of stability to the neighborhood. They employed hundreds of women clerical workers. The Union Square Savings Bank at 20–22 Union Square East was located in a small building with Corinthian columns (Figs. 3.4 and 3.5); it figured prominently in Isabel Bishop's neighborhood panoramas like *Dante and Virgil in Union Square* (Fig. 2.2) and provided the backdrop for Kenneth Hayes Miller's images of middle-class matrons (Fig. 4.6). The Corn Exchange Bank was a block away, at 34 Union Square East. Directly across the square, at 31 Union Square West, the Bank of Manhattan was headquartered in a tall building, constructed in 1901 and fronted by a semicircular

3.4 *Top:* The New York Edison Company Photographic Bureau, Union Square,
view of New York looking north from Fourteenth Street and University
Place, January 11, 1928. Photograph. Museum of the City of New York.

3.5 *Above:* Berenice Abbott, Union Square, Manhattan, statue of Lafayette
by Frédéric-Auguste Bartholdi, erected in 1876, March 20, 1936.
Photograph. Federal Art Project, "Changing New York." Museum
of the City of New York.

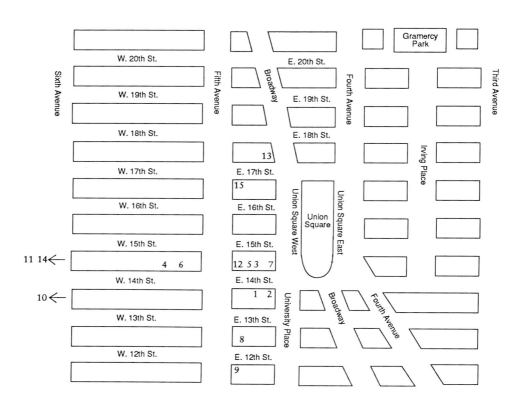

MAP 1.   Union Square, Artists' Studios.

1. Kenneth Hayes Miller's studio, 6 East Fourteenth Street, 1923 to 1928
2. Kenneth Hayes Miller's studio, 30 East Fourteenth Street, 1928 to 1952
3. Reginald Marsh's studio, 21 East Fourteenth Street, c. 1930 to 1932
4. Reginald Marsh's studio, 9 West Fourteenth Street, June 1932 to February 1933 and March 1935 to September 1935
    Isabel Bishop's studio and residence, 9 West Fourteenth Street, 1926 to 1934
5. Reginald Marsh's studio, 5 East Fourteenth Street, January 1934 to March 1935
6. Reginald Marsh's studio, 7 West Fourteenth Street, September 1935 to February 1937
7. Reginald Marsh's studio, 1 Union Square West (Lincoln Arcade Building), February 1937 to 1954
    Raphael Soyer's studio, 1 Union Square, c. late 1930s to early 1940s
8. Reginald Marsh's residence, 11 East Twelfth Street, February 1933 to January 1934
9. Reginald Marsh's residence, 4 East Twelfth Street, beginning May 1934
10. Raphael Soyer's studio and residence, 240 West Fourteenth Street (between Seventh and Eighth avenues on the south side of the street), c. 1930–1934
11. Raphael Soyer's studio and residence, 203 West Fourteenth Street (between Seventh and Eighth avenues on the north side of the street), c. mid-1930s
12. Raphael Soyer's studio, 3 East Fourteenth Street, c. mid to late 1930s
13. Isabel Bishop's studio, 857 Broadway, 1934 to 1982
14. Edward Laning's studio, 145 West Fourteenth Street (between Sixth and Seventh avenues on the north side of the street), c. 1928–1932
15. Edward Laning's studio, 12 East Seventeenth Street, beginning c. 1932

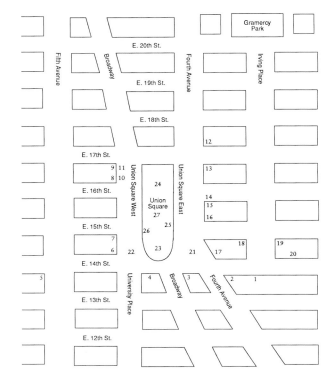

MAP 2.   Union Square, Commercial Sites and Park Monuments.

1. Luchows Restaurant
2. Central Savings Bank
3. Hudson Bay Fur Company, 856 Broadway
4. Ohrbach's, 48 East Fourteenth Street
5. Hearn's Department Store, 6 West Fourteenth Street and 74 to 76 Fifth Avenue
6. The Lincoln Building, 1 Union Square West
7. The Amalgamated Bank Building (formerly Tiffany's Jewelry Store, 1870–1905), 11–15 Union Square West
8. The Bank of Manhattan Company Building, 31 Union Square West
9. The Union Building, 33 Union Square West
10. *New Masses* Headquarters, 39 Union Square West, early 1930s
11. Hartford Building, 41 Union Square West
12. Guardian Life Insurance Company
13. Tammany Hall's new headquarters (occupancy 1929) and Manufacturers Trust Company
14. The Corn Exchange Bank, 34 Union Square East
15. Klein's Annex, 24–30 Union Square East (1928–1930, headquarters for the *Daily Worker; Freiheit;* and the Polish daily the *New World,* with the Cooperative Cafeteria on the ground floor)
16. Union Square Savings Bank, 20–22 Union Square East
17. S. Klein's, 103–107 East Fourteenth Street (old Steinway Hall property); 2–18 Union Square East (old Hotel America site)
18. Irving Place Theater
19. Consolidated Edison Company (site of old Academy of Music building)
20. Tammany Hall's old headquarters (until 1928)
21. Site of George Washington equestrian monument (bronze, Henry Kirke Brown), before 1930
22. Site of Abraham Lincoln statue (bronze, Henry Kirke Brown), before 1930
23. Site of George Washington equestrian statue in renovated Union Square Park, after 1930
24. Site of Abraham Lincoln statue in renovated Union Square Park, after 1930
25. Site of statue of Lafayette (bronze, Frédéric-Auguste Bartholdi)
26. Site of *Woman and Child* (bronze, Adolf von Donndorf)
27. Site of Liberty Pole—Charles Francis Murphy memorial (flagpole with base by Anthony de Fransisci)

portico with two Ionic columns (Fig. 3.1). Further south, at 11–15 Union Square West, New York's first labor bank, the Amalgamated Labor Bank, occupied Tiffany's old building. The Central Savings Bank stood at the southeast corner of East Fourteenth Street and Fourth Avenue. Finally, in 1929 Manufacturers Trust Company moved into the ground floor of Tammany Hall's new headquarters at the corner of Seventeenth Street and Union Square East.[24]

Neighborhood insurance and utility companies also hired vast numbers of women workers. The Guardian Life Insurance Company, with its high mansard roof, towered over the northeastern end of Union Square (Fig. 3.4). But the most significant addition to the square was the Consolidated Edison Company. Construction on the huge building began in 1915 on the site of the old Academy of Music at Irving Place between Fourteenth and Fifteenth streets. By 1928 the building was crowned by a magnificent 531-foot tower with a clock. By night the tower was brilliantly illuminated, and it served year-round as a landmark for the square (Fig. 3.5).[25] The artists would have watched the construction, and Bishop in her Union Square panoramas—even the small work showing Union Square torn up for reconstruction (Fig. 3.6)—made it a glowing symbol of progress. Similarly, in *Union Square* the novelist Albert Halper used the clock tower, with its "solemn, stately bongs," to structure the relentless progress of time through the novel and the everyday lives of its characters.[26]

By far the most important commercial change in Union Square was the growth of retail women's wear in the twenties: large firms employing hundreds of women sold thousands of dresses. According to some accounts, stores sold more women's apparel in one day on Union Square than in any other place in the country.[27] The prosperity of retail trade on Union Square continued virtually unchecked into the 1930s and was largely responsible for bringing to the district the crowds of women shoppers who became the mainstay of Miller's imagery. The most successful stores were Hearn's, Ohrbach's, and S. Klein's.

Hearn's was one of New York's oldest. Established in 1879, it remained in its location between Fifth and Sixth avenues on West Fourteenth Street when most other department stores moved uptown. By the elder Hearn's original 1879 account, parts of which were quoted by the Fourteenth Street Association in a 1925 *New York Times* article, he chose the site because there were more women on Fourteenth Street than in any other retail district in the city and because "I would not give a snap of my finger for all the trade we obtain from men."[28] Hearn knew his clientele. "I may mention that I found the best-dressed people, and consequently the class who are likely to spend the most money, on upper Broadway. Fourteenth Street came next in this respect, and Sixth Avenue next to that."[29] Hearn's would retain a predominantly middle- to lower-middle-class clientele throughout the Depression.

The twenties brought prosperity and continuing expansion to Hearn's. In 1926 the store added a Fifth Avenue entrance, leasing the property at 74–76 Fifth Avenue

3.6 Isabel Bishop, *Union Square during the Expansion of the Fourteenth Street Subway Station,* 1930. Oil on canvas, 16″ × 20¹/₄″. Midtown Payson Galleries, New York.

and thereby adding 50,000 square feet of selling and storage space; the store acquired a long-term lease at 6 West Fourteenth Street, directly opposite Isabel Bishop's studio at 9 West Fourteenth Street.[30] Unlike Ohrbach's and S. Klein's, which specialized in women's wear and accessories, Hearn's was a full-scale department store, less flashy than its uptown counterparts—Saks Fifth Avenue, Lord & Taylor, and Altman's—but capable of offering a wider range of goods and services to its expanding clientele. As one shopping guide noted, Hearn's could attract even the elite with its offerings in fine linens, fit for "ambassadorial dinner parties":

> Many women who never direct their chauffeurs below Fiftieth Street for months on end make their way to Hearn's when the linen supply is low. This store, with a fine feeling for the distinction between sheep and goats, has opened a special Fifth Avenue entrance for that part of its patronage which would never happen in from the Fourteenth Street side.[31]

The Hearn's shopper became an important subject in Bishop's earliest paintings, not only because Bishop was influenced by her mentor, Kenneth Hayes Miller, but also because her studio looked out on Hearn's. At the time she painted the two similar works *Hearn's Department Store—Fourteenth Street Shoppers* (1927) and

3.7 Isabel Bishop, *Department Store Entrance*, c. 1929. Destroyed.

3.8 "A Sudden Change in Fashions— As Illustrated in the Afternoon Ensemble," from the *Delineator* 115 (October 1929), p. 25.

Department Store Entrance (c. 1929; Fig. 3.7), Bishop was enrolled in Miller's mural-painting class at the Art Students League. There, as is evident in *Department Store Entrance*, she absorbed Miller's formalist and academic principles.[32] All the figures move parallel to the picture plane. The setting is shallow, with double doors that divide the picture almost exactly in half. Figure placement conforms to compositional demands. The arch of the entrance is repeated below in the curved cloche hats, the fur collars, and the hem of the woman's coat in the center.

Bishop identified her early subjects as middle-class shoppers and, where they appear, their businessmen husbands. Whether in store entrances on Fourteenth Street or in the vast space of Union Square, these middle-class urbanites were for her the regular denizens of Fourteenth Street.[33] Most of Bishop's shoppers wear simple, fashionable costumes. The woman at the center of *Department Store Entrance* (Fig. 3.7) wears an exaggerated version of the newest fashions (Fig. 3.8): the helmet-style hat; the coat with massive fur trim at collar, cuffs, and hem; and, beneath it, the longer dress with an uneven hem. Her costume and her proximity to equally fashionable male shoppers allows us to date the work to 1929. The shoppers in up-to-the-minute styles enhance the image of the neighborhood's stores as fashionable.

Samuel Klein received much of the credit for the success of retail enterprises as well as for the renewal of Union Square in the 1920s. His development of a vast complex of stores for bargain women's wear established and stabilized rents and fees for buildings in Union Square.[34] Klein's was a classic American success story. In 1912 he began as a poor tailor in a Union Square loft. In 1924 he purchased the old Steinway Hall building at 103–107 East Fourteenth Street, at the northeast corner of Fourth Avenue. He demolished the building and constructed the seven-story edifice that became his main store. In 1926–27, he purchased the adjoining property (the Hotel America) at 2–18 Union Square East, and by January of 1928 he occupied the entire corner (Fig. 3.9).[35] Then, in the heart of the Depression, Klein remodeled the three office buildings from 24 to 30 Union Square East. These buildings, adjacent to the Union Square Bank and a block from the other store, became Klein's annex (Fig. 3.5). The annex allowed Klein to sell his "better dresses" in a different locale, serving, in effect, to separate his lower-class bargain-basement shoppers from the middle-class patrons who in the Depression had less to spend on clothing. Prior to its construction, as one shopping guide explained, Klein's "better dress" department was not an easy place to shop:

> A note to be filed under the Penny Saved section in your mind concerns S. Klein, a shop found in the grubby environs of Fourth Avenue and Fourteenth Street. Head in here and ask, with aplomb, to be shown the way to the Better Dress section, whose prices range upwards from $9.50, I give you my word. I do not understand the racket, but I know that you can pick up astounding bargains here in dresses that do not turn green when you wear them out in the sunlight. All the employees are engaged in sitting on high platforms watching for shoplifters, so expect no service.[36]

3.9 S. Klein's, looking from the south side of East Fourteenth Street toward the
intersection of Fourth Avenue and Union Square East, 1928. Photograph.
United States History, Local History and Genealogy Division, The New York
Public Library, Astor, Lenox and Tilden Foundations.

S. Klein's, Fourteenth Street, and success became synonymous. In every way,
Klein's overshadowed its equally successful, though less visible, competitor, Ohrbachs, at 48 East Fourteenth Street on the south side of the square at the corner of
Broadway. Klein's overwhelmed Union Square with an extraordinary display of
signage (Fig. 3.9). Bishop in her work, unlike her colleague Marsh (see Figs. 2.2
and 2.4), omitted all advertisements. She preferred to emphasize the measured
sobriety of the building facades and the ranks of shoppers and to celebrate commercial success without the interruption of its garish trappings.

Klein's also overwhelmed Union Square with its extraordinary crowds of women
shoppers, who bought as many as ten thousand dresses per day. In March 1930,
there was a stampede of four thousand at the store, which forty special officers
failed to quiet.[37] Evidently, sale days regularly promised some chaos; the guidebook
writer Gretta Palmer cautioned, "Please, in the name of the defenseless Police
Department, do not choose a sale day for your visit. At this time, ropes are put
around the curbing, trucks are overturned and the event is counted a failure without
the breakage of one plate-glass window and an ambulance call."[38]

Several artists featured the Klein's shopper. In *Afternoon on the Avenue* (1932;
Fig. 3.10), Miller depicted an energetic shopper leaving Klein's (he included enough
of the name on the store window to identify the locale). Behind her, a burly policeman watches over the scene. Mary Fife, Edward Laning's wife, who was also a
Miller student, captured the chaos and humor of trying on clothes in *Klein's*

3.10 Kenneth Hayes Miller, *Afternoon on the Avenue*, 1932. Present location unknown.

3.11. Mary Fife Laning, *Klein's Dressing Room,* undated. Private collection.

Dressing Room (undated; Fig. 3.11). She shows two groups of women in twisted baroque poses, parodying the three Graces as they struggle into or out of new garments. The floor is littered with gloves, hats, and ornaments; drapery and bows flutter; limbs flail. Commentators marveled at the exuberance of the Klein's ritual, with shoppers treating bargains as a life-and-death matter.

By contrast, even though the dressing room in Soyer's *Shopping at Klein's* is communal, it remains a place of reverie where the quiet contemplation of both self and self-transformation becomes possible (c. 1940; Fig. 3.12). A young woman gazes thoughtfully at herself and a new garment in a standing oval mirror—an image we cannot see. Soyer's picture contrasts the graceful pose of this figure with the awkwardness of another, seen from behind, who steps into her garment.

Miller's dressing room and bargain counter appear genteel in comparison with Fife's and Soyer's. Women in *The Bargain Counter* (Fig. 3.13), though crowded together, confer deliberately over the goods rather than grabbing them from one another, the reported practice at Klein's. In *The Fitting Room* Miller, who as a man lacked access to women's dressing rooms, conflated the communal dressing room with that of the fashionable department store, where saleswomen provided help to customers (Fig. 3.14). The figures in both works are in repose, their movements stately, as if the business at hand is a ritual. The sense of stability comes again from Miller's use of old master models and his studied placement of the formal elements

3.12 Raphael Soyer, *Shopping at Klein's,* c. 1940. Oil on canvas. Present location unknown.

3.13 Kenneth Hayes Miller, *The Bargain Counter,* 1931. Oil on canvas. Present location unknown.

3.14   Kenneth Hayes Miller, *The Fitting Room*, 1931. Oil on canvas, 28″ × 34″. The Metropolitan Museum of Art.

in the painting. In *The Fitting Room* Miller borrowed the motif of the three Graces for the three women on the left. Then he used a series of repeating drapery folds to tie them into a harmonious group. The U-shaped fur collar of the women on the left is carried into the drape of the central figure and across to the shoulders of the woman on the right. Identical U-shaped folds underline the buttocks of the women with their backs to the viewer. These curves are repeated throughout the picture, in the arched background, in hat shapes, and in hairstyles.

To judge from both Miller's, Laning's, and Bishop's pictorial responses to the neighborhood and the enthusiasm of business leaders, Union Square had once again become influential. Visually and verbally artists and business leaders constructed an image of a growing and prosperous district, a desirable place to shop and do business, and a pleasant environment just to pass through. In January 1930, Clarkson Cowl assessed the change:

I have seen the old district between 14th street and Washington Square hold its own and redevelop until today we have a veritable city within a city where thousands of lovers of historic New York make new homes for themselves and perhaps, hand on to their descendants something of the sturdy Americanism for which the old ninth ward has long been famous.[39]

The rhetoric about the neighborhood's progress, financial stability, importance, and significance as a contributor to American community values was based in part on fact. On the eve of the Depression, however, many projects lay unfinished, and many dreams remained unrealized. The neighborhood's boosters never really succeeded in reversing a stubborn perception that Fourteenth Street could not sustain business ventures. Moreover, the vehicular tunnel originally proposed between West Fourteenth Street and New Jersey was eventually built from Canal Street. Fourteenth Street also lost the bid for a bus terminal to Times Square. With the onset of the Depression, projects that were under way ground to a halt. The developer Henry Mandel's proposed forty-three-story office building was never erected, leaving a gaping hole in the block between Fifteenth and Sixteenth streets on Union Square West, as seen in a 1929 aerial view (Fig. 3.15; see n. 26).

An even more unsightly space, visible in the same 1929 photograph, was the square itself. For almost eight years, from 1928 to 1936, the park was under renovation. As early as 1927, the Municipal Art Society of New York submitted plans to the Municipal Art Commission to redo the park, an old tree-lined space that had been a gathering place for unemployed men and a center for political rallies and speeches since the turn of the century.[40] In April 1928 plans were announced for the construction of additional passageways, mezzanines, and platforms to connect the Union Square station of the Broadway line with the Fourteenth Street eastern subway line. Since all the lines intersected beneath Union Square, the plans necessitated raising the level of the park, constructing a retaining wall around the square, and complete relandscaping. The plan also called for relocating the park's statues to alleviate some of Union Square's traffic problems.[41] The equestrian statue of George Washington was to be moved from the triangular point of land at Fourteenth Street and Fourth Avenue to the south end of the park, Abraham Lincoln from an analogous position at Fourteenth Street and Broadway (Fig. 3.4) to the north end of the Square, and Lafayette to the east side of the park, facing Klein's annex (Fig. 3.5 and Map 2).

Work on the park and the subway renovation began in August 1928 and was scheduled for completion in March 1929. Neighborhood businesses, proudly boasting that the new subway station would be the largest in Manhattan, looked forward to increased commerce. But from the beginning schedules went awry, plans were constantly revised, and frustration grew as the square remained in disarray. The Lafayette statue was moved in August 1929 as one of the first steps in improving the park.[42] Isabel Bishop's small oil *Union Square* (Fig. 3.6) shows Adolf von Donn-

3.15　The New York Edison Company Photographic Bureau, Union Square, general aerial view of New York from Fourteenth Street and Irving Place, March 27, 1929. Photograph. Museum of the City of New York.

dorf's *Woman and Child* statue, across the park from the Lafayette, surrounded by workmen and their carts and the torn-up earth of the square. In May 1931 Park Commissioner Herrick urged the speedy construction of the retaining wall and the installation of walks, benches, and fences to placate merchants and nearby residents who were complaining about the park's appearance. In August 1931 a *New York Times* editorial reported on years of slow work:

> The square has had anything but a tranquil history in recent years. The exigencies of subway building required that it be torn up and regraded. The work was done without adequate planning and consultation, and consequently much of it had to be done over again at considerable expense to the city. For months, the area has not even been fit for soapbox oratory. Local merchants . . . will be delighted when the park is restored to something of its former glory.[43]

The Depression naturally slowed funding for the park's completion. In June 1932 topsoil was brought in (in a public ceremony); but when further appropriations were rescinded, the park remained unfinished. Landscaping was finally completed in 1935–36, eight years after the initial work had begun.[44]

With the exception of Bishop's one small oil, the paintings of Union Square and Fourteenth Street by Bishop, Miller, and Laning avoided the ugliness of this "mud-

3.16 Reginald Marsh, East Fourteenth Street, late 1930s. Photograph. Museum of the City of New York.

caked oval" and the eyesores around the square (Figs. 3.6 and 3.15). Bishop filled the square with sparkling light and a happy community of middle-class people. Laning in *Fourteenth Street* unified the symbols of commercial success—the institutions of Fourteenth Street and its participants—by choosing a limited palette of blues, pinks, and golds (Fig. 2.3). By painting the elevated structures in pastels that recall the palette of fifteenth-century Sienese painters and by simplifying all the elevated structures, he denied their decrepit condition. Miller, in *In Fourteenth Street* (Fig. 2.1; Plate 1) similarly stripped down forms and settings to avoid painting the seedier aspects of the district. One of the numerous photographs of Fourteenth Street windows by Reginald Marsh (Fig. 3.16)[45] shows that they were filled to bursting with randomly arranged goods: an ideal of plenty rather than an aesthetic of simplicity governed the display. Miller removed all but a few items in the painting orchestrating them around the demands of repeating downward curves. His shoppers, with the three Graces at the front, are deliberately placed; nothing litters the sidewalk; the women are uniform types. No complex reflections detract from the overall clarity of design, of which Miller himself remarked: "It would be naive indeed to feel that one could go anywhere in the plastic art by just being spontaneous."[46]

Images by Miller, Bishop, and Laning avoided evidence of the Depression in the early 1930s and thereby enhanced the perception of the neighborhood as a pristine environment characterized by middle-class commercial success. By creating a carefully structured and evenly painted contemporary classical style and by fashioning monumental idealized figures, Miller and his students sustained the optimistic vision of a homogeneous American urban community enacting rituals of commerce that assert the society's well-being, just as its boosters did.

Marsh, in contrast, deployed his updated Ashcan realism to document a different part of the district—East Fourteenth Street between Fourth and Third avenues—that contained cheap stores, restaurants, and entertainments (Figs. 3.17 and 3.18). The Ashcan painter John Sloan provided precedents for some of Marsh's paintings of this seedier block of the neighborhood, chief among them *The Wigwam, Old Tammany Hall* (Fig. 2.5), whose design was based on a 1928 etching of the same subject. Inspired by the sale of the building, which had been owned by one of New York's oldest and most corrupt political organizations, Sloan depicted the darkened facade of Tammany next to the glowing entrance of the Olympic Burlesque. Before the theater, crowds of women and men—sailors, newsboys, and policemen—promenade and flirt jovially. This image of New York captures the air of good-natured prosperity that characterized the mayorality of James J. Walker (1926–32) before the exposure of his corruption forced him to resign.[47] Sloan later wrote of the etching, "Old Tammany Hall, the Headquarters of the bosses of New York City, has ceased to exist. It lurked, menacing, in dingy red brick, facing the tawdry amusements of East Fourteenth Street."[48] In the painting Sloan exaggerated the raucous gaiety of the scene.[49] He took a distant and slightly elevated position and separated the figures to clarify their interaction. Then he chose a strident palette of harsh browns, fiery oranges, and yellows to suggest the garishness of nighttime entertainment.

Marsh, like Sloan, was drawn to the block containing Fourteenth Street's less refined entertainment and commerce. He too depicted crowds of stereotyped figures set against tall building facades. Both *Fourteenth Street* (1932; Fig. 2.4) and *In Fourteenth Street* (1934; Fig. 3.19 and Plate 3) show the urban crowd on the street in quest of a cheap bargain—a chaotic pleasure search similar to the one Sloan depicted in *The Wigwam, Old Tammany Hall.* Marsh, however, compressed his space, filled the scene with figures to the point of *horror vacui*, and took the warmth of flirtatious interaction out of the scene. Like Sloan, Marsh celebrated, even reveled in, female beauty as he found it in lower-class or working women. Finding precedents in some of Sloan's mid-1920s etchings, works more illustrative and frankly sexual than Sloan's paintings, Marsh in his own etchings of the late 1920s coarsened and exaggerated the sexuality and tawdriness of Sloan's more decorous scenes.[50] For example, the woman whose legs Sloan frankly exposes in *Subway Stairs* (Fig. 3.20) resembles the women of his earlier etchings, fresh-faced and exuberant

3.17   *Top:* Reginald Marsh, Fourteenth Street Bowling Alley/Billiards. Photograph.
Museum of the City of New York.

3.18   *Above:* Reginald Marsh, *10 Shots, 10 Cents,* 1939. Watercolor and ink on paper,
27″ × 40″. The Saint Louis Art Museum.

3.19   Reginald Marsh, *In Fourteenth Street,* 1934. Egg tempera on composition board, 35⅞″ × 39¾″. The Museum of Modern Art, New York.

(*Return from Toil,* Fig. 3.21). Sloan sought out women with these qualities as his subjects and acknowledged his pleasure in them—the pleasure of a male viewer. "I enjoy a jolly subject like this just as I like a healthy kind of ribaldry. There is something clean and wholesome about ribaldry that is completely different from the salacious or pornographic."[51] Marsh's women in etchings like *Subway—Three Girls* (1928; set in the Fourteenth Street subway) and *BMT #3* (1929; Fig. 3.22) are chillier, more sophisticated, and more singularly self-possessed than the women in his paintings. This strategy increases the distance between the artist or viewer and the subject of the work; at the same time, it reflects the character of the flapper, the worldly wise and sexually experienced new woman of the jazz age.

3.20 *Left:* John Sloan, *Subway Stairs,*
1926. Etching, 7″ × 5″. Delaware
Art Museum, Wilmington.

3.21 *Below:* John Sloan, *Return from
Toil,* 1915. Etching, 4½″ × 6″.
Delaware Art Museum,
Wilmington.

3.22 Reginald Marsh, *BMT #3*, 1929. Etching, 7⁷⁄₈″ × 9⁷⁄₈″. The William Benton Museum of Art, The University of Connecticut, Storrs.

Marsh, as a younger artist, was less restricted by genteel norms of both art and society than was Sloan, who came to maturity in the Progressive Era, before movies were part of the cultural landscape. Marsh's women in his painting *Fourteenth Street Subway Stairs* (1932; Fig. 3.23), in contrast to Sloan's women, are sophisticated beauties with curving figures. They are heavily made up like the movie queens whose look they emulated with the help of mass-produced beauty aids that had become widely available. Because this look was still at the periphery of beauty culture before 1920, the kind of women Marsh painted were not part of Sloan's experience.

Marsh chronicled a Fourteenth Street different from that of his compatriots, one that featured the district's cheap entertainments. The south side of the block between Fourth and Third avenues, as recorded in Marsh's photographs (Fig. 3.17) and in journalistic accounts, was lined with burlesque shows, bowling alleys, penny emporiums, orange drink stands, dance halls, and pool parlors, along with cheap restaurants.[52] In the late 1920s and early 1930s, before the Irving Place Burlesque

3.23   Reginald Marsh, *Fourteenth Street Subway Stairs*, 1932. Tempera, 60″ × 30″.
Private collection.

3.24   Reginald Marsh, *Irving Place Burlesque*, 1930. Tempera. Present location unknown.

left the neighborhood for good, Marsh etched and painted several images of it in which he contrasted women as objects with dazed or leering men (Fig. 3.24). He capitalized on the burlesque's exploitation of the female body to show off two other, equally gaudy, Fourteenth Street entertainments. In *Ten Cents a Dance* (1933; Fig. 3.25) Marsh painted taxi dancers, women for hire for dancing—like the Depression dance marathons, a quintessentially thirties phenomenon. The sultry women in this frieze, in their lurid red and yellow garments, engage the viewer and seem available for more than dancing. In *Hudson Bay Fur Company* (Fig. 3.26) Marsh depicted the live models who displayed furs in the large second-story windows of the Hudson Bay Fur Company, using strip-tease poses to titillate the viewer. The painting links the show window to the burlesque runway, a vantage point different from that afforded Marsh when he photographed the actual window (c. 1939; Fig. 3.27).

The varied population of Fourteenth Street was what attracted Marsh. He worked to capture the confusion of the crowds confronted by the chaotic sights, sounds, and cheap sidewalk shopping attractions that also gave the neighborhood its flavor in the accounts of journalists, guidebook writers, and storytellers during

3.25   Reginald Marsh, *Ten Cents a Dance*, 1933. Egg tempera on panel, 36″ × 48″. Collection of
Whitney Museum of American Art.

the 1930s. This was the lower-class community that business leaders avoided discussing and the one that Miller, Bishop, and Laning homogenized into a prosperous
middle-class community—making their subjects resemble themselves. This gaudy,
constantly moving spectacle of Fourteenth Street engaged Marsh's fascination with
popular culture and its participants, subjects the upper-class Marsh portrayed as
the Other. In works like *In Fourteenth Street* (Fig. 3.19) Marsh focused on the
street's proximity to the neighborhood where many immigrant families and poorer
working-class people lived and its centrality for this population as a source of commercial entertainment and a place of commerce.[53] In his paintings, Marsh saw Fourteenth Street as the archetypal melting pot described by a *New York Times* reporter,
with many "races, colors and classes," from "river front and Bowery," from "a
thousand domestic Main Streets," and from "fifty neighborhoods in wise old New
York."[54] He saw its population as the one Klein's catered to when it posted its
warnings against shoplifting in a dozen languages.[55] And he saw it as Albert Halper
did in his novel *Union Square*, as a seething mass of humanity in which he found
only ethnic types, never individuals.

3.26 *Top:* Reginald Marsh, *Hudson Bay Fur Company*, 1932. Egg tempera on cotton, 30″ × 40″. Columbus Museum of Art, Columbus, Ohio.

3.27 *Above:* Reginald Marsh, Hudson Bay Fur Company, Fourteenth Street, c. 1939. Photograph. Museum of the City of New York.

Swarm after swarm of heads pass, wave on wave, all kinds of nationalities, the true melting pot of the town. Little dark Cuban women, big black Negresses from Jamaica, tony little kept women from West Side apartment houses, tall lanky Swedish girls with washed-out faded eyes, sturdy Polish housewives carrying big shopping bags—all crowd into the bargain stores and shove and push and jam near the counters.[56]

Because many from the Lower East Side were attracted to the inexpensive entertainments of Fourteenth Street, writers compared these crowds to those at Coney Island, the favorite amusement escape for working-class immigrants and Marsh's other favorite subject.[57] Moreover, guidebook writers and journalists were fascinated by the sidewalk salesman—the fly-by-night hawker who sold cheap goods and souvenirs on the run. They were awed by this exploitation of the poor by the poor and marveled at the array of goods offered for sale—"unbreakable combs, rubber toothbrushes, 'pitchers from Paris for men only' ";[58] "sliced cocoanut, gloves, scarves, neckties, popular song sheets, . . . magic roots which sprout full-blown gladiolas, peonies, or regal lilies; prophecies from a turbaned seer."[59] Halper captured the look, sound, and turbulent spirit of the sidewalk scene in *Union Square*:

There were also young men and boys who peddled songs printed on big, square sheets of paper, songs that told you all about the silver lining and how to chase the blues away. And further down were the high-pressure boys, the lads who spat and hawked their wares at you, offering, for your consideration, socks, bars of candy, twenty-five cent neckties ("they're worth two bucks apiece, mister, honest to Christ!"), shoelaces, needles for the lady of the house, and little Japanese toys to tickle the kiddies' fancy. But the cleverest lads of all were the fellows who sold worthless watches out of small, black leather bags, one eye out for passing suckers, the other on the policeman down the street.

The noise was terrific, everything was bedlam. Folks crossed the street against the traffic and were shouted at by our vigilant police. Everywhere you turned a vender shoved an object under your nose, yelling, screaming, urging you to buy. Some even clutched you by the arm, others followed you a way with whining voices. . . .

Barkers stood in front of almost every store, like at a circus, rattling off the bargain prices of fur pieces, shoes and dresses hot from the marts of fashion, pointing to the goods in the windows.[60]

Along with the hawkers there were those Halper called "the wrecked bits of humanity."[61] The blind, legless beggars—countless numbers of them—many on small platforms with wheels, were either veterans or clothed themselves in uniform to make a good impression. With their faithful dogs they made their way to the district at "the first crack of daylight" to gain an honest or dishonest living.[62]

Fourteenth Street also offered legitimate bargains in numerous smaller stores and thus became for first- and second-generation immigrants what Fifth Avenue was to those in the social register. To these new Americans the street symbolized abundance and democracy; there they could buy cheaper versions of everything rich people possessed uptown. One writer characterized Fourteenth Street as a place where

> The second generation quickly catches the spirit of American folk ways and appears in Fourteenth Street adaptations of Fifth Avenue modes. Youth clusters around the clothing store windows on its way home from work. Silk stockings are as sheer and skirts as short and jaunty of their kind on Fourteenth Street as on Park Avenue. The little shop girl with her $15 a week may within her circle rival a queen of the uptown social world in dressiness if she lives at home. On her way to and from business she studies the field of fashion as presented in the shop windows she passes.[63]

Iconographically and structurally, Marsh's paintings of Fourteenth Street shopping crowds are about consumer energy, chaos, and confusion. Marsh photographed the district and put its legless beggars and sandwich-board advertisers in his paintings (Figs. 3.17–3.19; Plate 3). Like Halper, he transformed the district into an image of Bedlam. Using the iconography of Michelangelo's *Last Judgment* from the Sistine Chapel (Fig. 3.28) in *In Fourteenth Street*, Marsh depicted modern commerce as both heaven and hell. At the center of the swirling maelstrom attracted to the temptations of Fourteenth Street's sidewalk commerce, the hawker, one of Halper's conniving clever lads with a black leather satchel, assumes the pose of the judging Christ—but in reverse. Marsh's hawker—a deceptive figure—raises his (sinister) left hand instead of his right and offers seduction instead of judgment. Furthermore, this figure and another salesman working the crowd below him are painted in grisaille. In an otherwise colorful group they are bloodless, shadowy figures, exploiting the crowd with cheap fly-by-night goods. The image suggests Marsh's ambivalence toward an urban scene that was energetic and exciting but also cynical and chaotic.

Marsh's ambivalence is even clearer when contrasted with the more overtly acerbic vision of the social realist painter Philip Evergood, who depicted the Fourteenth Street crowd beneath the Hudson Bay Fur Company. The figures in Evergood's *Treadmill* (c. 1936; Fig. 3.29), reminiscent of the satirist George Grosz's caricatures, show the bankruptcy of American commercial civilization. Vicious-looking men, and women in see-through dresses, cavort against a dizzying flat backdrop of flashing neon lights and signs. These women move provocatively before a storefront as similarly attired women display themselves in the windows of the Hobson & Co. store above, a parodic reference to the actual Hudson Bay Fur Company. The juxtaposition of the two friezes of cartoon-like figures suggests the close relationship between those who sell and those who purchase.

To capture the overwhelming visual and aural sensations of the district's gaudier commercial side, Marsh and writers like Halper resorted to a rhetoric that was inclusive and documentary as well as stereotypical and hyperbolic. Although they sought to catalog what was there, the stylistic exaggeration—whether in layers of

3.28 Michelangelo, *The Last Judgment* (detail).

3.29 Philip Evergood, *Treadmill*, c. 1936. Oil on canvas, 49″ × 29″. Present location unknown.

words or in densely crowded and detailed settings—suggests their ambivalent response. Ethnic stereotypes inscribe class difference in the scenes, as does the frequently elevated and distanced point of view, which constructs a middle- to upper-middle-class observer. In the chaotic compositions, moreover, those in the crowds are deemed out of order—an Other somehow less civilized. At the same time, these pictures also examine how modern urban society—through advertising, movies, radio, and news media—had multiplied sensations to the point of overload, so that both the individual and the community had become fragmented. The paintings thus simultaneously describe forces beyond individual control and specific daily events. Dislocation in Marsh's shopping crowds provides a point of contrast with the cheerful, stable crowds of Laning and Bishop. Their images encapsulate the myth of urban optimism in the 1920s, when the idea of civilization seemed a positive force in the march of progress. Marsh's images express a tension his friends and critics struggled to convey. Laning wrote that Marsh's New York was "vibrant, alive and various but it curiously resembles New York as a stranger sees it. The city remains always wonderful to him, something hectic, dazzly and in a sense meaningless."[64] Although Marsh celebrated the energy of the urban crowd, he recognized the alienation of individuals in it and thus showed an image of the 1930s formed when the ideal of urban civilization was increasingly in doubt.[65]

From a growing interest in the social sciences, which studied individual and group behavior, to an increase in radical protest, doubts about American civilization (understood in the Progressive Era as scientific advance, industrial and technological progress, and new forms of organizations and institutions) surfaced frequently in the Depression, particularly around Union Square. The district was more politically active at the end of the 1920s and into the early years of the 1930s than at any time in its long history as the center for radical politics. Membership in radical organizations and participation in individual political events increased dramatically as artists and writers from all political backgrounds felt threatened by the economic crisis.

Among the Fourteenth Street School artists, Soyer regularly attended meetings at the Communist-run John Reed Club; he taught classes there, worked on group murals, and made it his social center. Laning exhibited works in two of the club's major exhibitions, The World Crisis Expressed in Art in 1933 and Revolutionary Front in 1934, and he attended occasional meetings until he became involved in government projects. The only shopper image by Miller in the John Reed Club's exhibition The Social Viewpoint in Art in 1933 drew negative comments from leftist critics for its lack of social commitment to the working class. In May and June 1931 Marsh attended four "communism" classes at the Workers' School on Union Square, and his diaries record his attendance at a John Reed Club meeting on March 27, 1933. The following January he taught a morning class at the club. He watched two demonstrations on Union Square in the spring of 1933, noting after one of

3.30 Reginald Marsh, "Birthday Party,"
or "Union Square," *New Masses* 10
(February 20, 1934), p. 7.

them that he walked around all night talking with a friend (presumably about the event); in June he made his print of the square featuring the unemployed men gathered at the base of the George Washington monument (Fig. 3.30). From 1926 until the mid-1930s Marsh, following his pattern of working as an illustrator for magazines across the political spectrum, contributed over a dozen drawings and prints to the *New Masses*.[66] Isabel Bishop participated in none of these early decade events. Then, although she, Marsh, and Miller never signed the original call for the American Artists' Congress in 1935 (though Soyer did), she subsequently became a member and participated in its exhibitions. Like many liberals, she believed in its mission to support artistic freedom against the global threat of Fascism. Following the signing of the Hitler-Stalin nonaggression pact and the Soviet invasion of Finland, the congress splintered to include a group that could no longer support Stalinist policies. Bishop was one of these "Congress Seceders" who joined the Society for Modern Artists (also called the Federation of Modern Painters) to "promote the welfare of free progressive artists working in America." The group denounced all forces working against cultural development and all forms of totalitarianism, including those of Russia, Germany, Italy, and Spain.[67]

Numerous radical groups met in their headquarters around the square during the 1930s (See Map 2).[68] The district had been the scene of relatively little political agitation until the late 1920s.[69] Then, an increasingly tense political climate, nationally and internationally, brought May Day rallies, unemployment demonstrations, and protests against police brutality to the district. After the August 1927 execution of Sacco and Vanzetti, conflict began when police injured several of the five thousand sympathizers who had gathered for an all-night vigil.[70] In 1929 five thousand Communists staged the first May Day rally in Union Square since 1916.[71] Eighteen days later, when three hundred Communist party members displayed from the windows of the Communist party headquarters a sign reading "Down with Walker's Police Brutality," police entered the building without a warrant and arrested twenty-seven participants, including nine children.[72] The largest and most violent unemployment demonstration—with thirty-five thousand participants—erupted on March 6, 1930. By the end of the day, one hundred had been injured, and news accounts across the political spectrum condemned the zealousness with which plainclothes police "pummeled" the victims with their nightsticks.[73]

This last event galvanized the public against police interference, and under pressure, city officials guaranteed the right to free assembly in the square. Subsequent May Day rallies, though larger every year, remained peaceful throughout the Depression. These gatherings continued to reflect the changing political climate: 1935 was the last year in which Socialists and Communists marched in separate parades; 1936 brought a united demonstration against the threat of Fascism—"the quietest parade in years"—leading police to set aside their nightsticks. The 1937 parade stressed aid to Spain as its theme.[74]

Even as Union Square continued as a center for radicalism, municipal leaders and store owners, concerned about the effects of demonstrations on business, decided to make the district into a patriotic center as an antidote to radical activities. The Veterans of Foreign Wars received permits to stage their first in a series of annual May Day activities immediately following the Communists' rallies.[75] Much to local business leaders' delight, Park Commissioner Herrick announced a celebration of Washington's birthday for Union Square, specifically designed to rid Union Square of its Communist reputation and "cleanse its atmosphere."[76] Then in April 1932, with accolades from both Mayor Walker and President Hoover, local business leaders presented a Union Square centennial, also designed to renew patriotic spirit. President Hoover praised the neighborhood as a center of "industry, finance and commerce." Noticeably absent was any mention of the park as a center of free speech, assembly, and the quest for social betterment.[77] This elaborate centennial celebration, which featured a civic pageant and an Americanization meeting, helped spur the renovation of the park as a showpiece for American democratic values.[78]

Although all the Fourteenth Street artists made their imagery more responsive to the worsening conditions of the Depression, only a few of their images depict

3.31   Reginald Marsh, "No One Has Starved," 1932. Illustration for *New Masses* 11 (June 12, 1934), etching: sheet, 13^{1}/$_{16}$″ × 15^{1}/$_{2}$″; plate, 6^{5}/$_{16}$″ × 11^{7}/$_{8}$″. Collection of Whitney Museum of American Art.

demonstrations or gatherings on Union Square. Miller, the oldest and most conservative, artistically and politically, made only minor modifications to his matronly shopper type, showing her less fashionably dressed or in bargain-counter settings to suggest her economic constraints (Figs. 3.10 and 3.13). Laning, who adhered to his youthful mural style in his few Fourteenth Street images from 1931, depicted neighborhood political events in works like *Unlawful Assembly, Union Square*, a staid image in which two mounted officers direct the dispersal of a crowd containing only a few mildly agitated individuals, and *Street Orator* (Fig. 3.33). These were the first of a small body of works that Laning may have been inspired to paint during the brief time he participated in John Reed Club activities.[79] Bishop, who avoided political affiliations throughout the decade, painted a few images of unemployed men. These appeared as she began to move away from Miller's example in subject and style, adopting looser brushwork and a darker palette. Marsh during the worst years of the Depression looked not only to Fourteenth Street's inexpensive entertainment attractions, but also to Union Square and its growing number of unemployed. He may well have used his classes at the Workers' School as Soyer used John Reed Club meetings—as an education in socially conscious art, put to use in his drawings and cartoons for the *New Masses*.[80] These works, which incorporate a critical edge, are predominantly satires of the rich and, as in "Birthday Party" or "No One Has Starved," satiric images about unemployment (Figs. 3.30 and 3.31). Soyer in the 1930s darkened his palette to create his "brown paintings of the unemployed,"[81] worked in a more "naturalistic"—topical and descriptive—

3.32 Raphael Soyer, *John Reed Club Meeting,* c. 1933. Oil on canvas. Present location unknown.

manner, and transformed his studio settings into street scenes. Furthermore, he sketched and painted images of his fellow Communists at the John Reed Club (Fig. 3.32), whose meetings he attended regularly beginning in 1929, and the Artists' Union, formed in 1933. Though a quiet member rather than an activist, Soyer, of all the Fourteenth Street artists, remained the most regular participant in radical organizations.[82]

None of the images by Fourteenth Street artists depicts demonstrations on Union Square; none overtly criticizes the social or political order. Instead, the pictorial language remains consistent with that of other works in each artist's oeuvre and adheres to the basic attributes of Fourteenth Street realism. In *Street Orator* Laning applies the contemporary classical realism of his more generalized *Fourteenth Street* (Fig. 2.3) to a political protest (1931; Fig. 3.33). In this work a soapbox orator stands amid a relaxed crowd that includes matronly shoppers, businessmen, and workers. A policeman, at the right, converses in friendly fashion with one of the spectators, using his nightstick only to make his points.

A comparison of Laning's *Street Orator* with Morris Kantor's *Union Square* helps to distinguish the old-fashioned patriotism of Laning's work from the more

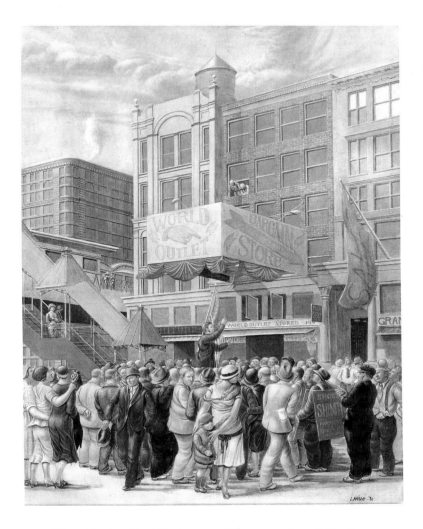

3.33   Edward Laning, *Street Orator*, 1931. Oil on masonite, 31″ × 24″.
Collection of Muriel and Howard Weingrow.

strident, politicized social realism of Kantor's (Fig. 3.34).[83] Kantor's orator is a faceless, muscular worker, the sleeves of his T-shirt rolled up to reveal strong arms, his fists clenched as he speaks to a crowd of male workers, listening with rapt attention. Loudspeakers and a reporter in the foreground will broadcast his heroic plea for justice, social betterment, and improved working conditions. The reporter and PA system also define the official nature of the rally.[84] Kantor's orator stands out in sharp contrast to the rectilinear silhouettes of modern buildings, whose omi-

3.34 Morris Kantor, *Union Square*, c. 1932. Oil on canvas. Present location unknown.

nous tiers of blank windows rise above the scene, their institutionalized power a threat to the masses. Yet a spatial perspective that telescopes sharply down and away from the foreground ultimately minimizes the scale of the architecture and enhances the heroic dimensions of the worker. His lone "voice" becomes a compelling call to political activism in the service of social and economic change.

Laning's picture is a small-scale easel painting, Kantor's a life-size panel. Laning's picture, to judge from the crowd, the location (Fourteenth Street rather than Union

Square), and the lack of loudspeakers, depicts one of the spontaneous speeches made daily by self-appointed speakers of various political persuasions who made their way to the district with something to say. Low storefronts with decorative finials, fluttering sale banners, and the pavilions and ironwork of the Victorian-style elevated impart a comforting sense of early twentieth-century American Main Street on the Fourth of July. In Laning's more intimate street scene the orator wears a business suit and stands before an American flag (in 1931 both anti-capitalist radicals and pro-American groups saw themselves as patriots and used American flags at their rallies).[85] By placing the orator in the background in a scene using conventional one-point perspective, Laning minimizes his importance, decreases the drama of the scene, and thereby, unlike Kantor, focuses on the ordinary and typical rather than the extraordinary and exigent. Laning's orator practically disappears into the setting, with its massive yellow awning and gaily colored signs, which also detract attention from his oratory.

Though Laning chooses a scene of potential discord, his contemporary classical realism dilutes any message about the power of the political process to alter or improve carefully constructed patterns of community life. The celebratory qualities of the picture—its bright colors, fluttering banners, and harmonious composition—along with the restrained behavior of the crowd recall Laning's archetypal affirmation of community life in *Fourteenth Street*. In his art the politically charged Fourteenth Street environment supported a more general renewal of the values of free speech in a democratic society.

Around 1932 Raphael Soyer also painted a neighborhood rally, called *The Crowd* (Fig. 3.35). According to Soyer, it is one of only two works he made under the "direct influence" of the John Reed Club.[86] In its present state, the image is a fragment of a larger painting, originally called *Union Square*, of a girl making a speech to a group of demonstrators. When the work was damaged, Soyer cut out what was salvageable: a group of demonstrators, part of the background above their heads, and, at left, a portion of the American flag on the speaker's platform.

Where Laning's contemporary classical realism allowed him to mask the tensions of the Union Square rally, Soyer's updated Ashcan school realism draws the viewer close to his subjects and suggests the complexity of their situation. He uses coarse brushwork and a dull palette of blues, browns, and grays to depict the listeners' rough garments, which suggest the downtrodden condition of their lives. But he also suffuses their open, attentive faces with a warm light, romanticizing their growing awareness of their plight and their hope for change. It is an image of quiet attention rather than strident agitation. In closely scrutinizing individual responses to the rally, it invites a more immediate empathy with members of the working class than do the generalized depictions of types in crowds in other Fourteenth Street School paintings.

3.35 Raphael Soyer, *The Crowd* (originally called *Union Square*), c. 1932. Oil on canvas, 25⅝″ × 22⅝″. Wichita Art Museum, Wichita, Kansas.

3.36 Reginald Marsh, untitled crayon drawing, *New Masses* 8 (April 1933), p. 8.

3.37 José Pavon, *Fourteenth Street*, c. 1935–36. Lithograph. Present location unknown.

Only one untitled crayon drawing by Marsh in the *New Masses* depicts any police brutality (Fig. 3.36). A small but powerful image, it pits a group of men fleeing in terror against a wall of anonymous policemen, who rise above them, brandishing sticks with a measured cadence that recalls the Napoleonic executioners in Goya's famous *Third of May, 1808*. To judge from the victims' backward glance, the police pursue them from behind as well—there is no escape from seen or unseen foes. Reversing his usual topical approach, Marsh eliminates any specific signs or references, so that the experienced fear can be attributed to a wider range of repressive forces, from local to international, rather than to a specific event. The drawing contrasts with the high legibility and the immediately comprehensible message more typical of political graphics in the early 1930s. José Pavon's lithograph of a Fourteenth Street anti-Fascist rally being dispersed by police includes storefront signs, political placards, strong light and dark contrasts to set the tone of conflict, and simply drawn anonymous figures to make an easily understood image for the viewer (Fig. 3.37). Similarly, William Gropper, in "Free Speech," one of his many images of police brutality, drawn for the *New Masses*, sets three enormous policemen wielding clubs against a small frightened worker (Fig. 3.38). A caricatural

FREE SPEECH

3.38 William Gropper, "Free Speech,"
New Masses 3 (August 1927),
p. 14.

display of distorted features and extreme contrasts of scale make the topic immediately clear.

For his graphic works related to Union Square activities, Marsh also drew on the tradition of John Sloan and his work for *The Masses*. Between 1912 and 1917 Sloan had been one of the major contributors to this radical publication, which had effectively combined art and politics in its drawings and articles. Featuring works by the cartoonist Art Young and the artists Stuart Davis, George Bellows, and Boardman Robinson (whom Marsh admired greatly) and articles by Max Eastman, John Reed, and Floyd Dell, *The Masses* took on virtually every Progressive Era cause, advocating feminism, free love, and birth control; criticizing organized religion and racism; and, as a Socialist publication, taking on the cause of labor and the working class. Artists for *The Masses*, as Rebecca Zurier has shown, rejected the widely accepted style of illustration that featured a precise line, substantial descriptive detail, and high finish; instead they popularized a rough crayon style. Based on the lithographic work of the nineteenth-century artist Honoré Daumier, this rougher style came to signify the directness and simplicity appropriate to making a "people's art."[87] With the renewal of the *New Masses* many artists who moved politically to the left found this style appropriate to portraying the economic and political problems of the Depression. Many of the crayon-style drawings, etchings, and lithographs Marsh made for the *New Masses* approach the style and sentiment of works for the earlier publication in their adoption of the direct medium and their depiction of working-class struggles. The audience for which Marsh made these drawings was entirely different from the audience for his paintings. To make them effective, he educated himself in the leftist doctrines and messages these works were meant to convey in classes at the Workers' School in the early 1930s, and he adopted for them the "people's medium" of the representational print rather than the easel painting, condemned as a tool of the capitalist bourgeois epoch.[88] As a consequence, many of these works carry a more satiric message than do Marsh's paintings.

In his study of satiric graphic work in the 1930s, Richard Masteller has used the term "cultural satire" to describe Marsh's graphics. Unlike lighthearted, less critical social satire, which pokes fun at the quirks of average people at work or play, and unlike blunt political satire, which uses simple symbols to attack capitalism and political corruption, as in the work of Gropper, cultural satire reveals the "psychological and spiritual consequences" of Depression era events. In works frequently characterized by substantial detail and dark tonalities, cultural satire unmasks, often subtly and indirectly, the systemic and frequently irresolvable contradictions of society, taking, as I have argued about Marsh's Union Square paintings, an ambivalent stance.[89] Marsh's print "Union Square," for example, situates the viewer well beneath the towering figure of the George Washington monument by exaggerating the scale of the pedestal (Fig. 3.30). The distance between the ideal of freedom embodied in the monument and the unemployed men below becomes insurmountable. At the same time, the monument itself becomes more heroic, a visual device that forces confrontation with the irony of the system. This print, made for the Contemporary Print Group, was the first in a portfolio entitled *The American Scene No. 1*. When the same print appeared in the *New Masses*, it was titled "Birthday Party," in ironic reference to the recent bicentennial celebration of Washington's birthday. That the scene could be used for two very different audiences suggests the multivalent context of cultural satire, especially as Marsh used it.

As painters engaged—by temperament, training, and personal preference—with the values of American Scene realism rather than a blunt social realism, the Fourteenth Street group avoided direct criticism of the social order in painting their subjects, even when depicting the political events of the neighborhood. They did the same in their images of the unemployed. From about 1932 to 1936, Marsh, Bishop, and Soyer moved into Union Square and portrayed the poor and the unemployed men who had migrated north to Union Square from the Bowery[90] and congregated at the bases of the five major monuments in the park.[91] In none of these works do the subjects stage demonstrations or suggest their dissatisfaction with the system whose failures contributed to their condition.

3.39 Isabel Bishop, *The Club,* 1935. Oil and tempera on canvas, 20″ × 24″. Midtown Payson Galleries, New York.

3.40 Reginald Marsh, *Alma Mater,* 1933. Tempera on masonite, 36″ × 24¹/8″. Collection of the Newark Museum.

3.41   Raphael Soyer, *In the City Park,* 1934. Oil on canvas, 38″ × 40″. Private collection.

Instead, the unemployed men in paintings like Bishop's *The Club* (1935; Fig. 3.39), Marsh's *Alma Mater* (1933; Fig. 3.40), and Soyer's *In the City Park* (1934; Fig. 3.41) wait patiently for their situation to change. In Bishop's and Marsh's work the figures have a classical dignity; none is individualized, thanks to a dark palette, soft obscuring brushwork, and the placement of the figures in a deep space. As a result, there is an air of timelessness to these topical works, as if the sad figures will continue patiently at their stations long after the Depression ends. Soyer's figures, by contrast, seem more transient. With his homeless models the artist created portraits of the unemployed. He then used a harsh golden brown ochre for their skin tone, sharply illuminated their faces, and placed the three men in the right foreground so

3.42　Philip Evergood, *North River Jungle,* 1933. Pencil on paper, 18^7/$_{16}$″ × 22^7/$_8$″. Hirshhorn Museum and Sculpture Garden, Smithsonian Institution.

close to the viewer that their plight cannot be avoided. While Soyer's painting personalizes and thereby reinforces the hardship of the many unemployed, the subjects remain, as Soyer himself described them, "silent, non-demanding" figures.[92]

A statement by Philip Evergood helps to distinguish between social realism and Fourteenth Street realism as it was understood at the time. Evergood contrasted the angry bums of his own expressionistic drawing, as in *North River Jungle* (1933; Fig. 3.42), with Marsh's unemployed men.

> When Marsh painted his Bowery bums he was seeing them through the eyes of a social observer and not through the eyes of a social thinker. Oh, yes, Marsh saw the sadness and the unfairness and Marsh was sorry for the bums, but he accepted this state of society and this picturesque scene, representing New York as inevitable. Hence, Marsh's bums are "classical," "acceptable" bums, acceptable as lost souls and classical in their tragic hopelessness. *My* bums, which I painted at the same time as Marsh, were dangerous bums, discontented bums, because mine had not accepted their lot. Mine were not congenital bums, but transient bums.[93]

As a committed social realist, Evergood faulted Marsh for his failure to give the unemployed a strong voice, along with the power to alter their situation.

By the mid-1930s, a number of changes in the political, social, and economic climate had contributed to the production of new themes in Union Square imagery for several of the artists. Though unemployment remained high, government projects brought relief, and with Roosevelt's re-election in 1936 a short period of recovery fueled a perception that conditions were improving.[94] Around Union Square, the new Popular Front movement united Communists, Socialists, and liberal New Dealers in the struggle for freedom and democracy against the threat of Fascism. In this more confident and hopeful climate, the Fourteenth Street artists produced images of working Americans, among them Soyer's and Bishop's clerical workers and shopgirls—additions to the already established iconography of women shoppers that completed the repertoire of neighborhood images.

The Fourteenth Street neighborhood was a timely symbol of both prosperity and despair between the wars. As an entrepreneurial and politically charged environment it elicited a wide range of commentary from artists, writers, and merchants in the district. Although none of the Fourteenth Street realists were radical innovators in their pictorial form, drawing instead on a body of traditions from both European and American sources and concerning themselves with ideas in mainstream art circles, they recombined established traditions in complex ways, often experimenting in different media. Their efforts resulted in works that cut across the political spectrum without fully advocating revolutionary social change.

The Fourteenth Street neighborhood was the stage for some of the larger changes reshaping American urban life—the sexual revolution, the increasingly restless pace of twentieth-century work and leisure, the development of mass culture, and the economic collapse, as registered in the lines of unemployed men. Artists selectively represented the life they saw around them, exploring changes in women's activities and shifting ideals of womanhood and participating, deliberately or inadvertently, through their paintings in the construction of gender identities in the period. The next four chapters move within and beyond the intersecting frames set out here— the discourse of new womanhood, the artists, and the neighborhood—to examine each artist's specific representations of new women.

CHAPTER FOUR

MOTHERS OF CONSUMPTION: KENNETH HAYES MILLER'S MATRONLY SHOPPER

The degree in which a cultural form embodies the aspirations of men to present their common humanity is one index of its value.

KENNETH HAYES MILLER

A woman's virtue and excellence as a housewife do not in these days depend upon her skill in spinning and weaving. An entirely different task presents itself, more difficult and more complex, requiring an infinitely wider range of ability, and for those very reasons more interesting and inspiring.

Ladies Home Journal, 1928,
on the woman shopper

In the early 1920s Kenneth Hayes Miller began to paint full-figured shoppers in contemporary dress. Like Dorothy Bromley, who soon after codified the revised new woman, a contemporary viewer of a Miller shopper would have classified this placid figure for what she was not—at one extreme, the youthful, swinging jazz-age flapper and, at the other, the grim, outmoded, and un-feminine feminist. Instead, Miller produced paintings whose pictorial strategies articulate middle-class society's conception of a newer and supposedly liberated model of post-franchise womanhood. His image, fully consonant with a consumption-based, family-oriented, heterosexual ideal, occasionally reveals the constraining ideologies of consumer culture and an awareness of feminist claims. More specifically, his matron can be linked to the ideal of the professionalized homemaker advanced by businessmen, advertisers, and home economists who helped promote the conservative ideology of the back-to-the-home movement in the 1920s. Miller's own intellectual experiences and values had much in common with those of pre- and postwar philosophers, social scientists, and psychologists whose views shaped traditional

4.1   Kenneth Hayes Miller, *Shopper,* 1928. Oil on canvas, 41″ × 33″. Collection of Whitney
Museum of American Art.

attitudes about women's roles. Such patterns of thinking, conscious or not, informed his image of the matronly shopper.

Miller's archetype in a painting called *Shopper* (1928; Fig. 4.1) is both old style and new style, modern and traditional. Like her counterpart in a 1928 Sears Roebuck catalog (Fig. 4.2), the shopper wears the latest in moderate-priced fashion—a dress with a straight silhouette, softly bloused and belted at the hips, a cloche, and a choker of big beads. But Miller's shopper appears too dumpy and round for these slender fashions—unlike the sleek *Vogue* model nonchalantly seated behind the wheel of her automobile, a symbol of both American progress and her own new-found liberation (Fig. 4.3). At odds with the fashionable media images from the 1920s, the shopper's figure type harks back to the plump, though frequently corseted, earlier generation of matronly women.

Behind the full-bodied shopper—her proportions are echoed formally in the rounded hats and the columnar backdrop of the Fourteenth Street store window display—stand a long line of classical goddesses and Renaissance beauties. Neither the conventions of advertising nor the increasing cultural preference for a slender athletic female body dictated Miller's choice of body type and pose. Instead, in his desire to keep "art" in a privileged position, he adhered to conventions of earlier art, fashioning a monumental figure type that never gained widespread visual currency or popular cultural acceptance but nonetheless embodied deeply felt and frequently voiced ideals of womanhood. For the *Shopper*, Miller borrowed the Venus *pudica*, or modest Venus pose, from Hellenistic examples like the Medici and Capitoline Venuses (Fig. 4.4) but then occupied the shopper's hands with an umbrella and her purchases. A work like Titian's *Woman with a Fur* provided an intermediate prototype, perhaps more direct given the similarity of the necklace and capped sleeves in both works (c. 1536; Fig. 4.5).[1] Finally, the full-bodied figure type of Miller's shopper is like Renoir's later bather images, which became very popular in American art circles at this time. These sources were among Miller's favorites, especially in the 1920s. By connecting his up-to-date woman with idealized goddesses, whose pose and proportions suggested enduring models of nurture, beauty, and fertility, Miller transformed the shopper into a goddess of commerce, a Venus of Fourteenth Street.

Miller orchestrated the picture of the shopper to make her an image of classical stability and repose. Placed close to the picture plane, she dominates the scene with her bulk. Her columnar stance—arms held close to her rounded body—partakes of the architectonic qualities of the massive supports behind her. Her own roundness and that of every object, from the cloche hats to her sloped shoulders, expresses softness and womanliness. Even painting techniques stabilize the image: Miller carefully outlined and differentiated all the shapes that make up the design. Brushwork remains controlled, and in the more fluid passages surface elaboration is subordinated to the creation of weight.

4.2 *Top, left:* "New York—Paris." Page from a 1928 Sears Roebuck catalog from *Everyday Fashions of the Twenties As Pictured in Sears and Other Catalogs,* ed. Stella Blum (New York: Dover Publications, 1981), p. 122.

4.3 *Top, right:* Cover of *Vogue* magazine, March 16, 1929.

4.4 *Above, left:* Medici Venus, early third century B.C., Roman copy. Uffizzi Gallery, Florence.

4.5 *Above, right:* Titian, *Woman with a Fur,* c. 1536. Oil. Staatsgalerie, Vienna.

This and other shopper images show additional signs that traditional and modern womanhood co-exist. The demure, self-protective pose of the modest Venus only partially masks the shopper's sexuality, signaled by her swelling figure, coy glance, and umbrella-as-phallus held between her legs. In images like *Leaving the Bank* (Fig. 4.6) the phallic bank columns that frame and tower above the shopper symbolize male power and allude to the absent male viewer in the scene or beyond the frame. The men for whom the matronly shopper consumes—either to make herself more beautiful or in her role as homemaker—rarely appear in Miller's works.

The Miller shopper appeared as a modern goddess of commerce in other situations as well. In *The Fitting Room* (Fig. 3.14) the women on the left recall the three Graces while the central woman, dressed in gold, takes a pose that is both generally classical (when compared to that of a Venus by Ingres, for example) and contemporary. Viewers of Miller's painting in the 1930s might well have recognized the Jean Harlow publicity pose and its overt display of a potent and, as some contemporaries would have argued, liberated sexual self (Fig. 4.7). In *Sidewalk Merchant* or *In Fourteenth Street* (Fig. 2.1; Plate 1), the three Graces re-enact the first beauty contest, the Judgment of Paris. Here, however, the Fourteenth Street hawker awards the prize; instead of a golden apple, he proffers packaged goods to a woman who has packaged herself like a beautiful commodity with the fashions and cosmetics of consumer culture; she is a visual display for the (male) viewer's gaze.

Miller placed his old-style new-style woman into settings whose formal designs not only enhance her womanliness but also function visually to stabilize or contain her sometimes powerful presence. In *Woman with an Umbrella* (Fig. 4.8) Miller again orchestrated curves and countercurves to exaggerate the woman's roundness and femininity. Placed close to the picture plane, filling the space with her substantial presence, she is framed by the curving columns, the open umbrella, the rounded cloche, and the enveloping fox (a favorite device that in several other works looks disturbingly alive). In *The Fitting Room* (Fig. 3.14) flat pilaster-like mirror frames anchor the women vertically while furs bind them together.

Whereas Miller's women in public settings appear up-to-date, if somewhat contained or controlled by the trappings of modern commerce, the full range of modern womanhood in his works suggests that in the private sphere the shopper fulfills the traditional, though updated, obligations of wife- and motherhood. Together his images enact the domestic ideals of the revised new woman. In *Mother and Child* (1927; Fig. 4.9), for example, although the mother sports bobbed hair and wears a robe in a style widely advertised in clothing catalogs and middle-class fashion magazines of 1926, Miller's use of a prototypical Renaissance model, like Bellini's *Madonna degli Alberetti* (1487; Fig. 4.10), imparts a sacred and special quality to modern motherhood that defenders of women's more "natural" wife-mother roles began to reassert in the late 1920s. Similarly, since Miller's images of nude women,

4.6　*Above:* Kenneth Hayes Miller,
Leaving the Bank, 1924. Oil on
canvas, 30″ × 25″. Collection
Gilbert and Editha Carpenter.

4.7　*Right:* Jean Harlow publicity
photograph for the movie
Dinner at Eight.

modeled after Renaissance Venuses, late Renoir bathers, or odalisques, are shown
in middle-class domestic settings, the rituals of self-beautification or modes of sexual
address resonate with contemporary discourses on intimate male-female relations.
In *Odalisque* (1926; Fig. 4.11), for example, a nude reclines on her living room
couch. Her seductive glance at the (implicit) male viewer coupled with the contemporary domestic interior suggests the more passionate and intimate sexual demands
of new women in companionate relations.

In other images of the late 1920s Miller explores the world of female friendship,
continuing to show the coexistence of old-style and new-style woman by chronicling
female interaction as it shifts from private, homosocial to public, heterosocial

4.8 Kenneth Hayes Miller, *Woman with an Umbrella*, 1928. Oil on canvas, 30″ × 25″. Nebraska Art Association, Nelle Cochrane Woods Memorial Collection, Sheldon Memorial Art Gallery, University of Nebraska–Lincoln.

4.9 *Top, left:* Kenneth Hayes Miller, *Mother and Child,* 1927. Present location unknown.
4.10 *Top, right:* Giovanni Bellini, *Madonna degli Alberetti,* 1487. Oil. Accademia, Venice.
4.11 *Above:* Kenneth Hayes Miller, *Odalisque,* 1926. Oil. Present location unknown.

4.12 *Above:* Kenneth Hayes Miller, *Women Greeting,* 1928. Present location unknown.

4.13 Giotto, *The Visitation,* 1305. Fresco. The Arena Chapel, Padua.

4.14   Kenneth Hayes Miller, *Casual Meeting*, 1928. Oil on canvas, 20″ × 24″. Collection of John P. Axelrod, Boston.

spaces. In *Women Greeting* (1928; Fig. 4.12) Miller stages a display of physical affection between two women in old-fashioned dress who meet indoors in a domestic setting. These ample matrons are clearly nurturing figures. Closely approximating the Renaissance prototype, exemplified by Giotto's fourteenth-century *Visitation* in the Arena Chapel in Padua (Fig. 4.13), the woman on the left encircles her companion's shoulder with her left arm and touches her breast with her right hand while her companion returns the embrace.

In *Casual Meeting*, also painted in 1928 (Fig. 4.14), two fashionably dressed women meet on a city street. They neither touch nor make eye contact with each other. Instead, the figure on the left glances down the street while the other meets the viewer's gaze. Between them in the distance is a male pedestrian. Distracted, perhaps, by the public world of commerce and male-female interaction, they project cool sophistication rather than sentimentality in their exchange.

4.15   Kenneth Hayes Miller, *Finishing Touches*, 1926. Oil, 28³/₄″ × 33¹/₂″. Collection of Jean and Sam Sapin.

In another up-to-date image, *Finishing Touches* (1926; Fig. 4.15), two women participate fully in the public pleasures permitted the modern new woman. Wearing fashionable hats over their short hair, they end their meal with coffee, a cigarette, an illicit glass of wine, and cosmetic repair, preparing themselves for the public and masculine gaze of the street. For all the seeming modernity of the women in *Casual Meeting* and *Finishing Touches*, their appearance is still shaped by Renaissance prototypes. Similar images of women painted by Miller's contemporary (and former student) Guy Pène du Bois show a greater reliance on modernist simplifications of form than on old master conventions.[2] As a result, the look of the women in *Americans in Paris* (1927; Fig. 4.16) more closely approximates that of the sleek prototype in *Vogue* magazine.[3] In his pictures du Bois, unlike Miller, accentuated angles; sharp, stridently colored shapes; and harsh lighting effects. Consequently,

4.16 Guy Pène du Bois, *Americans in Paris,* 1927. Oil on canvas, 28³/₄″ × 36³/₈″.
Collection, The Museum of Modern Art, New York.

du Bois's women have a contemporary look; Miller's matrons, even in their modern
guise, appear old-fashioned.

Miller's archetypal shopper in flapper costume (Fig. 4.1) contrasts strikingly with
the most widespread image of early 1920s womanhood: the flapper immortalized
by the illustrator John Held.[4] Held's flapper was young, savvy, and independent
and reflected some of the postwar woman's new self-sufficiency. Described in *Ladies
Home Journal* as a "sprightly and knowing miss in her teens"[5] and by F. Scott
Fitzgerald as "lovely, and expensive, and about nineteen,"[6] the flapper comfortably
sported daring clothes and engaged in pastimes that undermined all previous
notions of genteel womanhood (Fig. 4.17). Following the advice of Madison Avenue advertisers, the flapper ate less and smoked more to obtain the boyish silhouette
demanded by clinging fashions. In pursuit of pleasure she danced the Charleston,
the shimmy, and the blackbottom until dawn and by day indulged herself with new
mass-produced beauty aids and fashions. The real mark of her liberation (aside
from her job, if she had one) was the unrepressed expression of her sexuality—
kissing and petting on unchaperoned dates in the automobiles that aided and abet-
ted her newfound freedom. The flapper and her rebellious image were nurtured in
the 1920s by affluence and the attendant consumption of new products, by pro-

4.17 John Held, dancing flapper from
McClure's cover, August 1927.

hibition, by Freudian psychology, by advertising, and by the movies.[7] For those
who saw the 1920s as a decade of woman's liberation following enfranchisement,
the flapper was a potent symbol of women's independence.[8]

The young woman in Miller's *Party Dress* (1928; Fig. 4.18) resembles the flapper: she is slimmer than Miller's usual model and wears the latest skimpy dress; her
short hair is closely cut and marcelled in a new permanent wave. But she, like some
of her plumper shopping counterparts, appears self-conscious and uncomfortable
in her costume. She sits primly, eyes modestly lowered, contained by her chair, and
she clutches a boutonniere. Apart from her dress, she bears little resemblance to the
brazen Held flapper (Fig. 4.17), whose freedom is manifested in her flinging gestures, jutting chin, and jagged hemline. Assertive angles define her independent
"don't touch" affect, whereas soft curves express the vulnerability of Miller's reflective girl.

Miller's image resonates with a larger meaning when compared with a senti-
mentalized 1927 advertisement for Oneida Silver (1927; Fig. 4.19) that draws on
a more romantic style of illustration. A young woman holds the hand of the man
to whom she is presumably engaged (and in whose home she will use her new

4.18   Kenneth Hayes Miller, *Party Dress*, 1928. Oil on canvas. Collection of Barry and Rita Rothenburg.

4.19 Magazine advertisement for Oneida Ltd., 1927, from Carol Wald, *Myth America: Picturing Women, 1865–1945* (New York: Pantheon Books, 1975), p. 123.

silver).[9] He rouses her from her reverie to fulfill her dream of husband, protector, and provider. She in turn will be homemaker, mother, household manager, *and* expert consumer—like the woman in Miller's painting, whose title, *Party Dress*, describes the commodity by which she has made herself elegant and contemporary. But in this dress whose daring cut symbolizes freedom from constraint is a young woman tied by pose and demeanor to a romanticized vision of womanhood that considers her independence only temporary. This is an image of waiting and attendance for the man who will give her identity, status, and the opportunity to fill an expected role.[10]

Much of Miller's 1920s imagery is a counterpoint to the representation of the flapper. The combination of old master prototypes with modern fashion reveals a tension between an older female ideal of nurture, companionability, and stabilizing docility and the newer image of self-centeredness, vitality, independence, and sexuality. Miller's matronly (or, in the case of *Party Dress*, proto-matronly) type follows the comforting day-to-day rituals of contemporary domestic life. Her adoption of the modern costume—the outward sign of equality and liberation—without its accompanying behavior suggests that conventional stereotypes of femininity remain in force. Furthermore, such a superficial accommodation to appearances grounded in a deeper preservation of traditional patterns suggests what recent historians have demonstrated to be the represented flapper's preferred destiny in life. As the historian Alice Shrock has shown, in theater and film scenarios, and in the fiction published in mass-circulation magazines in the 1920s the flapper rarely remained independent. In the typical scenario, she rose from the middle class to a life of luxury. But eventually she became disillusioned with her freedom, recognized her need to serve a man, and "subsumed her wit and intelligence to help him."[11]

Thus Miller's late-1920s image, only marginally new style, was in its traditionalism both a visual antidote to the flapper of the early 1920s and an acknowledgement of her destiny as a homemaker. In this respect the image is consonant with that of the more decorous and mature revised new woman as writers like Dorothy Bromley and Lillian Symes defined her at the end of the twenties.

The flapper of the immediate postwar years was not just a Madison Avenue fabrication but a woman who by means of the flapper identity contributed substantially to the "revolution in manners and morals."[12] At the beginning of the decade she caused extreme consternation among her elders. Many religious leaders and social critics predicted society's downfall in light of such flagrant abuses of female modesty and moral respectability.[13] Others saw the flapper as a welcome sign of freedom.[14] Though newsworthy and a sign of liberation in her own day, the flapper was a short-lived phenomenon, historians like Lois Banner have argued, limited to the middle- and upper-middle-class population. By mid-decade, much of the furor over her appearance and sexual behavior had subsided.[15] Robert and Helen Merrell Lynd in their study of Middletown observed that with the dissemination of the flapper image in popular periodicals, many of her practices and fashions were adopted by women of all ages, classes, shapes, and sizes.[16] It became possible to copy the look of the flapper without adopting her daring behavior.

In reconsidering the substance and impact of the flapper and the guarded acceptance of the new working woman, historians have also reassessed woman's liberation in the 1920s. The historian Frederick Lewis Allen wrote in his 1931 study *Only Yesterday* that the ballot "consolidated woman's position as man's equal."[17] But such was not the case. The revolution in manners and morals and the flapper phenomenon had as their darker side the reversal of feminist gains and the weakening of feminist intentions. The franchise failed to consolidate a point of view as women continued to vote like their husbands and fathers. After some initial legislative gains, women were brought up short by a series of legislative failures—chief among them, the failure to pass the first draft of an Equal Rights Amendment. Though women entered college in increasing numbers, their enrollment as a percentage of total enrollment declined. And even though their numbers swelled the work force, women were consistently found in the lowest levels of business and industry. As old-guard suffragists retired, younger women failed to take up the slack.[18] In a booming postwar economy with a new "sense" of equality from the vote and in an intellectual climate whose somewhat superficial understanding of Freud made it unfashionable to be repressed, the young new woman focused on her personal liberation from Victorian social conventions rather than on effecting change by political means. Even though social feminists kept feminism alive in the 1920s, they tended to subordinate radical feminist desires for equal rights to social reforms stressing women's separate nature.[19] For the flapper, who became a popular sign of liberation, feminism was a matter of individual satisfaction at the physical and emotional level, not a collective quest for economic and political equality. Liberation was frequently limited to the imitation of male ways, like smoking and drinking. The flapper's expression of her sexuality could turn against her as her body became another commodity on display in a burgeoning consumer culture. Finally, polls taken in the 1920s showed that though some young women wanted to work for a time, most still longed for husband, home, and children.[20]

In his matronly shopper Miller constructs one version of the revised new woman: he shows women in contemporary dress participating in urban society, signifying one kind of equality and liberation in the 1920s. But because his images are rooted in a tradition of strong, nurturing female types, he portrays a woman who also guards her traditional role as a stabilizing force at home and in society[21]—exactly the woman to reassure the sociologists and businessmen who expressed concern about diminished family stability and individual autonomy resulting from rapid social and economic change in the 1920s and 1930s. Many of them promoted a new kind of household organization in which homemaking and consumption became bureaucratized activities.[22]

The experts who discussed social change, the family, and women's roles during this period focused on the unsettling shift from a rural, production-oriented economy to an urban, consumption-oriented economy.[23] Home functions like food preparation, housecleaning, care of the sick, childbirth, clothing production, and some home-centered leisure activities were taken over by hospitals, childcare centers, camps, and mass culture. Most commentators felt that technological advance, household inventions, and mass production were instrumental in simplifying home management.[24] With urbanization, smaller families moved to smaller quarters. According to Lawrence K. Frank, a woman operating under such radically altered conditions found that her prestige "as a competent housekeeper and mother of a family [had] diminished with the simpler function of the household and the decrease in number of children."[25] The home and family were no longer the "focus of human endeavor and interest," and women's "befogged condition" reflected the general helplessness of the individual in industrial and consumer society.[26]

Although the pattern of marriage, children, homeownership, and community life continued among middle Americans, some commentators saw drastic alterations in its social and economic underpinnings. Beginning in the early 1920s, when a spokeswoman for the American Home Economics Association proclaimed that it was time for a back-to-the-home movement, home economists, sociologists, psychologists, and business spokespersons tried to "elevate the homemaker's task to the dignity

4.20 F. A. Leyendecker, "A Modern
Witch." Illustration for *Life*
magazine cover, October 1, 1923.

of a profession." They redefined homemaking to take into account new social, economic, and psychological changes that had altered women's lives.[27] The overt aims of this back-to-the-home movement were to restabilize the family and to reaffirm marriage in ways that recognized the new woman's post-franchise equality. The covert ideology reinforced woman's containment in the domestic arena but made the public activity of consumption central to the domestic role.[28] This new conception of womanhood, combining modernity with enduring values, became the basis of Miller's matronly shopper.

Writers, whether proponents of the back-to-the-home movement or advocates of renewed family stability, found ways to reactivate the joys of domestic life and modernize the homemaker. Recognizing that the new woman had often worked before marriage and had developed high expectations of the marital relationship, many sought to centralize household activities. Some image makers suggested that household drudgery was challenging, fantastic, or even sexual, as a blissfully smiling kitchen witch astride a soaring vacuum cleaner makes clear (Fig. 4.20). These spokespersons addressed a majority audience, for while 10 million working women received considerable press as new women, 22.5 million remained at home.[29] They aligned themselves, furthermore, with an already well established movement for domestic science and home economics. Since the first decade of the twentieth century, conservative women, many of them anti-suffragists, had joined forces with scientific experts, clergymen, and politicians to preserve the sanctity of the home. Recognizing the diminished physical labor involved in home production, they restructured housework around tasks that could be performed daily instead of weekly or monthly and thereby gave languishing women new energy and a renewed sense of their "true" vocation. Essentially, domestic science, or home economics, was one of many new areas of scientific expertise in the Progressive Era, and 20 percent of all schools by 1916 offered courses in it. Between 1906 and 1917 enrollment in college home economics programs jumped from 203 to 17,778. The federal government established the Bureau of Home Economics in 1923, signaling to many of the women's groups supporting home economics its recognition of women's issues beyond the franchise. Many women used the new science to claim professional employment as home economists, to redefine their unpaid work in the home, and to refashion the domestic sphere through the new ideology of consumption.[30] Even with this rapid growth, some commentators continued to fault women's education for failing to prepare women for their true vocation; they saw women's extra-domestic pursuits as diversions.

> While the average girl today as always is looking forward to marriage and family life as her goal, yet she is not fitting herself seriously for this as a life work, but is turning to office, factory, school teaching, social work and other professions as a means of earning her living. . . . Neither parents nor educators are in the main preparing girls today for the performance of their economic functions within the home.[31]

In the 1920s, to counter what they saw as a dangerous rising trend toward "female bachelorhood,"[32] those who supported the values of the back-to-the-home movement undertook several tasks: first, to make more work for the homemaker whose burden had, theoretically, been lightened by inventions and changes in the marketplace;[33] second, to make the work itself more interesting and important; third, to redefine the role and status of middle-class women who through work or extra-domestic activities had realized new capabilities and developed increased expectations of themselves. Even if these women were persuaded to redirect themselves from political to personal goals, feminism and the *perceived* achievement of woman's equality continued to redefine women's homemaking roles. So did the heterosexual revolution—with its more sexually intimate marital ideal on the one hand and its condemnation of female-centered relations as sexually deviant on the other. Altered relations between the sexes and new styles of marriage and interpersonal relationships appeared as a response to Freudian psychology, contributing to changed marital dynamics.[34] All these social changes fueled arguments for the professionalization of housework.

Dr. Amey Watson's essay "The Reorganization of Household Work" is a model of its kind, reflecting the arguments made by businessmen and like-minded social scientists who linked efficient home management to the profits of business. In their economic role women would stabilize the family, a major concern of social scientists in the interwar decades: efficient consumption would rationalize home economy, thereby increasing family happiness. Like many writers, Watson borrowed the rhetoric and organizational strategies of those preoccupied with scientific expertise and business management.[35]

Watson asserted that the "function of management in the home is the heaviest and most important responsibility." Although anyone could take on the task, Watson assumed that women did it by nature: the woman is home manager because "*she* is qualified for the job, chooses to do the work and is willing to train *herself* while on the job" (italics mine). According to Watson, the efficient homemaker must make daily, weekly, monthly, and seasonal inventories for repairs, alterations, supplies; must oversee both the planning of meals—"for health, economy and contentment"—and the "thrifty and intelligent use of supplies, materials, equipment, time, and strength."[36] She included charts of the minimum essentials for operating a household (Fig. 4.21) and stressed the complexity of the work. "Even the skill to be a good cook takes more training and experience than is usually admitted," she wrote.[37] Despite the difficulty of organizing the work and orchestrating harmony among different personalities, sound management would result in "a feeling of satisfaction and craftsmanship . . . on the part of both workers and management."[38] The term *craftsmanship* made the housewife a skilled rather than an unskilled laborer and thereby elevated her status.

Household work was thus made more difficult and more intellectually challenging. Nowhere is the scrubbing of floors mentioned; nor are crying children.[39] Nowhere is the inadequacy of a single income—however soundly managed—considered, particularly for working-class mothers. That Watson assumed a middle-class readership is clear in her continual references to the management of domestic help.[40] In fact, women spent relatively little time on home management or scientific childcare (2 1/2 to 5 1/2 hours per week); most of their work was mundane: cooking, sewing, and cleaning. Food preparation alone occupied about 22 hours per week.[41]

If some tracts professionalized the homemaker, another growing body of literature revealed the gap between managerial myth and household drudgery. In 1926 Dr. Abraham Myerson wrote *The Nervous Housewife*, chronicling the anxiety and loneliness of housewives confronted by the monotony of housework that efficiency experts had encouraged them to standardize. Myerson argued that housework in an industrial society was glorified because it carried an emotional burden unjustified by the menial nature of the work. "In its aims and purposes housekeeping is the highest of professions; in its methods and techniques it ranks among the lowest of occupations."[42] Carol Kennicott, the main character in Sinclair Lewis's 1920 novel *Main Street*, was torn between conforming to Gopher Prairie's model of the housewife and pursuing her own needs for independence and creativity. The drudgery of

MINIMUM ESSENTIALS IN OPERATING A HOUSEHOLD

Invariables	Variables

I. PLANNING STANDARD OF LIVING AND OTHER POLICIES

Invariables	Variables
Balance between income and outgo of money, time and energy	Complex standard of living as money and other factors increase

II. PHYSICAL CARE OF MEMBERS OF THE FAMILY

Food

Invariables	Variables
Planning of meals	Increase in amount
Purchasing of food	Elaborateness of cooking and menu
Preparing	Type and extent of service
Serving	Standard of entertainment
Clearing away	
Paying for	
Entering in accounts	

Clothing

Invariables	Variables
Planning budget	Amount of clothing
Purchasing	Frequency of changing
Laundry, inside or outside of home	Quality of materials and consequent care needed
Pressing and cleaning	Varying standards in regard to rough dry or fine laundry work
Sorting, mending, and putting away	Varying standards of style, neatness and beauty
Making clothing, costumes, etc.	
Paying for	
Entering in accounts	

Shelter

Invariables	Variables
Cleaning house	Frequency and thoroughness of cleaning
Daily bedroom care	Type and amount of service
Daily bathroom care	Frequency of changing house linens
Laundry of house linens	Quality of materials and consequent care needed
House furnishings and equipment—planning, purchase and care of	Type of house furnishings, extent and delicacy with consequent care needed
Care of outside of house, grounds, garage	Extent of grounds and standards of care

Other Physical Factors
(1) Care of Children

Invariables	Variables

(a) Development of good physical habits
  regularity of meals washing and bathing
  feeding self dressing
  bowel habits other
  sleeping habits
	(a) Varying standards in regard to habits

(b) Fresh air and exercise under supervision	(b) Amount and complexity
(c) Supervised play inside including music, art, literature, etc.	(c) Type of supervision
(d) Nursing in illness	(d) Use of clinic or private physician
(e) Teamwork with physicians in planning child's regime	

(2) Care of Adults

Invariables	Variables
Nursing in illness	Extent and Type

III. PSYCHOLOGICAL, EMOTIONAL AND EDUCATIONAL CARE OF MEMBERS OF THE FAMILY

Invariables	Variables
(1) Constant oversight of infants and small children with understanding of their needs from the point of view of balanced growth of personality	(1) Extent and type of care
(2) Supervision of child's school work and cooperation with schools	

IV. SOCIAL PROLEMS INVOLVED IN CARING FOR FAMILY

Adjustments of relationships within family group
Working out relationships of family to community

4.21 "Minimum Essentials in Operating a Household," from Amey E. Watson, "The Reorganization of Household Work," *Annals of the American Academy of Political and Social Science* 160 (March 1932), p. 172.

"A WOMAN'S PLACE IS IN THE HOME"

William Gropper

International Woman's Day: March 8: Out of the kitchen into the struggle for freedom from capitalist exploitation and household drudgery for workers' wives.

4.22 William Gropper, "A Woman's Place Is in the Home," *New Masses* 7 (April 1932), p. 20.

housework and women's status were made clear in cartoons like William Gropper's in the April 1932 issue of the *New Masses* entitled "A Woman's Place Is in the Home" (Fig. 4.22).

To make homemaking attractive, business leaders called the housewife a "home executive" or a "domestic engineer" or made her a member of the household board of directors—an equal business partner with her spouse.[43] Dr. Benjamin Andrews echoed the sentiments of those who felt that social change and the franchise had liberated American women when he wrote that "two adults form a partnership with *equal* responsibilities, make *equal* contributions to its support, and draw out *equal* returns not only in the daily physical services of food, clothing and shelter but as well in the broadening of experience and all the satisfactions of life" (italics mine).[44]

These writers sidestepped the fundamental inequality of a woman's economic dependence on her spouse, stressing instead her managerial role and her ability to be self-supporting within the home. As they co-opted the language of feminism, and its specific claims to equality, they undermined those claims. As early as 1910, Andrews had even suggested that women were still producers in the home:

> To woman has fallen the task of directing how the wealth brought into the house shall be used. . . . If commodities can be so arranged and grouped for consumption as to make them yield more pleasure than if they are consumed in a haphazard way, then the one who secured the result performs just as distinctly an economic function as the one whom we call technically a producer.[45]

All these analyses equated the effective economic management of the household with family stability and family happiness, by far the most important goals. Perceiving that the family was threatened by major social changes—one of the most significant being women's extra-domestic activities—conservative and liberal thinkers alike struggled to make household responsibilities seem important by connecting them to popular business values and by professionalizing the homemaker. William Baldwin wrote *The Shopping Book* to show the helplessness of the woman consumer confronted by rationalized businesses and comprehensive advertising campaigns. But he too made the family America's number one institution, and even as he recognized her frustrations, he assigned the shopper an extraordinary level of power and responsibility. Baldwin provides a timely backdrop for the images of matronly shoppers:

> Running homes is the greatest single business in America, towering above steel production, transportation, the motor industry, and other familiar yardsticks of power and size. . . . The shopper is paramount. On the one hand she controls the comfort and attractiveness of the home—the standard of living as it is actually applied; in the other hand she holds the destiny of great industries.[46]

Miller's first women on the street were painted in 1920, shortly before he moved his studio to Fourteenth Street. He identified them as Fifth Avenue shoppers and called the pictures his fashion series;[47] during this period the famous avenue held pride of place as New York's boulevard of fashion, proclaiming "throughout its whole length the joys of material life in their most alluring forms."[48] With these early images, Miller created an elegant bourgeois type. *In Passing* (1920; Fig. 4.23) shows chic young matrons in fragile dresses and high-style furs, rendered in the high-key palette and fluid painting style of Renoir's late works. With rose-tinted, creamy complexions and chiseled features recalling the profiles of Greek goddesses, they are more refined than some of the later matrons. The independent woman of *Leaving the Bank* (Fig. 4.6) purposefully adjusts her glove after withdrawing money

4.23 Kenneth Hayes Miller, *In Passing*, or *The Shoppers,* 1920. Oil on canvas, 24″ × 20¼″. The Phillips Collection, Washington, D.C.

to fulfill her role as a consumer. The powerful classical columns that frame and support her also link her to the American financial success and self-confidence of the mid-1920s: they are the male architectural symbols of her financial security and status. In the early 1920s the cool self-confidence of Miller's figures suggests the public persona of women who had just gained the right to vote. A Milleresque woman appeared frequently in popular illustrations; one on the cover of *Leslie's*

September 11, 1920

Price—15 Cents
Subscription Price $7.00 a

Le~~~ie's

Illustrate~~~ ~~~paper

VOTING
BOOTH NO 1

The Mystery of 1920

4.24 "The Mystery of 1920,"
*Leslie's Illustrated
Weekly Newspaper,*
September 11, 1920,
cover illustration.

magazine is poised outside a voting booth (Fig. 4.24). Enfranchisement (which Miller supported) may have been one reason for the artist's growing fascination with painting the new and well-to-do urban woman. These early images emerged in a climate of postwar enthusiasm for her new role, as yet unknown.

Major changes in Miller's own surroundings and in the immediate political environment by the late twenties would have only a mild impact on his matronly type. For five years, since moving to his Fourteenth Street studios in 1923, Miller had watched the multiplication of stores for bargain hunters and had heard the increasingly vociferous critique of capitalism as an exploiter of working-class men and women like those who shopped and worked in the district. Speeches by the neighborhood's radicals and unemployment rallies in the first months of the Depression culminated in the large-scale demonstration on March 6, 1930, which the police broke up, causing numerous injuries. With the crash and the Depression, artists and writers were drawn to neighborhood organizations like the John Reed Club, and many began to engage social issues by depicting factories, struggling workers, and breadlines. Miller never involved himself in political meetings or demonstra-

4.25   Kenneth Hayes Miller, *Glove Counter,* c. 1937. Present location unknown.

tions, nor did he portray social realist subjects. Because he interacted regularly with his students, a number of whom participated in John Reed Club exhibitions or submitted drawings and cartoons to the *New Masses,* however, he would have been familiar with the debates on art and politics.[49]

Miller's only response to concerns expressed by artists and social critics preoccupied with the common man was to broaden the socio-economic base of his matrons. His shopper became humbler, plumper, and more awkward in appearance. In *Afternoon on the Avenue* (Fig. 3.10) the shopper, her child beside her, emerges from Klein's rather than a Fifth Avenue store. Instead of a fur, she wears an ill-fitting coat of unnameable fabric, the kind of second-hand garb one uptown journalist associated with the poor Fourteenth Street bargain hunter.[50] In *The Bargain Counter* (Fig. 3.13), in marked contrast with *Glove Counter* (an uptown department store painted c. 1937; Fig. 4.25), Miller's shopper patiently endures a

4.26   Reginald Marsh, photograph of Fourteenth Street and Broadway,
c. 1938–39. Museum of the City of New York.

crush of shoppers, trying to assess the value of merchandise, which in that year
would have been unlabeled. Like women in the photographs of Fourteenth Street
taken in the 1930s by Berenice Abbott or Reginald Marsh (Fig. 4.26), these women
are less than sleek. Many, like the mother in *Waiting for the Bus* or the foreground
figures in *Bargain Counter*, have coarse, homely features. Through subtle modifications in the fashions, locale, and facial appearance of the basic matronly type and
in his decision to depict ordinary women—perhaps wives of men feeling the pinch
of economic hard times—Miller constructed for the socially concerned viewer a
"common woman" to go with the "common man."

But it remained a superficial accommodation at best, one that was not present
in all the pictures.[51] Many of the women look contented. They attend to children
while they shop and happily assent to both mothering and consumption as part of
their role in home management. In *Department Store Shoppers* (1930; Fig. 4.27
and Plate 2), Miller's matron is a professional homemaker, working side by side
with an "expert" saleswoman to make purchases that will contribute to familial
well-being. The shopper in *Woman with Packages* (1934; Fig. 4.28) emerges from
a store, arms laden with packages. Her capacious form suggests her ability to consume. Her efficiency and her oneness with her role as consumer are conveyed in the
rhyming of simplified shapes that define her and her purchases. The rectangular

4.27   Kenneth Hayes Miller, *Department Store Shoppers*, 1930. Oil on canvas, 24″ × 17⅛″.
Hirshhorn Museum and Sculpture Garden, Smithsonian Institution.

4.28 Kenneth Hayes Miller, *Woman with Packages*, or *Contemporary Scene*, 1934. Oil on masonite, 34″ × 28″. Weatherspoon Art Gallery, University of North Carolina at Greensboro.

package repeats the shape of her purse, the curved package the shape of her fur collar. Miller never used models when he painted. He developed instead a standard female type, like a mass-produced product. The woman's head and hat are echoed in those of the mannequin to her right. She imitates and consumes what is displayed. And she shares the values implicit in those activities with the community of like-minded, similarly dressed women behind her. Her upward-turned face, like that of a baroque saint in ecstasy, glows with the joy of successful consumption. She is the contemporary Madonna of shopping, the pastime some recent historians have argued became a substitute for traditional religion.[52]

Both Isabel Bishop and Edward Laning adopted Miller's matronly shopper type for their panoramas of Union Square and Fourteenth Street, making her the image of progress tempered by continuity and tradition. In Bishop's *Dante and Virgil in Union Square* and in Laning's *Fourteenth Street* (Figs. 2.2 and 2.3) she appears with family and friends, an energetic participant in commerce playing a traditional, if updated, role. Her community is all-white and middle-class. No one is old or unemployed, though Bishop and Laning painted these images in the worst years of the Depression, and no one protests the inequities of capitalism, even though writers and artists described such protest as a noteworthy part of Fourteenth Street neigh-borhood life.[53]

Even where "protest" occurs, as in Laning's *Street Orator* (Fig. 3.33), the matronly shopper suggests stable patterns of community life. This image depicts a familiar ritual rather than a heated protest and reaffirms the value of free speech in a democratic society. Thus the matronly shopper in the foreground neither protects her child from "subversive" street politics nor fears a clash between crowd and police.[54] Instead she begins to turn back toward her child, who grasps her arm, demanding her attention—a common motif in Laning's early work in less topical images like *Fourteenth Street* (Fig. 2.3). In *Street Orator*, the shopper's gaze seems to linger for a moment on the shoeshine signboard, as she is caught between her two primary duties—childcare and consumption. Reaffirming popular and contem-porary historical assessments of post-franchise womanhood that in turn reinforce the back-to-the-home ideology, she rejects political involvement in favor of wom-anly responsibilities, leaving political activism to men, who make up the bulk of the crowd.[55]

A comparison of Miller's shoppers with those in William Glackens's *Shoppers* (1907; Fig. 4.29), one of the few American iconographic precedents on this theme, helps to define the social class of Miller's women. In Glackens's image elegant women are looking at equally elegant goods. At the end of the nineteenth century, social critics like Thorstein Veblen understood shopping for the upper-class woman as a compensation for her boredom, a way to pass the time. Veblen's *Theory of the Leisure Class* described shopping as a symbol of the husband's economic success; the American woman was permitted, even required, to "consume largely and con-

4.29 William Glackens, *The Shoppers*, 1907. Oil on canvas, 60″ × 60″. The Chrysler Museum, Norfolk, Virginia.

spicuously—vicariously for her husband or other natural guardian. She is exempted or debarred from vulgarly useful employment—in order to perform leisure vicariously for the good repute of her natural (pecuniary) guardian."[56]

Glackens celebrated the genteel, well-to-do woman shopping for handcrafted clothing. Miller glorified a new ritual in urban industrial society as average matrons were caught up in shopping for mass-produced ready-to-wear items. By the 1920s consumption had become democratic. And in the new ideology of consumption, Miller's matronly shopper was a professional, an equal partner with her husband, theoretically, in bettering home and family.

In relation to Miller's shopper in the dual contexts of a bargain shopping district and a twentieth-century culture of consumption the designation "middle-class" requires clarification. Because Miller never used live models in painting, because he generalized his women from both contemporary ideals and old master models, and because he subtly modified the body, facial type, and costume of the women he painted, the class identity of his shoppers remains indeterminate. Moreover, in the consumer culture of the twenties and thirties middle-classness—especially when attached to ideals of personal achievement, marriage, and family—meant the channeling of desires to build a community that would continue to serve capitalism. Miller's matrons, shopping for bargains in a working-class district, could be read as members of an assimilating working class, consuming their way into the middle-classness or Americanness that was said to confer legitimacy on their lives.[57]

Given the ambiguity of class in Miller's works, I would refine the distinction to one of condition rather than specific class position: his Fourteenth Street shopper was an average lower- to middle-class woman but not a downtrodden one. Her image affirmed the values of a democratic and capitalist society, and her occupation suggested that society's central institution, the family, would endure at all socio-economic levels with women at the managerial helm. With the Depression, this image implied that financial stability would re-emerge, consumption would continue, and society would prosper. Such attitudes are embodied in an idealized model of substantial and nurturing womanhood taken from earlier artistic sources. The choice of an old master model itself places value on continuity and tradition over radical cultural change. The image dovetailed with the ideology of the back-to-the-home movement, revealing pictorially how American society and artistic culture accommodated shifts in economic and social patterns while adhering to and perpetuating cherished values.

Miller's paintings of stable full-bodied matrons signified democratic prosperity and familial well-being and thereby endorsed the capitalist status quo. The leftist critic John Kwiat, in his review of the 1933 John Reed Club exhibition The Social Viewpoint in Art, argued a similar point—that the mere presence of certain urban types did not guarantee a social (meaning social realist or socially committed) viewpoint, and such images remained remote from the needs of the class-conscious worker. Kwiat claimed that the depiction of American life by painters like Miller and the Regionalists was a chauvinistic response on the part of critics and painters to superior French modernism: "The Club should not have invited in the name of an imaginary united front the prominent painters who could submit only tame picturesque views of cowboys, crapshooters and fat shoppers issuing from department stores." The "fat shoppers" were Miller's, in an unnamed and undocumented painting, the only one Miller ever submitted to a John Reed Club exhibition.[58]

A number of New Masses cartoons from the mid-1920s—some of the most notable by Miller students—came much closer to the socially committed viewpoint advocated by critics like Kwiat. Artists often exaggerated the shopper's girth to symbolize the greedy capitalist, well-off and well fed at the expense of others. Adolph Dehn (a friend and former student of Miller's) drew an idle shopper and called her unemployed to suggest a status given her by her husband's ill-gained wealth (Fig. 4.30). Peggy Bacon, a social satirist, contrasted the bulky capitalist's self-satisfied pose with the saleswoman's tiny frame in "The Little Jumper Dress" (Fig. 4.31).

Miller's uncritical stance is also clarified by a comparison of his works with those of other contemporary painters critical of capitalism. The Mexican muralist and revolutionary artist José Clemente Orozco, for example, painted shoppers in Fourteenth Street (1928–29; Fig. 4.32),[59] showing them as suffering victims. Unattractive angular figures are compressed between towering skyscrapers. In profile or facing forward, these women, with mask-like faces and shadowed eyes, move through the

4.30   *Above, left:* Adolph Dehn,
       "Unemployed," *New Masses* 1
       (May 1926), p. 5.

4.31   *Above, right:* Peggy Bacon,
       "The Little Jumper Dress,"
       New Masses 1 (July 1926),
       p. 22.

4.32   *Right:* José Clemente Orozco,
       Fourteenth Street, 1928–29.
       Present location unknown.

dense crowd like automatons, with no sense of one another's presence. Lloyd Goodrich suggested the prescience of Orozco's image:

> With a skyscraper and a few figures . . . he creates images that convey the feeling of New York more intensely than most painters with a thousand and one details. If the sombreness and sense of brooding tragedy in these pictures seem a little out of place in our optimistic atmosphere we can only reflect that perhaps he sees things of which we are not yet aware.[60]

That Orozco's image of urban women is far more oppressive and pessimistic than Miller's not only reaffirms the uncritical nature of Miller's art, but suggests that his matron is a reassuring image in troubled times. For those who argued in the early 1930s that economic recovery would occur only with continued buying, a woman consuming effectively was performing a patriotic duty. On Fourteenth Street, beginning in January 1933, Hearn's department store regularly advertised that a percentage of its daily receipts would be contributed to various agencies to help the poor. Through this program, staffed by volunteers, supported by celebrities who made guest appearances, and praised by Mrs. Roosevelt, Hearn's contributed to the Red Cross and the Emergency Unemployment Relief committee, to name only two. Such public-spirited relief activity encouraged increased consumption, and Hearn's began to pull out of an early Depression sales slump.[61]

Hearn's was not alone in linking consumption to civic duty. Samuel Klein, head of Fourteenth Street's most successful bargain emporium, appealed to American women to help stop the extraordinary growth in sweatshops that had occurred since the onset of the Depression. Explaining that increased demands for cheap, low-quality merchandise had encouraged fly-by-night firms whose workers labored long hours for poor wages, he proclaimed that women "desirous of doing something tangible to save thousands of workers from intolerable conditions . . . should make known their views." Klein, himself guilty of exploiting the labor force, argued further that responsible manufacturers should be encouraged "not only because of their public-spirited stand, but because they are actually featuring goods that will afford the most satisfaction to the ultimate consumer."[62] Klein's and Hearn's pleas placed responsibility for effective and now "moral" consumption squarely on the shoulders of American women.[63]

The ideology that emphasized woman's domestic and consuming roles received indirect expression in contemporary criticism of Miller's work. Though journalists for mainstream newspapers mocked what they perceived to be the dowdy appearance of actual Fourteenth Street shoppers,[64] one art critic, recognizing both the working-class locale of Miller's matron and her multiple tasks of domestic management, praised her as the "blousy and bulbous 'ideal' of the Five and Ten . . . in all the changing phases of a crowded day."[65] Other male art critics, implicitly or explicitly, praised the woman who did not conform to aristocratic ideals of youthful beauty. For example, Miller's friend Lloyd Goodrich likened her "bold voluptuous coarseness of feature" to that of a Roman matron rather than an "obviously pretty" Venus. Like many intellectuals seeking to understand and document the nobility of the average citizen in the 1930s,[66] Goodrich called her strong and vital. A "mature" and "robust" woman of the people, she was the female version of the common man who would pull the nation through its worst times.[67] Walter Gutman commented more directly on her stability and endurance and highlighted her motherly and "wifely" responsibilities by describing her as "maternal and companionable."[68] As early as 1924 Paul Rosenfeld had recognized in the Miller matron a familiar figure whose down-to-earth quality he paired with her sexuality in characterizing her as a "lusty" creature not unlike our "everyday selves."[69] For the male viewer in the Depression Miller constructed a strong, physically comforting, and capable help-mate rather than a conventionally beautiful companion.

Other critics commented unfavorably on the Miller type. One, reviewing Miller's 1929 exhibit at the Rehn Gallery, lambasted Miller's recent nudes (unlike his "once solid and sculptural" nudes) as "ingenious concoctions of rubber, unpleasant in color and texture, filled with gas. They are blown up almost to the bursting point and it is perhaps unfortunate that the little more needed for the explosion was not added."[70] Such criticism of Miller's monumental figures suggests that even if they were perceived as placid, they still took up too much space. These remarks also reflect the growing popularity of the slimmer body type common to film stars and female athletes, the two most widely celebrated exemplars of female beauty in the late 1920s and early 1930s.[71] Male viewers, conditioned by the newer ideal, may have found the Miller type increasingly less attractive, artistic precedents notwithstanding.

Miller's stated artistic goals were largely formal and contained few clues about his feelings toward the shopper or, for that matter, American women. But we can extrapolate his attitudes toward women from his views on American society and politics; from his intellectual pursuits, which fed the ideas in his paintings; and from his own life as he took advantage of the new woman's sexual liberation. These sources in the aggregate confirm that for him the matronly shopper was an affirmative icon of prosperity and family stability—a figure accommodating social and political change only superficially.

Miller was a patriot. He loved his country, accepted its values, and respected its political system: "I'm one of this nation, heart and soul, and I have an infinite desire to add a crumb to its treasure. I believe in my native land, my feeling for it is strong and deep-rooted."[72] When the artist Louis Lozowick asked Miller to endorse the Communist candidates William Foster and John Ford in 1932, Miller declined:

> Please do not add my name to your list as proposed in your invitation to me. I consider it would be a misfortune indeed, both as artist and as man, to be a member of a small minority antagonistic to the genius of our nation, a party which is not very tolerantly regarded by the great majority of all classes.[73]

Miller's celebration of the modern American shopper reflects his belief in mainstream national traditions and majority beliefs rather than in dramatic social or political change. In rejecting Lozowick's solicitation in such vehement terms, Miller affirmed his faith in democratic values, majority rule, and the status quo. Such ideals are embodied in his matronly shopper.

Miller's views toward women were shaped not only by his patriotism, but also by his reading and experience throughout the teens. Several of the works Miller read epitomized the ideology and conservatism of the back-to-the-home movement. One was the popular book *Love and Marriage* by the Swedish feminist Ellen Key, which Miller and his second wife, Helen, read in 1912, shortly after it was published in an English translation.[74] In this book and her other works—*The Renaissance of Motherhood*, *The Century of the Child*, *Love and Ethics*, and *The Morality of Women and Other Essays*—all discussed widely in the early teens—Key espoused controversial ideas about motherhood and women's sexuality.[75]

In *Love and Marriage* and *Love and Ethics*, Key proposed what seemed a radical system of "erotic ethics" to an American audience steeped in the genteel tradition.[76] Believing that puritan Christianity had no meaning for modern society, she deplored its failure to reconcile the demands of spirit and body and advocated greater personal freedom in the expression of sexuality, especially for women.[77] She also argued that love without marriage was moral and marriage without love, immoral; the institution of marriage itself should be revised, with divorce allowing for the "changing demands of love."[78] Although she believed that unconditional fidelity was virtually impossible, given the need for individual growth and the changes occurring in every other area of life, she never advocated free love. Instead, she urged temperance and restraint for the sake of love itself.[79]

Because she dared to question traditional attitudes toward marital fidelity and female chastity, Key was branded a radical, particularly by Americans. Yet by her own and other writers' assessments, her views on the social roles of women were highly traditional, her vision of motherhood decidedly "reactionary."[80] She believed fervently in the distinctiveness rather than the equality of the sexes and thus supported the nineteenth-century belief in separate spheres. Motherhood was woman's natural sphere, and her dependence on man was natural rather than social.[81] Key deplored the New Woman's desire for financial and personal independence through work and said that women should learn a trade only in case they did not become mothers. Observing that among women there would always be a number of "unmotherly . . . sexless, but useful working ants" who devoted themselves to careers, she saw women's quest for freedom as a "sick yearning to be 'freed' from the most essential attribute of her sex."[82] Rather than recommend improved working conditions for women, Key simply claimed that women's factory, clerical, or teaching jobs were so monotonous that they could never "bring greater freedom and happiness than the broad usefulness in a home, where woman is sovereign— yea under the inspiration of motherhood, creator—in her sphere and where she is working for her own dear ones."[83] As a concession to the New Woman's need for financial independence (not to mention the increasing financial need among families), Key proposed that mothers receive a government stipend for child rearing, a proposal that American audiences, fearful of any government intervention in individual families, wholeheartedly rejected.[84]

Key's ideas about motherhood reflected an ongoing conflict in the feminist movement that solidified in the 1920s into a polarity between those who supported protective legislation (woman's difference) and those who campaigned for the E.R.A. (woman's equality). Miller would have come to understand these positions by reading Key and by conversing with his young wife Helen who was moderately active in the suffragist movement.[85] Key represented the views of "female" feminists, Charlotte Perkins Gilman those of "human" feminists; both women's views were debated in several publications during the early teens.[86] Where Key believed in the fuller development of woman's sexual identity and her sacrifice of self to motherhood, Gilman argued that she should improve her human capacities, those commonly held by all men and women but previously ignored because of woman's all-consuming preoccupation with her separate womanly activities. By concentrating on their humanity over their womanliness, Gilman believed, women could participate more fully with men in improving society.

Gilman advocated a social rather than an individual motherhood, calling for benefits like communal kitchens for working mothers and professional childcare. Although Gilman supported Key's view that childcare was crucial to a better society, she felt that children would be best educated by both their mothers and specialists in childcare. Where Gilman longed for equality between the sexes in a fully humanized society, Key believed, according to one *Current Opinion* author, that women would find power over men through a "consecration and exaltation of motherhood which amounts to . . . a maternalization of life."[87]

In her opposition to what she called amaternal feminism, Key found the declining birthrate and the obliteration of sexual difference particularly appalling. To define the special role of twentieth-century mothers, she adopted Nietzsche's concept of motherhood, which placed a high value on individual development and was based on the evolutionary assumption that mothers were vital in improving the race. According to Key, Nietzsche

> emphasized not only the significance of motherliness in a physical sense, but also in a sense hitherto barely perceived, of *consciously recreating the race* [Key's italics]. He knew that the race instincts first of all must be developed in the direction of sexual selection so as to promote the growth of superior inborn traits. He knew also that women needed to be educated to a perfected motherliness, that they, instead of bungling this work as they are apt to do today, may come to practice the profession of motherhood as a great and difficult art.[88]

Key's observations here about the difficulty of the "profession" of motherhood and elsewhere about the erosion of family and the race resulting from woman's desire for equality, independence, and a working life outside the home anticipate the arguments of the back-to-the-home movement a decade later, when conservative pundits linked American social progress and woman's liberation to an ideal of the professionalized homemaker.

In the early years of the twentieth century a belief in women's special sex-related skills (Key's position) rather than a wholesale acceptance of their equality and independence (Gilman's position) helped women gain the franchise. To counteract a rising anti-suffragist movement, suffragist leaders borrowed from the separate spheres position the argument that women, as spiritual models and domestic experts, would bring a whole new moral tone to American life and politics. Thus woman's difference from man rather than her equality made her worthy of the vote.[89]

By the 1920s when Miller began to portray his matronly shopper, the New Woman's working life, her new freedom in society (symbolized by less restrictive fashions and behavioral codes), and her new political life had gained some acceptance, but an ideology of separate spheres, with its corollary maternal feminism, had gained the day, persisting in the back-to-the-home movement and continuing to be promoted by mainstream "social" feminists. So thoroughly did this traditional position permeate American culture that Charlotte Perkins Gilman, once the spokeswoman for women's individuality and equality with men, modified her views. Appalled, like many suffragists of her generation, by the hedonistic excesses of the flapper, she wrote in 1923, "Wifehood and motherhood are the normal status of women, and whatever is right in women's new position must not militate against these essentials."[90]

Miller would have been drawn to Key's arguments for both personal and intellectual reasons. Over the years, in modified form, they influenced his conduct as well as his image of womanhood. In 1912 Key's ideas on the amorality of marriage without love would have justified Miller's 1911 divorce from his first wife, Irma Ferry (ostensibly for infrequent sex), and his immediate remarriage to his young art student Helen Pendleton, with whom he had had a romantic and emotional, if not physical, attachment for at least one and one-half years prior to the divorce.[91] Key's ideas about the need for a freer expression of one's unconscious and natural sexual desires would have prepared Miller for his deep emotional and intellectual exploration of Freud's theories of sexuality and the unconscious beginning in 1915 and continuing well into the 1930s.[92]

Miller told his students that he wanted to put Freudian "things" into his paintings.[93] In many of his images of matronly shoppers, Freudian currents move just beneath the surface. Some of Miller's images seem to take on the culture's ambivalence about the expression versus the repression of sexuality as it played out in

4.33   Kenneth Hayes Miller, *Little Coat and Fur Shop*, 1931. Oil on canvas, 43″ × 31″. Collection of Palmer Museum of Art, The Pennsylvania State University.

the flapper phenomenon. The chilly idealization derived from old master sources masks the sensuousness of full-figured women nearly bursting forth from too-snug garments. In *Little Coat and Fur Shop* (1931; Fig. 4.33), the woman poses provocatively, her body swelling to fill her suit. Her genital area is framed by the open coat and overlaid by two highlighted and sharply protruding diagonal folds. These elements meet the formal and aesthetic needs of the composition, but given Miller's desire to include Freudian overtones, their further implications cannot be ignored. Moreover, the professionalized homemaker was presumably a modern woman, sexually and emotionally liberated; Miller's barely covert references to her sexuality, like the umbrella as phallus (Fig. 4.1), acknowledge the cultural construction of her sexuality according to the heterosexual ideals of a revised new womanhood in the 1920s.

Apart from the effects of Freud and Key on Miller's marital and extra-marital practices and the ideals behind the matronly shopper, Ellen Key's arguments from Nietzsche about the need for "good" mothers to promote superior traits would also have struck a responsive chord in Miller, who was raised with similar ideas in the utopian community in Oneida, New York.[94] Members of the Oneida community believed in human perfectibility through sexual selection and acknowledged female sexual pleasure.[95] Though Miller eventually shared traditional marriage- and family-oriented ideals that his family acknowledged by abandoning the Oneida practice (studio liaisons notwithstanding), he continued to espouse the idea of human perfectibility through natural selection.

Throughout the teens Miller continued to be fascinated with works that supported this evolutionist position.[96] One of the studies he praised, Madison Grant's *Passing of the Great Race* of 1916, argued that heredity influenced men's actions more than either environment or social conditioning. Grant used this theory to demonstrate the natural superiority of the Nordic race, which formed the basic American colonial stock. He argued that the unrestricted emigration from what he considered the racially inferior areas of southern and eastern Europe would destroy our national heritage. He concluded with a passage that spoke his distrust of egalitarian principles and universal suffrage.

> We Americans must realize that the altruistic ideals which have controlled our social development during the past century and the maudlin sentimentalism that has made America "an asylum for the oppressed" are sweeping the nation toward a racial abyss. If the Melting Pot is allowed to boil without control and we continue to follow our national motto and deliberately blind ourselves to all "distinctions of race, creed or color," the type of native American of colonial descent will become as extinct as the Athenian in the Age of Pericles and the Viking of the Days of Rollo.[97]

The racist thinking in Grant's work worried Progressive Era thinkers and social workers struggling to improve urban immigrant life. Many upper-middle-class Americans, however, rationalized his attitudes by arguing that the "purity" of American values, morals, and social and political systems could remain in force only if the Anglo-Saxon stock, which provided the true "spirit of Americanism," were perpetuated.[98] Extreme though it may have been, Grant's thinking reflected the growing anxiety in the conservative native-born circles to which Miller belonged that the massive influx of immigrants from eastern Europe and Mediterranean countries would bring about unwanted cultural and political change.[99] This thinking also fueled the xenophobia underlying the Red scare and Palmer raids of the early 1920s and promoted the chauvinism behind the practices of debunking and cultural stereotyping throughout the decade.[100]

Given Miller's upbringing and continued association with the Oneida sect and his intellectual preoccupations throughout the teens and 1920s, his receptivity to the ideas discussed above is hardly surprising. Key's elitist and reactionary ideas on exclusive motherhood, Freud's theories of sexuality, and Grant's racial theories appealed to Miller as to like-minded native-born middle-class intellectuals in these years, his brief flirtation with socialism aside (see pp. 45–47).[101] Such nationalistic thinking passed into the ideology of the back-to-the-home movement of the 1920s, the immediate historical context for the matronly shopper. The active, well-educated, and conscientious middle-class mothers to whom the arguments were addressed would keep American society stable and prosperous by helping to keep it purely "American."[102]

Although the Fourteenth Street milieu was anything but purely American in its demographics, Miller avoided virtually all individualization or ethnicity. Unlike his students Laning and Bishop, who showed the shopper in a crowd, Miller made only superficial accommodations to the Depression decade's preoccupation with the common people (themselves often recent immigrants) by varying details of costume, facial feature, and girth. Miller's matron was more often fair than dark-skinned, with light brown or Titian red hair, her eyes invariably light blue, green, or hazel.[103] Such obvious references to homogenized Nordic beauty and avoidance of the Near Eastern and Mediterranean ethnicity of Fourteenth Street suggest that Miller's idealized Anglo-Saxon mother would assure not only family and economic stability but also the continuity of her race.

The generalization of the Fourteenth Street shopper can be read as an avoidance of reference to class and ethnicity in an era devoted to celebrating the equality of the average American. In the context of consumer culture it can also be read as the quest for a purchased ideal of middle-classness. Such an interpretation is equally appropriate to Laning's and Bishop's mural-like images of Fourteenth Street crowds, painted in the early 1930s. In Miller's work, this idealization also becomes an assertion of America's need to retain and perpetuate the values many conservatives argued would see the country through hard times far better than increasing the number of government programs to assist the poor. Given Miller's age, a social and intellectual background that fostered individualism and elitism, and what some of his friends termed his zealously patriotic, even reactionary, politics,[104] this conservative interpretation of the early 1930s matronly shopper is as valid as the one that posits Miller's broadening of the social base of the image to adapt it to Depression era conditions and a viewing audience that became more class conscious in the early 1930s.

Miller and his students Laning and Bishop idealized the matronly shopper and glossed over features of a dingy working-class shopping environment. In the heart of the Depression, they focused on the successes of Fourteenth Street's commercialism, made the shopper into an average American woman, and placed her in settings that spoke about the promise and beauty of urban America. Her image thus participated in that affirmative and optimistic outlook that helped the middle class continue in hard times.

The image of the shopper also perpetuated a historical stereotype of a patient, enduring woman, whose dress and activity as a shopper seemed to acknowledge substantial changes in women's lifestyles—many resulting from consumer culture. Although fashion, self-conscious pose, and public settings signaled modernity, sexual liberation, and political emancipation, the matronly bearing of Miller's old master figures also embodied the conservative ideology of the back-to-the-home movement. Within this powerful ideology, rhetorical claims to equality and professionalism did little to alter women's roles. Even their public status as consumers remained essentially domestic. This traditional ideology served business, which needed a homemaker/shopper ally to keep the economy running, both before and after the crash. It also met a need for family and community stability to counteract the social fragmentation of modern society and the economic chaos of the Depression. The matronly shopper—sturdy and reassuring—satisfied a widely held, if obliquely articulated, need for stability and in so doing fulfilled her socially expected role.

CHAPTER FIVE

SEX FOR SALE: REGINALD MARSH'S VOLUPTUOUS SHOPPER

He accepts his girls for what they are—gaudy, full-bosomed and hungry for pleasure, yet immensely appealing.

THOMAS CRAVEN, "A Paean for Marsh"

You are a painter of the body. Sex is your theme.

KENNETH HAYES MILLER to Reginald Marsh

Reginald Marsh's voluptuous shopper first appeared in his Fourteenth Street paintings in 1932. Her sexually provocative look (Figs. 3.19 and 5.1) is derived from the popular stereotype of the movie Siren (Fig. 4.7), an elegant image of a femme fatale that emerged in the late 1920s and dominated the popular imagination for much of the Depression. The Siren was the flapper's successor. Her looks and behavior projected a new ideal of femininity within the discourse of new womanhood. Her image was fashioned by journalists, advertisers, and movie producers who molded Hollywood stars from Greta Garbo to Joan Crawford in the Siren image, created endless fictions about the Siren in films, and used her image to advertise movies or to sell products in entertainment publications. This glamorous stereotype became so pervasive that women appropriated elements of it for their own purposes, as they had with the flapper. Some of these young women, imitating the Siren's look by exaggerating its components, became the voluptuous shoppers of Marsh's Fourteenth Street paintings.

Marsh's voluptuous shopper so dominated his 1930s imagery that she came to be called the Marsh girl. How are we to read this figure of hyper-glamorized working-class femininity? Like Miller's matron, she embodied a conservative ideal of post-franchise new womanhood; this New Woman had abandoned collective activism to express her independence, sexuality, and self-conscious femininity by applying mass-produced beauty products. Where Miller's shopper inhabits a clear,

5.1 "Siren" under the ladder (detail of *In Fourteenth Street*, Fig. 3.19).

stable composition, Marsh's voluptuous shopper is often trapped in a texture of confusion and uncertainty. Marsh's paintings foreground the powerful energy and sexuality of the woman consumer. Where she towers above helpless admirers, she can be read as a figure of sexual danger, a threat to masculinity already compromised by unemployment. Yet in paintings that accentuate that potent sexuality, she is not only subject to the consuming male gaze but also vehicle for and victim of the consumer culture.[1] Thus, although the Siren stereotype informed Marsh's individual images of the voluptuous shopper, the paintings in which she is placed reveal the complex meanings that were part of the Siren image in the 1930s, whether or not that was Marsh's conscious intention. Thanks to his unusual strategy of combining forms and subjects from movies and movie advertisements with forms and subjects from old master works, the paintings uncover the contradictions of the Siren's persona, her power and passivity, desirability and unattainability.

With that argument about the Marsh girl more or less in place, I must digress to refine my claims—to make the pictures more problematic or at least to express my own discomfort with them. My perplexity arises from two sources, one critical, one personal. The critics, who either have slotted Marsh into virtually every available art-historical category or have equivocated in their response to his work, have described him as a romantic with an element of fantasy in his art, an objective documentary realist of everyday life in the thirties, an upholder of the baroque tradition, a Hogarthian satirist, or an affirmative celebrant of modern urban life. And no matter what the assertion, there seems to be a case for its opposite.[2]

Within this initial problematic of "the failing grip of categories," I have two particular concerns, first with disclaimers about Marsh's politics and second with the self-referential nature of Marsh's art.[3] Edward Laning, one of the artist's confidants, wrote that "Marsh held aloof from every sort of politics. While others argued, he drew and painted. As I look back on it, it seems to me that every faction believed he belonged to them, and I guess he did!" Because of Marsh's minimal participation in politics and his preoccupation with old master aesthetics, many art historians and critics have concluded that whatever his liberal leanings, they remained a distant issue in his art. Moreover, during the thirties, liberal and leftist critics faulted Marsh for refusing to take responsibility either for his lower-class subjects or, worse, for his elitist attitudes toward them.[4] After Thomas Craven aligned Marsh with the Regionalists Benton, Curry, and Wood in the famous *Time* article of 1934, Marsh, who had claimed "well bred people are no fun to paint," was attacked by Stuart Davis in *Art Front*. Referring indirectly to the artist's Yale background and training with Kenneth Hayes Miller, Davis wrote that Marsh had the "psychology of the bourgeois art school." Three years later Marsh defended his social and artistic position in an autobiographical piece:

1932–33. Deep depression. Art world and Fords and Rockefellers conquered by Mexicans. Emphasis on the social conscious. The hung head. *Time* magazine launches "American Scene" painters—I seem to be included. Great uproar on all fronts. What? Thomas Craven praises Americans!!! With Benton, Curry, et cetera, condemned by prominent, Communist abstract painter, big chief defender of culture, as Hearst's New York "American" scene Fascist opportunist—"Chauvinism," "Nationalism," cry the Communist boulevardiers!! Well, what should we do—be ashamed of being what we are—or imitate Orozco, Grosz, African Sculpture, and draw endless pictures of gas masks, "Cossacks" and caricatures of J. P. Morgan with a pig-like nose? . . . Whatever you say, there is a tradition to be proud of.[5]

That Marsh never made the political commitments of leftist artists seems especially clear in 1937, by which time he had almost completed his second of two government mural projects and had adapted his art to the broader ideological aims of American Scene painting. Nonetheless, in the early 1930s he worked diligently to educate himself in the debates on art and politics. His attendance at Workers' School classes and Union Square rallies, his contribution of satirical graphics to the *New Masses*, and his increased depiction of unemployed men suggest a desire to reach, not a broad proletariat audience—for that would have compromised his views about the relation between art and propaganda—but an audience with a broad point of view.[6]

Given this distinction, it is important to interrogate the largely unexamined and often conflicting gender and class politics in his paintings, often manifested in the figure of the voluptuous shopper. In doing this, I wish to reinstate in Marsh's painted works some of the "cultural satire"—that "psychological and spiritual" probing of social ills and social contradictions—found in the dense details and dark tonalities of his graphic works. These qualities in his paintings subtly increase the deep ambivalance of these works toward both the female subjects and the commercial themes Marsh represented in them.[7]

I want to address as well the division between the public and private (or self-referential) side of Marsh's art proposed by Marilyn Cohen in her interpretation of the artist's work. Cohen claims that the fascination with the affirmative, documentary, and public side of Marsh's art obscures the private darker motivations behind his themes; "characters, situations, and subjects repeated in his works have as much to do with the artist's psyche as with their actual presence in the contemporary landscape."[8] In art whose major theme is "spectacle," with seeing, watching, and sexuality its major components, the endlessly repeated Bowery bums, muscle men, and untouchable striding women (Sirens) are not just social types but "artistic projections of aspects of Marsh's own self." The eroticized yet inaccessible terrain of Marsh's female imagery suggests the artist's anxieties about his own masculinity, the Bowery bum and muscleman his conflicts about his artistic position, his obsession with productivity, and his fear of failure.[9] Although I have no wish to discount

Cohen's careful and persuasive arguments, I would like to blur the boundaries between public and private, social and psychic, to claim that the deeply personal anxieties and the ambivalent construction of gender relations we find in Marsh's presentation of the voluptuous shopper are also deeply social and pervasive in the Depression era.

The second source of my discomfort with the artist's pictures emerges from my own unease as a feminist interpreter of the paintings. My initial pleasure in comparing Marsh's dynamic and sexually energetic women with Miller's more complacent and passive matrons is immediately undercut by my reading of the overt sexism, classism, and racism inscribed in these images. It is a pleasure mediated, as for all viewers, by social and psychic formation, by knowledge and experience—in particular here by a historically situated awareness of feminist ideas. I assume here the feminist premise articulated by Rosemary Betterton, that all representations of the female body and female sexuality draw on "visual codes [that] reinstate the same relationships of sexual power and subordination." Images of women from various discursive sites are inevitably caught in a web of voyeurism and exploitation or defined in a regime of looking that oppresses women (in a museum, at the cinema, in advertisements, or in pornographic representation, to mention the most obvious).[10] Because the Marsh girl resembles a popular cinematic stereotype, because the Fourteenth Street paintings thematize situations in which predominantly lower-class women are visually on display for men—at the burlesque, the dance marathon, or the movies or on the street near display windows—and, finally, because they are easel paintings for a bourgeois audience interested in "high art," the paintings are constructed almost exclusively for a male viewer's gaze. This is not to say that Miller's, Soyer's, and even Bishop's paintings do not address a masculine spectator, only that in Marsh's paintings the visual and sexual objectification of women appears extreme—and thus my initial discomfort as a female spectator is more palpable.

In thinking about the structures of spectatorship, I am concerned not only with my own position but also, and primarily, with the historical viewing subject—the artist and the viewers of the work in the Depression. Laura Mulvey's analysis of the cinema is particularly useful in relation to an artist whose work has cinematic codes and qualities. In "Visual Pleasure and Narrative Cinema," Mulvey argued that the female spectator's pleasure in images of women comes from her assuming one of two viewing positions available to her. She might identify with the masculine, voyeuristic gaze—associated with looking from a distance—thereby assuming a position of power and control over the image. From this position, however, she would lose a sense of her own identity, not to mention a sense both of her own experience and of how her viewing pleasure might differ from that of the male.

The second viewing position, identified with narcissism, finds pleasure in closeness and self-identification with the image. But there can be a degree of danger in this position because woman's narcissistic obsession with self-image (in art, the theme of women looking at themselves in mirrors) has been linked to her innate frivolity, her concern with individual appearance, and her self-indulgence—in a demeaning image of woman that is "naturally" hers. Rosalind Coward, refuting biological explanations, reasons that because woman's desirability in our culture is attached to her social/sexual success, a woman examines ideal images of femininity for what she might appropriate to achieve that success. Coward also points out that women usually fault their own image when they match it against the ideal, a condition she calls "narcissistic damage."[11]

In her later work, Mulvey refined the notion of the female spectator. She identified as feminine a greater mobility in viewing that makes it possible to switch points of view or to appropriate some aspects of masculine and feminine viewing positions while rejecting others. Her revision was important for its recognition that "masculine" and "feminine" are not essential viewing categories but socially formed and historically shifting. Thus, as Betterton points out, it is possible to distinguish "between looking 'as a woman' and the fact of being one, between a feminine position and female experience"—to acknowledge simultaneously different viewpoints and read an image against the grain. Although a masculine viewer can engage in similar critical viewing, in a patriarchal culture whose forms most often address male viewers men are rarely forced to negotiate a viewing position in the same way.[12]

Teresa de Lauretis discusses the social construction of gendered subjects in representation in a way that broadens Mulvey's consideration of the structures of spectatorship; both analyses contribute to my own reframing of how and to what effect gender relations are played out in the figure of Marsh's voluptuous shopper. De Lauretis emphasizes a double premise about gender: first, gender *is* the representation of a social relation—of belonging to a class, or a group, or a category; second, "gender [also] *constructs* a relation" between entities (individuals) "previously constituted as a class, and that relation is one of belonging." The mutually exclusive yet complementary categories male and female together constitute an asymmetrical sex-gender system—a system of meanings that in every society is connected to economic and political arenas. For de Lauretis, "*the construction of gender is both the product and the process of its representation*" (de Lauretis's italics).[13]

Not only does de Lauretis give a complex *definition* of gender; she also asks how and where social subjects are constituted as "gendered." The process involves more than sexual differentiation—a psychic mechanism that posits a universal opposition between male and female. Male and female subjects result not only from the splitting of the subject through the unconscious but also from sexual relations, languages, cultural representations, and the experiencing of race and class. The "engendered" subject is multiple and contradicted at every turn, never unified or even simply divided. Finally, as de Lauretis points out, gender (and the gendered subject), "both as representation and as self-representation, is the product of various social technologies, such as cinema, and of institutionalized discourses, epistemologies, and critical practices, as well as practices of daily life."[14]

De Lauretis's discussion of how gender and representation construct social subjects, together with Mulvey's discussion of how viewing subjects take up positions with respect to representation allow a more nuanced and more historical reading of Marsh's voluptuous shopper. On the one hand, the Marsh girl figures one aspect of a revised new womanhood—itself a product of both the institutionalized discourses and the practices of daily life. As a Fourteenth Street shopper she expresses her independence and sexual liberation through consumption. As a stereotyped icon of female beauty, in paintings that foreground her potent sexuality, she becomes a mere sexual commodity, constructed for a male viewer's gaze.

These paintings of working-class women never displace the hierarchy of looking—of class and gender relations inscribed in them by an upper-class Yale-educated male artist who assumes a "naturally" bolder and more visually accessible sexuality in working-class womanhood. At the same time, however, the paintings interrogate that viewing position and the degrading conception of new womanhood forged through the stereotype by engaging in a veiled critique of consumer culture. This oscillating and ambivalent critique occurs because Marsh's construction of gender—of a sexually alluring image of post-franchise new womanhood—takes place at the intersection of competing discourses on advertising, on cinematic representation, and on the socially concerned forms of urban realism in the Depression.

Marsh's voluptuous shopper is easy to identify in his paintings of Fourteenth Street crowds and to distinguish from other Fourteenth Street women. Youthful, frequently blond, heavily made-up, she exudes sexuality. With snug-fitting clothes in flamboyant colors that accentuate every curve, she immediately calls attention to herself. Though she might double as a Fourteenth Street shopgirl, she appears in several major works of the early 1930s as a pedestrian.[15] In *Show Window* (1934; Fig. 5.2 and Plate 4), for example, two blondes survey a crowded display of fashions modeled by mannequins whose appearance approximates their own. In *In Fourteenth Street* (Fig. 3.19; Plate 3), Marsh's most ambitious picture of Fourteenth Street shopping crowds, several glamorous women stand out from the vast undifferentiated crowd of stereotyped city people. Most striking is the saucy baby-doll blond in a bright blue skirt and frilly blouse, striding forward yet isolated from the crowd between the lamppost and ladder at the left of the picture (Fig. 5.1). Another sultry blond in vivid blue stands quietly at the center of the composition, arms folded, a still, mysterious figure in the swirling crowd. To the far right, a third provocative blond in bright red enjoys an ice-cream cone. In *Fourteenth Street Subway Stairs* (1932; Fig. 3.23), a mincing brunette wearing a brilliant turquoise suit and carrying only a purse stands aloof from a group of women carrying briefcases and ledgers on their way to or from work. Her chic dress, chilly demeanor,

5.2   Reginald Marsh, *Show Window*, 1934. Egg tempera on board, 42″ × 34″.
The Saint Louis Art Museum.

5.3 Reginald Marsh, *Women on Fourteenth Street*, 1934. Tempera, 16″ × 12″. Present location unknown.

and placement accentuate her isolation, her exaggerated beauty, and possibly her different class position.

In *Women on Fourteenth Street* (1934; Fig. 5.3) Marsh focused more closely on the individual shopper. Here a tall, self-assured blond (on the right) takes a provocative, sexually challenging pose. Arms akimbo, she gazes directly at someone or something outside the picture. Another Fourteenth Street shopper in *Hat Display* (1939; Fig. 5.4) with the more robust body typical of figures in Marsh's late-decade watercolors, primps beside a window filled with mannequin heads.

This voluptuous woman played multiple roles in all Marsh's other paintings. In Fourteenth Street images, she was a burlesque queen (Fig. 3.24), a taxi dancer (Fig. 3.25), or a live model on Union Square (Figs. 3.26 and 5.5). More regularly, she was a Coney Island beach bather (Fig. 5.6).[16] The locales she frequented and the activities in which she participated mark her as a working-class woman. Marsh showed her caught up in the popular forms of mass entertainment that attracted members of her social class in the early years of the Depression. Unlike Miller's shopper, who remained a homemaker and was pictured in comfortable middle-class settings when not shopping, Marsh's shopper is always part of a public urban spectacle. A youthful single woman, she never appears with children. In the context

5.4 Reginald Marsh, *Hat Display,*
1939. Watercolor, 40″ × 26³/₈″.
Present location unknown.

5.5 Reginald Marsh, *Modeling Furs on
Union Square,* 1940. Watercolor,
28″ × 42″. Private collection.

5.6   Reginald Marsh, *Coney Island Beach*, 1934. Egg tempera on masonite, $35^{5}/_{8}'' \times 39^{5}/_{8}''$.
Yale University Art Gallery.

of an imagery dominated by scenes of mass leisure, shopping was another form of popular entertainment, not part of homemaking.

Although Marsh's women display themselves in ways that are alternately provocative, mysterious, aloof, or hesitant, all are portrayed as sophisticated and glamorous. All share an early 1930s look codified by Hollywood, whose films reached their largest audience in Depression America.[17] By 1929, the look of this woman was marketed in movie magazines, where advertisers used film stars to sell their products, reaching an extensive audience through cheap periodicals and tabloids that claimed to tell the "whole truth" about the new popular heroes and heroines of America—the movie stars. *Modern Screen*, advertised as having "the largest

5.7 "Modern Screen Patterns
Join the Easter Parade,"
Modern Screen (April
1933), p. 71.

guaranteed circulation of any screen magazine," at a monthly cost of ten cents, provides evidence of the close visual relationship between the Marsh girl and the Siren stereotype.[18]

In facial and figure type, pose, gesture, and fashion, Marsh's voluptuous shopper approximates in exaggerated ways the look of women in 1930s movie stills, photos of film stars, and fashion illustrations or advertisements. For example, the blond under the ladder in *In Fourteenth Street* (Fig. 5.1), with her parted red lips and heavy-lidded eyes, resembles Jean Harlow (Fig. 4.7) or Mae West. Her blue and white dress with puffed sleeves (Fig. 3.19; Plate 3) appears as an "utterly distinguished" and "adorable" up-to-the-minute frock in *Modern Screen*'s monthly page of fashion patterns in the April 1933 issue (Fig. 5.7). The woman with her arms folded at the center of the painting has a faraway gaze and wears a hat that partially shields her eyes. This woman is more enigmatic than her perky counterpart under the ladder and more aloof than the straightforwardly respectable women in the

5.8 *Right:* Marlene Dietrich, in *Modern Screen* (September 1933), p. 16.

5.9 *Below:* Conchita Montenegro and Virginia Bruce, in *Modern Screen* (October 1934), p. 57.

5.10   Berenice Abbott, Union Square, July 16, 1936. Photograph. Federal Art
Project, "Changing New York." Museum of the City of New York.

pattern illustrations. With her veiled and shadowy mien she resembles arch-Sirens
Greta Garbo and Marlene Dietrich, whose mysterious and alluring attributes exemplified the European origins of these important Siren qualities (Fig. 5.8).[19] The painting's old master veneer, which comes from Marsh's limited gray-brown palette,
sketchy brushwork, and deep flickering chiaroscuro, approximates the look of contemporary Hollywood portrait photographs, with their strongly contrasting lights
and darks and their blurred soft focus. In *Fourteenth Street Subway Stairs* (Fig.
3.23), the shopper in turquoise with her short black hair and gamin features is a
chilly version of Conchita Montenegro (Fig. 5.9). Finally, the suited blonde of
Women on Fourteenth Street (Fig. 5.3) takes her pose from stars like Virginia Bruce
who regularly modeled the latest fashions (Fig. 5.9). Indeed, the provocative pose
of "display" appears regularly in fashion plates or photos in which movie stars
appear as living mannequins.

Marsh's use of the Siren stereotype for his more garish image of the voluptuous
shopper indicates his intent to showcase this new model of feminine beauty. The
1930s viewer would have known this woman and what she stood for. At the same
time, however, Marsh placed his voluptuous shoppers in settings whose specificity
left no doubt that these beauties were also meant to be seen as the lower-class

women of Fourteenth Street. Marsh filled his compositions to the point of *horror vacui* with documentary material and incorporated fragments of his neighborhood photographs and drawings into his pictures. For example, the legless beggar at the lower right hand corner of *In Fourteenth Street* (Fig. 3.19; Plate 3) is taken directly from one of Marsh's neighborhood photographs.[20] Carefully lettered placards advertise beauty bargains and sales held, in all probability, at actual Fourteenth Street establishments. The neighborhood was filled with beauty establishments. Berenice Abbott's photograph of the south side of East Fourteenth Street (Fig. 5.10) shows Klein's Beauty Academy and the Manhattan Beauty School; Ida's Beauty Salon was located in Klein's building.[21] In *Show Window* (Fig. 5.2) Marsh recorded prices on markers labeled Ohrbachs, one of the district's most celebrated bargain centers.

Marsh's voluptuous shopper appears "real," but the documentary realism of these works coexists uneasily with exaggerated, isolated fantasy females in paintings whose compositions and technique were perceived to be like "movies in themselves."[22] Contemporaries observed, as have subsequent writers, Marsh's use of cinematic techniques. Some, pointing to sequential movement and the lack of a focal point in his frieze-like compositions, have compared them to 1930s newsreels. Others have noticed that his asymmetrical framing creates an anticipation of the next frame and that Marsh's paintings work best when seen together like the frames of a film. Still others have found resemblances between his shimmering brushwork and moving images and the insubstantial, flickering qualities of film.[23] Marsh frequently sketched elaborate sets for his paintings from neighborhood storefronts or movie marquees and only subsequently inserted female figures, sketched separately from a model. In casting the voluptuous shopper as the star against a Fourteenth Street backdrop, Marsh used the techniques and subjects of Hollywood's 1930s fantasies. And his paintings, like the movies of his day, imaged women as sexualized movie queens.

In their concern to understand the relation between movies and conduct, psychologists and sociologists in the 1930s frequently examined the cinematic techniques that they felt fostered viewer identification with a hero, a heroine, or a situation. The psychologist Malcolm Willey, for example, demonstrated that quantities of visual detail (often related to lavish settings in movies) and the exaggerated vitality of film in general were used by filmmakers to heighten viewers' emotions.[24] Marsh's paintings use similar devices to equally dizzying ends. The agitated surfaces of his settings generate a sense of continuous and accelerated movement. Moreover, he not only focused on the Siren stereotype by isolating her within crowds, but also took a particularly voyeuristic stance toward his female subjects, thereby accentuating the masculine viewing position. In fact, voyeurism was sometimes part of Marsh's process. His two-story studio at the top of the Lincoln Arcade Building contained a telescope, which he used to survey the crowds; *In Fourteenth Street* inscribes the unequal class relations implied by Marsh's elevated point of view. *Modeling Furs on Union Square* (Fig. 5.5) places the viewer at the same level as the second-story display window instead of below and looking up, as in either Marsh's photograph of the same scene (Fig. 3.27) or *Hudson Bay Fur Company* (Fig. 3.26), where the viewer's position is that of a male watching the burlesque. In *View from My Window* (1938; Fig. 5.11) Marsh is the voyeur, gazing across the square to the roof of Klein's, where a nude sunbathes with two companions. The power of the male look—in this case, the artist's—is underscored by the elderly man as the impotent viewer who cannot see the rooftop scene from his window below the bathers.

Marsh's awareness of cinematic devices, including the camera's eye, would have come in part from a long-standing fascination with the movies. As early as 1912, when he was fourteen, Marsh described the kinemacolor moving pictures of the coronation of George V: "Remember, it was all in color." When his family moved from Nutley, New Jersey, to New Rochelle, New York, Marsh regularly attended moving pictures and vaudeville shows at Lowes Theater, sampling everything from Shakespeare to live acrobatic performances.[25]

Marsh's records of his moviegoing in the 1920s are meager. But he made drawings to accompany film and theater reviews for both the *New Yorker* and *Vanity Fair* so that he kept in touch with new female and male stereotypes: the Siren, for example, began to appear in Cecil B. deMille extravaganzas in the mid-1920s. Marsh's diary entries suggest that his most active period of moviegoing was the early 1930s, when American preoccupation with Hollywood had reached an all-time high and when the Siren in her most sexualized form dominated the screen.[26] He attended a variety of American classics like *The Maltese Falcon* but also liked German films and watched newsreels. He saw Siren films like Mae West's *I'm No Angel* and occasionally recorded movies by their stars (i.e., "Garbo Film," "Buster Keaton film"). Beginning in 1934, with his marriage to the artist Felicia Meyer, Marsh's social life changed. He seems never again to have given movies the same attention.[27] Marsh had lived through and internalized the major changes in film iconography and technique, however, and made them part of his artistic and intellectual process.

Besides being fascinated with the movies, Marsh would have been well acquainted with the workings of the advertising industry. He witnessed firsthand the changes in a cityscape increasingly dominated by billboards and movie marquees. Edward Laning observed the influence on Marsh of the commercial world, suggesting that this environment was "an endless flow of free images which have no fixed locus but are woven through the entire physical fabric of our lives, in papers and magazines, on walls and billboards, in the air as skywriting, in electrical displays and in shadows projected on screens."[28]

In the late 1920s and through the Depression Marsh received illustration assignments that sent him to Coney Island and to Fourteenth Street, enabling him to stay

5.11 Reginald Marsh, *View from My Window*, 1938. Tempera, 29⅞" × 23⅞".
Present location unknown.

close to popular culture, mass entertainment, and a variety of attitudes toward the working-class audience. He worked for elite publications like the *New Yorker* and *Vanity Fair* that targeted a well-to-do readership in their extensive advertising. For them Marsh drew cartoons, characterizing a range of city neighborhoods and their inhabitants. He also worked for the *Daily News*, the first of New York's successful tabloids, intended for a mass readership. Between 1922 and 1925 he drew "the humors of city life," for a column called Subway Sunbeams, a practice that enabled him to improve his skills as a caricaturist. He also illustrated a daily vaudeville column for the *News* that included both his drawings and his ratings of the shows.[29] All these pursuits eventually fueled the illustrative, documentary, and sometimes mildly caricatural tone of his mature work in the 1930s. They also provided Marsh with themes he would continue to pursue throughout his life. They made him conscious of how film, fashion, and advertising were reshaping the American city by suggesting to its population new ways of seeing and being seen. He, in turn, mined popular culture and advertising to show how they were molding the contemporary environment and its population.

But Marsh had a far more intimate connection with the advertising industry— through William Benton, a former Yale classmate, a millionaire advertiser, a close friend, and one of Marsh's most important patrons. It was Benton who purchased Marsh's cartoons for the Yale *Record* after Marsh graduated. And, beginning in 1935, it was Benton who purchased a painting a month from Marsh.[30] Between 1929 and 1935, when Benton sold out to assume the presidency of the University of Chicago, he and his partner, Chester Bowles, ran one of New York's most successful advertising agencies. In the Depression, agencies that succeeded did so by developing new techniques and special skills: Benton and Bowles, looking to popular culture, made a series of advertisements using comic strip "situation copy." They developed expertise in the new fields of consumer studies and product research; and they capitalized on a theory Benton borrowed from a friend called "progress through catastrophe."[31] For example, Benton, recognizing the popularity of the "Amos n' Andy" radio show and ultimately purchasing it for Pepsodent sponsorship, rescued the faltering toothpaste company, whose sales quadrupled. Benton also established the number one program in radio broadcasting, the "Maxwell House Show Boat," eventually admitting that "the chain stores were selling coffee that was almost as good—the difference was undetectable—for a much lower price. But advertising so gave glamor and verve to Maxwell House that it made everybody think it was a whale of a lot better. It doubled and quadrupled in sales."[32]

Marsh had a close relationship with Benton, and he shared the upper-class, elite cultural and Ivy League educational background of most of the advertising industry's upper-echelon workforce—who were overwhelmingly male. The artist would have understood something of advertising's strategies and (perhaps less consciously) its at times ambivalent conception of its mass audience. With his working experience for class-diverse New York publications he would also have understood the stereotyping and slogan making by which advertisers like Benton glamorized and marketed goods. One 1930s writer on advertising characterized the slogan as "a very powerful device . . . intended to short-circuit the reasoning process."[33] The Siren and her lifestyle were products for a wide audience as well as a marketing device for businessmen promoting movies and fashion items. At the same time, Marsh's voluptuous Fourteenth Street shopper represented an audience Benton and his advertising colleagues addressed, one whose working-class desires seemed at odds with theirs and thus at times proved particularly troubling.

Because Marsh's voluptuous shopper is constructed out of competing discourses, I wish to look first at the Siren stereotype in relation to the discourse of new womanhood in the late 1920s and early 1930s. To understand the meanings behind this stereotype, we can examine the Siren's persona as defined by journalists, movie publicists, and advertisers as well as by Marsh, who borrowed her look from popular sources. The ideology that framed the discourse on the professional homemaker also helped to shape the Siren's image, for both the Siren and the housewife were seen as successors to the flapper, whose persona was understood (if not actualized) as that of the jazz-age rebel who had won freedoms for women. The Siren and the professionalized homemaker might capitalize on these, but in a decidedly unliberated way.

When the mysterious and alluring Siren began to appear in mid-1920s movies, everyone took notice. In a *New York Times* article of July 1929, boldly titled "Now the Siren Eclipses the Flapper," Mildred Adams codified her look and behavior for the *Times*'s middle- to upper-middle-class reader with great self-assurance.[34] Adams proclaimed that the "new woman" of the 1930s must renew her covenant with femininity, must strive to nurture and please men rather than compete with them—must, in short, remake herself into an attractive and essentially passive object of consumption rather than an active, independent woman. Adams urged women to abandon the frank, boisterous, and energetic behavior of the flapper and to relinquish clothes with boyish silhouettes. She advocated instead a new, European-style, femme fatale who would combine "high serenity, and seductive languor"; who would know how to wear feminine clothing "molded to her figure," veiling "line and curve only to accentuate them"; and whose behavior would give her a "mysterious allure that is at once the oldest and newest of feminine accomplishments."[35]

Like publicists who raised the homemaker's status by professionalizing her and granting her a new and supposedly equal status, Adams assured her readers of the Siren's "independence," her freedom to choose and control her life. Above all, Adams argued that the Siren was "modern," countering any reference to an "old, traditional, or ladylike" quality with an assurance that renewing these older attributes of womanhood indicated a new kind of liberation.

Adams, however, makes her assertions of progress and freedom to choose in a rhetoric that covertly supports subservience to men. Her notions of liberation were conciliatory, like those of the popular historians of the late 1920s and early 1930s whose arguments I examined in conjunction with Miller's matronly shopper. These historians claimed that liberation had occurred with changes in social conventions, but they paid no attention to the economic and political arenas. Like them, Adams argued that the flapper, having succeeded in changing manners, was now obsolete:

> By sheer force of violence she established the right to equal representation in such hith-erto masculine fields of endeavor as smoking and drinking, swearing, petting and upsetting the community peace. They need no longer be the subject of crusade. Indeed, the incurable flappers who go on fighting for them are as absurd as the good ladies who still carry the hysteric air of martyrs in the cause of women's rights.
> *They being won*, the new siren may elect to use them or not as she sees fit [italics mine].³⁶

Moreover, while suggesting that the Siren could borrow from the flapper-femi-nist, Adams clearly advocated the Siren's feminine and alluring persona. She criti-cized the pre–World War I feminists for having abandoned feminine charm. Indeed, she read the avoidance of charm as an insulting gesture, made by women who tried to meet men on equal terms. In her view, women would have fared better by using charm in the strongest sense of the term—to enchant, to bewitch, to subdue, or to captivate—in short, to gain power over men instead of struggling to achieve eco-nomic and political equality. She argued that the modern Siren could feel free to use her "brains" to manipulate men into doing what she wanted:

> She turns the tired businessman into a courtier and makes him like it. Ancient wisdom teaches her to be a confidante but seldom to confide, to understand rather than to seek to be understood, to charm and delight rather than to demand amusement. She has learned . . . that men are not angels, but beings very human who prefer flesh and blood to sugar candy heroines. And she has discovered abroad that the best technique of managing them keeps always a reserve of power, and that mystery which suggests untold possibilities is more successful than frankness which knows nothing worth revealing. So she puzzles the boyfriend by leading him away from headlong petting par-ties into the ancient devious ways of courtship.³⁷

We have encountered this rhetoric before—in the writing of Dorothy Bromley, who like Adams rejected old-style feminism, and in that of Lillian Symes, who like Adams deplored the flapper. For the old-style feminist and the flapper Adams sub-stituted an accentuated model of femininity that would reclarify the masculine and the feminine. Somewhat cynical about men, her Siren possessed hidden powers (instead of direct and hence masculinized power). Covert manipulation, substituted for bold confrontation, would dispel men's fear of women as a threat while still making men need, and even serve, women.[38]

Adams's article helps to clarify aspects of the Marsh girl. Adams proposed that a woman use charm to maintain a mysterious tension between desirability and inaccessibility. In this way she could achieve power over men. Deviously withholding her feelings, she could nonetheless make men reveal theirs. She became desirable by "delighting" men rather than by demanding amusement and by suggesting rather than explaining. So too the Marsh girl. Pictorially, she is powerful and dangerous, desirable yet unattainable—qualities suggested in *In Fourteenth Street* (Figs. 3.19 and 5.1; Plate 3). Glamorized like a screen Siren, more lovely by far than other members of the Fourteenth Street crowd, she becomes an object of desire, a visual commodity. At the same time, she is isolated pictorially from those around her. She occupies larger pockets of space and wears brighter colors than other figures in the gray-brown swirling mass. Such isolation and exaggeration make her fearful and inaccessible; her lack of emotion and individuality make her seem even more aloof. Here and throughout his work, moreover, Marsh places her in proximity to emotionally or physically crippled men; the baby-doll blonde and the crippled beggar move past one another in opposing directions. In Bowery images, the Siren strides purposefully past helpless drunks. At dance marathons, she frequently supports exhausted men. At the burlesque or looking down from Fourteenth Street windows (Figs. 3.24 and 3.26), she expands to take over pictorial space, towering above her helpless admirers or separated from them by window glass (Fig. 5.5).[39] Desire becomes a form of weakness for men who fall prey to this sexually dangerous working-class version of the Siren.

Although Adams's celebration of Siren behavior suggests that women were equal, free to choose their roles, and armed with power over men, the underlying ideology signaled the same delineation of gendered activity and natural capabilities that lay behind the concept of the professionalized homemaker. Whatever power she might claim—the Siren, from her "charm," and the professionalized homemaker, from her managerial status in the family—the middle-class woman for whom Adams and others wrote in the late 1920s and 1930s were encouraged to trade independence and equality for economic security.[40] According to Adams, the Siren's business was to be a Siren. She performed the important social service of being an attractive diversion, particularly in the Depression. Her behavior, Adams argued, was "one of those things for which a grimy and hard-working world is always grateful."[41]

The Siren, like the professionalized homemaker, appealed to both sexes. For men, she was an object of sexual fantasy. For women, she offered an escape from inadequate working conditions and poor job opportunities. No one suggested that the Siren engage in wage labor—though Adams's frequent references to "ancient" wisdom and devious ways of courtship allude not only to the mythical Siren's seductive powers but also to an older profession. No one suggested that lower-class women who needed to work were subject to the same "grimy" conditions of the modern world as men. Rhetorical claims to power and status notwithstanding, both Siren and professional homemaker stereotypes deferred to traditional ideologies where womanly nurture and self-sacrifice were ultimately of highest value. The great paradox of the Siren's claim to power was the resultant loss of power. Like all women she remained in the position of the other; she put male needs ahead of her own to gain economic *dependence*, and in so doing became an object to be consumed.

The anti-feminist ideology underlying Adams's *New York Times* piece, whose readership would have been middle- to upper-middle class, was disseminated to working-class women like those in Marsh's paintings through institutions of mass culture—movies and the beauty advertisements featured in tabloids, the popular confessional magazine *True Story,* and cheap film magazines like *Modern Screen,* a glance at which reveals that by 1933 the Siren's domestic habits, loves, and fashions were well established "norms," much preferred to those of the flapper.

The Siren's domesticity came to the forefront as movie stars married and had children. The title of a December 1933 article announced, "Divorces Take a Back Seat As a Fierce Marriage Epidemic Sweeps Hollywood." The article, which described Hollywood as a new matrimonial center, recorded Ginger Rogers's ambition to "make a million dollars, then marry and have at least 5 children."[42] Six months earlier, Universal Studios had billed Gloria Stuart as the "All-American Girl, married to a nice young Sculptor." While Siren stars like Stuart occasionally combined marriage and career, more often movie stars retired as they had children and made a home. Furthermore, for successful stars, retirement with the birth of the first child presented no financial hardship.[43]

"Glamour," the external and visible manifestation of the Siren's "charm," also had a domestic component. In April 1933, *Modern Screen* introduced a new feature column entitled Glamour—Hollywood's and Yours. Promising the "very latest"— the most "authentic" news about fashion, beauty, and the home, the monthly feature displayed Mary Pickford's spectacular mansion Pickfair as every woman's dream home and offered a "modern hostess department" to show the reader that "glamour had its practical [i.e., domestic] side." A regular part of this new feature, Hollywood Charm Gossip, brought "fascinating chatter" about the stars' wardrobes, homes, parties, and beauty secrets and even offered dress patterns so that readers could duplicate stars' wardrobes for themselves. The new column concluded, "If you're interested in your appearance, your clothes, your health, your home and your happiness—and what woman isn't, you can't afford to be without this every month."[44]

In *Modern Screen*'s features, everything glamorous reinforced a domestic rather than a working life for women, and the "models" for fashion and lifestyle were always actresses whose wealth exceeded that of all but a small fraction of *Modern Screen* readers.[45] In a painting called *Sentimental Girl* (1933; Fig. 5.12), Raphael Soyer represented a rather plain and slightly overweight young woman, clad only in a skirt and chemise, sitting on the edge of a cot in a drab interior, musing over the contents of the *True Story* magazine she holds in her lap. Her wistful hopes, reflected in part by the warm luminosity that suffuses the painting, are fed by the myths of the magazine. Such dreams in the middle of the Depression were one of the few avenues of escape for working-class women.

As *Modern Screen* offered Hollywood Sirens as models of behavior, Hollywood films of the late 1920s and early 1930s presented the Siren in several formulaic situations. Commonly, the Siren used her sexuality to obtain men's attention and love, often "sacrificing" herself for a gangster or a ne'er-do-well, the implication being that she had no marketable skills, nothing to sell but her body.[46] The Siren might also be a young woman who used her allure to capture a millionaire, as Mildred Adams recommended in her article on the Siren. In the immensely popular *Gold Diggers* films of 1929, 1933, 1935, and 1937; in *Dinner at Eight* (1933) with the archetypal Siren Jean Harlow in the leading role (Fig. 4.7); and in Anita Loos's screenplays *Gentlemen Prefer Blondes* (1928), *Red-Headed Woman* (1932), *Hold Your Man* (1933), and *Social Register* (1934) the Siren became, as one author has observed, the female version of Horatio Alger—her goal being to win the man so that she could continue the business of being a Siren.[47] The film historian Andrew Bergman summarized the situation of the Siren in 1930s films: "Each picture made evident the fact that no woman could perform work functions not directly related to sex. Once any fatal misstep occurred, complete ruin was certain, until a purification was effected which involved a virtual ceding of one's individuality for the love of a male."[48]

A number of films characterized the Siren as a powerful or successful woman, a nod to her new social status following enfranchisement. Erica Doss, in her essay on Marsh's *Paramount Pictures*, suggests that many of these women were portrayed as flawed or evil (in these qualities the women resembled both the mythical Siren and the woman criticized in turn-of-the-century anti–new woman rhetoric). In Cecil B. deMille's popular historical epics, a scheming woman like Claudette Colbert's Cleopatra was punished for her destructive sexuality. Other assertive Sirens of the 1930s were portrayed as somehow problematic or "disobedient" characters: Bette Davis in *Of Human Bondage* (1934), Barbara Stanwyck in *Baby Face* (1932), and Katharine Hepburn in *Christopher Strong* either capitulated to a male pursuer, repented their wrongdoing, or were punished for their misdeeds. Sirens as working woman held glamorous jobs, which they frequently relinquished for men.[49]

5.12 Raphael Soyer, *Sentimental Girl*, 1933. Oil on canvas, 36″ × 34″.
Collection of Bella and Sol Fishko.

The historian Lois Banner views the Siren somewhat differently—not as disobedient but as assertive and self-confident. She observes that in the 1930s women
appear in higher-status jobs in movies; though women in these roles marry less
frequently, when they do, they give up their jobs. These Sirens—even Jean Harlow,

who is extremely sensual—are also tough and wisecracking, their makeup, enlarging mouths and eyes, being further evidence of their defiance. Banner acknowledges that part of the Siren's allure was America's need for escape, but she also argues that the Siren was a strong woman in the chaotic 1930s.[50] Using Banner's interpretation of the Siren, we can argue that the exaggerated sexuality, mystery, and lurid makeup of Marsh's figures also functions to destabilize a Depression era discourse on the revised new woman as a nurturing, quiet, and stable domestic figure who would not threaten males with unemployment by seeking her own career.

Like screen magazine writers and filmmakers, advertisers, in marketing beauty and fashion items, played on women's sometimes professed, sometimes culturally orchestrated desire for men's love and protection. They used Freudian psychology to manipulate women's anxieties about their appearance as central to their ability to please men.[51] Their advertisements reflected the ideology of consumer culture in suggesting that the purchase of material goods was an expression of personality and spiritual values. For these advertisers the Siren supported the claim that beauty, allure, and mystery—what made women attractive to men—could be purchased. Advertisers, besides making women anxious, suggested that they had power over what they consumed and how they presented themselves—power that enabled them to make choices that would achieve their goals.

An advertisement for Irresistible perfume (Fig. 5.13) in *Modern Screen* depicted a close-up of a bare-shouldered blonde, her head seductively thrown back like Jean Harlow's in a movie photograph. Using the same terminology Mildred Adams had used, it identified charm and allure as essential to winning a man's love:

> The smart Parisienne has long practiced the subtle art of the correct use of perfume. She chooses her perfume for its effect, for its ability to make her truly irresistible. But no longer need you envy her choice, for now with Irresistible perfume, you can give yourself that indefinable charm, that unforgettable allure that has attracted men the world over. . . . One trial will convince you that it has the magic power to make you, too, more irresistible.[52]

Blue Waltz beauty products, also advertised in *Modern Screen*, used similar strategies in their copy. But instead of a close-up of a movie Siren, this advertisement shows a miniature tableau of upper-class life: a man in a tuxedo escorts an elegant woman to a dance. The caption reads: "To be beautiful and alluring is yours and every other girl's most treasured dream. Such beauty would mean popularity, romance, love! And, though it may seem beyond belief, it is not beyond possession. Beauty is not always a gift of the gods. It is more often the result of correct make-up."[53]

Advertising in the 1920s and 1930s promised a new life through correct consumption. In doing so, it frequently co-opted rhetoric signaling women's modernity and attached product claims to women's new political and social freedoms. Here,

Irresistible

Yes— and you, too, can be as
glamorous as a
Parisienne!

5.13   Advertisement for Irresistible
perfume, *Modern Screen*
(September 1933), p. 89.

though, the tactic remains indirect; women can choose the best perfume just as they could choose a candidate or a career. The "vote" was often compared implicitly with women's choice of product and their "right to a certain fashion or look. This strategy, hardly new, altered dramatically in the post-franchise era. To sell cosmetics before the First World War, advertisers employed a feminist vocabulary to suggest women use cosmetics to achieve greater self-respect. In the Progressive Era many feminists and social scientists believed that woman's spiritual side rather than her physical appearance made her beautiful: beauty was available to anyone who followed the "proper ethical path." In an era preoccupied with personal spiritual development along with political and social reform, experts advocated this natural approach to beauty, stressing proper diet and exercise over the use of cosmetics. This view of the natural woman also reflected the long-standing belief that woman's distinctive moral superiority was part of her separate sphere of influence. Pre–World War I feminists adopted this idea of women's special contributions to American moral and spiritual life as their strategy to gain access to public life and to win the vote.[54] Advertisers marketed cosmetics in pale colors to enhance women's natural beauty, capitalizing on a popular theme to sell products rather than working with any altruistic desire to back a feminist cause.

With postwar sexual and social liberation, however, the idea of woman's moral superiority fell by the wayside and, with it, the identification of beauty with the natural or spiritual woman. Two things remained: first, the idea that beauty was a natural right of all women and, second, a new commercial beauty culture. The mass production of cosmetics—dozens of creams, salves, bright lip and nail colors, and hair-care products—and an astonishing proliferation of beauty parlors created a new and widespread beauty culture in the 1920s.[55] Since women were no longer considered morally and spiritually superior, appearance superseded spirituality as a desideratum: beauty products alone could change any woman's appearance and, with it, her life. With this strategy advertisers forged an inseparable bond between the beauty branch of consumer culture, woman's evolving self-image, and a new ideal of womanhood.

In analyzing these changes in beauty culture, the historian Lois Banner recognizes that the pre–World War I feminist argument for woman's moral superiority was a way to maintain the differences between men and women. In this sense the separate and superior position was ultimately counterproductive in the quest for equality. But Banner also perceives that the argument for moral superiority had a positive side. Though the natural and ethical notion of beauty was as much a social construct as the commercial one that succeeded it, Banner concludes that it nonetheless "raised an important barrier to the commercial exploitation of women in the idea of physical appearance. With its demise, the modern commercial culture of beauty scored a significant triumph."[56]

In this context Marsh's Siren, the powerful 1930s stereotype, becomes a textbook demonstration of the triumph of the commercial beauty culture and its ideology and the concomitant loss of feminist values. Her ruby lips, painted nails, bleached hair, and heavily shadowed eyes and her charm and allure all take precedence over the self-respect, individuality, and independence that early feminists had sought to promote.

Behind the visual and verbal strategies in many of these advertisements lie advertisers' often biased and ambivalent conception of a mass audience. In his extensive study of advertising in the 1920s and 1930s, Roland Marchand writes about the missionary zeal with which an elite corps of male advertisers planned to market modernity and bring a culturally enriched life to their audience and their growing dismay at the "vulgar and depraved" audience of common folk, hungry for tabloids, true confessions, and escapist movies.[57] On the one hand, advertising's copywriters and artists learned from their audience; they recognized that movies often provided romance, adventure, or escape from what they assumed to be mundane lives. And they appropriated from popular culture such strategies as tabloid layout or the close-up (which, when used in an advertisement, could capitalize on the attractive features of an everyday object or demand self-scrutiny on the part of the viewer— the ad for Irresistible perfume is an example of both techniques, visual and verbal).

On the other hand, advertising men were often put off by what they perceived as a socially inferior audience. Though advertisers seldom made sharply drawn class distinctions, they nonetheless viewed their mass audience as culturally debased and intellectually inferior.[58]

For advertisers, women were the most important members of an audience they eventually divided into "class" (meaning the upper class) and "mass" (a *Saturday Evening Post* readership that blurred upward toward the corporate executive and downward toward the shopgirl, while excluding the lower third of the population as "economically unqualified"). As countless surveys demonstrated, women were the major purchasers. In the increasingly problematic and competitive market of the Depression, advertisers reached a consensus that consumers were to be swayed by emotion, not reason. And with that observation they produced a discourse on the feminine based on a series of gendered oppositions that made women the target of specific marketing strategies. Since women were characterized by "inarticulate longings" rather than rational needs, advertisements had to portray idealized tableaux, and advertising copy had to be intimate, glamorous, and colorful to alleviate the boredom of women's lives. Advertisements, according to one *Printer's Ink* contributor, must be "the magical carpets on which they may ride out to love," so that they may "daily see themselves as *femme fatales* [*sic*], as Cleopatra or Helen of Troy." Even though women's magazines showed women leading active and productive lives, advertisers stereotyped their audience as female moviegoers and *True Story* readers; frequently their depiction of women differed from their conception of their female audience. For advertisers, the feminine mass consumer was "capricious, irrational, passive and conformist," whereas they themselves were rational, productive, and creative (male) individuals.[59]

Marsh's paintings of working-class women shoppers develop this theme depicting the female shopper as a glamorous, de-individualized icon among a mass of fellow consumers. Furthermore, densely cluttered settings, like those in *Show Window* (Fig. 5.2; Plate 4) or *In Fourteenth Street* (Fig. 3.19; Plate 3) exemplify the proliferation of detail that characterized advertisements by the early 1930s—a style called tabloid technique. In desperate straits as businesses folded, advertising agencies competed for clients by adopting a Depression era rhetoric. Needing to squeeze money out of increasingly cautious consumers, they shifted from an opulent, art deco style to one that was less dignified and more direct and featured cruder layouts. As Marchand points out, for the "hard sell" advertisers adopted a different, more working-class, style of masculinity, engaging in "shirt-sleeve" advertising. "Such images of working-class exertion and vitality seemed to provide catharsis for the hard-pressed, white-collar professionals of the advertising trade, struggling to regain a sense of potency."[60]

I want to suggest that Marsh, in his Fourteenth Street paintings, provides one segment of *his* audience—white male advertisers with privileged backgrounds, like his patron William Benton—with *its* conception of its "tabloid" audience, including the demeaning image of "women [who] don't like to think too much when buy-ing."[61] Paintings of stereotyped women dressed in lurid colors and flaunting their sexual wares, as in *Ten Cents a Dance* (Fig. 3.25), used purchased goods to mimic Siren-style desirability. Women fashioning themselves after mannequins, like the stocky Fourteenth Street girl before a cluttered window in *Hat Display* (Fig. 5.4) or her elegant, slender upper-class counterpart in *Fifth Avenue No. 1* (1938; Fig. 5.14), would have reinforced the advertising man's belief in all women's capricious-ness and conformity. At the same time, such paintings, especially of working-class women, would have made an upper-class female viewer uncomfortable insofar as they caricatured her own chic self-image. For the most part, as one anonymous art critic stated, Marsh was "not a lady's painter."[62] Because of the extremes of sexual display, when Marsh's paintings are read in the context of the advertisers' discourse, some of them become cruel parodies, locker-room jokes like those the advertising men exchanged in the hidden arena of their in-house journals.[63]

Male art critics frequently participated in this talk about the Marsh girl. Thomas Craven's comment in the epigraph to this chapter reduces them to decorative con-sumers of pleasure. Adolph Dehn, a cartoonist and one of Marsh's close friends, spoke of "lots of attraction to the gaudy meaty girls of Fourteenth Street."[64] His equation of women with meat may not have been so far from the mark; in *Hat Display* (Fig. 5.4) a sign for grilled country sausage at twenty-five cents is posted next to one of Marsh's most full-bodied and seductively twisting women. Marsh often used signage, newspaper headlines, and notices in similarly punning ways, as in his 1940 painting *Dead Man's Curve* or *Dangerous Curves* (Fig. 3.3). Marsh too recognized the effects of his work:

> Maybe my pictures have too much shock in them for a lot of people—especially women—to hang on the walls at home. Not really shocking, just a kind of not-too-pleasant reminder of what they have shut out when they go home. . . . They don't want to be reminded in their living rooms and bedrooms of the people they see—or don't see—walking on the streets of New York. Makes them feel uncomfortable.[65]

However the Marsh girl may have been read in the advertising discourse, his-torically the Siren on which her image was based functioned as a Depression era stereotype. Her look and persona flourished in a climate of social and economic despair, and her enormous popularity suggests that she satisfied deeply felt cultural needs.[66] Beautifully groomed, expensively gowned, and elegantly coiffed, the Siren provided an illusion of wealth where none existed and thereby allowed the viewer to escape from economic deprivation into an image of plenty. Charming, alluring, and desirous of being kept, the Siren was more economically dependent than the flapper, whose bold, standoffish posture and mannish appearance were perceived as strident and assertive.

5.14 Reginald Marsh, *Fifth Avenue No. 1*, 1938. Tempera, 30″ × 24″. Present location unknown.

Depending on how the Siren was perceived, she might be a threat or a comfort. Marsh's working-class version might raise the specter of male anxiety about the sexual revolution. There is a simultaneous warning and allure in the forthright, aggressive sexuality of works like *Ten Cents a Dance* and *Hudson Bay Fur Company* (Figs. 3.25 and 3.26), where sexuality is also "at work." Here the Siren uses garish makeup and tight clothes as defiant challenges to the traditional complementary relationship between female passivity and male power. If she was a sexual threat, however, the Siren was not an economic threat to men who had lost their jobs; she could flatter and nurture male egos understandably damaged by the Depression era economy, no matter what their class position. With the onset of the Depression, women were pressured to remain at home and avoid taking jobs from male heads of households, and the question of working wives eventually developed into a nationwide controversy. A refeminized beauty who gave comfort and pleasure in exchange for economic subservience might allay cultural anxieties and perpetuate ongoing cultural myths about idealized womanhood—now in a less "sacred," more sexualized form. The Siren's overt sexuality, her striking femininity, moreover, reclarified sex roles that had begun to blur in the 1920s with the masculinized flapper image and the increase of women in the work force.[67] Though a different image, the Siren satisfied some of the same cultural needs as the professionalized homemaker.

This homemaker's image developed as early as 1921, out of prosperity and a postwar desire for "normalcy." Nurturing and homebound, she was also stable and businesslike—less frivolous, less exaggeratedly sexual, mysterious, and provocative than the Siren. The emergence of the Siren in the late 1920s signaled not only a redefinition of woman's sexual role but also her loss of control over her body and her life as she was made (at least in films) a compelling object of consumption. The only nod to liberation was in the presentation of her power, which derived from her sexuality. Where the professionalized homemaker could manage the household, the Siren merely decorated it with her body.

The Siren stereotype was a product of discourses *of* consumer culture in the interwar period—specifically of advertising and the movies. But she was also the subject of sometimes critical discourses *on* consumer culture. Sociologists and psychologists in the 1930s and, more recently, historians have focused on the Siren as a behavioral model—a vehicle of socialization for the young working-class immigrant women who shopped on Fourteenth Street. They have argued that Siren-style behavior altered values or was seen by these women as a desirable means by which to achieve a better lifestyle.[68]

Having argued that Marsh's paintings fashioned both a sexually charged and commercially motivated version of the revised new woman and a degrading image of working-class womanhood like that described by advertising's elite, I want to add a third category to the multivalent construction of gender that appears in these works. As I suggested in Chapters 2 and 3, Marsh's images of the neighborhood also engage the more socially concerned forms of urban realism in the 1930s, addressing, as a consequence, a more liberal audience. Read from this angle, the paintings reveal an ironic ambivalence—perhaps the oscillation between disdain and dismay—toward consumer culture as a process of socialization and toward those, like the voluptuous shopper, who are manipulated by it. Through stylistic and iconographic devices, the paintings reveal tension and anxiety produced in a population that adopted values and patterns of behavior from myths like those underlying the Siren stereotype.

In several of his Fourteenth Street paintings, Marsh placed his voluptuous shoppers in a pictorial context that suggests his awareness of tensions in consumer culture. In *Show Window* (Fig. 5.2; Plate 4) the viewer looks through a display window filled with Siren-style mannequins at two window-shoppers looking over the cluttered array of goods. The real shoppers mirror the look of the mannequins and seem as passive and unreal as their lifeless counterparts. This similarity—the lack of textural differentiation—and the absence of a strong dramatic focus blur distinctions between real and fabricated womanhood. All the objects—the real women, mannequins, purses, hats, and scarves—line up parallel and close to the picture plane. All are treated with the same loose sketchy brushwork, a combination of the nervous flickering patches of chiaroscuro that define the forms, and Marsh's agitated strokes, drawn in and actually hovering above the solid forms they define. Surfaces are further unified by Marsh's limited palette, primarily grays, pale blues, rusts, and browns. Together the painting techniques and the packed, unfocused composition make a tightly woven surface matrix of objects and shapes. Within the overwhelming plethora of goods and surface detail, it becomes difficult to disengage one object from another, or the real women from the pretend.

The real women shoppers, moreover, are virtually out of the picture, compositionally relegated to the lower right hand corner of the image. Gazing upward, they defer to the mannequin, who beckons seductively to them from her commanding position. Even in their own Siren-style beauty, which the picture accentuates, the real women have succumbed to an advertised stereotype. Their reduction to sexual commodities is manifest in the fragmentation of mannequins into various body parts and the placement of a price tag over a mannequin's genitalia. Sex is for sale at the center of the picture. Given Marsh's treatment of these women of Fourteenth Street as powerless in the face of the institutions of consumer culture, it is no wonder that Marsh's close friend Laning characterized the 1930s Marsh girl as "an automaton—a tremendous fantasy."[69]

The powerlessness of the voluptuous shopper and her fellow consumers is revealed more directly in Marsh's *In Fourteenth Street* (Fig. 3.19; Plate 3) through the link with Michelangelo's *Last Judgment* (Fig. 3.28). I have argued that the central hawker, whose pose inverts that of the judging Christ, tempts the unwary consumer with fraudulent goods. The pose of the still Siren in the blue dress, though she is above rather than beside the hawker, similarly resembles that of the Virgin in *The Last Judgment*. The Virgin assumes a twisted, self-protective pose; Marsh's mysterious Garbo-like figure, withdrawn into herself, casts her eyes to the right. Like the Virgin who cannot overrule the judgments of her son, the Siren-shopper is powerless to control the chaos around her; and her appearance suggests that she too has succumbed to the temptations of the latest Siren fashions.

Other beautiful women in the painting stand out as angelic figures. A blond woman wears a heart-shaped sign that can be read as angel wings, inscribed with advertisements for beauty bargains. While she offers a bit of heaven to the eager seeker after beauty, she is also a fallen angel, burdened by her task. The most prominent voluptuous shopper, under the ladder, seems initially to stand out as a lone figure of redemption (Fig. 5.1). Fitted with a modern halo and angel's wings, she floats among the mass of urban types who spill down and away from her and lands daintily on one pointed toe.[70] An isolated beauty, she promises salvation or at least the illusion of escape from the urban hell of lost souls swirling about her.

Though isolated pictorially to suggest her redemptive function, Marsh's Siren remains essentially powerless. Modeled on real Fourteenth Street women, she is represented as acting out the Siren's part. Marsh's characterization of her as a working-class version of the Siren stereotype makes this clear. And, though momentarily isolated as an angel under the ladder, as a Siren she can only be a fallen angel. She strides toward the picture's center, to join the other lost souls of Fourteenth Street in the confusion of the neighborhood's consumer hell. (Given her resemblance to Mae West, she may be a pun on the title of the Mae West movie Marsh had seen, *I'm No Angel*.)

Like the Siren, the souls in the crowd have lost their individuality. Marsh reduced them to urban and ethnic stereotypes, a strategy of simplification often used in advertising to short-circuit the buyer's reasoning process.[71] In their coarseness, many are like caricatures who contrast strongly with the beautiful isolated Sirens. Plump dark-haired women shoppers can be identified as Lower East Side immigrants from eastern Europe or the Mediterranean. They mingle with blacks, and to judge from costume, the occasional eager tourist, like the light-haired young man in a short-sleeved shirt and spectacles to the right of the crowd. The only identifiable individual is Kenneth Hayes Miller, whose studio was but a block away and whose presence localizes the neighborhood. He is passing behind the hawker, the self-absorbed artist-intellectual, oblivious to tawdry seduction.

Through the act of consumption, the figures in the painting and the Siren have come to resemble stereotypes in advertisements. Furthermore, virtually none of the figures interact; instead they focus on goods or activities. Consumption has replaced human interaction as authentic experience, and figures like the voluptuous shopper lose their free will, autonomy, and selfhood to the mass activity of consumption.

Indeed the parallels to *The Last Judgment* suggest the substitution of consumption for religion discussed by Jackson Lears.[72]

In a crowd scene like *In Fourteenth Street* Marsh takes the position of a distant observer looking down. In other works he gets closer to his subjects and through subtle arrangements of figures and body language reveals some of the covert meanings of the Siren image. *Women on Fourteenth Street* (Fig. 5.3) demonstrates the ironic gap between the Siren myth and Depression era reality for the average woman shopper on Fourteenth Street. The two shoppers, one in front of the other, stand so close that the figure in front and to the left seems to emerge from the figure in back and to the right. With their left arms in similar poses and their right arms concealed, they become pictorial complements or alter egos of a single women: one is self-assured, overtly seductive, and fashionable with directed gaze, feet firmly planted; and the other stands hesitant, tentatively balanced on one foot, arms self-protectively close to her body, guarding her purchases. This woman gazes absent-mindedly down at the pavement, neither pursuing the local bargain with the enthusiasm of a third woman, who bends over to read the sign, nor connecting herself to the world like her companion. She is also less chic. Her ill-fitting rumpled coat masks sexuality as much as the snug suit of the blond reveals it.

Pictorially enmeshed with the archetypal Siren behind her, the foreground shopper neither fully shares nor fully extricates herself from that model, at once a mythical and real support. The contrast between the two women foregrounds a question continually raised by advertisers: did they exercise power over consumers or derive power from them? Were women passive or in control?

Even as this picture blurs the distinctions between the condition of the Fourteenth Street shopper and the cultural fantasy, it points out the gap between them. Marsh's awareness of this tension-producing gap and his desire to explore its implications become evident in other works of the early 1930s. In *Twenty Cent Movie* (1936; Fig. 5.15), for example, young Sirens wait outside a theater boldly advertising sensationalist films. Both they and the men—a hip young black man and a Jimmy Cagney type—are so much like the film stereotypes they emulate that we feel transported into a film. In this painting (Marsh sketched the marquee advertisements from life, adding figures later) fact and fiction entwine inextricably.[73]

Twenty Cent Movie has an ironic historical context. The title refers to the closure, despite generally high attendance, of movie theaters during the Depression and the resulting drop in admission prices from thirty to twenty cents. Hollywood producers offered increased sensationalism, melodramatic romance, and more titillating sex to lure patrons to the theater. In response, censorship forces, headed by Catholic clergymen, whose concerns were buttressed by new sociological and psychological reports on the powerful effects of movies on conduct, rallied to make Hollywood adopt self-censorship, beginning in 1934. The only new guideline was that story lines distinguish more clearly between good and evil characters and sit-

5.15　Reginald Marsh, *Twenty Cent Movie*, 1936. Egg tempera on composition board, 30″ × 40″. Collection of Whitney Museum of American Art.

uations. Such a generalized and virtually unenforceable requirement indicated a recognition by producers and censors that sex and crime pictures were necessary to box office survival.[74] In light of this less than clear-cut censorship strategy, Marsh's 1936 image suggests the survival and popularity of cheap sensationalist films and, more important, their effectiveness in promoting social stereotypes and inculcating their values.

In *Paramount Pictures* (1934; Fig. 5.16), as in *Show Window* and *In Fourteenth Street*, Marsh continued to explore the gap between Siren myth and Depression era conditions and to suggest the way alluring mass-cultural stereotypes exploited female consumers. In this picture, a young woman stands directly in front of a movie marquee, her image emerging from the breasts of a larger-than-life poster image of Claudette Colbert as Cleopatra. Where two "actual" women in *Women on Fourteenth Street* (Fig. 5.3) were pictorial complements or alter egos, here the "actual" woman's image is compositionally enmeshed in an advertisement. Her own appearance depends on the glamorous fantasy depicted in the poster. In facial

5.16 Reginald Marsh, *Paramount Pictures*, 1934. Tempera on panel, 36″ × 30″. Marjorie and Charles Benton Collection.

features, makeup, and hairstyle the two women clearly resemble each other, so that reality and fantasy, moviegoer and movie Siren merge. At the same time, they remain distinct. Colbert is the archetypal Siren, before whose alluring and all-knowing gaze an adoring Antony melts. The real woman, however, waits alone. Her tired red eyes, perhaps the result of too long a working day, show that the fantasy she purchased has failed to fulfill its promise.[75] Mildred Adams's optimistic statements notwithstanding, she is far from free to go about the business of being a Siren.

Marsh's iconography combines film and fashion stereotypes and documentary elements with material from old master paintings; his style similarly takes devices from film and popular illustration and combines them with drawing, shading, and coloristic techniques that blur the stylistic boundaries between high art and the rough sketchy graphics and crayon drawings associated since the teens with a socially engaged "people's art." Marsh's sketchiness in these tempera paintings, however, differs markedly from that of the earlier *Masses* crayon drawings and from his own later crayon drawings for the *New Masses* (Figs. 3.30 and 3.36)—in part because these works address different audiences. Tempera is precious and fast drying; it allows little room for error and is thus often connected with ideals of careful craftsmanship. Moreover, it cannot be manipulated or "attacked" like either oil paint (as used by Sloan and other Ashcan painters) or crayon. Although Marsh uses the medium with facility, he applies tempera in a looser, more fluid, more rapid—in short, more "sketchy"—manner than is customarily associated with either the meticulous old master works of the thirteenth and fourteenth centuries or with the group of artists who revived the medium in the 1930s, among them Paul Cadmus, Thomas Hart Benton (who gave Marsh his tempera recipe), or Kenneth Hayes Miller and Isabel Bishop.[76]

By using a precious and craft-oriented technique of high art in a freer manner to portray his lower-class subjects, Marsh satisfied his own concern to address an audience with a broader point of view. Through his complicated stylistic and iconographic strategies, associated with the competing discourses on new womanhood, on advertisings' attitudes toward mass culture, and on a socially concerned urban realism, Marsh's paintings do much more than simply document Fourteenth Street life; they reveal how the Siren was created, how real women were socialized into Sirens, and how they were exploited by consumer culture. On the one hand, the paintings glorified Siren sexuality and thus shared the anti-feminist ideology of Mildred Adams and like-minded journalists. On the other hand, the pictures showed how media images in the Depression era entrapped women.

The paintings' multi-level exploration of the voluptuous shopper in a new consumer culture may be read, as I have suggested, as part of a larger attempt to comprehend how mass culture was altering modern behavior. If Marsh read a mass audience as vulgar and feminized, as advertisers read it, he also understood the *problematic* effects of the consumer culture as contemporary social scientists, psychologists, and consumer advocates understood it in the 1930s as they studied and analyzed how advertising and film were changing patterns of behavior and creating new values. Some of these researchers, for example, examined effects of movies on conduct as revealed in fan mail written by women and in psychological interviews.[77] Others debated the value of mass culture as a vehicle for assimilating the new urban immigrant population to American ways.[78] Still others studied individual and crowd behavior, wondering if individual consumers could evaluate and control their environment.[79] Although many of these studies were reasonably objective, others advocated a return to older ways and were critical of consumer culture, decrying the loss of individual will or personal autonomy as city dwellers succumbed to advertisements and movie themes promising a fuller life—a better personality and appearance through correct consumption. Some of the findings elucidate further Marsh's analysis of the Siren and consumer culture.

Excerpts from psychologists' studies of movie magazine fan mail and women's accounts of how movies influence conduct substantiate women's widespread adoption of the Siren ideology. A number of fans deliberately aped mannerisms and actions, fashions and lifestyles. One woman wrote, "For teaching me how to be graceful and attractive I would like to hand a well-deserved bouquet to Garbo. One could sit for hours and watch the exquisite grace of her bearing alone."[80] Movies also provided models of etiquette. One female reader decided it was "correct to wear gloves with formal evening gowns after watching Mary Astor do so in the movie *Ladies Love Brutes*."[81] Another suggested that movies were a means to realizing social aspirations, helping her "learn what to wear; how to dress; how a refined home should look into which my clever children could be proud to bring their friends. There is every opportunity in the movies for a keen quick eye to observe the better way of living."[82]

For this viewer films offered lessons in conducting her life and elevating her social status. *Modern Screen* used the lives of stars as models for its readers; here movie fantasy reinforced the magazine story model, so that movies too played a significant part in suggesting values to women.

Movies also showed aspiring Sirens how to manage men. One nineteen-year-old regularly practiced a "look" from the movies on a gentleman friend:

> When I discovered I should like to have this coquettish and coy look which all girls may have, I tried to do it in my room. And surprises! I could imitate Pola Negri's cool or fierce look, Vera Banky's sweet but coquettish attitude. I learned the very way of taking my gentleman friends to and from the door with that wistful smile, until it has become a part of me.[83]

Another nineteen-year-old cited the movies as her source of information on how to act at parties and dances and how to achieve "success" over a competitor.

I decided to try some of the mannerisms I had seen in the movies. I began acting quite reserved, and I memorized half-veiled compliments. I realized my "dates" liked it. I laid the foundation with movie material. Then I began to improvise.

Of course I had a rival in the crowd. Every time she began to receive more attention from the boys than I, I would see a movie and pick up something new with which to regain their interest. I remember one disastrous occasion. She was taking the center of the stage and I was peeved. I could think of nothing to do. Then I remembered the afternoon before I had seen Nazimova smoke a cigarette. . . . I got one, lit it, and had no difficulty whatsoever in handling it quite nonchalantly. The boys were fascinated and the victory was mine.[84]

If this Siren achieved her "victory" by adopting male patterns of behavior, like smoking, an unselfconscious fifteen-year-old reported how she had learned to defer to men in matters of "love" behavior: "When with the opposite sex I am rather quiet and allow them to tell me what to do. When they go to make love, to kiss or hug, I put them off at first, but it always ends in them having their way. I guess I imitated this from the movies because I see it in almost every show that I go to."[85]

In each of these narratives the young woman takes narcissistic pleasure in looking at movies because she identifies with the Siren and makes herself an object of male desire or pleasure even as she fashions her own image. These examples from a large body of firsthand accounts provide evidence that the Siren's look and persona played an integral part in the socialization of young women who attended movies. As an endlessly repeated image, the Siren stereotype became the most pervasive and persuasive exemplar of American womanhood in the early 1930s, even where other widely publicized models existed.[86] And in Marsh's paintings, although she is not the only kind of woman depicted, she is the one who is meant to be noticed.

In virtually all the literature directly or indirectly related to the Siren—journalistic celebrations, advertisements, firsthand accounts, fan mail, and expert studies—the ideology of charm and grace, "what every woman wants," was deeply entrenched. The sociologist Herbert Blumer, for example, observed in the conclusion of his scholarly study of movies that in adolescence the girl "in particular" has increasing "desires for beauty, for sophistication, for grace and ease, for romance, for adventure and for love."[87] Blumer never mentioned what desires emerge for adolescent boys. Moreover, he could not recognize that the desires he assumed were "natural" were those promoted by the very institutions he studied. His assumptions were those of a widely held anti-feminist ideology of the interwar period. What was omitted from his list—self-sufficiency, independence, a good job, a sense of equality, self-respect—was absent as well from the literature and visual imagery surrounding the Siren.

Recent historians are divided in their assessments of the relation between working-class women and consumer culture. Kathy Peiss portrays consumption as one aspect of working-class women's new independence and their exuberant resistance to bourgeois prescriptions for women. Joanne Meyerowitz sees these women as more independent and a source of new images of sexuality and womanhood. As a taxi dancer or a strip-tease store model, for example, the Marsh girl confronts the viewer with sexual assurance. Richard Fox and Jackson Lears see complex patterns of unintentional collaboration between consumers and producers while Stuart and Elizabeth Ewen examine power relationships and are less sanguine about the resistance and agency of women in the face of consumer culture. Along with several 1930s sociologists the Ewens have suggested that the women most affected by films and advertising were precisely those Marsh painted on Fourteenth Street: urban working-class women, some of them newcomers to the city from rural communities, others the first- and second-generation immigrants who lived mostly on the Lower East Side just below Union Square.[88]

Those among them who wished to elevate their social standing came to the Fourteenth Street stores searching for bargain versions of middle- to upper-middle-class fashions and for the glamorous look achieved by the stars. All these goods were advertised in magazines that throughout the 1920s increased their "style conscious" copy. In 1918, for example, fashion advertisements made up 18 percent of all the advertising in *Ladies Home Journal*; by 1930, they made up 30 percent. Thanks to mass production, cheap versions of movie fashions became available no more than a week after their expensive counterparts first appeared uptown at Saks Fifth Avenue.[89] *Modern Screen* made dress patterns of stars' wardrobes available to its readers (Fig. 5.7), and in the early 1930s a nationwide chain store called the Cinema Shop sold copies of stars' gowns from specific movies at moderate prices.[90] Everywhere the culture of consumption forged links with its two principal agencies of socialization, the movies and advertising. The psychologist Malcolm Willey, who studied the film mechanisms that instilled new values, recognized this collusion: "A commercial mechanism has been developed whereby manufacturers and retailers of women's clothing are acquainted in advance with the specific garments worn by popular stars in forthcoming productions, in order to be prepared to meet the demand that invariably follows the release of the picture."[91]

Having created a demand and a role model for young women, through film and advertising, the commercial market met that demand with merchandise that further encouraged young women to become Sirens. In his 1933 study on movies and conduct, Herbert Blumer discussed the particular susceptibility of urban ethnic populations to the socializing effects of movies:

> Where, as in disorganized city areas, the school, the home or the community are most ineffective in providing adolescents with knowledge adequate for the new world into which they are entering, the reliance on motion pictures seems to become distinctly greater. Where the molding of thought and attitude by established institutions is greater, a condition of emotional detachment seems to be formed which renders the individual immune to the appeal of much that is shown in motion pictures.[92]

This susceptibility that turned the average Fourteenth Street shopper into the consumer automaton embodied in Marsh's voluptuous shopper has been documented by Stuart and Elizabeth Ewen in their studies of mass images and the shaping of American consciousness. Their analysis of the twentieth-century immigrant woman's socialization by the movies touches on a phenomenon of Fourteenth Street that began as early as the turn of the century, during the largest wave of immigration.[93] Moviegoing created a strong sense of community:

> Visit a motion picture show on a Saturday night below 14th Street when the house is full and you will soon be convinced of the real hold this new amusement has on its audience. Certain houses have become genuine social centers where neighborhood groups may be found . . . where regulars stroll up and down the aisles between acts and visit friends.[94]

The early silent films, moreover—which were about the immigrant experience—taught immigrants how to become Americans and how to find opportunities for a better life in the New World. These movies thus bridged the gap between immigrants' old and new cultures. At the same time, other agencies of the consumer culture provided "a new visual landscape of possibility."[95] Although many of these visual forms—signs, advertisements, and "gaudy shop windows"—struck the new population as American, in the eyes of native-born middle- to upper-middle-class citizens (Marsh's own class) they were vulgar, distasteful, and even foreign. Natives who had grown up in a city unspoiled by the new visual forms of mass culture remained aloof, resisting and even mistrusting their effects. Immigrants, however, who arrived along with these new forms, accepted them as "beautiful" and their message as "true"; they were thus vulnerable to them as agents of socialization.[96] In accepting these messages, immigrants also accepted consumer values—passively, as in Marsh's depictions of them in the 1920s and 1930s, when consumer culture reached its heyday.

Second-generation immigrant women who came to maturity in the teens and early 1920s and shopped on Fourteenth Street increasingly looked outside their traditional family units for leisure and for guidance on how to behave in the New World. American models of womanhood replaced traditional ones from their native cultures. As immigrant women entered the work force, often as factory workers or low-paid saleswomen, they frequently looked to film stars as models of fashion and behavior.[97] By the early 1920s, as immigration subsided with the passage of restrictive measures by Congress, movies dealt less with immigrant life and presented new female stereotypes in new situations. The Vamp (played by Theda Bara), the Gamin (Mary Pickford), and the Virgin (Lillian Gish) provided models of behavior by which immigrant women could distance themselves from older family traditions. In Cecil B. deMille's extravaganzas featuring the glamorous Siren, the immigrant woman found a model of seduction who could, as the Ewens have argued, rise above her class and economic status through consumption. Movies and advertisements with the Siren thus pointed to new roles for women in general at the same time that they were agents of both urbanization and Americanization.[98]

Debates about the value of mass culture in assimilation and Americanization appeared before the war and continued during the 1920s. Among prominent academics, businessmen, intellectuals, and politicians who worried about the loss of what they perceived to be pure American values, Americanization was essential. Edgar D. Furniss, a social scientist from Yale, Marsh's alma mater, wrote in his 1925 study of labor problems,

> Americanization is the paramount need, not only for the immigrant, but for the very existence of the Republic. Unless the millions of immigrants present and future are made an integral part of the population, understanding our institutions, sharing the standards and ideals of the democracy, the Nation itself is imperiled.[99]

Some Progressive Era social scientists recognized the racist attitudes underlying the immigration restrictions passed in the early 1920s. In 1919 two American social workers satirized the melting pot, recognizing the centrality of consumption in making the immigrant an American:

> Come on all you foreigners, and jump into this magic kettle. . . . Your clothes are ill-fitting and ugly. Your language is barbaric. Of course we do not hold you personally responsible; for you have come from backward and antiquated civilizations, relics of the dark ages. . . . Jump into the cauldron and behold! You emerge new creatures, up to date with new customs, habits, traditions and ideals. Immediately you will become like us; the taint will disappear. Your sacks will be exchanged for the latest Fifth Avenue styles. . . . You will be reborn. In short, you will become full-fledged Americans. The magic process is certain. Your money back if we fail.[100]

In his works Marsh represented the ethnicity of the urban population, focusing on the leisure pastimes of the working class, like going to movies or amusement parks. Many of these pastimes were understood to help first- and second-generation immigrants assimilate to American ways.[101] Marsh's pictures of crowds often combined references to ethnic appearance and practices with more characteristically American behavior, so that his crowd scenes reveal the ongoing existence of—and occasional antagonism between—Old and New World cultural traditions.

In a work like *Coney Island Beach* (Fig. 5.6), for example, some women wear bathing suits and display themselves provocatively in the foreground. Others are clothed more decorously in summer dresses, preserving a sense of Old World modesty. Several women participate in acrobatic stunts, which bring them into close physical contact with men. Other women, however, recoil, their combined expression of modesty and violation borrowed from *The Rape of the Sabine Women*, whose motifs Marsh uses in this and in his other Coney Island beach scenes. Discarded Nestlés and Love Nest candy wrappers lying beside a Hebrew newspaper in the foreground document the immigrants' simultaneous adherence to old cultures and acceptance of American products.

Apart from depicting the culture of consumption as heaven or hell, Marsh's *In Fourteenth Street* (Fig. 3.19; Plate 3) is also a melting pot. Urban blacks, young and old, dark and fair, healthy and helpless retain their ethnicity yet are assimilated to American patterns of behavior through the act of consumption, one of the most self-conscious ways of behaving as an American. Style too becomes a metaphor for assimilation, specifically the artist's all-consuming lively brushwork and tightly packed compositions that hold people together. With rapid strokes, the artist put his figures in motion and created a unified agitated surface pattern. These devices suggest both the assimilation and the deindividualization wrought by consumer culture.

Although the intense furor over assimilation had subsided by the 1930s, the process itself continued, and Marsh and his Fourteenth Street compatriots continued to observe it. Miller and, in their early works, Laning and Bishop homogenized the urban population to suggest that the American standard prevailed. In *In Fourteenth Street*, as in Marsh's other images of the shopper, the voluptuous shopper-as-movie-Siren is fully assimilated, fully Americanized. Whatever her ethnic origins, they have been masked by the accoutrements of the Depression era icon.

But as I suggested earlier, the urban chaos in this work—Marsh's borrowings from Michelangelo's *Last Judgment*—indicates the price to be paid for adopting the appearances and values of consumer culture: the loss of autonomy, selfhood, and identity.[102] This loss of individuality and independence, though related to a historical muting of feminist demands for independence during the 1920s and 1930s, was also, as consumer advocates recognized, the lot of any consumer confronted by movies, tantalizing packaging, and advertising that provided inadequate guidelines for what to buy.[103] Marsh's paintings of working-class new women appear at an important juncture in the battle between advertisers and consumer rights advocates. Advertisers contemptuous of the "feminized" mass audience for its irrationality and poor taste during the Depression increased the sensationalist, hard-sell, hyperbolic style and content of their copy to induce consumers to buy. At the same time, consumer advocates, also noting the irrationality of the consumer—but not contemptuously—hoped to increase consumers' awareness of their rights. By the early 1930s consumer groups reported rapid increases in membership. In August 1931 the magazine *Ballyhoo*, which lampooned the most exaggerated advertisements, became an overnight success both inside and outside the advertising world. By the mid-1930s, as consumer organizations threatened to ask the federal government to regulate advertising and as New Deal proposals began to take shape, advertising trade journals called for greater self-regulation by the industry. In the rhetoric that often characterized advertisers' in-house discussions—what Roland Marchand has dubbed "the formulaic character of a halftime talk"—trade journals accused advertising men of being cowardly, weak-willed, and effeminate. Only the reinvigoration of hard labor, courage, and manliness could bring self-regulation and restore success.[104]

The theme of most consumer guides was the consumer-as-victim, lost in a visually chaotic world.[105] Stuart Chase and J.F. Schlink, for example, opened their popular 1927 book *Your Money's Worth: A Study in the Waste of the Consumer's Dollar* with a caveat: "We are all Alices in a Wonderland of conflicting claims, bright promises, fancy packages, soaring words and almost impenetrable ignorance."[106] Consumer land was a fantasyland. Businesses and advertisers often ignored the consumer's real needs, by either distorting their claims or denying the consumer adequate information. For some consumer advocates, advertising was another form of social control: "Advertising is big business. Advertisers are not philanthropists who are out to make us happy, and secure. They aim to make a profit."[107]

In Marsh's Fourteenth Street pictures there is a tension between the voluptuous shopper's isolation as a powerful urban goddess and her helplessness and loss of individuality. The manipulation was engendered by agencies of consumer culture that, in dictating her appearance, objectified her and denied her any autonomy. Her only "power" came from choosing what to buy and, more broadly, choosing to participate in the consumer culture. The paradox of the consumer who is both victim and decision maker exists in Marsh's crowds, where stereotypes actively seek consumer goods or passively, even helplessly, fall by the wayside. On the periphery of the crowd in *In Fourteenth Street*, for example, a dwarf on crutches and a legless beggar turn away from consumption, which offers no solution to their problems; at the top of the crowd, a frail woman in ragged clothes looks dazedly down; and to the right, Kenneth Hayes Miller remains aloof as he passes by. Besides tension and paradox, there is a stylistic unease in Marsh's work. While there is pleasure in observing the dynamic crowds, compositionally the figures are uncomfortably close. The brushwork and chiaroscuro make a lively surface, but everything in the crowd seems agitated and confusing. Through its iconographic and stylistic mechanisms Marsh's painting simultaneously calls into question advertising's view of its audience and makes a position for the viewer concerned about the working-class consumer in a capitalist society.

Writings on individual and crowd behavior also filled consumer texts. By the mid-1930s a mainstay of social thought was that the "common man" in an urbanized consumer culture could no longer effect responsible social and political change.[108] Though advertisers and social scientists arrived at their conclusions by different arguments and were opposed in their aims, both came to believe consumer behavior had become irrational and impulsive—advertisers pointed to feminized emotionality whereas social scientists blamed advertisers' hold on the consumer population. In his 1931 article for President Hoover's Research Committee on Social Trends, Robert Lynd, co-author with Helen Merrell Lynd of the well-known study *Middletown*, reversed his optimistic belief in the average man's ability to change culture from within.[109] Having observed the power of advertising in which merchandise was a panacea for "job insecurity, social insecurity, monotony, loneliness, or failure to marry," Lynd argued that consumers could no longer be perceived as "rational, soberly constant" individuals. Instead, they were "only partially rational bundles of impulses and habits shaped in response to an unsynchronized environment with resulting tensions."[110] The social scientist Kenneth Haas went even further, seeing the typical bargain crowd as primitive men and women who had lost all powers of reason or critical thought. He suggested that "the crowd mind should be classed with delusions and dreams. . . . They believe whatever the dominant idea of the occasion may be."[111]

Marsh's paintings are thus part of a larger dialogue about individual (both female and male) and group behavior in the 1930s that took place in the social sciences, in advertising, and in the forms of urban realism that address a concern for the "common man." In his paintings, Marsh uncovered a growing consensus that the historian Richard Fox has defined as a central tenet of consumer ideology—that people are irrational and subject to whatever institution gets to them first.[112] His paintings use the very forms and styles of advertisements and movies to show how these two institutions could be instrumental in the gendered construction of the individual—like the voluptuous shopper. As I suggested earlier, Marsh self-consciously trained himself, as he worked for popular publications, to observe changes in culture. From attendance at left-wing forums, he learned how capitalism was criticized. His teacher, Kenneth Hayes Miller, read widely in Freudian psychology and crowd behavior and shared these insights with his students.[113] At several points in the 1930s Marsh underwent analysis himself. His close friendship with William Benton gave him insight into the ways of advertising and the thinking of advertisers—men of his own class and educational background who shared his competitiveness and concern for personal success, both colored by the anxieties of the Depression. Marsh was well schooled in human behavior and strategies in consumer culture but, as I argue in Chapter 2, like many members of his social class, he was anxious about his own place in the world.

What then of Marsh? Have I given him too privileged a view of his culture, his own position, or his female subject? Have I positioned him as a man fearful of both the class and the aggressive sexuality of his female subjects? Have I been too hard on him for an elite and disdainful male voyeurism that reduces lower-class women to unintelligent but sexually enticing commodities? Or have I let him off the hook by charting an alternative—a viewing position held by a socially concerned observer of the systemic inequalities of capitalism—who finds in the disturbing surfaces and apocalyptic iconography no propaganda for social change but, instead, a pessimistic interrogation of commodity culture? Is his ambivalent oscillation between disdain and dismay or, as Laning asserted, between attraction and revulsion toward his subjects, quantifiable? I think not. Some of the energy and chaos in paintings of Fourteenth Street crowds, along with their powerful address to a male spectator, may reflect Marsh's desire to control an environment he found confusing, even unsettling. Sensing the progressive loss of selfhood in consumer culture, Marsh depicted its participants in an exaggerated, almost frantically active search for a new self within that culture.[114]

Marsh's Fourteenth Street pictures can be seen to participate fully in the intellectual and emotional concerns of American culture in the 1920s and 1930s. They embody aspects of the history of women between the wars, the history of consumer culture, and the effect of the movies and advertising as agencies of assimilation and socialization for the working-class constituency that Marsh found in Fourteenth Street, at the dance halls, and at Coney Island.

Marsh's paintings are ambiguous and even contradictory because in them the ideology of a revised new womanhood—"what every woman wants"—intersects with the ideology of consumer culture. Both ideologies proclaimed their adherents' power and autonomy. Following enfranchisement, women were perceived to be so liberated that they could reacquire sexuality, charm, and allure as marks of their power and independence from men. It was widely held that they could control their destiny and ensure success by choosing a marketed look and behavior. The consumer in general was accorded the privilege of an improved lifestyle through correct consumption.

Because the promise of consumer culture and perceptions of the revised new woman were far from givens in the 1930s, both ideologies covertly required passivity and gullibility on the part of the woman consumer. These were needed to maintain capitalism's economic and social hegemony in the shift from a prosperous to an unstable financial climate. The beautiful, sexualized women whom advertisers and filmmakers used to promote the Siren look and persona were objects of consumption rather than equal participants in American life. The Siren as a role model was less threatening to men than a career woman, more effective in contributing to the economy and American society as a consumer. She offered an escape from present reality and the promise of a better life in a society where women would be traditional women, and men would be strong working providers. On Fourteenth Street, Marsh found a population whose receptiveness to anti-feminist myths and consumer ideologies led to their exploitation. Knowing and ambivalent, he watched their comings and goings through Fourteenth Street's consumer culture.

CHAPTER SIX

"THE SWEET, SAD POETRY OF FEMALE LABOR": RAPHAEL SOYER'S WEARY SHOPGIRLS

I was always out. I saw these people. I studied their faces and their gestures,
their habits. And then I made compositions. . . . I watched them come out of
the shop, you know, and they were less fancy, more informal, more casual than
the other girls.

RAPHAEL SOYER on his
Shop Girls, December 27, 1982

There is no time for pleasure in her life, no time for the softer, sweeter, tenderer
things of womanhood. It is a life stripped of humanity, robbed of most that
makes life beautiful, and spent in one ceaseless, perpetual grind—simply *to
live*. . . . There are many among them, who, in spite of the difficulties in the
way of courtship, will become loved wives and mothers, and there are many
who will become prosperous business women, and do a creditable share in the
world's work.

MARY K. MAULE, "What Is a
Shop-Girl's Life?" 1907

In the late 1920s, Raphael Soyer gained critical attention with paintings of sparsely
populated city neighborhoods, family gatherings, and seminude or clothed female
models in intimate studio settings. Because of a high-key palette and the flat,
unmodeled quality of the figures, early works like *Odalisque* (1928; Fig. 6.1) have
a naive, almost decorative, quality. By the mid-1930s, however, the artist had
expanded both his subject matter and his repertoire of "realist" Depression era
conventions; darkening his colors and working in sharply contrasting values, he
made his figures more substantial. His depictions of unemployed men ensured his
reputation as a sympathetic chronicler of the Depression; in his paintings of women

6.1   Raphael Soyer, *Odalisque,* 1928. Oil on canvas, 25^1/$_8$″ × 20^1/$_8$″. Columbus Museum of Art, Columbus, Ohio.

6.2 Raphael Soyer, *Window Shoppers,* 1938. Oil on canvas, 36″ × 24″.
New Jersey State Museum, Trenton.

6.3 Raphael Soyer, *Office Girls,* 1936. Oil on canvas, 26″ × 24″. Collection of
Whitney Museum of American Art.

in the Fourteenth Street neighborhood, he also took up contemporary social issues.

By the mid-1930s, Soyer's casually posed female models began to appear in groups as urban types, placed outdoors in minimally described street settings that often featured store window displays.[1] The female types in *Window Shoppers*, for example (1938; Fig. 6.2 and Plate 5), encompass the multiple roles of the revised

6.4   Raphael Soyer, *Shop Girls*, 1936. Oil on canvas, 30″ × 40″.
Collection of Babette B. Newburger.

new woman; three working women (the one in a suit jacket carrying a briefcase is probably an office worker) survey rows of hats while a more simply clad mother holding her child has turned her back to the viewer to enter the store. In *Office Girls* (1936; Fig. 6.3) working women against a skyscraper backdrop hurry home. In *Lunch Hour* (1936), which Soyer originally called *Fourteenth Street Midinettes* (*midinettes*, literally "little noon girls," refers to young Parisian dressmakers or milliners), the artist showed young milliners mingling with other passersby on their lunch hour. And in *Shop Girls* (Fig. 6.4; Plate 6), the work I consider in this chapter, the artist depicted seven retail salesclerks coming out of a Fourteenth Street shop at the end of the day.

In *Shop Girls* we move, figuratively at least, to the other side of the counter. Without abandoning the realm of consumer capitalism, we turn from the woman consumer to the woman worker, and to a subject also treated by Kenneth Hayes Miller in several paintings of department store saleswomen helping their customers

(Figs. 3.14, 4.25, 4.27, and 6.12). But Soyer's female imagery stands in marked contrast to Miller's and Marsh's. First, Soyer's realism was based on artistic sources, studio practices, and compositional strategies that differed substantially from those of the other artists. Second, with the choice of shopgirls over Miller's department store salesladies, Soyer not only portrayed the typical effects of working life in Fourteenth Street's bargain emporiums and a struggling specialty shops but also addressed the ambiguous, even inconsistent, gender and class conflict of the retail sales profession. By the 1930s the once interchangeable terms *shopgirl* and *saleslady* described women of different social classes and educational backgrounds who worked for different kinds of stores. The shopgirl retained at least part of her turn-of-the-century persona as an unskilled, poorly educated working girl, often from a lower-class immigrant background. By the 1920s, she had lost her status to the newly professionalized saleslady, a "skilled seller" who worked in the fully ration-alized urban department store; by the 1930s she held mainly backstage jobs in department stores, bargain stores, and five and dimes.[2] Even though this feminized occupation was frequently considered either transitional work between school and marriage or even part-time work, store owners and job counselors billed the sales-lady as a new model of feminine achievement. Both working-class females and refined, middle-class, college-educated new women, who increasingly looked on work as a respectable pursuit, accepted these service positions behind the retail display counter.

The pictorial rhetoric of Soyer's shopgirls and Miller's salesladies reinforces distinctions that often remained blurred and relations that remained contradictory throughout the Depression. As Susan Porter Benson has shown in *Counter Cultures*, department store managers, customers, and saleswomen held different, shifting, patterns of expectation about class and gender—about women's roles as workers and consumers. In many stores, working saleswomen formed an informal "clerking sisterhood," an alliance that allowed them substantial flexibility in interpreting a masculine middle-class management's dictates on how and what to sell their female clients. Female customers were perceived variously by the sales staff, depending on the situation: as middle- to upper-middle-class "enemies," female shoppers conspired with managers to keep the socially inferior woman worker in her place, but as female "allies" they worked with saleswomen to close a mutually beneficial sale. Whatever the dynamic, such mobile configurations in saleswomen's work culture alternately enhanced the saleswoman's power and kept her in a socially and economically disadvantaged position.[3]

Soyer's painting foregrounds an escalating (though historically long-standing) tension in the discourse of new womanhood between "femininity" and "labor." This occurs because Soyer, like Marsh—though by different means—operates in multiple registers, constructing gender between intersecting discourses. Because the painting features individualized shopgirls, it explores a class-specific discourse on women and work. From this vantage point, Soyer's image is more fully engaged than works by other Fourteenth Street artists—and more concerned with the social effects of Depression era labor conditions and ideologies related to working-class women. But Soyer's means of attaining this heightened social awareness are subtle and covert rather than direct: his images have no specific work-related setting; the artist retained studio conventions for outdoor pictures; and his paintings evoke an earlier, and by the 1930s romanticized, image of the shopgirl as the long-suffering companion of the artist, a social outcast. By employing these accepted pictorial conventions, Soyer's painting continued to register within the discursive boundaries of American Scene realism rather than social realism. At the same time, however, the painting disrupts the rhetoric of success embodied in the saleslady by interrogating the idealized or glamorized models of womanhood found in works by artists like Miller and Marsh. Because the work addresses the politics of both class and gender within the overlapping discursive fields of urban realism and working-class womanhood, it embodies many of the conflicted social relations and shifting attitudes related to women and work in the Depression.[4]

Shop Girls pictures seven youthful white women emerging from a drab store at the end of a summer day. Their colorful short-sleeved blouses are rumpled, their hair unkempt; one carries a coat, another a hat. Several of the women look especially tired. Dark shadows frame the eyes of the woman with a magazine under her right arm who faces the viewer (Fig. 6.5). Her face is drawn and pinched like that of the woman holding her hat (Fig. 6.6). The woman in the center lowers her head, closes her eyes, and raises a limp hand to her throat in an inward-turning gesture of weariness. Even the women who communicate with unseen figures lack energy and animation. The flattened position of the open hand and the angled position of the arm and tilted head of the woman to the far left suggest that she must make a substantial effort to raise her arm and call to someone outside the picture.

The rudimentary storefront setting itself is cramped and dingy. Soyer painted the window backdrop, like the brown skirt of the figure who faces forward, with random brushstrokes, so that the surface appears unfinished, deliberately rough. He chose a dull palette of brown, rust, and ochre, enlivened by the garish corals, blues, and whites of the shopgirls' patterned blouses, the patterns and paint blotchy or coarse.

Compositionally, there is barely enough room for the figures. They occupy a shallow space parallel to the picture plane. Cut off above the knees, their figures fill virtually the entire canvas. The setting is minimal (a store window with three mannequins and a pilaster at the store entrance), and as a consequence the women are close to the viewer. This proximity of full-bodied individualized women forces us to experience the sense of crowding. The discomfort is most intense at the left side of the canvas, where four of the women are packed together at the store entrance. Even more important, it forces us to concentrate on these shopgirls as

6.5 Detail of *Shop Girls* (Fig. 6.4).

6.6 Detail of *Shop Girls* (Fig. 6.4).

women. Because they are in transition between environments and are isolated from the locus of any purposeful working, domestic, or leisure activity, these women are meant to be visually available to the viewer.

The melancholy, serious mood of the shopgirls themselves adds to the general dreariness of the environment. Within this somber emotional range, weariness, anxiety, and self-preoccupation are expressed through the use of carefully arranged poses, gestures, and facial expressions. Yet strange and somewhat inconsistent patterns of interaction contribute a feeling of tension or unease to the picture. The women are physically close. The linked arms that extend across the foreground and help to define the left-to-right movement of the figures and the actual painted merging of one form into another imply a camaraderie among the women. These are the sturdy limbs of labor, attached to stocky bodies that signify work rather than femininity. At the center of the picture, two horizontal forearms, their muscles carefully delineated, dictate the group's momentum, framing the vertical arm of the reflective figure at the center of the picture. Yet, for all this structural connection, there is little emotional interaction. Figures remain psychologically isolated, communicating not with one another but with people or events outside the picture. The extent to which these aspects of mood, physical condition, and psychological relationship can be attributed to the effects of work on these women will be demonstrated presently. But the curious disjunction between elements that suggest closeness and those that insist on separation permeates the work.

Adding to this disjunction are the ambiguous transactions that occur between subject and viewer. Most of the women show no awareness of, or response to, an observing presence. As viewers, however, we are physically close to these shopgirls, and two of the women look toward us: the foreground figure turns our contemplation of her back on itself by observing us. Because of the unfocused cast of her eyes (Fig. 6.5), her gaze is quiet and serious rather than demanding or sexually provocative. Indeed, unlike Marsh's paintings of alluring Sirens, this painting does not insistently address a masculine viewer. Soyer's women are portrayed as substantial and relatively unprovocative rather than curvaceously slender and self-consciously seductive. Furthermore, in confronting us, Soyer's central figure gently asserts her individuality and plays several possible roles. Through her gaze and the questioning, tentative gesture of her upturned palm, she may be interrogating us or someone beyond the confines of the picture. Or, because she stands slightly in front of the rest of the group and therefore detached from it, her enigmatic gesture may be intended to direct our gaze toward her fellow workers. In this capacity, she functions as both a player and a narrator, like St. John the Evangelist in Masaccio's *Trinity* or Peter and Christ in the sequential narrative of Masaccio's *Tribute Money* (Fig. 6.7). The latter work, along with Courbet's *Burial at Ornans*, was Soyer's favorite precedent for groups of figures ranged along a horizontal format.[5] Since *Shop Girls* lacks an explicit narrative, what is being indicated is not immediately evident.

A comparison between Soyer's *Shop Girls* and several other works helps to define further some of the artist's distinctive and generally subtle pictorial strategies for showing Depression era female laborers. Among images of American working women prior to the 1930s, John Sloan's 1915 etching *Return from Toil* (Fig. 3.21) provides one of the few iconographic precedents for Soyer's work. In Sloan's image a similar line of women parade through the streets at the end of the day. But unlike

6.7   Masaccio, *The Tribute Money*, c. 1427. Fresco. Brancacci Chapel,
Santa Maria del Carmine, Florence.

Soyer, Sloan stages a narrative of interaction within the picture. Compositionally these women are at a greater distance from the viewer than those in *Shop Girls*. They do not engage us, and we observe their energetic flirtations with male passersby—observed in turn by a dispassionately amused constable—instead of participating in their weariness. The linked arms, smiling faces, and lively interactions among Sloan's women signify a spirited camaraderie. They seem buoyed up by their jobs and the new opportunities available to them as working women. In *Shop Girls* the pace is slower, the mood changed. The daily event of leaving work is never, as one of Soyer's reviewers pointed out, a "glittering" public spectacle but one in a number of ordinary episodes that the artist carefully scrutinized.[6]

A comparison between *Shop Girls* and two more socially conscious images of the 1930s suggests that while Soyer evokes a mood of weariness, he offers neither overt protest to specific working conditions nor solutions for change. In *Eight Figures* (Fig. 6.8) the artist Lew Davis depicted seven women sewing in a New York City sweatshop.[7] Like Soyer's shopgirls, the women are emotionally and psychologically distant from one another. But the painting is a stronger critique of women's working lives because we witness the actual conditions of their labor. We watch them stripped down and bent over under the heat of a bare light bulb. Although both Soyer and Davis delineate the musculature of the working woman's arms, Soyer's women nonetheless appear soft because of his more painterly style. Thanks to Davis's firmer definition of forms and the rhyming of the curved sewing machines with tense rounded shoulders, the women seem to become the disciplined body of

6.8 *Top:* Lew Davis, *Eight Figures,* 1935. Oil on board, 29½″ × 48″. Marjorie and Charles Benton Collection.

6.9 *Above:* Joseph Vavak, *Women of Flint,* 1937. Oil on canvas, 25″ × 36″. National Museum of American Art, Smithsonian Institution.

labor merged with the metal machines over which they work, from youth (on the right) to old age (across the table). With Soyer's *Shop Girls* we see the women only at the end of their working day; in *Eight Figures* we see the machinery of exploitation along with the faceless male authority figure who stands over the women, whose wooden expressions suggest their inability to protest their plight.

In *Women of Flint* (1937; Fig. 6.9), the WPA artist Joseph Vavak painted a group of women workers and wives of workers who were part of a massive 1936–37 sit-down strike against General Motors. The most militant faction in this group was referred to as the red berets, whom Vavak immortalized in the group at the right. The women, like figures on a stage, circle in a barren outdoor setting, the strife marked only by the broken gear in the foreground. All the figures are brutally plain, spare, silent, their angular faces anonymous, their postures anguished. Sharply defined winter coats conceal their bodies, denying any hint of womanliness. It is a cold, unrelenting picture of despair; Soyer's *Shop Girls* seems warm and welcoming by contrast. And, like Davis's *Eight Figures*, *Women of Flint* contains a set of narrative strategies that make the picture more immediately comprehensible than Soyer's *Shop Girls* as an image of exploited or suffering working-class women.[8]

Instead of creating an explicit narrative, Soyer worked to convey a mood through a studied casualness in the arrangement of figures in relation to one another and through penetrating psychological portraits of his subjects. Contemporary critics frequently pointed out Soyer's "uncanny gift of finding the exact bodily gesture that parallels habit of mind" or his serious study of "human psychology" along with human bodies. For thirties critics, Soyer's studies conveyed topical rather than timeless or poetic ends, intensifying a viewer's reaction to a familiar scene of modern urban life. One writer observed that in capturing "the pathos of ordinary people caught unaware," Soyer's art proved "as sensitive a reaction to humanity as it is an accurate piece of reporting."[9] Soyer proclaimed, and critics agreed, that his old master model in this quest was the nineteenth-century French artist Edgar Degas, whose own deliberately haphazard arrangements and revelation of interior moods through pose and gesture Soyer particularly admired. Soyer was inspired both by Degas's images of working women, like laundresses, theatrical performers, and ballerinas, and by his more intimate pictures of models bathing or at their toilettes.[10] And, like the other Fourteenth Street artists Miller and Marsh, Soyer was literal and overt in some of his borrowings. A yawning, stretching laundress in Degas's *Ironers* (c. 1884; Fig. 6.10) may have provided sources for both the calling woman and the woman with her arm raised at an angle in *Shop Girls*. Other precedents for the careful orchestration of arm movements to create a sequence of suspended motions appear in some of Degas's frieze-like arrangements of ballet dancers.

The casual yet carefully arranged poses in *Shop Girls* are also products of the studio picture tradition, in which an artist's model is posed in a studio setting, occasionally with props. The focus is on the figure, often a nude or partially clothed

6.10 Edgar Degas, *The Ironers*, c. 1884. Oil on canvas, 32³/₈″ × 29³/₄″.
Norton Simon Art Foundation.

woman arranged as an aesthetic object for the (primarily masculine) viewer's contemplation and pleasure. In the nineteenth century, painters like Degas depicted
women bathing or at their toilette. By showing women engaged in intimate activity,
Degas's pictures create a mood or allude to a narrative. But he never transformed
his women into figures from myth, religion, or history according to academic standards. In fact, as Eunice Lipton has shown, nineteenth-century viewers, equipped
with a knowledge of bathing conventions and attitudes toward the body among
the bourgeoisie, would have immediately read and understood the bathers as prostitutes cleansing themselves. By the twentieth century, Degas's images—and their
influence on Soyer—came to be read less for their social meaning than in the context
of a growing preoccupation with formal and aesthetic issues. Many early modernists began to paint the model in a more straightforward fashion, as one of a number

of beautifully composed forms knitting together the picture's composition. This approach served to universalize, to remove historical specificity from the female figure, objectifying or demeaning the model.[11]

In his early work from the end of the 1920s Soyer borrowed his conventions for posing models from the more formal side of the studio picture tradition. In his studies of carefully arranged, flatly painted, evenly lit, and unemotional models like *Odalisque* (Fig. 6.1), Soyer was guided further by the example of three artists—the French painter Jules Pascin and the Americans Alexander Brook and Yasuo Kuniyoshi. In mainstream American art circles of the 1920s these artists were enormously influential and popular for their aestheticized depictions of nudes and still lifes. Such works took a noncontroversial position, avoiding the polemical realities of contemporary life and the more daring experimentation with formal abstraction conducted by avant-garde modernists.[12]

By the 1930s Soyer's studio pictures had changed in subtle ways. He began to individualize his models and add darker shadows to the tints of his underpainting to create greater luminosity and weightier figures. Then, like Degas, he moved them into settings, posed them, and added props to suggest a particular social context or situation related to the economic deprivation engendered by the Depression. In general, his studio pictures with female models are dark and somber, with the figure spotlit to probe her state of mind. Most of the women are ordinary, tired, rumpled, and sexualized through revealing but nonprovocative poses. Many seem sad. Most are bored or waiting—passive rather than purposeful. Most are reflective, inward-turning figures in settings that are bare or sparsely furnished with unmade dilapidated beds, hard chairs, and old lamps. These are pictures of poverty as opposed to luxury, melancholy as opposed to happiness. In the painting *Sentimental Girl* (Fig. 5.12), a plain, plump young woman, dressed in a revealing chemise, is captured in an awkward, self-conscious pose as she reflects on an episode from the *True Story* magazine she holds in her lap. In an empty room with nothing else to do she loses herself in daydreams through the publication understood to be *the* magazine of the working-class girl. In *Kathleen* (c. 1933; Fig. 6.11), a full-bodied woman with unkempt hair huddles, wrapped in an old coat. A bare sink with a small mirror above it provides the only decor. Kathleen, whom Soyer described as one of the few "radical" women he knew, posed several times for him in the 1930s. She appears in *Shop Girls* as the second figure from the right.

Soyer's shopgirls are like his melancholy studio models. As women who are only moderately sexualized, in part because of snug-fitting blouses, they receive the same kind of scrutiny from artist and viewer. Placed in the traditional reflective or unself-consciously casual poses of the model moving through the studio as the artist draws her, they too are in transit in a bare setting, available for the viewer's contemplation as womanly objects in a work of art. Although these studio conventions evade the specifics of setting and condition found in works by Davis or Vavak—specifics of

6.11 Raphael Soyer, *Kathleen*, c. 1933. Oil on canvas, 20″ × 24″. Present location unknown.

the actual working lives of women—Soyer's shopgirls are nonetheless meant to be seen as Depression era working women on Fourteenth Street. I am thus suggesting that *all* aspects of the picture I have been describing—the studio picture conventions, the individualization of the models, the tawdry setting, and the melancholy mood—can be interpreted in a specific historical context: shopgirls were frequently alienated lower-class workers, exploited because of the relationship between their sex, their class, and their occupations in places like Fourteenth Street.

In this respect Soyer's *Shop Girls* differs substantially from Kenneth Hayes Miller's nearly contemporary paintings of saleswomen. As a group Miller's paintings *The Fitting Room, Glove Counter, Department Store Shoppers,* and *Saleswomen* (Figs. 3.14, 4.25, 4.27, and 6.12) help to distinguish Soyer's view of Fourteenth Street retail salesclerks as alienated from the workplace and from one another. Instead of melancholy young women in transit, the viewer observes cheerful salesladies in bustling department store interiors helping matronly shopper clients. All

6.12   Kenneth Hayes Miller, *Saleswomen*, c. 1934. Present location unknown.

the saleswomen seem actively engaged in their tasks, whether they are folding stock, responding to a customer's query from behind the counter, fastening a client into a garment, or peering into a crowded dressing room to see if their services are required. Social interaction among women appears everywhere. In *Glove Counter* (Fig. 4.25), for example, a relaxed and very feminine saleslady chats amicably with one of her two clients while, across the aisle, three other store workers, momentarily without customers, pause to converse.

Miller's paintings enact a comfortable, feminized, middle-class democratic ritual in which women expertly assist other women in evaluating and eventually purchasing goods. Nowhere do men appear, even though men often filled managerial positions, keeping a close watch over the saleswomen. Nor do the subjects engage or interrogate the viewer. The workers are as contented and absorbed as the shoppers, and the saleswomen seem to labor effortlessly. They are equal partners with those who shop, as indicated by pleasant (though polite rather than intimate) exchanges of information between women of corresponding height and girth and deliberately graceful contrapposto pose. The equality of Miller's salesladies and their clients is underscored by the uniformity of type. Even though Miller's sales-ladies range from young girls to older white-haired matrons, as in *Department Store Shoppers*, they are unlike Soyer's shopgirls, who are identifiable individuals with distinctive facial features and body types. Miller's salesladies resemble their neatly attired customers, though most wear dark, solid color dresses with white ruffled or bowed collars and remain hatless to distinguish them from the shoppers. The full-figured bodies; round, full faces; almond-shaped eyes; and placid expressions in conjunction with the comfortable department store surroundings suggest middle-classness, arrived at by egalitarian interaction according to a standard of correct consumption.

Although Miller formed the saleslady image and Soyer the shopgirl image by adhering to traditional artistic sources to describe the contemporary environment and by using artistic conventions to make females into womanly figures in a work of art, their sources and artistic inspirations were as distinctive as their working methods. Miller never used a model, inventing instead an idealized female type.[13] Because of his practice of making formal harmonies in his design by rhyming like shapes, the women are objects, woven into the overall structural fabric. Younger saleswomen who deliberately pose in coquettish or overtly feminine ways (as in *Saleswomen* and *Glove Counter*) become part of the visual display—another com-modity behind the counter—deliberately addressed to the masculine viewer of the painting. Like the shoppers, Miller's salesladies remain standardized women; they are stable urban professionals, serving others in ample, pleasant surroundings.

Soyer, in contrast to Miller, always used models for his subjects and always individualized them. And unlike Marsh, who painted figures sketched from models only after substantially completing the settings, Soyer painted the figures first and made the background almost an afterthought, sketching in neighborhood millinery shops or office buildings. Some of Soyer's models were women he knew well—unemployed actresses and writers. Others were young women he saw on the street whose look he found appealing. Many suffered in some way from the effects of the Depression, and he remembered their stories long after they had modeled for him. On occasion, he allowed some of the more destitute to sleep in his studio, often several at a time. In a number of works he depicted their ennui or exhaustion, as in *Girl Asleep* (Fig. 6.13).[14] And, as we have already seen, Soyer found an altogether different artistic precedent for his shopgirls in the evocative models painted by Degas.

Though both Miller and Soyer focus on the womanliness of their models, Miller's images in general are more descriptive and anecdotal than Soyer's subtle and sug-gestive ones. A middle-class viewer/consumer would feel safe with Miller's carefully drawn and firmly contoured department store environment, with its plentiful dis-

6.13   Raphael Soyer, *Girl Asleep*, c. 1930. Oil on canvas, 24″ × 30″. Present location unknown.

play cases and its stable occupants. We are clear about the cordiality of their inter-changes and about the ritualized practices in which they engage. The same middle-class viewer might be less sure about Soyer's shopgirls because they are pictured as less secure in their tawdry environment. Since they are outside, they seem, by the standard of Miller's salesladies, to lack a purposeful activity. They interact with us only to invite us to participate in their ambiguous state of transition and to consider the apparently wearying effects of their work.

The transitional setting and the womanliness of the posed studio models in *Shop Girls* neutralize their economic status as workers. These are the only components of Soyer's pictorial strategy that move in concert with the prevailing ideology of woman's proper place—middle-class, domestic, and family-oriented—particularly as it was perceived in relation to sales work. By the 1920s sales work seemed an ideal job for women—to the feminists who wanted to ensure the right of women to continue working, to social scientists who wanted to reinvigorate homemaking, and to publicists for sales jobs. A particularly strong case for sales work was made by writers who noted its congruence with woman's traditional domestic sphere. Because selling dealt with what people wore or ate or put in their homes, it was, as one observed, "exactly as much a woman's job as housekeeping."[15] Such writers

6.14   Raphael Soyer, *Milliner*, late 1930s. Oil on canvas, 24″ × 16″.
Collection of Judge Irving Hill.

were recognizing, if not stating, that an already established feminized occupation would continue to pose no threat to the social status quo even if older or married women pursued it.

By serving others or prettifying the workplace, saleswomen like those in Miller's *Glove Counter* (Fig. 4.25) or Soyer's *Milliner* (Fig. 6.14) demonstrate the relationship of sales work to woman's sphere. Miller's lady, with a graceful gesture, raises her arm and rearranges her hair with her elegant fingers; the elevated arm reveals the gentle curve made by her breast, waist, and hip. The ease and grace of her pose make her a welcoming figure—the hostess for the guests at her counter as well as an attractive female figure for the viewer—and suggest that her elegance and femininity will accrue to the women who purchase her gloves. Similarly, Soyer's milliner arranges her wares in the otherwise bare setting to make them more attractive. With a vase of flowers instead of the mannequin, this young woman could just as easily be engaged in a traditional domestic task—arranging flowers before the arrival of guests. As workers, both women make things pleasant, comfortable, efficient, or attractive for the shopper. Such womanly workers, represented in a feminized occupation, signaled the movement of private-sector values into the public sphere. They defer—as store managers hoped they would—to superiors or customers as they would to spouses at home. Thus in both images women fit long-standing stereotypes, executing tasks suited to a womanly disposition.

Other writers who celebrated the joys of sales work described it not as an extension of domestic life but as a way to prepare for it:

> To the girl who has the perfectly natural and laudable desire to marry someday I would endeavor to show that a few years behind the counter of a big store is a far better preparation for the cares and duties of matrimony than pounding a typewriter or adding columns of figures 8 hours a day. The ability to control oneself in trying situations, which is one of the fruits of selling experience, is in itself a very valuable asset. Such control is based largely on forbearance and what greater factor than that is there in staying happily married.[16]

Even though married and older women entered the work force in increasing numbers in the 1920s, sales jobs were most often filled by young women between school and marriage or by married women who worked until the birth of their first child.[17] Thus both statistically and in popular perceptions these jobs were temporary and less important than other, male, professions. Although retail sales work provided job satisfaction and personal fulfillment—as feminists hoped it would—the department store job itself fit the ideology of women's proper place and did little to disturb the social status quo.

The suspension of Soyer's shopgirls outside the workplace, in transit between environments and observed for their womanly qualities, comes as less of a surprise when we examine contemporary attitudes toward them and their work. Feminine stereotypes and the perception of sales work as a short-term, dead-end job kept it from being taken seriously as a threat to men's work. The studio poses of Soyer's models and the minimal setting might convey the somber mood of the Depression to a liberal mainstream viewer, but they also reinforce the conservative belief that a woman's appearances and attributes would prove more enduring than the specificities of a job.

The womanliness of these figures, however, particularly when contrasted to that of Miller's, is counteracted by the tawdriness of the setting, the rumpled appearance of the women, their weariness, their anxiety, and their interrogation of the viewer. The differences are rooted in the history of two different stereotypes of women retail sales workers—the shopgirl and the saleslady. Soyer's paintings, which fuse historical and contemporary stereotypes of the shopgirl, encompass the complex issues related to class, femininity, and the working woman in the Depression.

By the 1930s both the shopgirl and the saleslady had well-defined and distinct characteristics. The shopgirl was an older historical type whose social class, educational background, and working conditions had been carefully researched by middle- to upper-class women social reformers in the decade and a half before World War I. Many such reformers, their careful research notwithstanding, filtered their observations through standards of femininity glossed by a moderate version of new womanhood that still insisted on woman's sphere along with new roles in the public arena. Woman, as Mary Maule proclaimed, deserved the rights due her because of her different nature—the "softer, sweeter, tenderer" attributes of womanhood alone. That she could make a valid claim to either marriage *or* career reflected the ambivalence of many women about managing both. Still, by bringing to light the poor conditions under which the shopgirl labored, these reformers hoped to improve the situation of female workers who were entering the rapidly expanding field of department store sales.[18]

As defined by these writers, the shopgirl was a woman who usually came from a large lower-class family, often immigrants, of limited means. She either lived at home and contributed to the family income or shared cheap tenement lodgings with others similarly employed. At most she would have finished high school. Lacking any specialized training, she turned to sales or to less desirable domestic or factory work.[19]

On the job, the shopgirl was usually a passive attendant rather than an active seller. Management required only that she staff the counter, keep the display in order, and show customers goods on request. Reformers claimed that she worked for subsistence wages for the longest allowable hours in department stores or in small shops that often exploited her so grievously that she occasionally resorted to prostitution to make ends meet.[20] Limited by her class and educational background, she was kept under strict surveillance by supervisors who gave her virtually no opportunity for advancement.

Moral issues aside, reformers concluded overwhelmingly that whether living on her own or at home, the shopgirl worked from economic need and was entitled to better wages. In taking this position, the writers struggled against the belief, held by many employers of wage-earning women, that women worked for extras—for pin money. The pin-money argument flourished on the belief that women lived at home, had fewer expenses, and could make a small wage go further; it never took into account women's differing life situations, nor did it assume that a woman might always work. As early as 1887 one New York City department store employer, asked about the shopgirl's wages and background, summarized the principal tenets of the pin-money argument:

A saleswoman gets about the same right along. Two thirds of the girls here are public-school girls and live at home. You see that makes things pretty easy, for the family pool their earnings and they dress well and live well. We don't take from the poorer class at all. These girls earn from four and a half to eight dollars a week. A few get ten dollars, and they're not likely to do better than that. Forty dollars a month is a fortune to a woman. A man must have his little fling, you know. Women manage better.[21]

When asked why his firm could not pay better so that women might be able to save some money, he replied:

We give as high pay as anybody, and we don't give more because for every girl here there are a dozen waiting to take her place. As to saving, she doesn't want to save. There isn't a girl here that doesn't expect to marry before long, and she puts what she makes on her back, because a fellow naturally goes for the best-looking and best-dressed girl. That's the woman question as I've figured it out, and you'll find it the same everywhere.[22]

Even with substantial evidence to the contrary, particularly for working-class women, the pin-money argument and the perception that women would marry and no longer work persisted. The female sales force shared the sex segregation of their workplace and the sex-based wage differential with millions of women factory workers and professionals.[23] This wage exploitation and the working and living conditions under which she labored became defining features of the shopgirl type. Essentially, she was poor. Because of her precarious economic situation, she was vulnerable to the psychological pressure of store surveillance and solicitation by male patrons. These aspects of her life were often embellished in "true-life" accounts and short stories by O'Henry. Such works transformed her into a minor heroine, sometimes ignoring the conditions under which she worked to admire her fortitude; economic deprivation defined the prewar shopgirl's image and personal courage her persona.

As Benson points out, the "subjective" and "fictional" also shaped the sales-woman—how she was perceived by others and how she thought of herself. In the guise of a romantic cultural heroine, the shopgirl/needlewoman had origins in the French *grisette*. After becoming a major player in Henri Murger's popular *Scènes de la vie de bohème* of 1847–49, the impoverished grisette was often portrayed as the attentive, self-sacrificing companion of the social outcast artist or poet. A comfort in financial distress, an inspiration as model and muse, the impoverished shop-girl/grisette willingly stood aside if the artist achieved fame and a higher social station. Documenting her attributes in a 1907 article called "*Grisettes and Midi-nettes,*" Mrs. John Van Vorst observed the passing of both the starving romantic artist of bohemia and the self-effacing grisette. After 1870, the artist became a man of the world, the Baudelairean flaneur who associated with women of his own bourgeois class. And the shopgirl of the new generation, Van Vorst claimed in observing the outpouring of social commentary, had become a cause less "for poetic inspiration than for sociological research . . . [T]he touching poetry of the *grisette* has been transformed into the problematic realism of the *midinette*." Van Vorst, once a factory mill worker, wrote of the difficult life of the contemporary shopgirl:

> So the *grisette* has disappeared, and in her place we have the more practical, more pro-saic, more modern, and more to be pitied little working-girl, to whom has been given also a nickname which in itself suggests the nature of her existence. She is called the *midinette* (little noon girl). From twelve to one-o'clock this laborer has the hour of free-dom which counts to the extent of submerging in forgetfulness the ten other working hours of the day.[24]

In her article Van Vorst looked at the contemporary French *midinette*—for her, any worker in the fashion/needle trade—to draw parallels with the American worker. Rather than adopting the muckraking stance of many of her contemporaries, Van Vorst found virtues of "self-sacrifice, endurance and heroism" in the *midinette*'s ability to manage a tiny wage. This young woman, she argued, took pleasure in self-sufficiency and in the pursuit of love, playing the "coquette" to make her conquest.[25] While Van Vorst celebrated the *midinette* for her gentle nature, she also mourned the demise of the passive and devoted ideal of woman-hood embodied in the grisette. For her the grisette was the working-class version of the steel-engraving lady, set against the new woman as Gibson girl in Caroline Ticknor's 1902 piece contrasting traditional and modern womanhood.

Van Vorst's two working-girl types relate to Soyer's shopgirls. Soyer's fascina-tion with Degas's nineteenth-century working women—among them milliners—extended to his own depiction of a solitary milliner, the adoption of millinery store fronts for many of his outdoor scenes featuring women, and his original title for the work now called *Lunch Hour: Fourteenth Street Midinettes*. More important, perhaps, is what may be read in these works as the conjunction of the "problematic realism" of the socially downtrodden *midinette*, to evoke rather than describe the hardship of female labor in the Depression, and the more melancholy figure of the working girl as artist's model.

When asked about the struggles he experienced in his choice of career, Soyer acknowledged that "it was a very romantic idea to be an artist," suggesting his willing acceptance of bohemian life, with the studio at its center. Soyer included himself in a community of fellow artists, many of whom he honored by making them subjects of his paintings beginning in the mid-1930s. He "talked to himself" frequently through the self-portraits that chronicled not just his changing appearance but his changing professional status or sense of the artist type. His relationship to his models was one of close friendship, respect, and mutual endeavor rather than sexual liaison; in this Soyer models were unlike their self-sacrificing predecessors. They were women largely from his own social class or bohemian milieu, with similar interests in art, literature, dance, or drama. Soyer always felt he inscribed himself somewhere in his work and identified with his models and with the unemployed; both, like artists, were social outcasts. This identification is visible, I would argue, in the parallels between his melancholy images of himself—one as the blue-shirted, smoking Depression era worker (Fig. 6.15)—and his portrayals of models as fellow workers with the same hollow-eyed serious mien. In effect Soyer adopted and transformed the grisette and the somewhat newer *midinette* to make his shopgirl resonate within the accepted discourse of art and society in the 1930s. It was a discourse he drew on as a member of the community of socially conscious artists in the Depression.[26]

In the prewar period, reformers used the term *shopgirl* interchangeably with *saleswoman* because most of these workers were from similar socio-economic backgrounds. Moreover, they used the term compassionately to refer to an impoverished retail sales worker. By the 1920s, when Miller and then Soyer began to paint urban life, the terms were no longer interchangeable. The shopgirl was still perceived as a poorly educated woman from a lower-class background, but store managers and employment counselors gave less focus to the conditions of her job, invoking instead the new model of success. The saleswoman was now characterized as a department store professional, often middle-class and college educated, sometimes married, and not always young.[27] In addition, the saleslady became the "improved" shopgirl, one who through education and retraining could better her position. By showing the shopgirl fatigued and in transit, Soyer takes a compassionate view of her historical plight as hard-working and exploited. And unlike Miller, who only depicts the saleslady, Soyer refuses to acknowledge what many boosters of the new department store sales staff wanted everyone to believe—that all store workers, thanks to benefits and training, shared an equal opportunity.

Several institutional, social, and economic changes since the prewar period help to account for the sharper division between the shopgirl and the saleslady. By the

6.15 Raphael Soyer, *Self-Portrait,* 1930s. Oil on canvas, 16″ × 14″.
Present location unknown.

1920s the urban department store had expanded into a business with all the respectability of a bank or an insurance company. As the historian Frederick Lewis Allen
observed, retail sales work became a highly desirable occupation for a new class of
woman.

> Up to this time girls of the middle classes who had wanted to "do something" had been
> largely restricted to school-teaching, social-service work, nursing, stenography, and
> clerical work in business houses. . . . In 1920 the department store was in the mind of
> the average college girl a rather bourgeois institution which employed "poor shop
> girls;" by the end of the decade college girls were standing in line for openings in the
> misses' sports-wear department and even selling behind the counter in the hope that
> some day fortune might smile upon them and make them buyers or stylists.[28]

Adding to the new respectability was a substantial improvement in wages and working conditions in New York stores for all members of the sales staff. Starting salaries, once as low as three dollars, were ten to sixteen dollars per week plus commissions. Hours were usually nine to five-thirty, and most store workers had morning and afternoon breaks in addition to an hour for lunch. A number of stores closed on several summer Saturdays, and after a year of work employees received a week of paid vacation. Large department stores had medical staffs, mutual-aid associations, and elaborate training programs for employees.[29] In the prosperous 1920s some of the wealthiest stores had country retreats where employees could spend a restful week of vacation. To judge from the literature on department stores and their employment opportunities as well as the contented appearance of Miller's salesladies, the days of the struggling shopgirl were long gone.

In her 1929 study *The Saleslady* the sociologist Frances Donovan initially corroborated these perceptions. She interviewed an older saleswoman who stated that it was no longer a disgrace to work in a department store and that the shopgirl attitude was dead. The woman explained that she was now treated well, and that she no longer feared either her customers or the floor manager. Donovan also noted that both European and American stores were adopting terms like *co-worker* or *store associate* to replace *shopgirl*, which had become in some store owners' minds "an epitaph [epithet]" of "disrespect."[30]

Management's "disrespect," unlike the "sympathy" of Progressive Era reformers, resulted from a class- and gender-based discourse, through which management claimed that lower-class, poorly educated shopgirls could not successfully sell to the middle- or upper-middle-class clientele they sought to attract. Salespeople, as one store manager reported, "frequently speak and act in ways which do not commend them to people of refinement."[31] By the teens and 1920s, store executives decided that a cordial and well-informed sales staff might improve profits. They embarked on programs to raise the educational level of their workers and professionalize the sales staff—in short to eradicate some of the class discrepancies between workers and customers and between members of the sales staff.

Welfare programs, ostensibly designed to improve the overall well-being of store workers, served management as well. (Later, such programs were given the more neutral designation "personnel work" to avoid charges of paternalism). Lunchrooms, medical programs, libraries, and personal-improvement classes made for happier workers, prevented union organization, and created an improved environment for socially conscious shoppers who might take management to task for mistreating working women. Store managers also knew that a decent standard of living would contribute to staff morale. Consequently, they included commissions in the wage system and discounts on store merchandise so that women employees could dress well.[32]

Training programs promised to transform the staff from a passive to an active, pleasant, and efficient sales force. In the 1920s stores instituted a series of such programs to help salespeople learn everything from filling out sales checks to "skilled selling," which meant an education in good taste, "improved standards of living, better habits of thought, higher interpretations and ideals."[33] Such an education would ensure that a saleswoman's class identity approached, at least superficially, that of her clients. Management also encouraged women to capitalize on qualities long recognized as womanly. The capacity to respond sympathetically to other women (and hence manipulate them) and to understand all things domestic became a key ingredient in the saleswoman's training. Sales training capitalized on women's gender identity by reinforcing the belief that women were natural consumers.[34] The results of this training are depicted in a work like Miller's *Department Store Shoppers* (Fig. 4.27), in which two women with equal expertise confer on yard goods for the home. The saleswoman, neatly dressed in the neutral attire worn by all the sales staff, exhibits both her respect for her client and the authority that comes from all the learned and instinctive responses of "skilled selling." Furthermore, Miller's use of an idealized matronly type for both seller and buyer blurs the signs of class distinctions between them.

Finally, along with reeducating the lower-class store worker and providing her with both welfare and financial incentives and promotion opportunities, management actively sought a new kind of saleswoman. Many applicants for sales positions were required to take aptitude and psychological tests. Stores sent representatives to women's colleges to recruit graduates from "good educational and social backgrounds—social in the sense of environment"—for sales training and management programs.[35] A number of stores also had visiting "squads" of college students who would work in all departments over a period of several months to get a feel for the entire store operation. The journalist Helen Law reported on one store executive for whom "the orderly mind which college education gives is a valuable asset." Along with colleges, several new schools of retailing provided well-trained candidates for sales jobs.[36]

In spite of the apparent favoritism shown in hiring the middle-class college-educated saleswoman over the old-style shopgirl, many store owners still held that the best sales force was "cheap help cheaply paid," that is, one that management could mold to its own practices.[37] No matter what its actual hiring policies and wage scales, however, management was quick to assure the public of the democratic makeup of its sales force. Samuel Reyburn, the president of Lord & Taylor in New York, explained in a 1930 speech to the National Retail Dry Goods Association:

We don't prefer the college or theoretically trained woman and we don't prefer the practically trained woman in collecting the material out of which we build this organization. We want both of them, and after we get them we want each to forget the class consciousness that she indulges herself in, in appreciation of her particular training. College-trained men and women are often a little bit too proud of the fact that they have that certificate—and many practically trained people I know, on the other hand, are just as egotistical and conceited about their training. Both of these classes of people have something to contribute.[38]

Practically speaking, however, there was a selective hiring process, and tensions existed between groups from different social and educational backgrounds in department stores. Frances Donovan, an attractive college-educated woman who went undercover to look for a sales job for her sociological study *The Saleslady*, was immediately hired over other applicants with sales experience because of her appearance and education.[39]

Donovan observed a natural camaraderie among saleswomen of all backgrounds that ended with the working day.[40] She also witnessed the arrogance of college students in management programs, pointing out precisely what Mr. Reyburn claimed the stores would avoid.[41] She came to understand, through sometimes touching interactions with her co-workers, what other writers also observed. Certain types of lower-class women were less visible in the stores than in earlier times. When they were part of the staff, they had little chance to advance in what were, by the 1920s, middle- to upper-middle-class stores whose management claimed to employ a better class of workers and not shopgirls. In Philadelphia, John Wanamaker refused to hear staff members referred to as shopgirls or help, arguing instead that men and women in his store exemplified the dignity and respectability of labor.[42]

The image of the professionalized department store saleswoman received substantial press in the 1920s because it satisfied the needs of several groups in and outside the stores. Gender aside, this saleswoman was a model of success, getting ahead in an era that valued business achievement. Articles describing her and her work stressed opportunities for quick advancement, dangled five- to ten-thousand-dollar per year executive salaries before readers, and reveled in the statistic that 50 percent of executive positions were held by women. In this context, retail sales work was exciting because it promised money, power, and status. But such success was not the norm, and the smoothly run sales process was often jarred by colliding class and gender interactions. Male managers who sought control over female saleswomen through training had little control over the actual process of selling; sales tactics developed by a cohesive department of women on the sales floor often sabotaged a trainer's best efforts. But such tactics could also produce effective sales, thereby undermining managerial authority. The desire of managers and customers for a well-trained and authoritative female sales staff collided with their desire for a deferential one.[43]

The rhetoric of success and professionalism surrounding this evolving saleswoman stereotype resembled that of feminists who argued for women's right to work, to be independent, and to achieve personal satisfaction; in both instances it served a narrow middle-class end.[44] It ignored the lower-class women who continued to work in factories, dime store sales jobs, small specialty stores, and Fourteenth Street bargain stores throughout the 1920s and 1930s. These women worked from economic need rather than for personal fulfillment or for pin money. The shopgirl had not disappeared, in spite of improvements in department store life and intensive training programs. She had been made invisible by an ideology of progress and personal success that celebrated the possibilities for the dominant middle class in the 1920s.

Some of the rhetoric shaping the discourse on women in the sales force appears in Fourteenth Street School paintings of the 1930s. A comparison between Soyer's *Milliner* of the late 1930s (Fig. 6.14) and Miller's *Glove Counter* of the same period (Fig. 4.25) makes it clear that Miller painted the new model of professionalism and achievement—the successful middle-class saleswoman—whereas Soyer painted the poorer shopgirl. Miller's saleswoman is confidently poised behind her counter of goods, whose plenty, like the grandeur of the department store space opening before her, signifies prosperity. Though young, she is mature; she wears the typical plain dress of the department store saleswoman, like Ohrbach's saleslady Miss Clara Mayer (Fig. 6.16).[45] Soyer's milliner, like his shopgirls, offers a striking contrast. She appears considerably younger. Dressed in a bulky jacket and a blouse with a wrinkled collar, she works with a single object in a bare interior. Coarsely brushed surfaces emphasize the setting's drabness, the shallow space its confinement. Everything in her appearance and surroundings indicates a subsistence wage that leaves little for pretty clothes or entertainment to brighten her spirits. She has no customers or co-workers. Her serious demeanor suggests that she is conscientious about her work—that she is worthy of both respect for her efforts and recognition of her difficult working surroundings and the isolation of her working life.

Miller's images embody action, interaction, and business. The saleswomen are at one with the prevailing middle-class ideology of woman's proper place—and fall within the discourse of a revised new womanhood. In comfortable department store interiors, they work and behave in the womanly ways that are expected of them and bring them success. Through the image of this professionalized worker Miller's paintings avoided the harsher conditions of working-class life and the inequities of gender ideology and muted such problems with the cheerful trappings of prosperity. Soyer's works confronted both by focusing on the historically hardworking shopgirl.

Paintings by Miller and Soyer belong to representational discourses on women and modern commerce that originated in the nineteenth century in works commodifying women by relating them to the display of goods for sale. In James Tissot's

6.16 Photograph of Miss Clara Mayer, "The American Shopgirl," from "Women in Business II," *Fortune* 12 (August 1935), p. 85.

Milliner's Shop (Fig. 6.17), as in Miller's *Glove Counter*, a young woman is a welcoming figure in an elegant boutique—as decorative as the ribbons and fabrics that surround her. Another woman, off to the left, becomes an available part of the display as a gentleman looking through the store window divides his admiring gaze between her and the goods. It was part of her womanly role to be admired, and, given the perception of sexual availability attached to the nineteenth-century milliner's occupation in France, even eventually acquired. Working women were part of a traffic in signs of modern life—and were available for ready visual consumption, if not for purchase. Degas's solitary milliner in *The Millinery Shop* (Fig. 6.18) works on finishing a hat, pins held between her lips as she appraises her work. In a plain setting she works beneath a colorful array of hats, none of which she actually wears. Her pose as she turns away from the finished product suggests her inability to acquire the beautiful hats that are available to the elevated buyer or viewer. Moreover, her absorption in her work belies to some degree the rhetoric of sexual availability attached to the milliner. Like Soyer, who succeeded him, Degas subtly evoked the inconsistencies of what the nineteenth-century critic George Moore called "the sweet, sad poetry of female labor."[46]

Apart from features he appropriated from Degas, Soyer's pictorial rhetoric—specifically the bare settings and the ennui of his figures—is close to that of periodicals like the *New Masses* that published images of the shopgirl. Throughout the

6.17 *Right:* James Tissot, *The Milliner's Shop (La Demoiselle de magasin),* 1883–85. Oil on canvas, 57″ × 40″. Art Gallery of Ontario, Toronto.

6.18 *Below:* Edgar Degas, *The Millinery Shop,* 1879–84. Oil on canvas, 39″ × 43″. The Art Institute of Chicago. Mr. and Mrs. Lewis Larned Coburn Memorial Collection.

6.19 F. S. Hynd, "Mid-Afternoon,"
New Masses 1 (May 1926), p. 27.

1920s, artists producing cartoons for this publication recognized that salesgirls in poorer establishments continued to have dreary lives. In a May 1926 drawing from the *New Masses* entitled "Mid-Afternoon" (Fig. 6.19) the shopgirl stands idle and alone in front of a tiny hat store on a deserted street, far from the bustle and glitter of Fifth Avenue. In "Sunday Morning" (Fig. 6.20), another *New Masses* cartoon, from December 1931, the wage-earning woman performs the Sunday ritual of doing her laundry to prepare for another week of work, the burden of which is expressed in the tired curve of her bent back and her lowered eyes. These images, at least in their sobriety of mood, differ from John Sloan's images of working women from earlier decades. Whether returning home from work (Fig. 3.21) or performing their own outdoor toilettes on Sunday morning (Fig. 1.9), Sloan's women are represented as exuberant and happy. They take pleasure in their freedom and sensuality as well as providing it for the viewer. Though Soyer's paintings lack the narrative specificity of either Sloan's paintings or the cartoons, they share with the earlier works a rough fluidity in the application of paint that by the 1930s, combined with lower-class subjects, had become an index of socially concerned art.

I have been tracing the historical development of two stereotypes of women working in retail sales to show how Miller depicted the successful middle-class saleswoman, Soyer the weary, anxious lower-class shopgirl. Both artists, however,

6.20 Mary O. Johnson, "Sunday
Morning," *New Masses* 7
(December 1931), p. 14.

portrayed retail sales clerks during the Depression. What vision was shaped by their
pictures? How do their strategies relate to specific conditions of the 1930s—the
employment picture in and around Union Square and changes in the discourse of
new womanhood as the working women assumed a larger role?

Unemployment was the central anxiety of the 1930s. To judge from the pictorial
record of all the Fourteenth Street artists, it was a male rather than a female problem. With the exception of Miller, who never painted unemployed men, Marsh,
Bishop, and especially Soyer all contributed to the iconography of the Depression
era's most compelling image of despair—the jobless man. They pictured these
men—on Union Square, in breadlines, and in scenes of Bowery dereliction—in somber browns and blacks. Where Marsh pressed men together to show their endless
numbers and collective despair, Soyer and Bishop portrayed only a few at a time
and individualized their ennui. In Soyer's *In the City Park* (Fig. 3.41), a scene of
perpetual waiting, three despondent men crowd together on a park bench in Union
Square. As in *Shop Girls*, however, Soyer placed the brightly illuminated individualized faces of the unemployed men close to the viewer so that we cannot avoid
seeing their boredom and despair.

In representing the unemployed male, the Fourteenth Street School artists painted
the historically acknowledged and accepted victim of the Depression economy. But
the situation was almost as bad for women. Although only 25 percent of the total

American work force were women, they made up one-third of the total unemployed. And 23 percent of New York women were out of work by early 1934. By mid-decade, the employment picture for saleswomen was more serious than for any other low-level white-collar position. In New York, more than 50 percent of the saleswomen, the lowest paid of all women professionals to begin with, reported a 50 percent drop in earnings. No economic aid for them was forthcoming.[47] The proportion of public relief funding allocated for women did not match the proportion of unemployed women in the work force, and aid efforts were usually concentrated on male heads of families. Female unemployment, moreover, received little publicity, even though the suffering of unemployed women was similar to that of men. Like men, they felt personally responsible for the loss of jobs, their appetites deteriorated, and they wandered about aimlessly or hid in their rooms. Yet few of them applied for relief; of five hundred early applicants for New York City funds, for example, only ten were women. There were no large-scale institutions for women's relief and no public flophouses. Women seldom joined breadlines. In the struggle to make ends meet, many took domestic posts or resorted to peddling apples or pretzels, often on Union Square. When totally destitute, many simply approached men who would take them in.[48] The anxious and weary appearance of Soyer's shopgirls was understandable given the conditions of existence for many 1930s salesclerks.

There are no images of unemployed Fourteenth Street women for two principal reasons: these women were less visible than their male counterparts, and their unemployment was not as significant a public issue. Moreover, the Fourteenth Street neighborhood was filled with shoppers and women who worked in stores or offices—it was a neighborhood of active women who, even if not gainfully employed outside the home, were involved in what the district offered.[49]

Indirectly, however, Soyer addressed the issue of women's unemployment. The women in his *Shop Girls*, in their transitional state, are never stable or secure in the working world. Furthermore, Soyer's other images of women in the Depression, unlike Miller's, show studio interiors in which women wait patiently with nothing to do because they have no work and nowhere else to go (Figs. 5.12, 6.11, and 6.13). In its theme and in the poses of its figures *Solitaire* (1934; Fig. 6.21) alludes to the issues of gender and unemployment that became acute in the Depression. A seated female figure in an unbuttoned skirt, her breasts half-revealed to the viewer by a loose chemise, plays cards while an anonymous male companion lies behind her, facing the wall, his back to the viewer. The contrast between her upright and his recumbent pose, between her identity and his nonidentity, between her card playing and his inertia suggests the solitude and isolation of each. But she is the more sexually available and attendant while he turns away, figuring shame in his posture—at his failure to work or to perform sexually, both failures of masculinity described by social commentators throughout the Depression. Whatever the mean-

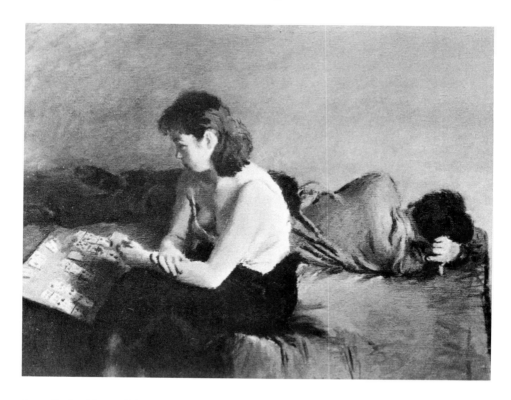

6.21 Raphael Soyer, *Solitaire*, 1934. Oil on canvas, 22″ × 28″. Private collection.

ing of a work like *Solitaire*, Soyer, in many of these images, gives lower-class, unoccupied women, who were otherwise out of public view, a place of recognition in his art. They are the counterparts of his weary shopgirls in the same way that Miller's active shoppers are counterparts of the saleswomen. In this context, Soyer's imagery has, as social documentation, a greater consciousness of the plight of the unemployed woman in the Depression.

The tension, anxiety, and constriction in Soyer's *Shop Girls* reflect both the unemployment that continually threatened salesclerks in bargain institutions and the conditions of the jobs themselves. Not only were these the lowest paid of all white-collar jobs for women, but also, in the cheaper stores, hours were long. Many clerks, on their feet for hours, suffered from flat feet, varicose veins, inflamed joints, nervous irritability, and anemia. For fear of losing their jobs, women refused to use the stools behind the counter that were required by law.[50] And surveillance by superiors continued to be a problem. One girl who took a job at a five-and-dime reported, "I had a grotesque consciousness of secret, unknown eyes on me—watching my every movement from some unseen vantage point."[51]

By 1934 the New Deal's NRA (National Recovery Administration) codes had appeared, intended to alleviate some of the wage problems. Fourteenth Street stores like Klein's and Ohrbach's were now required to pay a minimum wage of fourteen dollars per week (up from a low of about seven). Unfortunately, the codes were difficult to enforce, and stores regularly ignored them or found ways to circumvent them.[52]

Examples of the exploitation Soyer's shopgirls might have experienced come from 1930s sources exposing practices at Klein's. The evidence is particularly disturbing because Samuel Klein actively promoted the NRA codes in mercantile circles. Furthermore, he was widely acclaimed in newspaper and magazine stories for his Horatio Alger–like rise to wealth and commercial success and for his personal beneficence toward workers, to whom he gave annual Christmas bonuses.[53]

Having initially praised the new codes, Klein made several attempts to avoid them. In November 1933, he petitioned the NRA to reduce the minimum wage he paid from fourteen dollars per week to twelve. Prior to the NRA codes, Klein's wages had ranged from six to eight dollars per week. When his plea was refused in both New York and Washington, Klein said he would be forced to abandon the straight five-day week and operate under schedule C of the retail code, which provided for a forty-eight hour six-day week at fifteen dollars per week. He also stated that the denial of his plea would add $300,000 to his annual wage budget—this from a man who did a $25-million business and whose personal annual income in the middle of the Depression was $1 million.[54]

The most telling evidence of what life was like for a Fourteenth Street shopgirl comes from Stella Ormsby's account of her job at Klein's. Ormsby wrote "The Other Side of the Profile" for the *New Republic* in 1932 in response to a glowing story about Klein that had appeared in the *New Yorker*. She worked in the basement of Klein's, the site of the best bargains, with dresses selling for about two dollars. Soyer's empathetic image of tired, bleary-eyed, and rumpled shopgirls takes on a new resonance alongside Ormsby's account of her day.

The basement is a long winding, angular affair, calling to mind the Times Square subway station. . . . Every day between two and three thousand people find their way into this cellar, which is low-ceilinged and without windows. The unwholesome air alone makes it an ordeal to remain down below for more than an hour. The few electric fans are absolutely ineffectual to counteract the heat and smell of sweat.

My hours are from nine-thirty in the morning until seven in the evening, including Saturday, and my job consists in trailing customers and readjusting dresses they throw down from the racks. The work is so deadly monotonous that it would try the patience of a moron. I walk many hours a day in performing my job, and what with the rush and crush of the milling crowds, the foul air and the noise and the bawlings out from the supervisors, I find myself at the end of the day in a state of utter exhaustion. I get home brutally worn out with barely sufficient strength to eat my supper and get to bed to regain enough vitality for the next day's grind. My weekly salary is eight dollars handed to me in an envelope which cautions me to resolve to make "payday savings that future days may be happy days."[55]

Ormsby went on to describe the difficulty she had in getting a job and the shady practices under which she suspected she had been hired. Her description of Klein's search for cheaper labor is echoed in his petition to the NRA for a lower wage in 1933:

It was only after five months of persistent hunting for work that I landed my present job. Several weeks ago, an advertisement in one of the daily newspapers announc[ed] that Klein's would hire new help. With over three hundred other girls, I was on the premises two hours before the stipulated time. The employment manager lined us all up and went through the line selecting a girl here and a girl there in what seemed to me a wholly arbitrary fashion. Fifty were selected and the rest told to leave. After two days of red tape—physical examination, references, credentials and lecturing, the purpose of the last being to whoop up pride and enthusiasm in us for the Klein establishment—I was finally "trained" for my job. I soon learned from the older girls that the reason for the "new" help was that the girls whom he had displaced were receiving ten dollars per week and that they were all discharged in favor of the new group who were getting only eight. How true this is I cannot say. But it is the sort of thing anyone working in the basement would find it hard *not* to believe. Also that the girls hired after my group are getting seven and seven-fifty would seem to indicate that that is what happened.[56]

Klein was later accused by an NRA representative of discharging employees for having union affiliations. While Klein claimed that layoffs were seasonal (because his store sold no gifts, Christmas season was always slack), a report by the NRA official found him in violation for "a systematic, deliberate, all-embracing scheme to thwart the workers' rights to self-organization," including a store-wide system to prevent employees from joining a union. Klein accused the New York NRA of "breeding communism." Workers who had been laid off continued to picket Klein's until February 1935, when Klein settled with them and agreed to put them on a preferential list for rehiring.[57]

Artists and writers were both witnesses of the period of labor unrest on Union Square and participants in it. Continuing through March 1935, there were daily pickets and a series of large-scale Saturday demonstrations in front of Ohrbach's.[58] The facts of the strike were captured in Regional Marsh's 1936 painting *End of the Fourteenth Street Crosstown Line* (Fig. 6.22). Behind the laborers taking up the old trolley car line, store workers picket Ohrbach's for the store's failure to union-ize.[59]

6.22 Reginald Marsh, *End of the Fourteenth Street Crosstown Line,* 1936. Tempera on board, 23³/₄″ × 35⁷/₈″. The Pennsylvania Academy of the Fine Arts, Philadelphia.

By 1936, when Soyer painted *Shop Girls*, Klein's and Ohrbach's had been forced into greater leniency toward union representation, thanks in part to the four steady months of picketing and conflict. Soyer would have witnessed these events just before beginning the painting. Though less explicit and overtly documentary than Marsh's work, Soyer's painting *Shop Girls* portrays some of the hardship attendant on poor working conditions and uneasy management-worker relations. The compositional proximity of these tired women to the viewer makes the truth more blunt. The gesture toward her fellow workers of the shopgirl who confronts the viewer can be read as a worker pointing to signs of workplace unrest. Through her upturned palm she not only questions the observer about the conditions in which she and her co-workers find themselves but also quietly asserts herself.

Apart from unemployment pressures and the hardships she encountered in the workplace, a 1930s shopgirl, like other working women, was subject to changing attitudes about women in the workplace. Even though her feminized occupation remained acceptable for both young and older women—like those Miller depicted as saleswomen—a growing sentiment against married women in the work force affected all discussions of working women.[60]

Feminist arguments about women's right to work became hollow when the Depression struck and thousands of male heads of families lost their jobs. Advocates of working wives had spoken only to a small middle-class audience, ignoring the needs of married working-class women. Because these advocates understated economic motivations by emphasizing women's need for personal fulfillment—a central feature in the discourse of new womanhood—they only reinforced the notion already popular among proponents of the ideology of women's proper place—that women worked for pin money and personal satisfaction rather than from economic need.[61] The unfortunate persistence of this argument, even when statistical evidence pointed in the opposite direction, contributed to a growing sentiment against working wives just when many needed their jobs, indicating that the pin-money claim provided an easy justification for an underlying desire to remove all married women from the work force.[62]

Public sentiment against working wives ran so high during the Depression that it diffused all attempts to assert any woman's right to work.[63] To combat some of the employment problems, feminists and job counselors adopted a series of defensive strategies, not only to help women maintain their jobs but to help them find jobs as well. These writers and speakers now insisted that all women worked from economic need rather than for self-fulfillment or from personal ambition. Some even restated the old claim that women would prefer not to work at all because they valued home life over any job. Furthermore, employment advisors increasingly urged young unmarried women to consider sales or clerical positions where they could avoid competing with men.[64] The jobs themselves became vehicles for reasserting the ideology of women's proper place. Finally, in the middle of the decade, when writers on occupational trends noticed that employers emphasized the appearance and personality of a job candidate over her qualifications—a distinction from the 1920s—job counselors encouraged women to reassert their beauty and womanly charms and be aware of their secondary and temporary role. All these strategies neutralized previous arguments about working women and reinforced the ideology of woman's proper place.

In many of the Fourteenth Street paintings some form of attractiveness, prettiness, or glamour defines working and shopping women. A saleswoman's prettiness, whether consciously intended by the painter or not, also represented the way women workers were expected to look and behave. Contemporary critics who spoke favorably of Soyer's work, however, described his women by character rather than appearance as honest, humane, and sincere. Carl Zigrosser, who found this type of woman at concerts and meetings, felt she was "peculiar to the big city in the 1930s. . . . a working girl, not a debutante, sometimes sturdy, sometimes with a wistful charm, always self-reliant, never the automaton of the mass, always with some spark of individuality glowing within her."[65] Critics who were less positive considered Soyer's women drab, unhappy, and, more to the point, either lower class and not beautiful or, later, "lower-class beauties."[66] Beauty, as a standard quality critics responded to in Soyer's work, resided in the paint and poses of the figures—the artist's traditional means of defining women as attractive in a work of art. In *Shop Girls*, for example, the women's brightly colored or partially transparent blouses reveal full curving figures. Three women wear bright lipstick. Compared with the palette of *Shop Girls*, that of Soyer's images of unemployed men (for example, Fig. 3.41) is duller. In addition, the artist placed his male models in slouched and disconsolate poses; the women's attitudes are generally more upright and more appealing. Fundamentally, Soyer's use of studio conventions inscribes in these figures not beauty per se but one kind of femininity observed during the Depression.[67] This quality helped to make working-class women an acceptable subject of American Scene realism; the same quality also served to express the womanly ideology which permeated the salesgirl's job in the 1930s.

Though gently sexualized by studio poses, Soyer's working women remain more anxious than alluring, in contrast to some of Miller's saleswomen. The clerk with her back to the viewer in *Glove Counter* and the clerk to the right in *Saleswomen* (Figs. 4.25 and 6.12) assume the provocative pose typical of movie stars' publicity photographs (Fig. 4.7). Marsh's standards of beauty for women, bewitching glamour and charm, appear in their most extreme form in his *Hudson Bay Fur Company*, a work that depicts a regular Union Square event (Fig. 3.26). Alfred Kazin tells how crowds in the thirties gathered daily to watch the live fur models, "gawking" at them as they circled "round and round like burlesque queens" in a lighted corner window two stories above the square.[68] Marsh placed viewers below the central model so that they look up at the store window as if at a burlesque stage and take advantage of the strip-tease pose. In this tawdry corner of Union Square, working saleswomen become objects of delectation.[69] Marsh captured the sexual exploitation in the ideology of woman's proper place—the suggestion that women's sexuality would help them keep their jobs.

Because of job scarcity, this ideology, which had served to maintain the social stability of the nuclear family in the 1920s, now took on a larger economic meaning. It exercised more rigid control over women's lives in the 1930s—even those of women holding socially acceptable sales or clerical jobs. Marsh's photograph of the Hudson Bay Fur Company (Fig. 3.27) shows how distant the store model actually was from the sidewalk spectator and how Marsh transformed and sexualized her. The photograph also suggests that the store window was an unpleasant working environment, with cramped space and bright lights. Such unpleasantness was a fact of life in many of the retail establishments around Union Square.

The term *shopgirl* by the 1920s described a lower-class store worker who was given little respect or responsibility in an enterprise. Historically it also signified a working woman who suffered under the conditions of her work, unlike the saleswoman, who was a model of success. By choosing this shopgirl type and showing her fatigued, Soyer revealed the effects of her working existence on Fourteenth Street and focused attention on her life in the Depression. By showing her in transit, young and feminine, he reinforced the ideology of woman's proper place that considered her occupation temporary. Crucial to the multivalence of the work is the tension in which these features are held. *Shop Girls* disrupts the discourse of femininity by intersecting it with one of class and labor. Shopgirls had to work to survive and were thus alienated from an ideology that claimed their economic efforts were temporary and for "extras." They are also alienated from work that exploits them as women. Whether or not it was his intent, Soyer expressed that alienation by suspending them outside both the workplace and the domestic environment and by having them interrogate the viewer and ultimately the social order that sustained the conditions of their labor. Soyer's image embodies the contradictions and complexities of the ideology and of working women's situations during the Depression.

Raphael Soyer, one reviewer wrote, "tells a story of his own people, and naturally this sympathetic approach to his sitters renders his work all the more communicating."[70] Numerous reviewers echoed this environmentalist assumption of American Scene painting—that a realism created from the artist's own milieu was the most authentic art. Indeed, Soyer's early life and working experiences would have heightened his empathy for workers laboring under poor conditions for meager pay. Through his own experience, in his own marriage and family, and his observation of his models, Soyer was well acquainted with the problems of working women and with the importance of their right to work. He would have understood that lower-class immigrant women worked from economic need rather than for personal fulfillment. Through the 1920s, while he studied art and struggled with his early work, he himself endured firsthand the hardships of the hourly wage earner, an experience other Fourteenth Street artists never had.

Even more interesting in the contemporary reviews of Soyer's work is their negative response to lower-class femininity. Reviewers, consciously or not, used language that reduced women to lower forms of life or made them helpless. But because of the high quality of his art, they either forgave the painter for such flaws or saw the power of his depictions. Emily Genauer, who spoke of his "drab, unhappy and drooping" models, described his shopgirls as "pathetic." In *Office Girls* (Fig. 6.3), painted as a pendant in the same year as *Shop Girls*, the women were, according to one reviewer, "not particularly enticing," being "thin, wiry, alert . . . still showing the nervous strain of their days." Even though these women were "the mainstay of our commerce," this reviewer felt that their work undermined their femininity. One of the most revealing descriptions came when Soyer's *Gittel* (Fig. 6.23) won the award for the best portrait in oil at the Pennsylvania Academy's 1934 annual exhibit. Though Soyer himself characterized Gittel as a brilliant woman of ambition—a poet and singer—the *Art Digest* reviewer saw *Gittel* as the "essence of

6.23 Raphael Soyer, *Gittel*, 1932. Oil on canvas, 49$\frac{1}{2}$″ × 27$\frac{1}{4}$″.
The Regis Collection, Minneapolis, Minnesota.

piquant feminine undernourishment, a frail drab little *thing* in genteel rags." Indeed, the reviewer noted that Soyer's women were merely "*creatures . . .* delicate questioning souls in a world with little sunshine or happiness" (italics mine). But, he concluded, *Gittel* was "diabolically well-painted." Another reviewer, a year later, observed Soyer's potential but noted, "Technical facility is always a source of danger, and when it is allied with a powerful gift for depicting types it becomes a positive menace." Art could make class more powerful (and more threatening).[71]

Soyer's consciousness of issues of class and his concern about the exploitation of workers accompanied a heightened quality of what both critics and Soyer himself called naturalism. Along with his more traditional training and sources, Soyer developed both his sense of urban realism and its relation to social, cultural, and political issues through regular attendance at John Reed Club debates, the Artists' Union, and later the Artists' Congress. Soyer's principal motives for these activities were his pressing need both for a community of fellow artists—he wanted a way out of his self-involvement, and these activities became vital to his personal growth—and, more important for analyzing works like *Shop Girls*, for a greater sophistication about social and political events. He wanted to raise his consciousness, and he believed then and throughout his career that an awareness of such issues gave psychological depth to his paintings.[72]

Soyer was always reluctant to acknowledge the politics and ideology of his pictorial strategies, particularly in works of the mid-1930s:

> The John Reed Club of Writers and Artists helped me to acquire a progressive world view, but I did not let it change my art, which never became politically slanted. I painted what I knew and what I saw around me—many pictures of the unemployed, of homeless men, because I saw them everywhere, in parks, on sidewalks, sleeping on girders of abandoned construction sites. I sympathized with them, identified with them.[73]

In Soyer's view *Shop Girls* would have been "politically slanted" had it shown, for example, policemen breaking up a demonstration of shopgirls picketing a specific store. Instead, as he described the picture's genesis, he watched some shopgirls coming out of a store and re-created their casual movements with models in his studio. What Soyer then "saw" and embedded in his picture, however unconsciously, was the complex repository of attitudes that mainstream culture had invested in the working girl in general and the shopgirl in particular over an extended period of time. He also saw the physical and psychological effects of difficult working conditions on her life. These signs, none of them dramatic or overt, none "propagandistic," appear, as I have suggested, as spatial inconsistencies, awkward or cramped passages, and complex interactions—specifically interrogations between subject and viewer. They are pictorial tensions that speak to patterns of tension in the larger occupational and social structure; there is no exact correspondence between a particular compositional device and some specific facet of women's working lives. That the painting simultaneously affirms and disrupts the discursive underpinnings of the ideology of woman's proper place is part of the inconsistency within the social order itself.

The interrogation and confrontation of *Shop Girls* are also present in other multi-figure works by Soyer from mid-decade. The mode of address in all these works stems from a conjunction of personal events in Soyer's life with political and aesthetic shifts on the American Left, where Soyer was an engaged participant-observer. In 1935, shortly after all chapters of the John Reed Club were disbanded by the Soviet Union for failing to follow the broader anti-sectarian policies of the emergent Popular Front movement, Soyer went to Europe for the first time since immigrating to the United States in 1912. In Paris he and his wife, Rebecca, witnessed the initial spirited demonstration of the Popular Front as Algerians linked arms and shouted, "A bas la guerre." They were present at the opening of the World's Congress of Writers against War and Fascism. In Spain just prior to the outbreak of the Spanish civil war they were struck by the presence of soldiers, the pervasiveness of anti-fascist slogans, and the extreme poverty among the people. Throughout Europe they were aware of a heightened level of anxiety, of political tension.[74]

In his 1967 autobiography Soyer also recalled his responses to several European exhibitions he visited at that time. In comparing his own work to some of the more politicized European works, he was struck by an obvious dissimilarity; before a painting by George Grosz he became "dissatisfied with the mildness, the 'sympathy' the unexaggeratedness of my art."[75]

On his return from Europe, Soyer was on the executive committee to plan the February 1936 meeting of the First American Artists' Congress, the Popular Front organization formed by leftist artists following the demise of the John Reed Club. It was Soyer's most active participation in a political event until that time, and he was the only one of the Fourteenth Street School artists to sign the Artists' Call. In the wake of his experiences in Europe and his regular attendance at John Reed Club meetings it was natural for Soyer, along with hundreds of other artists, to commit himself to a movement whose stated intent was to "achieve unity of action among artists . . . on all issues which concern their economic and cultural security and freedom and to fight war, Fascism, and Reaction, destroyers of art and culture."[76]

Among Soyer's paintings from the 1930s are many socially engaged works of the period 1935–37. Works like *Shop Girls* and its pendant *Office Girls*, which one reviewer praised for its "direct spirit we can call American," and paintings depicting male victims of unemployment are more prevalent in these years than the studio interiors Soyer produced in the late 1920s and early 1930s and again in the 1940s. In *Fé Alf and Her Pupils* (1935; Fig. 6.24), Soyer portrayed the leftist modern dancer Fé Alf in a militant confrontational stance, her feet firmly planted, her hand tightly holding the mallet, her gaze leveled at the viewer.[77]

6.24   Raphael Soyer, *Fé Alf and Her Pupils*, 1935. Oil on canvas, 40″ × 37⁷/₈″. Collection of The Newark Museum.

In 1936 Soyer also painted one of only two "activist" images he claims ever to have attempted; in it he took up the theme of militancy related to the Spanish civil war, the event that galvanized the Popular Front. In *Workers Armed* (Fig. 6.25— see also *The Crowd*, Fig. 3.35) Soyer drew inspiration directly from Daumier's 1863 painting *The Uprising* (Fig. 6.26). In Soyer's work armed men and women packed closely together call out and march toward an unseen enemy. The crowd is brilliantly illuminated, and one young man looks out toward the viewer, soliciting support. In this work Soyer aligned himself specifically with other liberals and radicals who faulted American neutrality as well as the government's embargoing the sale of munitions to either side in the war. Because Hitler and Mussolini regularly supplied the fascist insurgents with arms, the Loyalists were left at an extreme disadvantage. Soyer legitimated the aesthetic component of his political art by invoking Daumier, an established "old master" of political themes and of the direct manner of painting that had come to be associated with a social or a people's art. In this way he took up a common aesthetic strategy of Popular Front artists. Broadening their aesthetic base to include both representational and modernist styles of oil painting, they diffused the charges of propaganda leveled at political graphics calling for direct action that had been produced and approved by the American Left in the more sectarian period of the early thirties. Soyer found in the liberalized political, cultural, and aesthetic strategies employed in the Popular Front era the means to respond to the threat of fascism and to express his solidarity with the cause of Spanish Loyalists in their civil war.[78]

The tension and interrogation in *Shop Girls* was thus part of a broader agenda that included the American artist's rising concern with international politics and its effects on the community at large in the 1930s. Similar concerns filtered into debates about the role of working women. In her study of the Depression's effects on these women, for example, the sociologist Lorine Pruette argued that they must protect their rights against the "fascist" tendency to return them to the home. She stated further that no family or society could develop when women were denied the "right to function according to their abilities, needs and desires."[79] Even as Soyer's *Shop Girls* directs the viewer to speculate on the conditions under which women labored, the individual figures continue to assert their need for that work. *Window Shoppers* (Fig. 6.2 and Plate 5), a work that portrays several of women's possible roles, can be read according to this late-thirties political agenda as a reassertion of women's rights in a democratic society.

Even though Soyer's art was more confrontational in these mid-decade years than it had been, it never became revolutionary or propagandistic—that was not what Soyer wanted. Nor apparently is that what the broadened critical agenda of the leftist press required of revolutionary artists, especially during the Popular Front era and the years immediately following. How to create a revolutionary art was debated in *Art Front*, the periodical published by the Artists' Union from October 1934 to December 1937. Soyer would have been well acquainted with the periodical because his brother Moses wrote for it; and debates in print carried over to the regular Wednesday night meetings of the Artists' Union that Soyer attended.[80]

By the fall of 1935, among leftist intellectuals and within the Communist party, there was a general reorientation away from a militant revolutionary posture toward the more peaceful collective aims of the Popular Front movement; Communists joined Socialists, Democrats, and members of the middle class to preserve

6.25 Raphael Soyer, *Workers Armed*, c. 1936–37. Oil on canvas. Private collection.

the values of democracy and social progress against the threat of fascism. At the same time, there was an attempt to broaden and liberalize the aesthetic debate about revolutionary art. Reviewers in *Art Front* explored ways by which an artist could make a revolutionary art without sacrificing the quality of the work or producing mere propaganda.[81] Harold Rosenberg, for example, wrote that no single work by an artist needed to make a full revolutionary statement:

> The principle—art is propaganda—recognizes the fact that the picture-world of the painter includes within it elements of many kinds, some confined to the world of simple appearance, some introducing into appearance action-motives and a critique of values; and that this picture-world, as an entirety, deflects the mentality of society in one direction or another.[82]

6.26   Honoré Daumier, *The Uprising,* undated. Oil on canvas, 34$^{1}/_{2}''$ × 44$^{1}/_{2}''$. The Phillips Collection, Washington, D.C.

Whereas Rosenberg discussed pictorial possibilities and implied that an artist's total style could embody many social ideas, the artist Louis Lozowick claimed that a revolutionary art opened up a new range of possibilities for subject matter within the artist's environment. In a July–August 1936 issue of *Art Front*, Lozowick's long list of subject possibilities included relations between and within classes and the "worker as victim" as important new avenues of investigation.[83]

Soyer's working women were new subjects. The shopgirl, as she came to be understood, was virtually unknown in the iconography of American art. By selecting her as his subject, Soyer was bringing to consciousness an image of the female working-class wage earner, who had been supplanted by the saleswoman, a middle-class model of success. Her victimization is expressed not only by painted effects of weariness but also, more subtly, by her suspended but moving state. She is between environments, linked to (but not interacting with) her fellow workers, alienated, in short, from her workplace, from her class, and from traditional mainstream beliefs about the role of her gender. Though never part of his expressed artistic intentions, Soyer's carefully coded pictorial strategies can be read at the conjunction of competing discourses on art, society, politics, and gender. He experienced these in moving from his own social milieu as an immigrant artist to the established world of American art in the late 1920s and 1930s and from there to the meeting places of the decade's most spirited debates on art and politics. The reading of the image I propose here is possible only when we begin to unravel the work's meaning within and between these sites of production and reception.

Although we lack complete evidence by which to evaluate Soyer's own response to feminist arguments for—or public sentiments against—women's work during the Depression, we can conjecture that the artist's values and personal experiences would have made him sympathetic to women's right to work. By showing women in transition and by asserting their womanliness, Soyer's painting affirms their acceptability as youthful, temporary members of the work force. By making them objects available for contemplation, through traditional studio picture formats, the artist made them into a work of art, thereby confining them to a constricted social space defined by looking. Even as the paintings reinforce the mainstream ideology that women had their proper place, the women are brought close to the viewer and return the viewer's gaze. This tactic, when combined with an individualized working-class subject, reinscribes class into the image as part of the viewer's social world; class is no longer a force made distant through a deeper space, a stereotyped figure, or a middle-class setting of consumption. By such means, the painting engages the working ambiance around Union Square more fully than other works by the Fourteenth Street School. It stages a muted interrogation of the social order for the viewer. And finally, Soyer's *Shop Girls* holds in visual suspension the ambiguous and problematic relationship between femininity and labor in the Depression.

CHAPTER SEVEN

THE QUESTION OF DIFFERENCE: ISABEL BISHOP'S DEFERENTIAL OFFICE GIRLS

I didn't want to be a woman artist, I just wanted to be an artist.

ISABEL BISHOP, December 16, 1982

I hope my work is recognizable as being by a woman, though I certainly would never deliberately make it feminine in any way, in subject or treatment. But if I speak in a voice which is my own, it's bound to be the voice of a woman.

ISABEL BISHOP, 1978

Both "masculine" and "feminine" are not essences, but social categories formed through changing social experiences. They are not only imposed from outside us, they are also experienced subjectively as part of our understanding of who we are. But in a patriarchal culture it is clearly the case that women are forced to adopt a masculine viewpoint in the production and consumption of images far more often than men are required to adopt a feminine one.

ROSEMARY BETTERTON, "How Do Women Look?" 1987

For Isabel Bishop the middle years of the Depression brought a succession of professional and personal milestones. Following her first one-woman show at the new Midtown Galleries in 1933, she met and married Dr. Harold Wolff in 1934. She left her studio–living quarters at 9 West Fourteenth Street, facing Hearn's Department Store; moved with her husband to a residence in the Riverdale section of the Bronx; and leased a new studio at 857 Broadway, with a view of the northwest corner of Union Square (see Map 1). In 1936 she gained considerable attention when the Metropolitan Museum of Art purchased *Two Girls* (Fig. 7.1). Reviews of her one-woman exhibition in that year and again in 1939 acknowledged her independence of Kenneth Hayes Miller's influence and proclaimed her well on her

7.1 Isabel Bishop, *Two Girls,* 1935. Oil and tempera on composition board, 20″ × 24″. The Metropolitan Museum of Art.

way to being one of America's best women artists. By 1941 she was elected to the National Academy of Design—the establishment of the American Art world.[1]

Bishop's shift away from Miller's sphere of influence occurred when she set aside the Milleresque shoppers, women at their toilettes, and still lifes featured in her 1933 Midtown Galleries show. By 1936, when Raphael Soyer painted *Shop Girls,* Bishop had begun to paint Union Square's other working women—the office workers who made up the clerical staffs of the banks, public utilities, insurance companies, and small offices in the district. Whereas the view from her old studio had inspired early works like *Dante and Virgil in Union Square* and *Department Store Entrance* (Figs. 2.2 and 3.7), her new studio looked down on the square itself, populated by those she called its "regular denizens": the unemployed men congre-

7.2 Isabel Bishop, *The Kid*, 1935–36.
Oil on gesso panel, 20″ × 17″.
Present location unknown.

gating at the base of monuments who became the subject for paintings like *The Club* (Fig. 3.39) and for many drawings and etchings, and the young working women, occasionally waitresses but more often than not office girls, who worked nearby. Bishop frequently sat in the park and sketched these girls as they relaxed during their noon-hour break, or she asked them to come to her studio and pose. With the relandscaping of Union Square, completed in 1936, nearly six years after the subway renovations, the park was a pleasant place to go.

Bishop's paintings of youthful, female office workers in the 1930s are sometimes bust-length portraits of individual girls in work clothes, often wearing the exaggerated hats popular in the second half of the decade. Works like *The Kid* (1935–36; Fig. 7.2), *Young Woman's Head* (1936; Fig. 7.3), *Laughing Head* (1938; Fig. 7.4), or *Tidying Up* (c. 1938; Fig. 7.5 and Plate 7) are penetrating close-up studies of character, physiognomy, and mood. In other works, like *Lunch Counter* (1940; Fig. 7.6), *Lunch Hour* (1939; Fig. 7.7), *At the Noon Hour* (1939; Fig. 7.8 and Plate 8), or *Two Girls with a Book* (1938; Fig. 7.9), two office workers appear together, usually outdoors and always in shallow, undefined settings.[2] Stylistically, these works combine the artist's respect for established artistic traditions with her modernist practice of structuring and articulating the picture plane. Arranged against a faint grid and thick repeating horizontals, Bishop's studied surface compositions

7.3 Isabel Bishop, *Young Woman's Head*, 1936. Oil and tempera on gesso panel, 20″ × 17″. Private collection.

7.4 Isabel Bishop, *Laughing Head*, 1938. Oil, 13″ × 12″. The Butler Institute of American Art, Youngstown, Ohio.

7.5   Isabel Bishop, *Tidying Up,* c. 1938. Oil on canvas, 15″ × 11¹/₂″. Indianapolis Museum of Art.

7.6   Isabel Bishop, *Lunch Counter*, c. 1940. Oil and egg tempera on masonite, 23″ × 14⅛″. The Phillips Collection, Washington, D.C.

7.7   Isabel Bishop, *Lunch Hour,* 1939. Oil and tempera on gesso panel, 27″ × 17½″.
Collection of Mr. and Mrs. John Whitney Payson.

7.8   Isabel Bishop, *At the Noon Hour,* 1939. Tempera and pencil on composition board, 25″ × 18″. Museum of Fine Arts, Springfield, Massachusetts.

7.9   Isabel Bishop, *Two Girls with a Book*, 1938. Oil and tempera on gesso panel, 20″ × 24″. Private collection.

are animated by fully realized figures, modeled in a soft chiaroscuro and painted with pale amber tints reminiscent of old master paintings. At the same time, her images also draw together conventions of genre paintings—as evidenced by quiet scenes of everyday life around Union Square—and figure studies, in which posed models assume the burden of pictorial expression. Placed in shallow, minimally defined settings outside the working environment, Bishop's relaxed young office workers remain self-absorbed or interact with one another but never directly engage the viewer. They lean on walls, eat ice-cream cones, converse quietly, share a book, or discuss a letter. Often they touch or link arms during their interchanges, suggesting a womanly closeness or camaraderie. Dressed in slightly wrinkled office attire, the women themselves are neither glamorous nor unattractive. Although

Bishop's pictures of neighborhood women were frequently compared to those of her teacher Miller and their close friend Marsh, the comparisons had more to do with their common urban site and the old master origins of their figures than with the types of women they painted. None of Bishop's women become sexualized stereotypes, and none are old enough to be matrons. Her sedate young women bear little resemblance to Marsh's Union Square workers, the blonde bombshells found in images like *Hudson Bay Fur Company* (Fig. 3.26). And, though stocky rather than svelte, Bishop figures are not made up of the repetitious rounded forms and idealized faces of Miller's shoppers. These are quiet, pleasant genre pictures; nothing about these young women seems striking, garish, unusual, or confrontational.

Bishop's representations of young working women depict a less sexually charged feminine ideal, one deemed more appropriate for the workplace. By embodying in her pictorial language a middle-class ideology of office work that prescribed business conduct proper for women in the 1930s, the artist simultaneously constituted and negotiated class and gender difference. A growing number of interwar publications on women and work championed this same ideology. Statistical surveys and government reports set out the facts about the office worker's job, charting institutional, social, and economic changes brought about by new office technology and the upheaval of the Depression and predicting the office worker's future.[3] These studies were less sanguine in assessing the constant changes in her occupation than were the popular periodical studies and advice manuals that helped to define the ideal office worker and contributed to the myth of occupational and social mobility connected to office jobs.

No matter what the focus of their study, writers for all these publications, many of them women social scientists, social workers, or job counselors, offered women a competitive model of success grounded in a discourse of gender difference and social mobility. Specifically, they argued that if a woman served her superiors with wifely loyalty, behaved deferentially, and dressed modestly, she might advance in her job. More important, in bringing her "natural" caretaking and homemaking skills to the office, she would be preparing herself for the successful marriage that both she and society considered her ultimate achievement.[4] Like the literature of the period, Bishop's pictures constructed an ideal of a modest, deferential office worker without reference to the material circumstances of the typical office worker's life. Her paintings can be aligned with mainstream 1930s thinking on women's roles that was part of the moderate discourse of the revised new woman. Within that discourse, Bishop's works also embody notions of female achievement and class mobility that can be linked to an ideal of liberal individualism. This ideal shaped the way Bishop characterized her subjects and perceived her own role as an artist.

"Difference," Griselda Pollock reminds us, "is not essential but understood as a social structure which positions male and female people asymmetrically in relation to language, to social and economic power and to meaning. . . . To perceive women's specificity is to analyse historically a particular configuration of difference."[5] According to Pollock, such gender imbalance in a particular social structure and its supporting ideology fosters a variety of possible and contradictory positions for an individual, all subject to constant conflict and negotiation. Many of these negotiations are played out in visual and verbal texts, themselves products and producers of ideology that are subject to the codes and conventions of their own institutional practice. As a female artist viewing her female subjects, Bishop—sometimes unwittingly—participated in contemporary discussions about women's roles and office work in the 1930s. The way she presented her subjects, within the range of representational practices available to her, simultaneously blurred and clarified the sites where gender and class difference were debated in the 1930s. To paraphrase Rosemary Betterton, I also wish to suggest that Bishop moved between a masculine and a feminine viewpoint in producing her images, thereby carving out a more prominent viewing position for the middle-class female viewer of her work.

By the time Bishop introduced the female office worker into the iconography of American scene painting she had become, like the saleslady, a highly visible member of the workforce. One out of every three New York City working women held some kind of clerical position. The institutions near Union Square alone provided close to ten thousand jobs (see Map 2). At the four main neighborhood banks, women computed interest, counted money, checked securities, made bookkeeping entries, and tabulated customers' accounts. At the Guardian Life Insurance Company, which towered over the northeast corner of the square, employees checked premium rates, risks, and policy expiration dates; sent out bills; and kept elaborate records on all their customers. At the Consolidated Edison Tower on Irving Place just off the square, young women kept meter records and did all the billing.[6] Other buildings in the district housed smaller firms that employed clerical workers for similar routine tasks. Bishop herself observed that "there were an awful lot of small businesses around," and she believed that many of her models and clerical subjects were from these smaller offices.[7]

According to contemporary statistical surveys the women who filed, sorted mail, and typed were usually white, native-born, unmarried, and recently out of high school; Bishop's office girls confirm the demographic profile. In clerical work, the field that had expanded most rapidly for women between 1890 and 1920, native-born white women had always taken approximately 90 percent of the jobs.[8] These women tended to be under twenty-five years of age. A number of polls from the 1920s suggest that white middle-class female workers preferred marriage to a career, and many dropped out of the work force when they married or, more frequently, when their first child was born.[9]

In the 1930s the young female clerical worker continued to dominate the business work force. A 1934 survey of New York office workers found that the median age ranged from twenty-four to twenty-seven years, with women in banks, insurance companies, and utilities on the low side of the median. A number of businesses, particularly insurance companies that required substantial clerical help, preferred to hire inexperienced workers. Employers usually liked to train and promote from within the organization as upper-level vacancies occurred. Because an immediate superior could rapidly instruct a beginner in routine tasks, most businesses found it uneconomical to search for a worker with particular job skills.[10] According to a Department of Labor Women's Bureau study in the early 1930s, few New York employers required a specific educational background of prospective female employees. Job counselors, however, warned girls against leaving high school to accept clerical jobs because of their dead end-nature. Finally, some companies refused to employ women over thirty for beginning office positions unless special skills were required, and almost no employer wanted college-trained workers at the lower levels: "College women are not satisfactory for the general run of clerical work; they quickly become dissatisfied, and we have always had high turn-over with such women, so usually do not hire them except for jobs that require special training."[11]

To judge from the extreme youth of most of Bishop's office workers, they were beginners and were probably unmarried. The 1930 Census reported that only 18.3 percent of women in clerical jobs were married, as against dramatically higher percentages for women in trade, domestic service, and manufacturing and mechanical industries. By 1934 the percentage had dropped even further.[12] Observers of occupational trends analyzed the statistics in several ways. The economist Grace Coyle, who looked to the economic and psychological states of the women, argued that in agriculture, industry, and domestic service women continued to work after marriage from economic need, whereas women professionals had a desire for "independence, self expression and the use of expert skill."[13] Clerical workers fell somewhere between: they usually married men who could support them, and the work was not challenging enough to keep them in the work force.

At the same time, however, employer and fellow employee pressure against the married clerical worker was stronger than in almost any other occupation. It was much easier, for example, for married women to acquire and retain department store sales positions than office jobs. Some of the pressure was exerted by the traditional ideology of woman's proper place. Coyle suggested that both husbands and employers wanted "to defend the 'American home' from subversive tendencies," and therefore to keep married women at home. Other pressure came from female co-workers. With increased competition for jobs in the Depression, single women workers wanted married women to leave the jobs to those who needed them. In any case, many of the larger institutions had such strict policies against the employment of married female workers that women chose not to report their marriages or retained their maiden names to avoid losing their jobs.[14]

The place of Bishop's women in the office hierarchy is difficult to generalize. Although occupational categories varied with the type of business, larger offices had more specialized and stratified positions; in smaller offices where there were fewer workers—and where Bishop believed many of her subjects worked—office girls shared several tasks. Because the categories of office work required different levels of education and skill, each had a different status. File clerks and junior clerks were at the bottom of the clerical ladder. These were the youngest, least experienced, and least educated, some of whom had left school to take their positions. Next came file and general clerks; Bishop probably painted some of these women since insurance and utility companies employed vast numbers. For these jobs a general high school education was sufficient.[15]

Office machine operators, followed by typists, were next in the occupational hierarchy, making up but a small proportion of the clerical population. Since most women who learned typing also took high school or business school shorthand, they moved into the next higher and more populous category of stenographer. These women, especially in smaller offices, usually performed a variety of tasks beyond taking and transcribing dictation. Bookkeepers, cashiers, and general telephone operators were also at the level of the stenographer. Finally, the secretary was at the top of the occupational scale. She had mastered all the skills of the occupations below her, was given more responsibility, and usually had the privilege of working for a single employer. She was often a woman who had worked her way up from a stenographic position in the company.[16]

From the information compiled, one can begin to draw a composite of Bishop's office worker. She was a young high school graduate, unmarried, on the job for only a year or two. The tentativeness in *The Kid* (Fig. 7.2) or in the shy interaction of the women in *Lunch Hour* (Fig. 7.7) suggest her inexperience and her employment in one of the lower-level occupations. The figure in *Young Woman* (1937; Fig. 7.10), however, is on her own, poised and self-confident. Middle- to upper-middle-class urban viewers of this work, familiar with the business world, might well have identified her as a stenographer working her way up the office ladder.

Bishop's pictorial strategies and her depiction of the appearance and behavior of these women suggest that both her attitude toward the working girl and her conception of that girl's life and job differed from those of Raphael Soyer. Bishop's paired office workers, in *Lunch Counter, Lunch Hour* (Fig. 7.6) and *At the Noon Hour* (Fig. 7.8; Plate 8), seem more relaxed than those in Soyer's *Office Girls* (Fig. 6.3). Unlike Soyer's figures—cropped at the waist, placed against the picture plane, and packed closely together—Bishop's are complete, placed on shallow stage-like settings with enough room to move. Soyer's women move quickly through the environment; Bishop's women are still; either they lean against a wall or sit or stand in relaxed contrapposto poses.

7.10 Isabel Bishop, *Young Woman*, 1937. Oil and egg tempera on masonite, 30¼″ × 22¼″. The Pennsylvania Academy of the Fine Arts, Philadelphia.

Both Soyer and Bishop depict ordinary women, and both individualize their models. They define the self-presentation of femininity as emotional expression. But Soyer's women are uniformly melancholy or serious. The directness with which they confront the viewer or go about their business suggests further that they have acquired some measure of knowledge and experience. The emotional range—from joy to wistfulness—that Bishop observed in her women was broader and her depiction of moods more subtly nuanced than Soyer's, thanks to the complex transitions between light and dark through which Bishop explores the characterizing topographies of these young women's faces. Bishop used this technique in the patterns that describe, for example, the pointed and slightly jutting chin and narrow eyes in *Young Woman's Head* (Fig. 7.3) as contrasted with the smoother surfaces of the full fleshy face in *Laughing Head* (Fig. 7.4).

Soyer's women are psychologically isolated from one another. Group solidarity is achieved only by compositional devices superimposed by the artist. In *Shop Girls* (Fig. 6.4; Plate 6), linked arms tie the women together, and several other figures who are spatially apart are actually merged through paint. The crooked arms of the two principal figures in the foreground of *Office Girls* (Fig. 6.3) unify the figures, but there is no suggestion that the women are acquainted; their isolation or self-preoccupation within groups thematizes urban anonymity. Alone among the Fourteenth Street School artists, Bishop regularly painted physically and emotionally intimate interchanges between women. In *At the Noon Hour* two women lean against the wall chatting, and one links her arm companionably through the other's. Their shoulders and thighs also touch. The same closeness appears in *Lunch Hour*, where two women rest against the edge of a Union Square fountain, their shoulders touching as they turn toward one another, sharing secrets over the pleasure of an ice-cream cone. In *Two Girls with a Book* the girl on the left drapes her arm over her friend's shoulder, gazing at her and her book as she traces a line in the text.

Bishop's emphasis on the warmth of these interchanges and the degree of her subjects' engagement with one another overrides, without fully obliterating, the sensuous projection of their femininity toward the viewer. In this aspect of her female imagery, Bishop differs from Soyer and, even more, from Miller and Marsh. Where Soyer's models seem "gently sexualized" on one level, his sympathetic response to them as individuals remains stronger than any projection onto them of masculine desire. With Marsh such a projection is overt to the point of exaggeration; with Miller it is somewhat less obvious. Even where Bishop's models assume more self-conscious poses of display, their provocativeness is never depicted as assertive, nor are they blatantly sexualized. Compare, for example, Marsh's *Fourteenth Street Siren* (Figs. 3.19 and 5.1; Plate 3) with the taller woman in *At the Noon Hour* (Fig. 7.8; Plate 8). Bishop's model stands with her right foot before her left, her left hip slightly forward, her right arm akimbo. But her looser dress (almost all of Bishop's women wear softly draped or loosely tailored costumes) masks the

7.11   Isabel Bishop, *Double Date Delayed, No. 1,* 1948. Oil on masonite, 22³/₁₆″ × 18³/₁₆″.
Munson-Williams-Proctor Institute Museum of Art, Utica, New York.

curves of her figure. And her energies are directed as much toward her friend as toward an unseen masculine viewer for whom she puts herself on display. In *At the Noon Hour,* perhaps more than in the other images that feature young women in a shared activity, Bishop captured what she referred to as

> a moment in their lives when they are really in motion, because they, of course, are looking for husbands and, at the same time, they're earning their living. . . . The time that I try to catch them, that I'm interested in trying to present, is when they are in their lunch hour, the hour of respite, when both these things seem to me to be communicated—that is their double purpose.[17]

While it is part of the structure and economy of looking that women in art are available to the masculine spectator, Bishop's paintings construct a larger space for the feminine viewer, producing in turn a greater exclusion of the male.[18] Bishop relegates masculine intervention to the margins of feminine interaction much more directly in a later painting, *Double Date Delayed, No. 1* (1948; Fig. 7.11). Here two young women lean across the upright figure of the male, conversing intensely as if he were absent. Banished from the conversation, he is further constrained by their enclosing postures, his discomfort expressed in his slumped pose with hands held together between his thighs.

In paintings of paired working women, the masking of overtly sensuous behavior blunts the intensity of the masculine gaze. These works also envision a same-sex sphere so circumscribed, thanks to the intimacy between the women, that a female viewer—another woman—may comfortably be drawn into the intimate circle. Finally, the space in which looking occurs is itself intimate. Because of the fluid surfaces and a close-value palette employing a narrow range of pastel colors, a viewer is made to draw closer to the works both to distinguish the figures and to observe the intricate surfaces that surround them. Within this closer range the gender-specific transactions occur.

In fact, when these works began to be exhibited in the late 1930s, some of the critical discussion—concerning viewing itself as well as the relative "strength" of Bishop's women—broke down along gender lines. Where Emily Genauer praised Bishop's "clearly defined faces and figures," her "superb draftsmanship and modelling," and her "sensitivity," other critics faulted her "indistinct, nebulous manner" of defining forms. Edward Alden Jewell of the *New York Times* complained of the need for "an uncommon amount of squinting" to see figures that were themselves too "pallid and frail and washed out to emerge." James Lane, who later spoke of Bishop's "unconventional and glorious" women, initially found them shy, "bloodless and lacking in vigor." Forbes Watson felt that Bishop's "extremely close searching for subtle values" sometimes led to a "neutrality approaching timidity."[19] As male critics described her, Bishop's young woman was a descendant of the fragile steel-engraving lady.

Late nineteenth-century images of women in interiors portrayed the social phenomenon of women's separate, often ritualized, activities; the term *homosocial* has been used to describe this separate, predominantly domestic, realm of female interaction. In Bishop's paintings, women are depicted carving out a similarly separate and intimate arena, now in the modern urban environment—where women are most susceptible to the masculine gaze. Seen in this light, the works impart a degree of quiet strength to these female intimacies.

Apart from the homosocial content of Bishop's work, its social spaces are similar to those Soyer represents. In both artists' works women are "in transit," outdoors, suspended between environments. But Bishop's environments are so ambiguously defined by her intricate painting techniques that her women are potentially anywhere and nowhere within the settings. *At the Noon Hour* shifts constantly between foreground, background, and figures, with value shifts and horizontal brushstrokes suggesting several spatial interpretations. One is that the wall on which the two women rest their elbows projects from a storefront glass, on which LUCKIES is printed; this possibility is reinforced by the proximity of the lettering to the picture's surface. Another is that the wall is freestanding and the storefront is all the way across a street behind the women; this is supported by the distance we read into the storefronts in the upper right background. A third interpretation is that we see a reflection of the street across from the women in the storefront glass behind them. Since the letters BSO just above the head of the taller woman appear to be further away than the larger letters, this interpretation also seems plausible. No matter how the picture is finally read, the space is ambiguous, and the women potentially relate to more than one environment.

Although the appearance of Bishop's youthful workers corroborates the historical profile of Depression era office workers, a tension exists between the depiction of ordinary women posed in a seedy neighborhood and the beauty of light, color, and carefully manipulated surfaces that eradicate all references to work. Bishop's firmly modeled figures in works like *At the Noon Hour* occupy spatially ambiguous settings created either by thick globs of paint that accentuate the surface of the canvas or soft veils of horizontal strokes that blur contours and link figures to one another or to their background. Though formally posed, her women are surrounded and overlaid by this fluid, constantly shifting atmosphere. Such an abstraction of pictorial setting disguises her female subjects' specific identity as workers outside the home and suggests that their spatial and temporal positions are tentative rather than fixed. The figures themselves are equally dynamic, their hands and arms animated by quavering pencil strokes. The fragility and transience resulting from this technique are heightened by the warm light and close gradations of pastel colors that illuminate the women's youthful faces.[20]

There are other things we need to know about these women. What, for example, did their jobs allow them to do, and what did their appearance and behavior signify in the late 1930s? They are outdoors, away from their working environments, look-ing pleasant and content and seeming to suffer little from their jobs. But there is also a sense that they renew themselves through repose, quiet conversation, or the refreshment of an ice-cream cone. Their clothing, generally fashionable, looks rum-pled, owing to Bishop's scumbled surfaces and sketchy pencil marks. In *Lunch Hour*, for example (Fig. 7.7), the wrinkles and limpness of the jacket worn by the figure at right detract from an overall impression of tidiness. Such naturalistic touches keep these predominantly optimistic works from being over-idealized or over-romanticized representations of office workers' lives.

Well-established perceptions about office work help us situate Bishop's pictorial language in the broader discourse of women and work. By the 1930s popular books like *If Women Must Work, Manners in Business,* and *She Strives to Conquer* cel-ebrated office work as the ideal stopgap for young women between school and marriage: in offices, hours were shorter than in factories or stores or domestic ser-vice, the surroundings more pleasant, and the pay better.[21]

Women who took clerical jobs were also attracted by less concrete variables, many of them linked to office work's most seductive, if least tangible, offerings. Ruth Wanger, somewhat simplistic and superficial in her analysis for a high school audience, noted that "office positions are very popular with women. They are what we call 'white collar jobs.' . . . It means there is no hard manual labor that would soil your clothes or wear them out quickly. As most women like to dress attractively, they want to find positions that do not call for old clothes."[22]

Clerical jobs were valued not only because offices were quieter and cleaner than factories but also because office work provided a chance to get ahead—to achieve what economics professor Grace Coyle defined as "the rise to business success so highly esteemed among us."[23] Within the office a young woman could rise to the top of the stenographic pool or even, in rare cases, achieve executive status. The social interaction in an office was considered superior to that in a factory or depart-ment store. In a small office a young woman whose parents had been manual labor-ers could transcend class and social background through interaction with better-educated superiors. The work itself remained free of the stigma of manual labor, allowing the office worker to achieve a middle-class standard of femininity. Inter-personal relationships in an office could stimulate a woman to greater personal achievement and loyalty to her institution. The institution in turn could reward her with promotions and better pay.[24]

Given this situation, the fluidity of Bishop's surfaces can be read in two ways: it destabilizes the position of the woman as a worker with access to economic power even as it unfixes the boundaries of gender and class to project the possibility of such access.

In fact, the blurring of boundaries seems to have been Bishop's goal. As early as 1939 the artist equated her formal quest for "painterly mobility," manifested in her intricate painted surfaces, with the possibility of social betterment for her subjects. Mobility, as she worked it out during her career according to a loose Wölfflinian model of stylistic analysis, was not movement per se but the *potential* for movement.[25] "To express that potential by visual means is a very subtle business. You can't describe it in words, it has to be expressed in the modeling. To express it in the modeling there has to be created in the onlooker . . . a sense of physical continuity as by a subtle and delicate web throughout the picture."[26]

Bishop viewed the continuous horizontal strokes in her works as the web that links her figures to the environment and thereby suggests mobility in these otherwise still figures. In extensive discussions of her 1930s imagery held prior to her 1975 retrospective exhibition, Bishop reiterated her goal of showing these office workers' potential for upward mobility in American society. Her theory of painterly mobility as a metaphor for social mobility was also based on her sense that one could identify the lower classes.[27]

> It seemed to me that in order to say what I felt I wanted to say about them, girls or men had to be classifiable. I don't think you can classify the upper middle class. The upper middle class is not definable in our society, but these young people are class-marked in the sense that you understand they are socially limited. But what I feel about them—and I really do feel strongly about these things—is that I know so many instances where, if they want to move, in a social sense, they can. . . . and it's that mobility that connected for me.[28]

Bishop amplified her statement, emphasizing her optimistic view of upward mobility.

> I was conscious of their being class-marked, but not class-fixed. If I succeeded in making them seem to the onlooker that they could turn and move in a physical sense, this opened up a subjective potential which could include the mobility of content. I mean it made it possible to suggest, or at least the suggestion was already there, to my mind, that if a physical movement takes place who can tell what other kind of movement might take place.[29]

Bishop's concern with her subjects' potential came in part from her own early awareness of class and gender difference. The artist's childhood home was located next to the urban working-class neighborhood in Detroit where her father was a poorly paid high school Latin teacher. Because both parents were from upper-middle-class families and wished to maintain the appearance of that position, social contacts with the neighbors were minimal. Bishop recalled in a 1975 interview that "though we didn't have the money, we identified with the big houses on the next block. I wasn't supposed to play with the children on my block or be connected with them but I wanted to be. I thought, 'Oh they have a warmer life than I do—they all know each other and see each other and we are isolated.' "[30]

Caught between two social classes, Bishop learned about the restrictions and exclusions of each and acquired her own attitudes about social limitation and social mobility. When she came to New York in 1920, her fortunes changed. She received a monthly stipend from a well-to-do relative that allowed her to concentrate on her education and to move in circles with artists of her own social, educational, and now economic circumstances. Her economic support continued until 1934, when she married Wolff, a prominent neurologist.[31] Bishop recognized that her changed economic situation allowed her greater occupational and social mobility—advantages not accessible to her subjects—but she was nonetheless optimistic about the relation between social mobility and individual initiative. The artist credited much of her own success to a rigorous six-day per week work schedule and to her slow, thoughtful production of images. Her story, and the one she envisioned for her subjects, was, in some ways, a version of the Horatio Alger success story, now told with female characters.

Bishop's depiction of warm, intimate relationships between working women was in part the outcome of a working process in which a female producer of images of female subjects promoted same-sex interactions that drew in both the artist and the female viewer. It was not until Bishop stopped painting friezes of shoppers in the Miller mode and turned to images of Union Square workers that she began to employ nonprofessional models on a regular basis and to sketch from everyday life in Union Square. She also made clear at the time of this transition that she wanted to portray more than modern women's "superficial" exteriors:

> I don't think I could ever use a professional model again. It makes a great difference, because I try to paint people who are trivial outside and show that they are decent and good inside. . . . There is a great discrepancy in American women. . . . Their hats and clothes make them look like flibbertigibbets, light as air, when they are not. Traditionally, we show silly people in silly clothes, and the housewife with her hair done up and in a gingham apron. But that is an anachronism. It isn't true of the modern world.[32]

When she began to use nonprofessional models, she also expanded her method, making dozens of sketches, followed by etchings, to capture a specific moment or gesture for a painting. In effect, Bishop was setting up female-centered working conditions in the space of her studio with women who were, like herself, meant to be understood as modern working women.

The depiction of same-sex intimacy was in part a reference to her own onetime wish to join her working-class neighbors' "warmer" interactions. Yet the dynamics of the artist-subject and artist-model relationship must also be read as the simultaneous acknowledgment or assertion *and* diffusion of class and gender difference. Bishop admitted in interviews that by the time she was an established artist, she no longer envied her subjects' lives. Nor did she want now to take part in them. Moreover, she was very clear about the types of women she portrayed and invited to her studio. Though art critics occasionally described her subjects as shopgirls, Bishop claimed that she had never painted "any of them"; their class and occupational status were lower than those of the office worker.[33]

A 1936 newspaper article characterizing the artist-model dynamic involved in the production of *Two Girls* defines the professional distance Bishop maintained in interactions with her subjects. She asked a waitress from Childs', where she regularly had breakfast, to model. Miss Riggins agreed and brought a friend, Miss Abbott, with her to the studio. Almost every day for six months the two waitresses sat for Bishop. As Miss Riggins described it, she and Miss Abbott—the two women married and lost touch with each other until the newspaper piece brought them together—talked about everything from movies to boyfriends to fashion while Bishop worked. Bishop wrote of the period, "I never did know their first names. They'd come up from Childs' and just sit and talk. I don't know what about. I couldn't tell if I had to. I made dozens of sketches of them. Finally I thought I had something."[34] Although Bishop's same-sex interest in her subjects enabled her to depict a relationship of female intimacy, class and professional distance kept her from forming bonds with her subjects. This distance can be read as respect, professionalism, or neutrality, but it is also consistent with objectifying the models in terms of class. Though class distance in Bishop's works is never what it is in Marsh's, it remains, now strongly modulated by the commonality of gender.

Even so, Bishop wished to blur class and gender divisions, to infuse her imagery with her own optimism about the possibilities for working women. Though she idealized her ordinary models through the use of pastel tones and light, she never wished to divest them of their individuality. A comparison of photographs of her models for *Two Girls* with the painting (Figs. 7.1 and 7.12) demonstrates that she retained the look of the actual women while suffusing their features with a soft light that emphasized their youthful seriousness. Of Miss Riggins, the woman in profile, Bishop wrote,

> I didn't think she was extremely beautiful or American or Hindu or 14th street or anything. I said, There's an interesting face. It didn't matter what she wore or how she fixed her blond hair. I wanted to paint her as she was, somehow and give the feeling that it didn't matter about the outside appearance the looking glass shows. I wanted to do her as a person.[35]

By seeing her women as self-sufficient individuals in a subtly shifting environment rather than as sexual stereotypes, Bishop conveyed her own optimism about working women and American life in general toward the end of the 1930s. She also attempted to suggest that these women could transcend the limitations of class, sex, and occupation, much as she had by achieving success from a marginalized position as a woman artist in the mid-Depression. She believed that they had freedom of

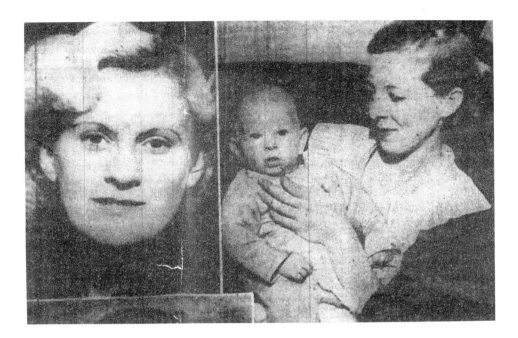

7.12 *Left*: Mrs. Anna Sweeters (Miss Abbott) and *right*: Mrs. Rose Hirschberg (Miss Riggins) with her daughter Sally. Photographs accompanying William Engle, "Portrait of *Two Girls* Bought by Metropolitan, Reunites Two Ex-Waitresses Who Posed for It," *New York World-Telegram*, February 27, 1936, p. 3.

choice, even if economic evidence suggested the contrary. Bishop's professed attitudes and her general liberal humanist stance can be read in terms of women's potential for achievement and in light of the broader political assertions of individual rights in the Popular Front movement. Bishop's late participation in the Artists' Congress and her secession from it to join the more pluralist Society for Modern Artists suggest her awareness of her own social and political agenda.

As a consequence of her upbringing, her experience as a woman artist in a male-dominated set of art institutions, the value humanism placed on an old master tradition, the discourse of new womanhood that celebrated the virtues of individual achievement, and her place within a specific political context of ideas, Bishop brought middle-class values and expectations to the studio, where she produced her "realist" representations of working women without engaging them in situations that spoke about their lives. In Bishop's view neither the working women nor Union Square's unemployed men, who also became subjects in her paintings, were the victims of society, or of an inegalitarian culture, or of ideology. Bishop wrote or spoke about this often in conjunction with the unemployed men she painted. She denied that she was socially conscious in painting these men in the Depression, claiming that they were "aliens by temperament," eccentric and not to be pitied: "I don't say their economic disadvantages haven't something to do with their condition but essentially they are persons who are eccentric. They are really hedonists. I got to know them as I had a series of them come up here [to her studio]. They would bring each other and they would take anything they could lay their hands on." She also acknowledged that her intent in her images of these men was nothing like that of Soyer, who sympathetically portrayed men unemployed as a result of the Depression whereas Bishop's men were a regular feature of any society. As a genre painter preoccupied with the characteristic movements of the human figure, she endeavored to capture their routines. Her more "generalized" intent allowed her to position herself outside the debates on art and politics that frequently intruded on discussions of subjects connected to the Depression.[36]

Although the park remained relatively seedy throughout the 1930s, Bishop felt safe sketching there and was accepted as a regular by the unemployed men. She recounted (interview, December 16, 1982) that on one occasion, however, a drunken man reproached her for making fools out of the men who lived in the park. When she chose not to respond to his continued questions, others gathered around and began to accuse her of exploiting them by selling her sketches to *Life* magazine. She ended by giving them the sketches and edging her way out of the park, where a policeman asked her if she really needed to sketch inside, suggesting it was hardly the proper environment for a lady. Bishop felt that her refusal to answer her accusors' questions transformed her from a regular occupant of the park into a capitalist "lady"; had she simply responded to the men, the hostilities would never have occurred.

In his 1975 article on Bishop, the critic Lawrence Alloway faulted Bishop's upper-middle-class worldview, in which social mobility results from diligence. The artist's theory of painterly mobility as a metaphor for social mobility remained unconvincing, Alloway argued, because "the fact that you can cross the street does not mean that you can cross social barriers in the same way."[37]

In fact, by 1936, just as Bishop began painting office workers, many of the occupational advantages that had once made clerical work seem a path to upward mobility were rapidly disappearing. The economists, social scientists, and job counselors who compiled statistical studies and wrote the rapidly growing body of advice literature for women entering the working world came to recognize that office workers' lives and expectations had altered drastically.[38] Wages dropped dramatically with the Depression, and socially conscious researchers, aware of the cost of living for workers, claimed that reports of high wages had been exaggerated even before the crisis.[39] *Fortune* magazine, in its lengthy analysis of the office worker's life, attributed low office wages to the youth of most office workers, who were under thirty and retired from the workplace with marriage: "The American office, to a great part of its female workers, is not a career but a device by which a woman works her own way through maidenhood" and into marriage.

> Capitalistic economy, which takes into account not only economic but social factors, has profited from this circumstance as might be expected. If the great majority of office girls were in business not for the business but for their lingerie then there would seem to be no particular reason why business should not reciprocate in kind. The girls, since their ambition was elsewhere, would not complain and business, since its ambition was itself, would profit. The consequence is a low, sluggishly rising, and generally despondent wage scale paid by business with a fairly clear conscience and accepted by the young ladies *faute de mieux*.[40]

In short, the ideology of office work, buttressed in part by statistical evidence, operated with that of woman's proper place to justify keeping the wage scale low.[41] Underscoring employers' views on women's lack of economic and career motivations was evidence that males in clerical positions earned twice as much as women and advanced more rapidly.[42]

Apart from diminished wages, working hours during the Depression were frequently extended in smaller offices and jobs combined. While some institutions failed during the crisis, creating an ever diminishing job pool, others stopped hiring. Of all the low-level white-collar fields, except sales, office workers suffered most from unemployment.[43] When businesses started to hire again following the brief economic upturn in 1936, there was a new problem—an oversupply of office workers. "Business at its rosiest could not possibly absorb all these girls," wrote Helen McGibbon. Many job counselors faulted the high schools for overdeveloping office-training programs and for failing to counsel women away from the standard feminized occupations like office work and teaching.[44] Since competition for these jobs was keen, women accepted low wages and beginning positions rather than have no job at all. As one writer observed, "Too many girls everywhere are still walking into employment agencies, vague and untrained, with the hopeless statement: 'I'll take anything.' "[45]

Technological change and the reorganization of offices bred dissatisfaction among those who found jobs. With more sophisticated office machines and the scientific application of mass production, workers who had previously executed a variety of related activities now performed repetitive tasks in stenographic pools, supervised by an office manager who distributed projects like a factory foreman. With the increasing centralization and specialization, some offices adopted methods of payment used in factories, setting piece rates for typing, billing, and transcribing.[46]

The streamlined procedures that helped businesses reduce higher-level staff and distribute work more efficiently had negative effects on the office girl. Because they reduced the number of coveted secretarial positions, they necessarily altered her expectations for improving her status. Work became boring, and offices reported more illness among those engaged in single repetitive tasks. The office machine operator lost track of how her job contributed to the business as a whole, and as a result her loyalty to the institution diminished and she felt alienated from co-workers and superiors alike. As job mobility diminished—one contemporary survey reported that 88 percent of office managers sought clerks who would be satisfied to remain clerks—the office girl became another cog in a vast production machine.[47]

In luminous outdoor settings, away from the workplace, Bishop's youthful office workers seem impervious to changes in the office environment. The only possible markers of labor and class are their costumes and occasionally sober expressions. More than other Depression era images, Bishop's paintings appear to preserve a disappearing ideal of female labor. This ideal was foreign to Raphael Soyer, even though he, like Bishop, used everyday outdoor settings, sketched on site, and arranged figures in studio poses. But with his spatial configurations, lighting, and palette in a work like *Office Girls* (Fig. 6.3) Soyer conveys some of the tension, monotony, and fatigue of women in routine jobs. They are crowded in an urban setting, placed directly against the picture plane, and surrounded by other figures. The pace of urban life prevents human interaction and repose. One figure rushes quickly by and another looks out, engaging the viewer with her weariness. Soyer's backdrop, unlike Bishop's soft veils of color and light, is one of dark, roughly painted office buildings. Finally, the figure of an unemployed man, at left, serves as a reminder that the economic crisis continues.[48]

Though Soyer was more cognizant than Bishop of the effects of the workplace, his image, like hers, avoids direct engagement with the socially problematic issues of women's labor. Drawings from the Communist periodical the *New Masses* use the direct, sketchy conventions of graphic media to show the clerical worker as exhausted, or at least hardworking—conventions that since the turn of the century had come to be associated with images of social protest.[49] In M. Pass's 1926 drawing of a typist (Fig. 7.13) the monotony, fatigue, and meager rewards of repetitive clerical work are crystallized in the image of a typist agonizingly bent over her machine. Similarly, William Siegel's "Office Worker's Lunch Hour" (Fig. 7.14) shows a poorly clad young woman looking up from her portion of bread (in contrast to the delights of the ice-cream cone), seeking release in the light from the urban prison that surrounds her. By contrast, Bishop's paintings avoid negative social commentary or any expression of a need for dramatic change. Instead, the clerical worker relaxes in an obscured outdoor milieu. Having fashioned a deliberate construction of womanhood according to her interpretation of artistic conventions, Bishop contributed to what in turn became part of the rhetoric defining the exemplary office worker.

7.13 M. Pass, drawing of a typist,
      New Masses 1
      (May 1926), p. 27.

7.14 William Siegel, "Office
      Worker's Lunch Hour,"
      New Masses 5
      (April 1930), p. 13.

7.15   Rembrandt, *Hendrickje,* undated.
Oil on canvas. Louvre, Paris.

   Like other painters who drew on the tradition of old master painting, Bishop regarded her women as figures to sustain aesthetic beauty in a work of art. Rembrandt, who often portrayed ordinary women, provided Bishop with a more appropriate model for her working women than either Titian or Rubens, whose more sensuously beautiful nudes inspired Miller and Marsh.[50] Bishop's works, like many of Rembrandt's portraits, depict reflective women or women responding to someone or something outside the confines of the picture. The more enigmatic figure of the woman on the right in *Lunch Hour* (Fig. 7.7) recalls, for example, Rembrandt's quiet portraits of Hendrickje (Fig. 7.15). Rembrandt's warm understanding of human relationships, like those depicted in *The Prodigal Son* and *The Jewish Bride,* touch Bishop's interpretations of intimate exchanges between women, which for some critics are even more sympathetic. Indeed, Lawrence Alloway wrote that her portrayal of women "has an acumen and an empathy that . . . neither males nor sexually mixed subjects elicit." Alloway argued further that Bishop needed two women to obtain these qualities, for "without that she cannot depict the web of mutual responsiveness which is at the core of her meaning and which is rarely found in the history of painting couples."[51]
   Even though her subjects may not be glamorous or beautiful, Bishop thought of women as beautiful forms—subjects of beauty in a painting; they are woven into

the texture of the painting as surface, color, light, and space. Bishop modified many of her Rembrandtian sources, particularly techniques from some of Rembrandt's later works. She spotlights certain areas of the faces while leaving other areas in shadow, and she obliterates contours. She sometimes applies paint with a heavily loaded brush (see, for example, the hair and faces of the two women in *Lunch Hour*), creating thick impastos or flickering highlights. Although no one source for either subject or technique is exact, Rembrandt was important in Bishop's capturing the modest humanity of her young office workers—in her creating a different model of womanhood and a different kind of working woman.[52]

Bishop's idealization of young women using an established model of artistic beauty assumed a particular meaning in the 1930s, when the office worker's prettiness became increasingly important to her job. Job counselors suggested what job applicants should wear and how they should behave, resorting to strategies that capitalized on conservative ideas about women and their role. They encouraged the practice of sex-typed behavior—the occasional use of flattery or sex appeal—but more often advocated modest dress and deferential manners.[53]

If Bishop's young women look reasonably fashionable, it is because they had to be. Dozens of job advice manuals contained some version of the following counsel:

> A business girl may be a mental giant with every qualification for the job she seeks, but that won't help her half so much as wearing the right clothes and make-up and looking clean. Theoretically, one's appearance should have nothing to do with getting a job, but it actually counts 75%. . . . Gone are the days when a girl could look dowdy at the office and get away with it. You no longer hear an employer say of his secretary "she doesn't look like much but how can she type!" He is more apt to say, "I've an A-1 secretary now, and *is* she a looker!"[54]

Employers justified their selection by equating good looks with good work. But they also wanted the proper decor for their offices, and women were encouraged to make themselves into ornaments.[55] When asked if he selected pretty, well-dressed women more often than others, one employer replied that he did, especially around June when graduation presented him with more "girls" than jobs. The reasons were clear:

> Partly to make our office look attractive. Partly because good looks, a good carriage and clear skin, are symptoms of good health which is of serious interest to an employer. And partly because we think that the kind of girl who takes pains to make the most of herself in every small detail of her appearance will also be orderly and painstaking in her work. It isn't always true that a girl who pencils the curves of her lips skillfully is quick and deft. But the converse is often true, that the girl who is careless of her appearance is not a good office worker. So we don't hire her.[56]

Despite such preferences, most writers agreed that "prettiness" depended more on good grooming than on glamour or sex appeal. Bishop focused on this particular preoccupation in *Tidying Up* (Fig. 7.5; Plate 7). With a light touch, she captured the young new woman "revising" herself in that most awkward of grooming moments, when she grimaces into her compact to check for lipstick on her teeth. Job manuals in the 1930s, forerunners of 1970s and 1980s dress-for-success guides, advocated moderation in all details of dress and fashion. Writers recommended against large flashy jewelry, bright makeup, and bright-colored clothes. Recognizing that most business girls operated on small salaries (and marveling at the clerical worker's ingenuity at dressing well for so little), counselors suggested conservative clothes, coordinated around a single color (preferably black, navy, gray, brown, or dark green), that would last for several seasons. Most appropriate were tailored dresses and suits in plain colors with white or matching blouses. Ornate trim belonged on afternoon dresses, which were out of place in the office. The higher women went on the occupational scale, the more simply they dressed.[57]

By such standards, many of Bishop's office workers appear appropriately fashionable. The subject of *Young Woman* is the very model of fashion success (Fig. 7.10). Her short jacket with its single button and wide lapels resembles styles from the middle of the decade. With her tailored suit, neatly brushed blond hair, and poised demeanor, she looks like the self-confident business woman about to be met by an American Express travel representative in a 1937 advertisement that reads, "A lady alone enjoys the luxury of American Express Travel Service" (Fig. 7.16). Other Bishop women seem less well turned out, like one young woman in *Lunch Hour* who wears a blouse with puffy sleeves. In *At the Noon Hour* (Fig. 7.8, Plate 8) the women wear dresses with flounces—the kind of sheer, fluffy dress deemed inappropriate for office work. Among successful office workers like Miss Kay Bell, pictured in the *Fortune* article of 1935 (Fig. 7.17), the tendency was toward understatement. When the private secretary trimmed her dress, the effect was still severe and geometric.

Despite Bishop's disclaimer (see p. 294) contemporary critics singled out these women by their dress and called them shopgirls, lower-class workers in a lower-status occupation. And even if they were mistakenly identified, they were not necessarily dressed for success. The reviewers linked assumptions about the class makeup of the neighborhood to the women themselves despite Bishop's light-filled ambiance, which eradicates the neighborhood's reported tawdriness. The critics' comments suggest how these women were seen by the middle- to upper-middle-class audience viewing Bishop's work. Bishop's stated intent notwithstanding, these young women were limited by their social backgrounds, which marked their speech, or by their clothing, which, though fashionable, was clearly purchased at Fourteenth Street bargain stores. One reviewer called the shopgirls "portly faced female subjects" seen with "the mixed collection of humanity gathering on New York's

7.16 Advertisement for American Express Travel Service, *Harper's Bazaar*, September 1, 1937, p. 159.

7.17 Photograph of Miss Kay Bell, from "A Portfolio of American Office Workers," in "Women in Business II," *Fortune* 12 (August 1935), p. 52.

squalid avenue of shoppers, 14th street." Another went so far as to attribute to the women he identified as shopgirls in *At the Noon Hour* a lower-class manner of speech: "They talk in that peculiarly harsh and grating dialect called New York-ese—Toird Avenue, terlet water, olive orl, idear, Greenpernt and Americer."[58] Job counselors claimed that the successful well-bred office girl would bring a well-modulated voice and correct usage to the office from her previous social training. By the late 1930s schools and business colleges offered self-development courses that included voice culture to help the aspiring office girl with an accent or dialect to modify her tones.[59]

Besides trying to be pretty, fashionable, and well-spoken, the young office girl competed for jobs by cultivating a modest, deferential manner. She adopted the new womanhood exemplified by Dorothy Bromley's "feminist–new style," her voice and gesture demonstrating the "feminine" qualities intended by "nature." Bishop's pictures show a narrow range of behavior in pose, gesture, and expression. Often serious, these women appear gentle and straightforward in their attentiveness to one another. Many stand in relaxed poses, confining their gestures to subtle inward motions. Their demeanor seems passive and responsive rather than provocative. When the subjects seem flirtatious, as in *Young Woman's Head* (Fig. 7.3), they are charming, never raucous or overtly sexual. Fundamentally, they are more receptive than argumentative, and they never affront.

The right personality supposedly had everything to do with obtaining, keeping, and advancing in one's job. Counselors devised recipes, which included a dash of polyvalent charm mixed with the right blend of efficiency. Hazel Cades in *Jobs for Girls* defined this "right attitude" as a perfect balance of irreconcilable polarities.

> It is difficult to define charm, and popularly it is not supposed to be a factor in business, but it is and if you have it you are apt to stand a better chance of getting the job you want. . . . Sometimes in business it is called the right attitude and it is really a combination of friendliness and reticence, of assurance and modesty, of ambition and willingness to do anything, of today's accuracy and tomorrow's vision. It is the ideal attitude of the girl who is willing to take any job and work hard at it while she admits no ultimate limitations.[60]

Job counselors recognized that women were relegated to mechanical and boring jobs. They no longer hid the nature of clerical work. Now, however, they encouraged women to show an interest in their menial tasks, strengthening the chain of production through personal dedication to the company and its goals.[61] By encouraging the right attitude, job counselors perpetuated a myth of easy advancement even as a decrease in the number of skilled secretarial positions lessened the possibilities for rapid upward mobility.

Job prospects were brighter for women willing to be passive and compliant. Hortense Odlum, even from her position as president of Bonwit Teller's Fifth Avenue Store, advised that "the greatest asset of the business woman is feminine charm and feminine clothes. . . . Don't wear the pants, men are the leaders."[62] Odlum believed that it was fine for women to work, as long as work never undermined their femininity and they remained aware of their naturally subordinate role as women.

From all quarters women were advised to defer to everyone else's needs. In a book implausibly titled *She Strives to Conquer,* Frances Maule advised women to surrender their will and freedom to the interests of superiors. Other writers advised women to dust a male boss's desk, run his wife's errands, and perform a host of other domestic tasks—no matter what the cost in overtime or the personal sacrifice—to get ahead. *Fortune* magazine's long 1935 article on women in business was the most overt attempt to validate women's subordinate role in the workplace. Its author claimed that a woman's intention to marry and her willingness to be directed by a man relieved her of the ambition that would have made a man restless in her job.[63] Moreover, the boss needed her in this job because social and economic change had created a "new woman," one vastly different from the dutiful upper-class Victorian model. A man, instead of being master in his home, was now the mate of "a more or less unpredictable woman," and he "resented it." The new office worker (especially the private secretary) replicated the woman his father had married, a daytime wife who knew "all the affairs, all the friends, all the friends' voices, all the idiosyncrasies, all the weaknesses of one man."[64]

A woman's "power" in the workplace came from her ability to behave in a deferential "womanly" manner according to an ideology that valued her subordination to the demands of male superiors. Since office work depended on a woman's extending her reputedly natural domestic skills to the public sphere—where she made the work environment more pleasant and inviting and managed the office efficiently—she achieved a success with which men could not compete, one that, as the *Fortune* author concluded, "was a triumph for [her] womanhood and not for [her] ambition."[65]

The pictorial narrative structure of Edward Hopper's painting *Office at Night* (Fig. 7.18), one of the few paintings of the period that shows a secretary in an office, encapsulates the contradictions in popular advice literature. It gives visual form to the ambiguous power and gender relations embodied in the boss-and-private-secretary or male-and-female relationship. The secretary has power. A fully realized figure, she towers above her boss and controls not only the access to and organization of office information (the filing cabinet) but also office "production." In the visual field, Hopper emphasizes the secretary's desk and typewriter. They protrude into the lower lefthand corner of the painting, and along with the filing cabinet and the boss's desk they become an important third term in the painting's triangular configuration of work. The secretary's power is subverted, however, by the very stance that affirms it. She is the ultimate office ornament, a male painter's construction of objectified womanhood; her impossibly twisted seductive posture displays her breasts and buttocks simultaneously for both the male viewer and, should he look, the boss. She "controls" the office decor with her beauty and her simple attire—a plain blue dress with a white collar. But her dress clings to her body, whose curves are emphasized by the chair arm which insinuatingly penetrates the

7.18 Edward Hopper, *Office at Night,* 1940. Oil on canvas, 22³/₁₆″ × 25³/₁₆″. Collection Walker Art Center, Minneapolis.

space beneath her buttocks. With her pose and her dramatic black hair and makeup she oversteps the boundaries of charm to overtly sexual, and therefore questionable, behavior, which the fair-haired male checks by not meeting her gaze. Ironically, her eyes are so shaded by heavy makeup that her mysterious gaze can be (as Victor Burgin points out) either directed and predatory (hence filled with power) or down-cast and modest (hence deferential). Although she appears able to move freely in the office, pictorially everything blocks her access to the seat of power behind the man's desk: the filing cabinet and desk intersect to create an unbridgeable gap. Another gap exists between her desk and his. She generates no activity but waits for instructions. Because the narrative is in suspension, the contradictions are not resolved.[66]

7.19 Isaac Soyer, *Office Girls,* 1939. Oil on canvas, 26″ × 24″. Present location unknown.

Although the clerical workers in Isaac Soyer's *Office Girls* (1939; Fig. 7.19) are absorbed in serious conversation, they too are placed before the viewer or office visitor as sexually attractive office ornaments. They congregate around a desk, where the central figure pauses momentarily over her typing. The legs of the woman on the left, exposed above the knee, are highlighted and silhouetted against the darker desk. The figure on the right bends over on a diagonal to prop her head in her hands, her brightly illuminated, snugly clothed buttocks projecting toward the viewer. The pose, unselfconscious in an all-female group, acquires a heavy erotic subtext as the figure takes over the entire right side of the canvas.

Male artists like Soyer and Hopper focus on the office worker as ornamental and sexual, available to the male; Bishop refused to sexualize her models. Even though a degree of objectification occurs that can be read as a difference of class, Bishop still sees them as modest, pleasant young workers. Deferential behavior, it was argued, allowed women either to compete for jobs and rise through the ranks *or* to attract a man and retire from the workplace, the other avenue of success for the office worker. Against all feminist arguments that women worked for personal fulfillment and from economic need, the *Fortune* author asserted that the *imitation* of marriage explained and justified the existence of the female secretary, whereas the *probability* of marriage made women willing to work at low wages in positions where advancement was almost impossible.[67]

In the 1930s job counselors urged women to engage in social activities "with an eye out always for a satisfactory marriage." No one wanted to pound a typewriter forever, and women entering the field were encouraged to overlook the tediousness of the work since it would be temporary. Writers warned women against obvious office romances, and one counseled them not to set their sights on men beyond their own social station, for the rising executive was more interested in the "junior leaguer or the society girl outside."[68] Comments like these suggest that a persistent stigma—grounded in class bias—attached to the woman who worked.

Still, it was frequently argued that office girls made ideal wives. A woman office worker had studied the male temperament firsthand. Borrowing a page from the "companionate marriage" and professionalized homemaker manual, she understood that marriage resembled a business partnership. She also knew the importance of her husband's business relationships and would willingly entertain on short notice to further them. The wife, who had all the advantages of sharing a home with a man, could learn a great deal from the secretary, who did everything to make life easier for him:

> A fault-finding wife who thinks only of her own selfish interests and what she can get out of her husband for herself or the children, is little better than the gold-digging stenographer whom she fears. Often a man becomes so fed up with discord at home . . . that he naturally turns to the girl who stands by him eight hours a day with praise instead of blame. . . . You very seldom see the wife who works shoulder to shoulder with her husband, who keeps herself pretty and attractive for his sake if not for her own, losing him to his secretary, or to any other woman.[69]

The ideology of woman's proper place permeated the advice literature for office workers and other job holders in the 1930s. Work was a preparation for marriage, a vehicle for finding a husband, and even a permissible pursuit for a wife if an economic necessity. But it was rarely seen as a substitute for marriage. In *Letters to Susan,* an example of a popular form of advice literature in the 1930s, a middle-class mother responded to her college-age daughter who had been offered a training-level position in a chemistry lab. Susan was engaged to Mark; although her mother urged her to accept the position because economic conditions remained uncertain, marriage, she insisted, ought to be a woman's main job.

> She ought to give it most of her time and the best of her energy, and she can't do it if she's employed and being paid to give just those same things to her employer. . . . A man needs his courage restored and a woman who works 8 hours can't do that. In marriage either husband or wife must be willing to make the outside the home needs of the other predominant.[70]

Preceding the letters in this volume, each of which addressed a different issue, was a preliminary essay entitled "The Situation," detailing the changed conditions in women's lives in the postwar world and offering some suggestions on how women should prepare for them. A woman's destiny was less clear than a man's because she had now to earn her own living and "manage her life successfully if someone else earns it for her." Unlike a man's life, hers was a gamble because she had to wait until her emotions "reached fulfillment" or until they were "permanently channeled into the pursuit of some major interest."[71]

Unlike a man, who actively selected his interests and goals from an array of possible choices, a woman was presumed to be concerned primarily with domestic life. Consequently, she had to await the right opportunity and react to it. She had to learn to respond to external stimuli—whether a male superior's work assignment or his social invitation—rather than develop skills that would allow her to initiate and direct her own behavior. To be selected by men for work and marriage and to be successful on the job and in the home, she had to display compliant, womanly qualities, and she had to wait. Furthermore, what she waited for was still dictated by an ideal of womanly service. Woman's work, at home or in the workplace, enhanced the lives of those around her: "Some kinds of women's work lead to the creation of beautiful things, some to the relief of distress and soothing of pain, some to the training of little minds, while still others go to the making of laughter or to the comfort and pleasure of all."[72]

Bishop's paintings often portray a young woman, in repose and relaxed, who waits or responds to stimuli around her. In such works as *Laughing Head* (Fig. 7.4) a solitary woman gazes at something beyond the confines of the picture and smiles or laughs. Within the picture plane she is unfettered because an ambiguous, shifting setting places no limits on her options; but these are the options of a temporary and transitional working life. The warm shimmering illumination that distinguishes the artist's painterly surfaces and sets her subjects' faces aglow suggests optimism, but it is so generalized that it in fact belies the inegalitarian conditions of office workers' lives during the Depression. Bishop's paintings also avoid the tawdrier features or downtrodden side of Union Square that Marsh and Soyer more readily acknowledged.[73]

In devising strategies by which women could succeed in the white-collar business world, writers of advice manuals promoted a contradictory set of instructions. They perpetuated a patriarchal model of individual success based on competition—a model that was particularly strong in white-collar businesses in large cities like New York. This model assumed equal access to opportunity through hard work, thus downplaying both gender and class difference. Yet these writers also relied on and ultimately reinforced well-established conceptions of gender difference, particularly attitudes about a woman's nature, her capabilities, and the roles she could be expected to fill. The belief that a woman needed to be more womanly to get ahead, even if such behavior restricted her to feminized occupations, was held by men and women alike. Thankful for jobs during hard times, many women were willing to dress in the prescribed fashion, behave modestly, and ultimately ignore their fellow office workers' collective demands for better wages and working conditions. Writing in the *Woman's Press* and in *Independent Woman*, 1930s activists who struggled to improve the clerical worker's situation often met resistance from women schooled in the traditional models of "success" perpetuated in the advice literature.[74] As one writer summed up the situation, "Women who hope to be cooking their lunches in their own homes before the year is out are not women to be organized in unions for the improvement of their pay."[75]

Bishop's post-franchise generation of professional women believed equality was a matter of individual responsibility achieved within established institutions. Although Bishop herself believed strongly in "women" (many of her close friends were women artists), she did not advocate "feminism" in the sense of women's collective endeavors. She never participated in any women's organizations or separate exhibitions for women. Attempting to downplay gender difference in favor of individual achievement, she claimed she wanted to join the art world, not "to be a woman artist" but "just . . . to be an artist."[76]

Though she earned early critical and financial success in the mainstream art world—jurors for important national exhibitions awarded her prizes for both graphics and painting, and major museums purchased her works—she was always characterized as America's best *woman* artist. Moreover, critics placed careful limits around her achievement. Most reminded the public that she was Kenneth Hayes Miller's "pupil" and had made "slow" progress. Henry McBride spoke of Bishop working "the *little* plot of ground she has preempted" and of her "restricted" range. In 1937, one critic even claimed that Bishop's most obvious qualities were "modesty and charm."[77] Critics, colleagues, and friends alike attributed to her the very prerequisites for success that she had inscribed in her subjects.

Bishop became one of the first artists to give the office worker a place in the urban iconography of easel painting. Her images of these clerical types—stocky and unglamorous yet ennobled through artistic conventions that focused on a woman's figure and face—negotiate gender and class difference according to an ideology of office work whose sometimes contradictory notions of mobility and femininity were shared by the artist. Although she depicted her women as self-possessed individuals rather than sexualized objects, she never envisioned them as productive workers in the society in which she saw (and had herself seized) great opportunity. Nor did she see them suffering from an entrenched set of attitudes about roles and occupations. Both the occupational and social spaces of her lower-level workers remained distant from her own and she interacted with her subjects only as studio models. The ambiguous spatial envelope around her casually posed figures, however, suggests a contested middle-class ideal of femininity that has been destabilized by the Depression, a time when the demands of work and family were particularly acute. If Bishop's painterly suggestion of mobility and potential remains unconvincing as a metaphor for women's social or economic progress, it nonetheless embodies 1930s perceptions of mobility and femininity assigned to the young, deferential office worker whose proper working life was lived in a transitional space between the public and the domestic spheres. As visual representations of the contradictory discourse on women and work, Bishop's paintings helped to reinforce the belief that even outside the home, a woman had her proper place.

CONCLUSION

In American Scene easel painting of the 1920s and 1930s there are virtually no radical feminist images of women. Depictions of women's oppression occasionally appear in leftist cartoons or images by WPA artists. But no work attempts to portray what radicals in the National Woman's party unsuccessfully campaigned for in the first E.R.A.—a statement of women's collective and full-scale equality with men. Instead, embedded in the painting, the politics, and the gender ideologies of the period are liberal accommodations, inscribed in a revised discourse of new womanhood that shifted women's roles toward more moderate ideals of femininity in the wake of the franchise. Paintings of urban women by artists of the Fourteenth Street School gave shape to these new standards, using female types and pictorial strategies that negotiated changing features of new womanhood.

I have argued that these artists inserted themselves into this theater of aesthetic and social mediations. Thus, though Kenneth Hayes Miller's generalized and capacious matron was never a model for a wide audience, she personified the new woman as consumer and represented social values of normalcy, nurture, domesticity, and companionability. Many of these values were prescribed for home and family in the prosperous 1920s by conservative pundits who sought an alternative to the boisterous boyish flapper. In contrast to Miller's shopping matron, Reginald Marsh's voluptuous model drew from the widely known cinema stereotype, the Siren. A mysterious and alluring, if inaccessible, fantasy in the early years of the Depression, the Siren had a provocative sexuality that worked in opposing modes, foregrounded in Marsh's paintings. Her bold mask of cosmeticized beauty could be read as a defiant declaration of the new woman's sexual liberation—her figure as an expression of male anxiety about unleashed female sexuality. But her exaggerated looks could also seem to reinstate sharp distinctions between masculinity and femininity. Clarifying sex roles by reducing working-class women to sexual commodities reassured some middle-class men whose manhood had been compromised by the loss of productive work.

Indeed the conjunction of "work" and "femininity" was debated throughout the Depression. The middle-class New Woman's earlier claims to economic independence and career satisfaction, both before and after marriage, fell by the wayside. In the competitive job market of the Depression, "right-to-work" claims yielded to the demands of family, the companionate marriage, and motherhood. Certain already feminized occupations, however, like sales and clerical work, were reaffirmed as womanly in a market otherwise hostile to working women. Raphael Soyer addressed the problems and Isabel Bishop the possibilities of feminized occupations. Soyer's shopgirls, working-class figures, represent alienated female labor, quietly interrogating a social order that systematically ignored their plight. Bishop's images of office workers carve out a transitional space for women's intimate interactions, a space in a public arena where women were most on display. Unlike Soyer's, her pictures tend to blur class distinctions, thus perpetuating the myth of access to individual female success.

These images are not simply female types mirroring aspects of womanhood "out there" in the culture, already well established and understood by any viewer who might have come across them. Nor are they Depression era updates of old master paintings, contained within the supposedly unproblematic institution of "art." Nor are they merely "American Scene" paintings, embodying a period look, a national iconography, and a mainstream politics of liberal humanism that ennobles the average individual as an equal participant in American democracy. Although I have discussed these works within and against such boundaries, I have argued that neither the artists nor their viewers saw them in such straightforward ways.

To place any one of these pictures in a single category of meaning or to apply any one mode of analysis foreshortens the historical complexity of pictorial production and signification. Paintings by the Fourteenth Street School work concurrently in and against each discursive category so as to defy easy summary. The pictures attest to what Cecelia F. Klein has called the "extreme complexity" and "exceptional flexibility" of the pictorial process that allows artists to manipulate signs of gender, class, race, and age, making possible "the production of a wide range of semantic assertions."[1] All these artists worked as painters of modern life, chronicling the urban scene by updating recognizable artistic traditions. But they also combined pictorial components in disparate ways, producing for a viewer often conventional (though sometimes oppositional) understandings of contemporary womanhood.

In arguing for the complexity of realist depictions that some art historians have called illustrative and merely topical, I have viewed these works as interpretations and constructions of gender that maintain relations of power. How did such images in easel paintings act on viewers? How widespread were their effects? The paintings were exhibited regularly in private galleries, major museums, and international shows. Some won prizes; others were appraised in critical reviews. When the Metropolitan Museum purchased Bishop's painting *Two Girls*, New York newspapers carried feature stories. In 1934 Marsh's work gained national recognition as the outstanding, example of urban regionalism in *Time*. By contrast, Miller's art addressed the art-world insider. Although they gained currency and popularity among an expanding audience for art, however, these paintings, unlike movies or advertising, played no part in the widespread dissemination of masculine or feminine imagery. With few responses to these works beyond the art press, how can we speak of their "constitutive effects?"

Several issues are important here: realist ideology, gender roles, and political commitments. The first addresses the assertions by apologists for American Scene painting. Whether discussing mural painting—intended for a vast public—or easel painting, which in adopting similar realist strategies could lay claim to similar communicative aims, critics described realists as motivated by a powerful quest for "truth." They also broadened the definition of realism itself, recognizing the mediating process of artistic form. No longer a "superficial" realism, faithful only "to what the eye perceives," the critic Virgil Barker intoned in 1934, "authentic realism is faithful rather to what the mind conceives. . . . realism may therefore assume many forms. . . . but in each case there is the achievement of a consistent conception of the world, and the communication of it with conviction and convincingness."[2] The true American artist would "naturally" convey true American values—the "consistent conception" lying behind a national realist art.

As important American Scene works, paintings by the Fourteenth Street School realists disseminated deeply held beliefs about American society. No matter what the actual viewing audience, the paintings belonged to the larger realist canon of more widely seen murals and prints in the Depression. At the same time—and this brings me to the second issue, feminist claims about representation—paintings that imaged women were produced and received according to mainstream assumptions about both American realist art and gender roles. Artists and spectators alike relied on prevailing conventions of gender as they produced and viewed painted figures. When their particular strategies are read in the larger context of representation in words and images—from social science and journalism to cinema and advertisements—the pictures themselves can be seen as constructing and maintaining conventional gender roles. They shared the aims—and to some extent the rhetorical means—of other cultural practices that produced the restricted and problematic femininities of the period. Their visual strategies were formed within the institutional boundaries of art, their meanings grounded in moments of production and reception when, for the middle-class viewer addressed by such works, there was "no aspect of present day social history more controversial in character or more delicate in its implications than that of the new status of Woman."[3] As a consequence the pictures share with other representations the tasks of understanding and shaping femininity for a larger audience; no longer simply part of a circumscribed American art history, they belong to a broader "regime of representation" that produces gendered identities at a given historical juncture.[4]

The fact remains, however, that debates in artistic circles frequented by the Fourteenth Street School artists focused not on feminism or the conditions of women's lives, but rather on the relation between art, society, and politics and the role of art in effecting social change. How do the representations of working and shopping women figure in these debates? I have tried to show that though none of these works was read as "propaganda," each artist's female type was produced at a slightly different historical moment within these debates and, depending on the politics of the critic, was interpreted accordingly. When Miller, after painting Fifth Avenue matrons, depicted a Fourteenth Street bargain hunter, for example, American Scene critics praised the democratic ideals implicit in the change; by contrast, leftist critics insisted that even if he painted certain types, his works were nonetheless tied to the bourgeois conventions of old master easel painting. Although Marsh's early 1930s paintings of Siren shoppers are also "bourgeois" easel paintings embodying none of the didactic or revolutionary proletariat themes advocated by the Left during its most sectarian period in the first half of the Depression, they appeared when Marsh himself was also engaged in depicting men on breadlines, making crayon drawings for the *New Masses,* and attending a few classes at the Workers' School. Moreover, though they lack the rhetorical directness of the political graphics produced in these years, their sketchy illustrative qualities, combined with a quantity of information about a working-class neighborhood, accommodate political concerns obliquely, allowing, as I have suggested, a more socially concerned reading of these types. Finally, Soyer's and Bishop's paintings of working women were painted during the Popular Front era in the second half of the decade. The more liberal aesthetic and political agenda surrounding the idea of revolutionary art made a space in which Soyer's work could be read as both accomplished painting and generalized social commentary. The shifting color and light surrounding Bishop's female figures celebrated broader ideals of individual achievement in a democratic society.[5]

Although the paintings featuring women should be read in light of these changing ideas about art and politics, that women in them are also subjects of aesthetic "contemplation" mutes the political impact of the works. For artists committed to painting contemporary life according to traditional aesthetic values, lower- and middle-class working and shopping women were signs of modernity, urbanism, and—because of the public nature of city space—sexuality; they were valued, moreover, as "average" Americans. By contrast, men depicted at work or unemployed raised the specter of labor conflict and class struggle at the heart of the leftist political agenda. Female figures were less implicated in this political rhetoric.

At a time of feminist conflict and heterosexual and domestic retrenchment, the Fourteenth Street School artists were among the few easel painters to acknowledge woman's growing participation in public life. The spaces of consumption and work in which women appeared signified to a liberal mainstream viewer both the progress and the integrity of democratic society. At a time of economic crisis and social concern, the artists broadened their viewers' social world, inscribing class and sometimes ethnicity into their female imagery. In addition to suggesting possibilities for women, they occasionally staged quiet inquiries into the circumstances in which women shopped or worked.

These artists, however, continued to work within old master and contemporary visual traditions that objectified the female form by constructing particular kinds of looking, modes of address that maintained established hierarchies of power and sexual relations. Though their aesthetic strategies participated in the containment of women by assuming that women are different from men—an unequal Other— the artists were attentive to distinct positions for and visions of women. Miller saw "otherness" through consumption, as domestic leisure; Marsh worked the boundaries of seduction and consumption; Bishop saw difference in terms of class; Soyer used the artist-model studio convention to demystify the lives of working women. In the end, the artists' diverse collective vision adjusted itself to social values and gender roles articulated by mainstream feminists and middle-class Americans who continued to subscribe to the ideals of a separate identity and proper place for women. Through such ongoing accommodations—such continual re-visions—the paintings made their contribution. From their own shifting vantage points on contested ideals of new womanhood the artists, through their works, kept in play the multiplicity of debates about women and the contradictory experience and representation of "new women" and a "new womanhood" between the wars.

INTRODUCTION

1. By 1929, industry was spending $15 per year on advertising for every American. Between 1909 and 1929, expenditures for advertising in periodicals rose from $54 to $320 million; in newspapers, they rose from $149 to $792 million. Robert S. Lynd, "The People as Consumers," in *Recent Social Trends in the United States: Report of the President's Research Committee on Social Trends* (New York: McGraw-Hill, 1934), p. 973.

2. Richard Wightman Fox, "Epitaph for Middletown," in *The Culture of Consumption*, ed. Richard Wightman Fox and T. J. Jackson Lears (New York: Pantheon Books, 1983), p. 105.

3. Chapter 3 discusses some of these businesses; see Map 2 for their locations.

4. Lois Scharf, *To Work and to Wed: Female Employment, Feminism, and the Great Depression*, Contributions to Women's Studies no. 15 (Westport, Conn.: Greenwood Press, 1980), p. 10.

5. Lorine Pruette, ed., *Women Workers through the Depression: A Study of White Collar Employment Made by the American Women's Association* (New York: Macmillan, 1934), p. 96.

6. Carroll Smith-Rosenberg, "The New Woman as Androgyne: Social Disorder and Gender Crisis, 1870–1936," in *Disorderly Conduct: Visions of Gender in Victorian America* (New York: Oxford University Press, 1986), p. 245. Smith-Rosenberg points out that the discourse was used in arguments about the naturalness of gender and the legitimacy of the bourgeois social order. The new woman as mannish lesbian—the literary figure she describes—threatened a social order that by the 1920s privileged the heterosexual over the homosocial sphere of women.

7. Nancy Cott, *The Grounding of Modern Feminism* (New Haven: Yale University Press, 1987); and Rayna Rapp and Ellen Ross, "The Twenties' Backlash: Compulsory Heterosexuality, the Consumer Family, and the Waning of Feminism," in *Class, Race, and Sex: The Dynamics of Control*, ed. Amy Swerdlow and Hanna Lessinger (New York: Barnard College Women's Center; Boston: G. K. Hall, 1983), pp. 93–107.

8. I make a distinction here between the *category/designation* "New Woman" and the *historical phenomenon* of the New Woman. Teresa de Lauretis's distinction between the fictional/discursive construct "woman" and "women"—"the real historical beings who cannot as yet be defined outside of those discursive formations, but whose material existence is nonetheless certain"—is useful. I want to be clear about my shifts from the discursive (i.e., representational) and hence social constructs to the historical exemplars of new women, even as the relationship itself may remain indirect: "The relation between women as historical subjects and the notion of woman as it is produced by hegemonic discourses is neither a direct relation of identity, a one-to-one correspondence, nor a relation of simple implication. Like all other relations expressed in language, it is an arbitrary and symbolic one, that is to

say, culturally set up." Teresa de Lauretis, *Alice Doesn't: Feminism, Semiotics, Cinema* (Bloomington: Indiana University Press, 1984), pp. 6–7.

9. My "characterizations" here draw on Lynda Nead, "Representation, Sexuality, and the Female Nude," *Art History* 6 (June 1983), pp. 227–236; Toril Moi, *Sexual/Textual Politics: Feminist Literary Theory* (London and New York: Methuen, 1985), pp. 157–158; Mary Poovey, "Feminism and Deconstruction," *Feminist Studies* 14 (Spring 1988), pp. 51–65; and Joan Scott, "Deconstructing Equality-versus-Difference: Or, the Uses of Poststructuralist Theory for Feminism," *Feminist Studies* 14 (Spring 1988), pp. 33–49.

10. Tickner, "Feminism, Art History, and Sexual Difference," *Genders* no. 3 (Fall 1988), pp. 96–97. In her formulation of *text* and *intertextuality*, Tickner looks to Roland Barthes, "From Work to Text," in *Image-Music-Text*, ed. and trans. Stephen Heath (New York: Hill and Wang, 1977); and Victor Burgin, *The End of Art Theory: Criticism and Postmodernity* (London: Macmillan, 1986).

11. Scott, "Deconstructing Equality-versus-Difference," p. 34; Tickner, "Feminism, Art History, and Sexual Difference," p. 97.

12. In the introduction to their edited volume *Feminist Criticism and Social Change: Sex, Class, and Race in Literature and Culture* (New York: Methuen, 1985), p. xxiv, Judith Newton and Deborah Rosenfelt speak about the value of reader-response criticism for its ability to see both male and female positions and historically changing interpretive communities. The notion of an "interpretive community" comes from the reader-response theories of Stanley Fish, *Is There a Text in This Class? The Authority of Interpretive Communities* (Cambridge: Harvard University Press, 1980); see also Catherine Belsey, "Constructing the Subject: Deconstructing the Text," in Newton and Rosenfelt, pp. 52–53; and Scott, "Deconstructing Equality-versus-Difference," p. 35.

13. Scott, "Deconstructing Equality-versus-Difference"; all quotations from p. 35.

14. Nead, "Representation, Sexuality, and the Female Nude," p. 231.

15. Linda Alcoff, "Cultural Feminism vs. Post-Structuralism: The Identity Crisis in Feminist Theory," *Signs* 13, no. 3 (Spring 1988), p. 431; and Catherine Belsey, "Constructing the Subject: Deconstructing the Text." There may be a contradiction between Belsey and Alcoff, though both are looking for some "agency" or way to effect political change. In this context, however, they are not thinking of the subject in terms of the artist but in terms of either a "reader" who recognizes himself or herself in a text (Belsey) or a feminist author trying to deal with woman as a concept (Alcoff).

16. Griselda Pollock, "Van Gogh and the Poor Slaves: Images of Rural Labour as Modern Art," *Art History* 11 (September 1988), p. 409. In her work on Van Gogh, Pollock offers three distinct configurations in which to think about the artist, or what she refers to as the "author name." One is the "historically located producer," who works within structures of "artistic production, consumption and their attendant discourses" in specific ways that the art historian can make comprehensible. A second is the "effect of the texts" (presumably visual and verbal) to which the producer's name is attached, "a set of procedures, competences, effects, concerns, stylistics, etc.," that the author name designates at "the point of their consumption." Finally, there is the artist as a divided and "inconsistent" classed and gendered subject. He or she operates as an "intending agent," one engaged in a highly motivated practice, but within determining structures outside his or her control. The subject is thus "articulated through visual and literary codes of his or her culture" and in turn inscribes across them his or her "particular history and the larger social patterns of which all subjects are an effect."

17. "Art, U.S. Scene," *Time*, December 24, 1934, pp. 24–25.

18. For this range of responses, dependent on the focus of their studies, see Matthew

Baigell, *The American Scene: American Painting of the 1930s* (New York: Praeger, 1974); Patricia Hills, *Social Concern and Urban Realism: American Painting of the 1930s* (Boston: Boston University Art Gallery, 1983); Patricia Hills and Roberta K. Tarbell, *The Figurative Tradition and the Whitney Museum of American Art: Paintings and Sculpture from the Permanent Collection* (New York and Newark, Del.: Whitney Museum of American Art in association with the University of Delaware Press, 1980), pp. 76–78, 82–84.

19. Thomas Albright, "Street Artist of the Depression," *San Francisco Chronicle*, November 27, 1983, pp. 14–15; Hilton Kramer, "Marsh's Search for a Style," *New York Times*, June 24, 1979, sec. 2, p. 31; Kramer, "Miller's Art: City in a Dimmed Light," *New York Times*, January 17, 1970, p. 25; Kramer, "Reginald Marsh, New York Romantic," undated clipping from *New York Times* News Service; and Kramer, "The Unhappy Fate of Kenneth Hayes Miller," *New York Times*, March 11, 1979, sec. D, p. 31.

20. For a study of gender in New Deal culture see Barbara Melosh, *Engendering Culture: Manhood and Womanhood in New Deal Public Art and Theater* (Washington, D.C.: Smithsonian Institution Press, 1991).

21. Melosh, *Engendering Culture*, has helped me to frame this account.

22. Cott, *The Grounding of Modern Feminism*.

23. Poovey, "Feminism and Deconstruction," p. 58. Poovey distinguishes between a conservative recuperative practice and a historicized demystifying one. She wants to show the importance of deconstruction as a tool within the latter practice for feminists interested in history, race, and class.

CHAPTER ONE

1. See Carroll Smith-Rosenberg, "Bourgeois Discourse and the Progressive Era," in *Disorderly Conduct: Visions of Gender in Victorian America* (New York: Oxford University Press, 1986), pp. 176–178.

2. John D'Emilio and Estelle B. Freedman, *Intimate Matters: A History of Sexuality in America* (New York: Harper and Row, 1988), chapter 8; and Smith-Rosenberg, "Bourgeois Discourse and the Progressive Era," pp. 176–178.

3. Both D'Emilio and Freedman, pp. 194–196; and Kathy Peiss, *Cheap Amusements: Working Women and Leisure in Turn-of-the-Century New York* (Philadelphia: Temple University Press, 1986), have shaped this chapter's discussion of working-class women, leisure, and sexuality. For other, more general, discussions, see Elizabeth Ewen, *Immigrant Women in the Land of Dollars* (New York: Monthly Review Press, 1985); and John Kasson, *Amusing the Million: Coney Island at the Turn of the Century* (New York: Hill and Wang, 1978).

4. Kathy Peiss, in *Cheap Amusements*, pp. 174–178, points out the existence of competing cultural styles and values among working-class women. In contrast to their pleasure-seeking sisters, many immigrant women pursued a middle-class ideal of respectability and found the elevating forms of leisure in neighborhood clubs fully satisfying. Still others organized themselves around the ideals of labor and helped to improve their own working conditions.

5. Nancy Cott, *The Grounding of Modern Feminism* (New Haven: Yale University Press, 1987), pp. 3–10, 33–38. Among the most active feminists were the lawyer and cultural radical Crystal Eastman; the industrial investigator Frances Perkins, who became well known as Franklin Roosevelt's secretary of labor; the anthropologist Elsie Clews Parsons; the writers Rhetta Childe Dorr and Inez Haynes Gillmore; and the socialist trade unionist Rose Pastor Stokes. They were joined by other women journalists and educators and by sympathetic men

like *The Masses* editors Floyd Dell and Max Eastman (brother of Crystal and husband of Ida Rauh) and the columnist Will Irwin.

6. Katherine S. Anthony, *Feminism in Germany and Scandinavia* (New York: Henry Holt, 1915), p. 6, as quoted in Cott, *The Grounding of Modern Feminism*, p. 49.

7. Cott, *The Grounding of Modern Feminism*, p. 39.

8. This paragraph summarizes Cott's analysis, pp. 41–47. For a discussion of the birth-control movement in the context of feminism in the teens, see Linda Gordon, *Woman's Body, Woman's Right: A Social History of Birth Control in America* (New York: Penguin Books, 1977; reprint 1986), pp. 186–245. For a more detailed discussion of feminism in Greenwich Village, see Ellen Kay Trimberger, "Feminism, Men, and Modern Love: Greenwich Village, 1900–1925," in *Powers of Desire: The Politics of Sexuality*, ed. Ann Snitow, Christine Stansell, and Sharon Tompson (New York: Monthly Review Press, 1983), pp. 131–152.

9. Cott, in chapter 1 of *The Grounding of Modern Feminism*, makes this brief coherence a major accomplishment of feminism in the teens.

10. Homer Fort is quoted in Fairfax Downey, *Portrait of an Era As Drawn by C. D. Gibson* (New York: Scribner, 1936), p. 196. Other information on Gibson and the Gibson girl can be found in Lois W. Banner, *American Beauty* (Chicago and London: University of Chicago Press, 1983), pp. 154–174; Robert Koch, "Gibson Girl Revisited," *Art in America* 1 (1965), pp. 70–73; Henry C. Pitz, "Charles Dana Gibson: Creator of a Mode," *American Artist* 20 (December 1956), pp. 50–55.

11. In *Imaging American Women: Ideas and Ideals in Cultural History* (New York: Columbia University Press, 1987), Martha Banta considers the effect of types on both daily conduct (the tendency of the Gibson girl to condition fashion and behavior among women) and larger cultural ideals—like a sense of nationhood. For Banta, Gibson was the most effective turn-of-the-century illustrator at imaging a wide range of cultural desires (pp. 15, 211–218).

12. Charlotte Perkins Gilman, *Women and Economics*, as quoted in Banner, *American Beauty*, p. 156.

13. Caroline Ticknor, "The Steel-Engraving Lady and the Gibson Girl," *Atlantic Monthly* 88 (July 1901), p. 106.

14. Ticknor, p. 107.

15. Ticknor, pp. 107–108.

16. Banner, *American Beauty*, p. 156.

17. Banner, *American Beauty*, pp. 156–157; Downey, *Portrait of an Era*, pp. 264–265; and Pamela Neal Warford, "The Social Origins of Female Iconography: Selected Images of Women in American Popular Culture, 1890–1945," Ph.D. diss., Washington University, St. Louis, 1979.

18. Koch, "Gibson Girl Revisited," pp. 71–72.

19. Downey, *Portrait of an Era*, p. 186.

20. This account of the portrait's origin, from I. N. Phelps Stokes, *Random Recollections of a Happy Life* (New York: 1932), pp. 115–118, is recounted in Stanley Olson, *John Singer Sargent: His Portrait* (New York: St. Martin's Press, 1986), p. 206.

21. Carter Ratcliff, *John Singer Sargent* (New York: Abbeville Press, 1982), p. 168.

22. Ratcliff, p. 167.

23. Olson, *John Singer Sargent: His Portrait*, p. 206.

24. See Trevor J. Fairbrother, *The Bostonians: Painters of an Elegant Age, 1870–1930* (Boston: Museum of Fine Arts, 1986), pp. 40–92.

25. Bernice Kramer Leader, "Antifeminism in the Paintings of the Boston School," *Arts*

Magazine 56 (January 1982), 112–119; see also Leader's dissertation, "The Boston Lady as a Work of Art: Paintings by the Boston School at the Turn of the Century," Columbia University, 1980.

26. Leader, "Antifeminism," pp. 117–118. Leader cites Philip Hale's portrayals of his artist wife, Lilian Westcott Hale, who achieved greater financial and professional success as an artist than her husband. Though Philip encouraged her professional life, he was active in the anti-suffrage campaign. When she served as his model, she was "romantically beautiful, face relaxed and dreaming," never painting at her easel.

27. Quotation from the *Philadelphia Times* coverage of a symposium of prominent women's anti-suffrage views, as quoted in Leader, "Antifeminism," p. 116.

28. The inaugural exhibition American Women Artists, 1830 to 1930, at the National Museum of Women in the Arts provided an occasion for seeing both self-portraits and portraits of women artists by their peers. Information on the artists comes from the catalog, Eleanor Tufts, *American Women Artists, 1830–1930* (Washington, D.C.: International Exhibitions Foundation for the National Museum of Women in the Arts, 1987).

29. *American Women Artists, 1830–1930*, cat. no. 19; Fairbrother, *The Bostonians*, p. 220; and Martha J. Hoppin, *Marie Danforth Page: Back Bay Portraitist* (Springfield, Mass.: George Walter Vincent Smith Art Museum, 1979). Danforth began her studies at age seventeen with Helen Knowlton (who collaborated with William Morris Hunt) and then moved to the Museum of Fine Arts School, where, thanks to the sponsorship of Edward Everett Hale, she studied with Benson and Tarbell between 1890 and 1895. Because she needed to care for her ailing mother, she had to refuse the school's travel prize awarded to her in 1894. Following her marriage to Page in 1896, she received her first commissions for copies of famous portraits and worked as an illustrator and a poster artist. By 1902 she had held her first one-woman exhibition of fifteen portraits at Walter Kimbell and Company. The following year she finally took her European tour and spent a portion of the time in Spain copying works by Velázquez. In the teens and twenties, she received prizes at national and international exhibitions, earned substantial fees as a portraitist (her paintings of children were especially popular), and was elected an associate of the National Academy of Design in 1927.

30. See Fairbrother, *The Bostonians*, p. 67. The Pages had no children until Marie adopted two young girls in 1919, when she was fifty. Hoppin, *Marie Danforth Page*, p. 11.

31. Fairbrother, *The Bostonians*, p. 67.

32. Little is known about Margaret Foster Richardson. She came to Boston for art training from Winnetka, Illinois, studying first at the Normal Art School in Boston and then with Tarbell. Primarily a portraitist, she received the Harris Bronze Medal at the Art Institute of Chicago in 1911 and the Maynard Portrait Prize in 1913 at the National Academy of Design. Tufts, *American Women Artists, 1830–1930*, cat. no. 16.

33. William Dean Howells, *Criticism and Fiction* (1891; reprint, New York: Hill and Wang, 1967), p. 128. The discussion of Howells, Caffin, and Santayana and the genteel tradition is indebted to Patricia Hills's discussion in "John Sloan's Images of Working-Class Women: A Case Study of the Roles and Interrelationships of Politics, Personality, and Patrons in the Development of Sloan's Art, 1905–1916," *Prospects* 5 (1980), pp. 172–174.

34. Charles Caffin, *The Story of American Painting* (New York: Frederick A. Stokes, 1907), pp. 340–344. For a discussion of late nineteenth-century notions of the decorative in relation to images of women and prevailing notions of femininity, see Bailey Van Hook, "Decorative Images of American Women: The Aristocratic Aesthetic of the Late Nineteenth Century," *Smithsonian Studies in American Art* 4 (Winter 1990), pp. 45–70.

35. George Santayana, "The Genteel Tradition in American Philosophy," in *Winds of*

Doctrine: Studies in Contemporary Opinion (New York: Scribner, 1926), p. 188. Presented as an address in 1911; published in 1913.

36. Kenneth Russell Chamberlain, interviewed by Richard A. Fitzgerald (unpublished transcript in the library of the University of California, Riverside), p. 28, as quoted in Rebecca Zurier, *Art for the Masses: A Radical Magazine and Its Graphics, 1911–1917* (Philadelphia: Temple University Press, 1988), p. 140.

37. Leslie Fishbein, introduction to *Art for the Masses*, pp. 14–15; and Suzanne L. Kinser, "Prostitutes in the Art of John Sloan," *Prospects* 9 (1984), p. 234.

38. Bennard B. Perlman, *The Immortal Eight: American Painting from Eakins to the Armory Show, 1870–1913* (Cincinnati, Ohio: North Light, 1979), p. 89.

39. Milton W. Brown, *American Painting from the Armory Show to the Depression* (Princeton: Princeton University Press, 1955; reprint, 1972), pp. 9–17. See also Robert Haywood, "George Bellows's *Stag at Sharkey's*: Boxing, Violence, and Male Identity," *Smithsonian Studies in American Art* 2 (Spring 1988), pp. 3–15; and Rebecca Zurier, "Real Men, Real Life, Real Art: Gendering Realism at the Turn of the Century," paper delivered at the American Studies Association annual meeting, Baltimore, Md., November 1, 1991.

40. T. J. Jackson Lears, *No Place of Grace: Antimodernism and the Transformation of American Culture, 1880–1920* (New York: Pantheon Books, 1981), pp. 107–108.

41. Helen Farr Sloan notes, as quoted in Zurier, *Art for the Masses*, p. 56.

42. Only five of Sloan's paintings from his early period show women working. In four women are cleaning, and in a fifth they are planting. In these works, women's work is "necessary ritual cleansing and renewal, with purification and regeneration the essential content." Hills, "John Sloan's Images," p. 175.

43. D'Emilio and Freedman, *Intimate Matters*, pp. 200–201. In summarizing the shifting foundations of turn-of-the-century sexual norms, the authors cite both commercialized leisure and the existence of lifelong intimate relationships among college-educated new women.

44. At the time he executed this work, Sloan was changing his previously somber palette to the higher-key tonalities of the Maratta color system. His declaration that "lavender light was on my mind" refers to the dominant tones of the painting and reflects his formal preoccupation. David W. Scott and Edgar John Bullard, III, *John Sloan, 1871–1951*, exhibition catalog (Washington, D.C: National Gallery of Art, 1971), p. 124.

45. Kinser, "Prostitutes in the Art of John Sloan," p. 238.

46. Though Kinser does not discuss this painting, my analysis of it as a possible narrative of prostitution is based on her discussion of *The Haymarket* (1907), *Sixth Avenue and Thirtieth Street* (1907), *Chinese Restaurant* (1909), and *3 A.M.* (1909).

47. Theodore Dreiser, *Sister Carrie: An Authoritative Text, Background and Sources, Criticism*, ed. Donald Pizer (New York: Norton, 1970), p. 1. Kinser points out this connection between Sloan and Dreiser.

48. Peiss, *Cheap Amusements*, pp. 62–67.

49. Peiss, pp. 108–113.

50. I want to re-emphasize here Peiss's claim (see n. 3) that not all working-class women sought the same forms of leisure. Many continued to follow parental desires for traditional patterns of courtship. Others went to women's clubs managed by middle-class reformers that offered more intellectual opportunities. Many of these women felt a need to understand American social habits as a means to assimilation and class mobility.

51. Although there is no specific evidence of a response by female working-class viewers of Sloan's work, I am drawing on the evidence of their responses to various institutions of

commercialized pleasure. In proposing a different viewer and in suggesting that the painting's narrative strategies made possible a variety of subject positions, I draw on Laura Mulvey's and Rosemary Betterton's theoretical work on female spectatorship along with the notion expressed by Stanley Fish that we read a text within a specific "interpretive community." Here the theoretical female spectator is positioned within a community of working women. Rosemary Betterton, "How Do Women Look? The Female Nude in the Work of Suzanne Valadon," in *Looking On: Images of Femininity in the Visual Arts and Media*, ed. Rosemary Betterton (London and New York: Pandora Press, 1987), p. 218; Stanley Fish, *Is There a Text in This Class? The Authority of Interpretive Communities* (Cambridge: Harvard University Press, 1980); Laura Mulvey, "Visual Pleasure and Narrative Cinema," in *Art after Modernism: Rethinking Representation*, ed. Brian Wallis (New York and Boston: New Museum of Contemporary Art in association with Godine, 1984), pp. 361–373.

52. Peiss, *Cheap Amusements*, pp. 185–188. This double edge is a central theme in Peiss's argument.

53. For a summary of the way that early moviemakers both used and undermined the ideals of new womanhood, see Peiss, pp. 153–158.

54. Leila J. Rupp, "Feminism and the Sexual Revolution in the Early Twentieth Century: The Case of Doris Stevens," *Feminist Studies* 15 (1989), pp. 289–309, points out this variety within the new woman typology. For a discussion of the early emergence of the flapper, see James R. McGovern, "The American Woman's Pre–World War I Freedom in Manners and Morals," *Journal of American History* 55 (September 1968), pp. 315–333.

55. Susanne Wilcox, "The Unrest of Modern Woman," *Independent* 67 (July 8, 1909), pp. 62–63.

56. Louise Connoly, "The New Woman," *Harper's Weekly* 57 (June 7, 1913), p. 6.

57. Norman Hapgood, "What Women Are After," *Harper's Weekly* 58 (August 16, 1913), p. 29.

58. Bram Dijkstra, *Idols of Perversity: Fantasies of Feminine Evil in Fin-de-Siècle Culture* (New York: Oxford University Press, 1986), p. vi. See also Alessandra Comini, "Posters from the War against Women," review of Dijkstra in the *New York Times Book Review*, February 1, 1987, pp. 13–14.

59. Sloan's images were untitled in the *Collier's* article "Women March," by Mary Alden Hopkins (May 18, 1912), pp. 13 and 31. See Rowland Elzea and Elizabeth Hawkes, *John Sloan, Spectator of Life* (Wilmington: Delaware Art Museum, 1988), pp. 101–102.

60. Carrie Chapman Catt, "Why Women Want to Vote," *The Woman's Journal* (January 9, 1915), p. 11, as quoted in Cott, *The Grounding of Modern Feminism*, p. 30.

61. Cott, *The Grounding of Modern Feminism*, p. 30.

62. Estelle B. Freedman, "The New Woman: Changing Views of Women in the 1920s," *Journal of American History* 61 (September 1974), p. 387. Freedman notes, for example, that male historians writing in the early 1930s, like Preston William Slosson and Frederick Lewis Allen, claimed that women were liberated but based their assessments on women's roles in the family, the home, and the fashion and entertainment industries. See Preston William Slosson, *The Great Crusade and After: 1914–1928* (New York, 1930), pp. 130–161; and Frederick Lewis Allen, *Only Yesterday: An Informal History of the Nineteen-Twenties*, First Perennial Library edition (New York: Harper and Row, 1931; reprint, 1964). By contrast, Inez Haynes Irwin focused on organized women's activities and their political life in *Angels and Amazons: A Hundred Years of American Women* (Garden City, N.Y., 1933); see also Sophonisba P. Breckinridge, *Women in the Twentieth Century: A Study of the Political, Social, and Economic Activities* (New York, 1933).

63. Cott, *The Grounding of Modern Feminism*, pp. 9–10, 20.

64. Editor's statement, "The New Woman," *Current History* 27 (October 1927), p. 1.

65. Cott, *The Grounding of Modern Feminism*, p. 272.

66. Harriet Abbott, "What the Newest New Woman Is," *Ladies Home Journal*, August 1920, p. 154.

67. Freedman in "The New Woman," p. 374, points out that between 1927 and 1933 there was a sudden proliferation of literature on the new woman, unequaled until the historical reassessment that began in the early 1960s. For an evaluation of these two stances toward feminism, see Cott, *The Grounding of Modern Feminism*, p. 271.

68. Dorothy Dunbar Bromley, "Feminist—New Style," *Harper's Monthly Magazine* 155 (October 1927), p. 554.

69. Bromley, p. 557.

70. Lillian Symes, "Still a Man's Game: Reflections of a Slightly Tired Feminist," *Harper's Monthly Magazine* 158 (May 1929), p. 678.

71. Symes, pp. 678–679.

72. Lillian Symes, "The New Masculinism," *Harper's Monthly Magazine* 161 (June 1930), pp. 98–107.

73. Symes, "Still a Man's Game," p. 678.

74. Henry R. Carey, "This Two-Headed Monster—the Family," *Harper's Monthly Magazine* 156 (January 1928), p. 171; Symes, "The New Masculinism," pp. 98–107. Carey's piece was also a direct refutation of what he perceived as the rampant selfishness of the economically independent woman in Bromley's "Feminist—New Style." His "Virist—New Style" also claimed independence from his job so he could become women's equal in "the art of recreation."

75. Symes, "The New Masculinism," pp. 105–107.

76. Lois Banner, *Women in Modern America: A Brief History* (New York: Harcourt Brace Jovanovich, 1974), p. 142. Rayna Rapp and Ellen Ross, "The Twenties' Backlash: Compulsory Heterosexuality, the Consumer Family, and the Waning of Feminism," in *Class, Race, and Sex: The Dynamics of Control*, ed. Amy Swerdlow and Hanna Lessinger (New York: Barnard College Women's Center; Boston: G. K. Hall, 1983), pp. 102–103.

77. Elizabeth Onativia, "Give Us Our Privileges," *Scribner's* 87 (June 1930), p. 597.

78. Banner, *Women in Modern America*, p. 142.

79. Benjamin R. Andrews, "The Home Woman as Buyer and Controller of Consumption," *Annals of the American Academy of Political and Social Science* 163 (May 1929), p. 41.

80. Lois Scharf, *To Work and to Wed: Female Employment, Feminism, and the Great Depression*, Contributions to Women's Studies no. 15 (Westport, Conn.: Greenwood Press, 1983), pp. 5–12.

81. Before the franchise, the largest women's reform groups saw labor legislation as a device to win over women to the suffrage movement. Among groups supporting legislation were the Women's Trade Union League, the League of Women Voters, and the Women's Bureau. Alice Kessler-Harris, *Out to Work: A History of Wage-Earning Women in the United States* (New York: Oxford University Press, 1982), pp. 205–210.

82. Cott, *The Grounding of Modern Feminism*, pp. 120–129; Rosalind Rosenberg, *Beyond Separate Spheres: Intellectual Roots of Modern Feminism* (New Haven: Yale University Press, 1982), xiii.

83. Kessler-Harris, *Out to Work*, p. 206.

84. Cott, *The Grounding of Modern Feminism*, pp. 73–74, 124–129; Rapp and Ross, "The Twenties' Backlash," p. 93.

1. Alison Lurie, *The Truth about Lorin Jones* (Boston: Little, Brown, 1988), p. 320.

2. Lurie, *The Truth about Lorin Jones*, pp. 326–327.

3. John I. H. Baur, *Revolution and Tradition in Modern American Art* (Cambridge: Harvard University Press, 1951), pp. viii, 87–90, 8.

4. Milton W. Brown, *American Painting from the Armory Show to the Depression* (Princeton: Princeton University Press, 1955; reprint, 1972), pp. 182–186.

5. There has been disagreement about the notion of a school since the early 1950s. On the occasion of the Art Students League retrospective for Miller just after his death (September 23–October 11, 1953), Stuart Klonis, director of the league, claimed Miller was "the only teacher working in America who, in the tradition of the Renaissance, produced a school of painters." This assertion was quickly refuted by the critic Margaret Breuning, who argued that there was no "common tradition of technical expression" among painters like Marsden Hartley, Edward Hopper, Yasuo Kuniyoshi, Niles Spencer, or William Palmer—and many others who had been Miller's pupils. *Kenneth Hayes Miller: A Memorial Exhibition* (New York: Art Students League, 1953), no pagination; and Margaret Breuning, "Little Touched by a Changing World," review of the 1953 memorial exhibition for Kenneth Hayes Miller at the National Academy, *Art Digest* 28 (October 1, 1953), pp. 19, 31.

6. I compare Soyer's account of the 1930s from his *Self-Revealment: A Memoir* (New York: Maecenas Press, Random House, 1969), pp. 70–79, and his essay "An Artist's Experiences in the 1930s," in Patricia Hills, *Social Concern and Urban Realism: American Painting of the 1930s* (Boston: Boston University Art Gallery, 1983), pp. 27–30. Soyer also wrote *Diary of an Artist* (Washington, D.C.: New Republic Books, 1977), *Homage to Thomas Eakins*, ed. Rebecca L. Soyer (South Brunswick, N.J.: T. Yoseloff, 1966), and *A Painter's Pilgrimage* (New York: Crown, 1962).

7. Interview with Lloyd Goodrich, December 30, 1982. Though he knew Soyer less well than the other artists, Goodrich felt that he shared with them a conviction that the human figure should be used as a design element—something that abstract art lacked. See also Lloyd Goodrich, *Kenneth Hayes Miller* (New York: Arts Publishing Corporation, 1930), *Raphael Soyer* (New York: Abrams, 1972), and *Reginald Marsh* (New York: Abrams, 1972).

8. Griselda Pollock, "Van Gogh and the Poor Slaves: Images of Rural Labour as Modern Art," *Art History* 11 (September 1988), p. 409.

9. Noyes's sister married John Miller, Kenneth's grandfather. Noyes's mother, Polly Hayes (Miller's middle name), was President Rutherford Hayes's aunt. Lincoln Rothschild, *To Keep Art Alive: The Effort of Kenneth Hayes Miller, American Painter (1876–1952)* (Philadelphia: Art Alliance Press, 1974), p. 19.

10. John D'Emilio and Estelle B. Freedman, *Intimate Matters: A History of Sexuality in America* (New York: Harper and Row, 1988), p. 112.

11. Louis J. Kern, *An Ordered Love: Sex Roles and Sexuality in Victorian Utopias—the Shakers, the Mormons, and the Oneida Community* (Chapel Hill: University of North Carolina Press, 1981), pp. 224–225. D'Emilio and Freedman, on p. 113, define the Oneidan conception of free love. The system of *coitus reservatus* is to be distinguished from the other traditional method of birth control, *coitus interruptus*, in which the male ejaculates outside the female to prevent conception; to the Oneidans this method would have meant loss of both semen and self-control.

12. These ideas are summarized in D'Emilio and Freedman, *Intimate Matters*, p. 120; Kern, *An Ordered Love*, p. 247; and Rothschild, *To Keep Art Alive*, pp. 19–21.

13. D'Emilio and Freedman, p. 120; Kern, p. 247; and Rothschild, pp. 19–21.

14. Rothschild, pp. 24–25. Miller's letters indicate some work done for the *Century* and for *McClure's.* Initially he taught a course on illustration at the Chase school. Rothschild argues that these early experiences gave Miller his lifelong interest in "the linear technique of etching."

15. Rothschild, *To Keep Art Alive,* pp. 25–26.

16. Kern, *An Ordered Love,* pp. 230, 259–260.

17. Kern, p. 270.

18. Ellen Kay Trimberger, "Feminism, Men, and Modern Love: Greenwich Village, 1900–1925," in *Powers of Desire: The Politics of Sexuality,* ed. Ann Snitow, Christine Stansell, and Sharon Tompson (New York: Monthly Review Press, 1983), p. 133.

19. Trimberger, p. 134.

20. Trimberger, pp. 134, 149.

21. Specific information on Miller's activities comes from Rothschild, *To Keep Art Alive,* pp. 35–36. In a letter to his cousin Rhoda Dunn, dated September 8, 1918, Miller professed admiration for Max Eastman's "American Ideals in Poetry," an essay in "the current issue of *The New Republic,*" Kenneth Hayes Miller Papers, Roll 583, Archives of American Art, Smithsonian Institution, Washington, D.C.; Paul Rosenfeld, *Port of New York: Essays on Fourteen American Moderns* (New York: Harcourt, Brace, 1924; reprint, Urbana: University of Illinois Press, 1961), pp. 135–144; for general discussions of the Greenwich Village milieu that help to place Miller's activities and attitudes see also Trimberger, "Feminism, Men, and Modern Love," p. 135; and Arthur Frank Wertheim, *The New York Little Renaissance: Iconoclasm, Modernism, and Nationalism in American Culture, 1908–1917* (New York: New York University Press, 1976), pp. 172–173.

22. Letter from Miller to Rhoda Dunn, dated October 19, 1915. In a letter to her dated September 8, 1918, Miller relates that Dr. Frink has had remarkable success with Helen in psychoanalysis: "Besides the benefit to her personality . . . she has gained ability and insight for the psychoanalytic technique which with practice she might use to practical—perhaps even professional purpose." Roll 583, Archives of American Art.

23. The artist Minna Citron, a former student of Miller's and a close friend of the artist's daughter, Louise, provided the information on marital dynamics in an interview, December 22, 1982. Evidently Helen's friends encouraged her to take a lover as well.

24. Interview with Minna Citron, December 22, 1982.

25. Raphael Soyer, "The Lesson: The Academy, the League, the Classroom," *Arts Magazine* 42 (September 1967), p. 35.

26. For a selection of some of these characterizations, see artists' remarks in *Kenneth Hayes Miller, A Memorial Exhibition*; Alan Burroughs, "Kenneth Hayes Miller," *The Arts* 14 (December 1928), pp. 301–306; and Harry Salpeter, "Kenneth Hayes Miller, Intellectual," *Esquire,* October 1937, pp. 89, 197–203.

27. Notes from Miller to Helen, dated July 28, 1921, and June 26 and October 8, 1923. Letters to Helen Pendleton Miller, Kenneth Hayes Miller Papers, Roll 583, Archives of American Art.

28. Letters from Miller to his mother, dated February 4, 1911; March 1, 1912; and December 20, 1915. Roll 583, Archives of American Art.

29. Letter from Miller to his cousin Rhoda Dunn, October 16, 1917.

30. Letters from Miller to Helen, dated December 31, 1912; July 7, 1925; July 13, 1925; and May 27, 1926; and letters from Miller to his cousin Rhoda Dunn, dated September 21, 1909; February 13, 1915; and September 8, 1918. Kenneth Hayes Miller Papers, Roll 583, Archives of American Art.

31. Harry Salpeter, "Kenneth Hayes Miller: Intellectual," p. 197.

32. For the most comprehensive biographical summary see Marilyn Cohen, "Reginald Marsh: An Interpretation of His Art," Ph.D. diss., New York University, Institute of Fine Arts, 1986; early information on Marsh's grandfather and father also appears in Frederick A. Blossom, "Reginald Marsh as a Painter," *Creative Art* 12 (April 1933), p. 257.

33. Interview with Lloyd Goodrich, December 30, 1982. Goodrich claimed that Fred Marsh designed and built three family homes as well as motor cars and miniature theaters and made a technologically advanced phonograph recording in 1910.

34. Lloyd Goodrich, *Reginald Marsh* (New York: Abrams, 1972), p. 295. Unless otherwise noted, Marsh's biography is based on Goodrich.

35. Goodrich, *Reginald Marsh*, p. 20. According to Goodrich, Marsh once reported that he had barely passed the art courses, instructed by "pedants" who "taught drawing from the antique and painting in still life . . . in a way that would make their 'old master' heroes turn in their graves."

36. Trimberger, "Feminism, Men, and Modern Love," pp. 146–147; Wertheim, *The New York Little Renaissance*, pp. 230–231.

37. Malcolm Cowley, as quoted in Wertheim, p. 230.

38. Enrollment Cards, the Art Students League of New York. Marsh enrolled in John Sloan's painting class from October 1921 through February 1922 and in his illustration class for the month of May 1922. That same year he signed up for Miller's "studio" in March. He spent four months of the 1922 season in Miller's life drawing and painting classes, and the following November in a painting course with George Luks. He concluded his formal studies with Miller in the 1927–28 season when he spent five more months in life drawing and painting, with an additional month of study in January 1929. At the league, students signed up on a month-by-month basis, following an academic (September to May) calendar with individual teachers. Miller's classes in the early 1920s were designated either life drawing and painting or studio. The latter designation may have referred to Miller's Wednesday afternoon teas at his studio on Fourteenth Street.

39. For a discussion of Burroughs's career, see Gwendolyn Owens, "Pioneers in American Museums: Bryson Burroughs," *Museum News* 57 (May 1979), pp. 46–53, 84.

40. Betty Burroughs, in an interview with Marilyn Cohen, characterized the Marsh family as nouveau riche (with enough wealth to be upper middle-class) and their life as bohemian. See Cohen, "Reginald Marsh: An Interpretation," p. 21.

41. Cohen, "Reginald Marsh: An Interpretation," pp. 19–20.

42. Interview with Lloyd Goodrich, December 30, 1982.

43. Reginald Marsh Papers, Roll D-308, frames 1–172, Archives of American Art, Smithsonian Institution, Washington, D.C.

44. Reginald Marsh Papers, Roll D-308, frames 1–172, Archives of American Art.

45. One can follow the events leading to the divorce in Marsh's diaries. He first saw a lawyer on October 5, 1932. During November and December, he paid bi- and triweekly visits to a Dr. Spaulding (a psychiatrist?). On December 21 Marsh left for Reno, Nevada.

Caleb Marsh, whose birth is recorded in Marsh's diary, is never mentioned by Marsh biographers. According to Raphael Soyer, to whom Marsh told the story, Marsh had been thrilled with the birth of Caleb, believing that the child was his. When Betty subsequently informed him that he was not the father, he was devastated (interview with Soyer, March 13, 1987). Edward Laning (interviewed by Marilyn Cohen, October 10, 1979) believed that Marsh might have been sterile as a result of a childhood illness and thus anxious about his masculinity. Cohen, "Reginald Marsh: An Interpretation," p. 220 n. 55.

46. Desk diary entries dated May 24, 1933, and June 30, 1933, Reginald Marsh Papers, Roll NRM-2, Archives of American Art.

47. Marilyn Cohen, *Reginald Marsh's New York: Paintings, Drawings, Prints, and Photographs* (New York: Whitney Museum of American Art in association with Dover, 1983), p. 34.

48. By February 1937, after occupying four different Fourteenth Street studios, Marsh moved into his two-story studio at 1 Union Square West, in the Lincoln Arcade Building, which he would occupy until his death. Marsh records these moves in his desk diaries—from 21 East Fourteenth Street, his first studio; to 9 West Fourteenth Street on June 1, 1932; to 5 East Fourteenth Street on January 19, 1934; back to 9 West Fourteenth Street on March 2, 1935; to 7 West Fourteenth Street on September 14, 1935; and finally to 1 Union Square West on February 2, 1937. Reginald Marsh Papers, Archives of American Art; see Map 1.

49. On one occasion he wrote: "I've hardly talked with or seen a soul since my last letter [this is confirmed in Marsh's August 1934 diary entries], working, planning, rambling and staring, meditating; I think this is the way a painter should live." Reginald Marsh Papers, Archives of American Art, letter dated September 9, 1934.

50. Cohen, "Reginald Marsh: An Interpretation," p. 170.

51. Though never a natural athlete (perhaps because his childhood illnesses forced long periods of inactivity), Marsh was constantly testing himself, always recording his scores in golf, swimming, and tennis in comparison with those of others. Marsh's diary for April 12, 1912, Reginald Marsh Papers, Archives of American Art.

52. Lloyd Goodrich, *Reginald Marsh*, p. 18.

53. Edward Laning, *East Side, West Side, All Around the Town* (Tucson: University of Arizona Museum of Art, 1969), p. 95.

54. Interview with Lloyd Goodrich, December 30, 1982; Interview with Raphael Soyer, December 27, 1982; and Raphael Soyer, "Reginald Marsh," *Reality: A Journal of Artists' Opinions* 3 (Summer 1955), pp. 5–6.

55. Barbara Ehrenreich, *The Hearts of Men: American Dreams and the Flight from Commitment* (Garden City, N.Y.: Anchor Books, 1984), pp. 68–84.

56. Laning, *East Side, West Side*, p. 95.

57. Interview with Raphael Soyer, March 13, 1987. Even before he entered psychoanalysis, Marsh would have become aware of its processes as a student of Kenneth Hayes Miller's in the 1920s. Several appointments with a Dr. Spaulding are recorded in Marsh's 1932 desk diary prior to his departure for Reno, Nevada, to obtain a divorce. Although the consecutive appointments in a stressful time suggest that Dr. Spaulding may have been a psychiatrist, I have not determined that this is the case. Marsh's calendars of the mid-1930s indicate regular appointments with a psychiatrist, Dr. Belcher; he saw Dr. Brodman, a psychiatrist interested in the psychology of artists, late in the 1930s and into the 1940s. Since Soyer and Marsh had adjoining studios in the Lincoln Arcade Building, at 1 Union Square West, beginning in 1937, Soyer's recollections undoubtedly date from sometime in the late 1930s or early 1940s, long after Marsh's mother's death in 1927. Dr. Brodman's wife kindly sent me photocopies of three letters, one undated and two dated 1945 and 1946, in which Marsh thanks Dr. Brodman for treatment and discusses paintings he is sending to the doctor. See also Cohen, "Reginald Marsh: An Interpretation," p. 211 n. 11.

58. Laning, *East Side, West Side*, pp. 89–91, and Edward Laning, *The Sketchbooks of Reginald Marsh* (Greenwich, Conn.: New York Graphic Society, 1973), p. 25.

59. Bishop could trace her lineage to both English and Dutch settlers in the eighteenth century. Her mother, Anna Bartram Newbold, was a descendant of the famous eighteenth-century botanist John Bartram. Her father was a member of a New Brunswick, New Jersey, family for whom Bishop House, the offices of the history department at Rutgers University, was named. John Bishop, one of the largest landowners in that area's early town-

ship, subsequently became a member of the governor's council. The family also rose to prominence in the shipping business in the early 1800s, when New Brunswick became New Jersey's first port. James Bishop was a New Jersey Whig representative to the Thirty-fourth Congress of the United States in 1855–57 and a principal founder of St. James Methodist Church of New Brunswick. "Isabel Bishop," *Current Biography Yearbook* (New York: Wilson, 1977), p. 63; and *Sunday Home News* (n.p.), June 21, 1970, clipping fragment, Isabel Bishop Papers, Archives of American Art.

60. Cindy Nemser, "A Conversation with Isabel Bishop," *Feminist Art Journal* 5 (Spring 1976), pp. 15–16. Helen Yglesias, *Isabel Bishop* (New York: Rizzoli, 1989), p. 10. Yglesias's book provides much new information about Bishop's childhood and her relationships with her parents. Yglesias mentions that one of Bishop's sisters, a gifted artist, was older by fifteen years. Thus the first set of twins would have been born in about 1887, the second in 1889.

61. Yglesias, *Isabel Bishop*, p. 10. This discussion of her childhood occurred sometime in the 1980s.

62. Yglesias, *Isabel Bishop*, p. 10. Bishop's parents were especially divided over religion: her father worshiped regularly at the Episcopal church; her mother dismissed Christianity as a "minor sect." The most scandalous display of her mother's nonbelief occurred when Bishop was eight or ten. Her mother, who had to appear in court, refused to swear on the Bible, claiming, "I don't believe in God." Bishop condemned her mother's actions—violations of convention that deeply humiliated her father. "I felt so sorry for my father. I thought it was terrible of her." Over the years, her own semiregular church attendance paid homage to her father's beliefs.

63. Yglesias, *Isabel Bishop*, p. 11. Information on Bishop's early class is found on the enrollment cards, Art Students League of New York.

64. Enrollment cards, Art Students League of New York. Bishop's observations on Weber and Henri were made during my interview with her, December 16, 1982.

65. Bishop, as quoted in Yglesias, *Isabel Bishop*, p. 12.

66. Nemser, "A Conversation with Isabel Bishop," pp. 16–17.

67. Sally Moore, "Isabel Bishop: Half a Century of Painting the Flotsam of Union Square," *People*, May 26, 1975.

68. Edward Laning, "The New Deal Mural Projects," in Francis V. O'Connor, *The New Deal Art Projects: An Anthology of Memoirs* (Washington, D.C.: Smithsonian Institution Press, 1972), p. 80; Howard E. Wooden, *Edward Laning, American Realist, 1906–1981: A Retrospective Exhibition* (Wichita, Kans.: Wichita Art Museum, 1982), pp. 6, 19; Yglesias, *Isabel Bishop*, p. 15; Reginald Marsh, desk diaries, 1931–34, Roll NRM-2, Archives of American Art. A comparison of these sources may correct the confusion about who participated in the 1931 and 1933 European trips. Marsh's desk calendars for the late spring and summer of 1931 show that he never left New York. An entry for May 30, 1931, states, "Miller sails, Brooks sail" (the plural may indicate Alexander Brook and his wife, Peggy Bacon). An entry for July 7, 1931, reads, "Majestic arrives bearing Ken, Isobel" (Marsh often misspelled Bishop's first name).

69. Interview with Isabel Bishop, December 16, 1982; Yglesias, *Isabel Bishop*, p. 14. Listings of the works exhibited at Midtown Galleries are in the Isabel Bishop Papers, Archives of American Art.

70. Yglesias, *Isabel Bishop*, pp. 16–17.

71. From the available literature, it is not clear when and how the stipend ended. According to a 1941 article, Bishop admitted "that if it were not for a small sum of money left her in a will and the income of her husband, Dr. Harold G. Wolff . . . she would have real trouble following her art career." Donna Ford, "Other Women's Lives," *Worcester*

Telegram, May 20, 1941, no pagination. The source of this small inheritance is unknown.

72.	In a taped interview with me (December 18, 1982) and in interviews with Nemser ("A Conversation with Isabel Bishop," p. 17) and with Yglesias (*Isabel Bishop*, p. 12) Bishop credits the painter Guy Pène du Bois with helping her realize how much she was influenced by Miller, to her detriment. In the early 1930s, du Bois, who had been her teacher one summer, arrived at her studio for one of his irregular visits, looked at her work, and asked, "What are you doing?" As Bishop told me, "Well, I was doing from morning until night and trying hard and struggling with it, but he felt there was nothing in it." Bishop also recalled that critics were quite "hard" on her about Miller's "influence." Although some of that criticism was apt, its persistence long after Bishop established her own manner of working suggests a bias in the criticism itself: women are always subject to authority, always "influenced."

73.	Yglesias, *Isabel Bishop*, p. 16.

74.	Yglesias, p. 16.

75.	Yglesias, p. 17.

76.	Yglesias, p. 19. The artist Jack Levine described her as a pluralist who always led from a position of neutrality.

77.	Yglesias, *Isabel Bishop*, p. 17.

78.	Reginald Marsh Papers, Roll NRM-3, Archives of American Art. The last sentence in this part of the letter reads, "So—no wonder Miller's been padding his nest." This enigmatic statement places me in the center of "Polly's dilemma." Do I interpret this as evidence of a more intimate relationship between Bishop and Miller, now coming to an end? We have evidence of Miller's reputation for becoming involved with a succession of female art students. Bishop (in her interview with me) said that she was very close to Miller's entire family. In 1928 Miller wrote to his mother: "Louise [his daughter] will have a really brilliant Christmas as Isabel Bishop is giving her a fur coat: she is rather stunned by such good fortune which seemed to have dropped from the skies." Bishop also subsidized a major study on Miller by Lloyd Goodrich, published in 1930. They may have traveled alone together in Europe; as I indicated in n. 68 above, Marsh's diaries for 1931 show that he did not accompany them in their travels that year as Bishop has claimed, though her memory could simply have elided separate events fifty years after the fact. In 1933, when they traveled to Europe together, Marsh left Bishop and Miller after ten days. (They all arrived in Berlin on July 10 and traveled to Munich on July 13; on July 19 Marsh took the train alone from Munich back to Berlin, where he caught a plane for Moscow.) There is not enough evidence to argue with any certainty for a more intimate bond; if there were one, it would have intensified the inequality of power in a relationship from which Bishop felt obliged to extricate herself. At the same time, if there were even an "assumed" perception of involvement on the part of members of Miller's and Bishop's social circle, it may have removed or postponed for Bishop the possibility of too early a marriage, which she also feared.

79.	Margaret Breuning, review from the *New York Evening Post*, quoted in "Women Art Critics Attack Organization of Modernist Women," *Art Digest* 3 (March 1, 1929), p. 9. She claimed that the older National Association of Women Painters and Sculptors was formed at a time (initially in 1889 as the Woman's Art Club of New York, in 1912 as an association) when a separate exhibition structure was necessary. For an overview of several early women's organizations, see Julie Graham, "American Women Artists' Groups: 1867–1930," *Woman's Art Journal* 1 (Spring–Summer 1980), pp. 7–12.

80.	Helen Appleton Read, as quoted in "Women Art Critics," p. 9.

81.	Rayna Rapp and Ellen Ross, "The Twenties' Backlash: Compulsory Heterosexuality, the Consumer Family, and the Waning of Feminism," in *Class, Race, and Sex: The*

Dynamics of Control, ed. Amy Swerdlow and Hanna Lessinger (New York: Barnard College Women's Center; Boston: G. K. Hall, 1983), pp. 100–101.

82. It is difficult to say how conscious Bishop's choices were; her 1980s insights are those of someone with historical distance and an awareness of feminist issues. One has a sense that she was making careful choices but that she did not deliberately manipulate circumstances she fully understood.

83. Raphael Soyer, *Diary of an Artist*, p. 181. Parts of Soyer's narrative of his childhood, his education, his early career, and his experiences in the 1930s appear in his earlier books, *A Painter's Pilgrimage, Homage to Thomas Eakins*, and *Self-Revealment: A Memoir*.

84. Interview with the artist, March 13, 1987. Soyer learned Hebrew along with Russian because his father took the twins to these private tutorials. In gratitude for their lessons, several of the students also taught the twins some French and German. Borisoglebsk is in the province of Tambov approximately 325 miles southeast of Moscow.

85. For the structure of Eastern European communities and the place of the scholar see Elizabeth Ewen, *Immigrant Women in the Land of Dollars* (New York: Monthly Review Press, 1985), pp. 38–39.

86. Moses Soyer, "Three Brothers," *Magazine of Art* 32 (April 1939), p. 201; and Raphael Soyer, *Diary of an Artist*, p. 207. The twins would copy their father's drawings of cossacks; he would correct these and hang the best pictures on the walls as both encouragement and praise. He also made intricate designs for table linens for their mother, who would select the color schemes and execute the embroidery.

87. Ewen, *Immigrant Women*, p. 52; Cynthia Jaffee McCabe and Daniel J. Boorstin, *The Golden Door: Artist Immigrants of America, 1876–1976* (Washington, D.C.: Smithsonian Institution Press for the Hirshhorn Museum and Sculpture Garden, 1976), p. 158. In his interview with me on March 13, 1987, Soyer characterized his father as a "social democrat," rather than a radical or a Communist, and an ardent Zionist (who longed for a Jewish state).

88. Raphael Soyer, *Diary of an Artist*, pp. 206–207. In "Three Brothers," p. 201, Moses described his father as a remarkable man who had toiled hard all his life without deviating from his youthful ideals—he was "self-taught and self-made in the real American sense of the phrase" and adored by contemporaries and colleagues as a brilliant teacher and scholar. In my interview with Raphael on April 26, 1984, he suggested that the picture Moses painted of their early days in New York was too "rosy." Life was particularly difficult for their mother. She had wanted to study and to learn English, but a lack of money and time made these pursuits increasingly difficult. Her recognition of lost possibilities in the New World, with its opportunities and its less repressive ideology of male and female roles, may well have contributed to the debilitating depression that eventually necessitated her institutionalization.

89. For a discussion of Old World and immigrant notions of childhood and adolescence, see Ewen, *Immigrant Women*, pp. 98–100; Soyer quotation from *Diary of an Artist*, p. 202.

90. Frank Gettings, *Raphael Soyer: Sixty-five Years of Printmaking* (Washington, D.C.: Smithsonian Institution Press, for the Hirshhorn Museum and Sculpture Garden, 1982), pp. 8–9. Harry Salpeter, "Raphael Soyer: East Side Degas," *Esquire*, May 1933, p. 156. As early as 1917, the Soyers also discovered printmaking. Their mother gave them twenty-five dollars to buy an etching press, which they set up in the back room. At the academy, Raphael attended Joseph Pennell's lectures on etching, which emphasized the work of Rembrandt and Whistler. Several years later, he found his first "patron," the printer Jacob Friedland, who "seemed to be a prosperous man." In exchange for studio space, models, and lithographic stones, Raphael gave Friedland a painting per month.

91. Soyer, *Diary of an Artist*, p. 211.

92. Moses Soyer, "Three Brothers," p. 204.

93. Raphael Soyer, *Diary of an Artist*, p. 212. Soyer is specific about the three-month stipend from his uncle. The Art Students League enrollment cards, however, show that he spent five months with du Bois at two different periods; two months of classes are recorded for December 1920–January 1921, three for January–March 1923. Perhaps Soyer wanted to return to du Bois after spending a year back at the National Academy (or at least the spring of 1922), and his uncle made the next three months possible.

94. Raphael Soyer, *Diary of an Artist*, p. 213, compares Luks and Miller. It is difficult to know if Soyer shied away from Miller because he feared Miller's "influence"; critics discussed it in the early thirties, and students may have talked among themselves at the league. Soyer told me (December 27, 1982) he disliked Miller's work. He met Miller only once, when they served on a jury together—where Miller was, as Soyer put it, "very loyal to his students." At the time, Soyer may have felt that Miller and his students, and the weekly teas, were a closed circle he could never enter. And he still needed part-time work. He tutored students in Hebrew and found seasonal work in embroidery shops, activities he alternated with painting.

95. Soyer, *Self-Revealment*, p. 58. Soyer also discussed his early behavior with me (December 27, 1982). His shyness prevented him from meeting several of the artists he admired in the late twenties. He particularly regretted avoiding the artist Jules Pascin, who had influenced him (as had Louis Bouché, Yasuo Kuniyoshi, Alexander Brook, and Peggy Bacon); under Pascin's influence Soyer hired his first nude model. Evidently Pascin made a great effort to know American artists. When he saw Soyer's first one-man show at the Daniel Gallery and expressed a desire to meet him, Soyer failed to make the appointment. Within the year, in 1930, Pascin had taken his own life.

96. Soyer, *Diary of an Artist*, p. 218. Although Soyer doesn't recall meeting Kuniyoshi, Salpeter ("Raphael Soyer," p. 157) reports that he attended these sketch classes.

97. Elizabeth McCausland, "The Daniel Gallery and Modern American Art," *Magazine of Art* 44 (November 1951), pp. 280–285. In the early 1920s Charles Daniel showed watercolors by John Marin and Charles Demuth; oils by Niles Spencer, Preston Dickinson, and Charles Sheeler; and works by the artists who most influenced Soyer, among them Jules Pascin, Louis Bouché, Alexander Brook, and Yasuo Kuniyoshi.

98. Interview with the artist, December 27, 1982. A lack of records, beyond the New York telephone directory, makes Soyer's movements hard to trace in the late 1920s and early 1930s. The Soyers lived at 203 and 240 West Fourteenth Street as well as at 229 West Fourth and 96 Charles Street. Soyer had a studio at 3 West Fourteenth Street, perhaps for several years. See Map 1.

99. Lloyd Goodrich, *Raphael Soyer*, p. 336. For a discussion of teachers in the Depression, see Lois Scharf, *To Work and to Wed: Female Employment, Feminism, and the Great Depression*, Contributions to Women's Studies no. 15 (Westport, Conn.: Greenwood Press, 1980), pp. 75–77.

100. Soyer, "An Artist's Experiences," pp. 27–29.

101. Soyer, *Self-Revealment*, p. 16; interview with the artist, March 13, 1987. Fannie was the first of the children to die, in 1963. According to Soyer, she was "steadfast, responsible, dedicated," and she loved school. In dedicating *Self-Revealment* to her in 1967, Soyer made his "secret and intimate appraisal of her," placing her "on a plane with a Marie Curie or a Käthe Kollwitz."

102. Ewen, *Immigrant Women*, pp. 193–196.

103. Gettings, *Raphael Soyer*. Throughout this catalog Soyer discusses his models; he

expanded on this subject in our interview of March 13, 1987, from which the characterizations of his models are quoted.

104. It is unclear from Soyer's account of the event whether the presence of the model with the artist and the model's recognition that "she was not expected" carried sexual innuendos. Soyer sketched the men present at the meeting: Nicolai Cikovsky, William Gropper, Adolph Wolf, Walter Quirt, and Nemo Piccoli. After Soyer became a teacher at the club, it exhibited the work of one of his students, Ruth Gikow, who went on to become a painter; Soyer wrote the catalog introduction for the show. Women, if Soyer's sketches give any indication, were more of a presence at Artist's Union meetings. Soyer, *Diary of an Artist*, p. 222, and Soyer, "An Artist's Experiences," pp. 28–29. See Soyer's *John Reed Club Meeting* (Fig. 3.32).

105. In her publication *Women and the American Left: A Guide to Sources* (Boston: G. K. Hall, 1983), p. 169, Mari Jo Buhle notes a "precipitous decline" in the radical feminist press during this period. The Communist party had little use for feminist journalism except for tactical purposes. Many radical women journalists turned to more middle-of-the-road literary publications, principally the *New Masses*. *Working Woman* maintained an ultra-left position, predicting incipient class warfare. In March 1933 the publication adopted a magazine format; in November 1934 Gwen Bard began to write and illustrate the "Fashion Letter." Apart from her work and occasional drawings by Mary Morrow, the magazine's principal, almost monthly, illustrator was William Gropper, with occasional submissions by Ben Shahn, Dan Rico, and John Arrow. For a general discussion of John Reed Club activities, see Helen A. Harrison, "John Reed Club Artists and the New Deal: Radical Responses to Roosevelt's 'Peaceful Revolution,' " *Prospects* 5 (1980), pp. 241–268.

106. Barbara Melosh, *Engendering Culture: Manhood and Womanhood in New Deal Public Art and Theater* (Washington, D.C.: Smithsonian Institution Press, 1991).

107. Interview with the artist, December 27, 1982. Soyer claimed that when his friends brought him to the John Reed Club, he himself had no idea that he was already well known.

108. "New Instructors at the Art Students League," *Art Digest* 8 (October 1, 1933), p. 25. Interview with the artist, March 13, 1987.

109. Richard Beers, "As They Are at Thirty-four," *Art News* 32 (January 13, 1934), p. 13; and "Brook and Soyer Enter the Metropolitan," *Art Digest* 7 (September 1, 1933), p. 7.

110. Soyer, *Diary of an Artist*, p. 218. Soyer told me (December 27, 1982) that he also took his work to the Downtown Gallery but that Edith Halpert wanted him to leave the paintings. He was reluctant to do so and went on to the Valentine Gallery, which at the time showed work by Picasso, Soutine, Modigliani, and some of the Impressionists along with a few Americans: Louis Eilshemius, Milton Avery, and John Kane.

111. Interview with the artist, December 27, 1982; and Soyer, *Diary of an Artist*, pp. 218–219.

112. Carl Zigrosser, *The Artist in America: Twenty-four Close-ups of Contemporary Printmakers* (New York: Knopf, 1942), pp. 60–61.

113. The discussion of a mainstream here and in the following paragraph comes from Randy Rosen and Catherine C. Brawer, *Making Their Mark: Women Artists Move into the Mainstream, 1970–1985* (New York: Abbeville Press, 1989), pp. 7–9.

114. Patricia Hills and Roberta K. Tarbell, *The Figurative Tradition and the Whitney Museum of American Art: Paintings and Sculpture from the Permanent Collection* (New York and Newark, Del.: Whitney Museum of American Art in association with the University of Delaware Press, 1980), pp. 71–76.

115. Hills and Tarbell, *The Figurative Tradition*, p. 7.

116. The Art Students League yearly catalogs give a complete roster of league instructors. See Hills and Tarbell, *The Figurative Tradition*, p. 70.

117. See Hills and Tarbell, *The Figurative Tradition*, p. 14.

118. Forbes Watson, "Opening Studio," *The Arts* 10 (October 1927), p. 220; for a discussion of Watson's criticism see Peninah R. Y. Petruck, *American Art Criticism, 1910–1939* (New York: Garland, 1981), pp. 134–176.

119. Raphael Soyer, *Self-Revealment*, p. 68.

120. See Hills and Tarbell, *The Figurative Tradition*, p. 15.

121. When I interviewed them, both Raphael Soyer and Isabel Bishop spoke highly of the magazine. It satisfied their needs, and both claimed to be faithful readers.

122. Hills and Tarbell, *The Figurative Tradition*, p. 13.

123. Statement of purpose in the Forbes Watson Papers, Roll D-48, Archives of American Art, as quoted in Petruck, *American Art Criticism*, p. 37.

124. Forbes Watson, editorial, *The Arts* 3 (January 1923), p. 1.

125. Alan Burroughs, "Young America—Reginald Marsh," *The Arts* 3 (February 1923), p. 138.

126. Lloyd Goodrich, "*The Arts* Magazine: 1920–1931," *American Art Journal* 5 (May 1973), p. 84.

127. Goodrich told me about the circumstances of the publication of his book on Miller in an interview, December 30, 1982. See Goodrich, *Kenneth Hayes Miller*; and Alan Burroughs, *Kenneth Hayes Miller*, American Artists Series (New York: Whitney Museum of American Art, 1931).

128. See in particular Marsh's desk diaries for 1931–32 for references to bowling and for entries about his almost daily social activities with Laning, Bishop, and Miller. Reginald Marsh Papers, Roll NRM-2, Frames 145–395, Archives of American Art.

129. Cohen, *Reginald Marsh's New York*, p. 3; Laning, "The New Deal Mural Projects," p. 80; Nemser, "A Conversation with Isabel Bishop," p. 16.

130. Cohen, "Reginald Marsh: An Interpretation," p. 14.

131. Interview with the artist, April 26, 1984.

132. Interview with the artist, December 27, 1982. Soyer in 1937 had a studio with Marsh in the Lincoln Arcade Building at 1 Union Square West, and occasionally they shared models. The two artists probably knew each other fairly well by the early 1940s, for Marsh confided some intimate details of his life to Soyer and Soyer included Marsh's portrait in his group portrait of 1966, *Homage to Thomas Eakins*.

133. Though Isabel Bishop did not know Soyer until the early 1950s, she became familiar with his work through the Whitney shows. She claimed that she had thought of Soyer as a disciple of both Brook and Kuniyoshi, whose work she defined as the "accepted" style of American art in the 1920s. She called it the Woodstock style, which she described as "the National Academy of Design touched by Cézanne," referring to the American painters' tendency to work from models posed in the studio and to treat their canvases with Cézanne's facture and manipulations of pictorial space.

134. Undated anonymous review for a traveling show featuring works by Miller, Marsh, Soyer, Kuniyoshi, Sloan, Sheeler, du Bois, and Dickinson, from the *Minneapolis Daily Star Review*. Whitney Museum Papers, Roll N-591, Archives of American Art, Washington, D.C.

135. Matthew Baigell, *The American Scene: American Painting of the 1930s* (New York: Praeger, 1974), p. 23.

136. Reginald Marsh, "What I See in Laning's Art," *Creative Art* 12 (March 1933), p. 187.

137. Miller's ideas were most clearly expressed in a lecture entitled "The Third Dimension in Painting," which he delivered at the league in the early 1920s. His students, moreover, recorded his ideas, which also survive in accounts of the critiques he gave at the league. Finally, in the 1920s and early 1930s perceptive responses to his work were published, focusing on his essentially formalist intentions. Rothschild, *To Keep Art Alive*, chapters 5 and 6; Goodrich, *Kenneth Hayes Miller*; and Burroughs, *Kenneth Hayes Miller*.

138. Rothschild, *To Keep Art Alive*, pp. 70–75.

139. Fry introduced the doctrine of significant form in his 1909 piece "An Essay in Aesthetics," published in the *New Quarterly* and republished in Fry's book of essays *Vision and Design* (1920). It was after this time that Miller codified his own views. See Sandra S. Phillips, "The Art Criticism of Walter Pach," *Art Bulletin* 65 (March 1983), p. 109 n. 22. Clive Bell also promulgated the idea of significant form in his 1913 book *Art*, implying, according to W. Eugene Kleinbauer, *Modern Perspectives in Western Art History* (New York: Holt, Rinehart and Winston, 1971), p. 7, that forms, lines, and colors are significant in themselves.

140. Rothschild, *To Keep Art Alive*, p. 74.

141. In November 1982 I interviewed Jack Henderson, N.A., one of Laning's oldest friends and colleagues. He said that Laning had often expressed a desire to be reincarnated as a fifteenth-century Sienese painter.

142. Petruck, *American Art Criticism*, pp. 35–37; and Meyer Schapiro, *Modern Art, Nineteenth and Twentieth Centuries: Selected Papers* (New York: George Braziller, 1978), pp. 151–154.

143. *Paintings by Nineteen Living Americans*, exhibition catalog (New York: Museum of Modern Art, 1930). The artists in the show (December 13, 1929–January 13, 1930) were chosen by ballot.

144. Petruck, *American Art Criticism*, pp. 68–85.

145. Baur, *Revolution and Tradition*, p. 89. Baur observed that Soyer's attention to closely knit design prevented his sympathetic paintings from becoming sentimental.

146. Bennard B. Perlman, *The Immortal Eight: American Painting from Eakins to the Armory Show, 1870–1913* (Cincinnati, Ohio: North Light, 1979), p. 46.

147. In his autobiography *It's Me O Lord* (New York: Dodd, Mead, 1955), Rockwell Kent, a onetime student of Miller's, distinguished among three of the major art teachers, Chase, Miller, and Henri:

> As Chase had taught us just to use our eyes, and Henri to enlist our hearts, now Miller called on us to use our heads. Utterly disregardful of the emotional values which Henri was so insistent upon, and contemptuous of both the surface realism and virtuosity of Chase, Miller . . . exacted a recognition of the tactile qualities of paint and of the elements of composition—line and mass—not as a means toward the re-creation of life, but as the fulfillment of an end, aesthetic pleasure. . . . Yet the importance of style as intrinsic to the expression of thought is undeniable; and Miller's emphasis upon some of its elements was of value to me if for no reason but as a corrective of Henri's disregard of it. (p. 83)

148. Petruck, *American Art Criticism*, pp. 139–143.

149. Marsh claimed that these old masters allowed him to see the energy in groups of moving figures. In 1944 he wrote that he loved going to the beach at Coney Island—another crowded New York scene: "I like to go there because of the sea, the open air and the crowds—crowds of people in all directions, in all positions, without clothing, moving—like

the compositions of Michelangelo and Rubens." Reginald Marsh, "Let's Get Back to Painting," *Magazine of Art* 37 (December 1944), p. 296.

150.   Interview with the artist, December 27, 1982.

CHAPTER THREE

1.   Albert Halper, "Behind the Scenes of *Union Square*," *Wings* 7 (March 1933), p. 5.

2.   John Hart, *Albert Halper* (Boston: Twayne, 1980), pp. 45, 50.

3.   *The WPA Guide to New York City: The Federal Writers' Project Guide to 1930s New York*, originally published as *New York City Guide* (New York: Random House, 1939; reprint, New York: Pantheon Books, 1982), pp. 200–201, 322.

4.   Gerald R. Wolfe, *New York: A Guide to the Metropolis* (New York: New York University Press, 1975), pp. 170–173.

5.   Frank Beckman, "I Remember When . . ." *New Yorker News*, Spring 1964, p. 24.

6.   *The WPA Guide to New York City*, p. 201.

7.   "The Rebuilding of Fourteenth Street," *New York Times*, August 29, 1926, sec. 10, p. 2.

8.   "The Rebuilding of Fourteenth Street." Mitchell's Fourteenth Street Central Mercantile Bank had increased its capital by $27 million in three years.

9.   Reginald Marsh made one of these new buildings his New York home following his 1933 divorce. "Many Advantages in Midtown Area," *New York Times*, September 6, 1925, sec. 10, p. 1.

10.   In her catalog, *Reginald Marsh's New York: Paintings, Drawings, Prints, and Photographs* (New York: Whitney Museum of American Art in association with Dover, 1983), p. 24, Marilyn Cohen clarifies this meaning, but her statement that "*Dead Man's Curve* does not refer to the shape of a road" fails to recognize Marsh's pun on an actual Union Square location.

11.   "The Rebuilding of Fourteenth Street"; "Favor Union Square for Bus Terminal," *New York Times*, December 3, 1926, p. 10; "Times Square Terminal for Buses Planned," *New York Times*, December 31, 1926, p. 2. In the article dated December 13, Nathan Ohrbach, president of the large Union Square store, said that the need for a central city terminal transcended local concerns and would be an advantage for suburban and city passengers, allowing buses to come down both East and West sides and cross to a terminal in Union Square, below the major congestion. "Extension Asked of Fourteenth Street Subway," *New York Times*, May 10, 1926, p. 39.

12.   "Explains Progress in Midtown Zone," *New York Times*, September 23, 1928, sec. 12, p. 24.

13.   "Many Advantages in Midtown Area."

14.   "The Rebuilding of Fourteenth Street." Mr. Adams, the advocate of Americanization, was president of Styles and Cash, 135 West Fourteenth Street.

15.   Christ's triumphal entry into Jerusalem is a particularly appropriate iconographic source for Henry Kirke Brown's equestrian statue of George Washington. The monument, dedicated July 4, 1856, commemorates Washington's triumphal arrival in New York in 1783 after he had driven the British out of the city. Joseph Lederer, *All Around the Town* (New York: Scribner, 1975), p. 53.

16.   Although Bishop's inclusion of Dante and Virgil may seem to imply that modern urban life is hell, the artist had in mind a very different idea, based on a vernacular translation of Dante's *Inferno*:

When I was working on this picture I was preoccupied with two things—one, trying to formulate visually my feeling about Union Square and, at the same time, immersing myself in a literal translation of Dante. Dante's *Inferno* in this down-to-earth "unpoetical" translation has to me a marvelous *homely* quality, almost a "genre" feeling in its reference to the definite, particular and concrete features of objects. They are thus given an every-day character even in the midst of the fantastic underworld! This "genre" aspect connected in my mind with my feeling for Union Square, which I felt to be "homely," ugly, and in that quality, lovable (instead of fearful) as the setting for hordes of human beings. At a point in the *Inferno*, Dante and Virgil find themselves confronted by a multitude of souls. This was my picture.

Bishop made the picture for her father; it was to hang in her parents' new home in White Plains after he retired. Given her mother's work on a translation of Dante throughout Bishop's childhood, the work had personal meaning for the family. Elizabeth H. Hawkes, *American Painting and Sculpture* (Wilmington: Delaware Art Museum, 1975), p. 122; and Helen Yglesias, *Isabel Bishop* (New York: Rizzoli, 1989), pp. 15–16.

17. Henry Adams, *Thomas Hart Benton: An American Original* (New York: Knopf, 1989), pp. 156–160; Marsh and Laning both spent time with Benton as he produced the New School murals—Benton, in fact, helped Marsh perfect his tempera technique. For a discussion of the environmentalist theories that fueled both the American Scene movement and the mural movement see Matthew Baigell, *The American Scene: American Painting of the 1930s* (New York: Praeger, 1974), pp. 41ff. and Forbes Watson, "A Perspective on American Murals," in *Art in Federal Buildings I: Mural Designs 1934–1936*, ed. Edward Bruce and Forbes Watson (Washington, D.C.: Art in Federal Buildings, Inc., 1936), pp. 3–5.

18. "Critics Unanimously Condemn Modern Museum's Mural Show," *Art Digest* 6 (May 15, 1932), p. 7.

19. A. Millier, "Murals and Men," *Art Digest* 9 (September 1, 1935), p. 6.

20. Of the three Union Square works Bishop exhibited in her first one-woman show at Midtown Galleries, one was in a private collection; Laning's *Fourteenth Street* (one of approximately six neighborhood scenes) was purchased by the Whitney Museum in 1933, and Bishop acquired *Unlawful Assembly* from Laning for her private collection. The other two works went into private collections much later. These were early works, some of them explorations for subsequent projects, that the artists kept in their possession or, in Bishop's cases, destroyed much later.

21. "Building Activity in Union Square," *New York Times*, July 15, 1928, sec. 11, p. 1.

22. "Union Square Attracts Banking Locations," *New York Times*, September 29, 1929, sec. 12, p. 2.

23. "The Rebuilding of Fourteenth Street."

24. "The Rebuilding of Fourteenth Street." See also the caption information for photograph 1002-C7/C8, dated 1930, "Photographic Views of New York," Microfiche Collection, New York Public Library.

25. *The WPA Guide to New York City*, p. 203.

26. Albert Halper, *Union Square* (New York: Viking Press, 1933), p. 378. In addition to banks and insurance and utility companies, developers planned a number of office buildings for the district. In 1928 Consolidated Edison bought the old Tammany Hall building for an addition ("Wigwam Sold Again at $100,000 Profit," *New York Times*, January 2, 1928, p. 2; and "Plan Eighteen-Story Building for Tammany Hall Site," *New York Times*, September 8, 1928, p. 29). Shortly afterward, the 1871 iron-front Domestic Building was

sold to the Broadway and Fourteenth Street Development Corporation, which planned to construct a twenty-one story building ("Office Building to Replace Union Square Landmark," *New York Times*, January 8, 1928, sec. 12, p. 2). In April 1928 Henry Mandel Associates, Inc., leased the property at 21–23 Union Square West to add to their existing property on the corner of Sixteenth Street and Union Square West. By June construction plans for a forty-three-story office building were in the works ("Mandel Adds Leasehold to Site on Union Square," *New York Times*, April 28, 1928, p. 32; "Work Started on Forty-three Story Structure by Henry Mandel," *New York Times*, June 17, 1928, sec. 11, p. 2; and "Building Activity in Union Square").

27. "The Rebuilding of Fourteenth Street."

28. "How Hearn Store Took Present Site," *New York Times*, August 9, 1925, sec. 10, p. 2.

29. "How Hearn Store Took Present Site."

30. "Hearn Will Have Fifth Avenue Entrance," *New York Times*, February 13, 1926, p. 16.

31. Gretta Palmer, *A Shopping Guide to New York* (New York: McBride, 1930), p. 170.

32. Until 1931 or 1932 Bishop was tied closely to Miller's influence (see Chapter 2, n. 72). Guy Pène du Bois visited her studio and questioned her about her early works. Some of them she destroyed prior to her 1975 retrospective exhibition because in her view they were "all wrong." Interview with the artist, December 16, 1982.

33. Interview with Isabel Bishop, December 16, 1982.

34. "The Rebuilding of Fourteenth Street."

35. Caption information from photographs 1002-F1, dated January 29, 1928, and 1002-F2, dated February 24, 1933, "Photographic Views of New York," Microfiche Collection, New York Public Library.

36. Palmer, *A Shopping Guide to New York*, pp. 45–46.

37. "Woman's Scream Stampedes Four Thousand Shoppers," *New York Times*, March 30, 1930, p. 6.

38. Palmer, *A Shopping Guide to New York*, p. 46.

39. "Growing Activity in Fourteenth Street Section," *New York Times*, January 11, 1930.

40. "Park Change Plans Approved by Board," *New York Times*, February 17, 1927, p. 12.

41. "To Shift Statues to Aid Straphanger," *New York Times*, April 22, 1928, p. 1.

42. "Lafayette Statue Moved," *New York Times*, August 7, 1929, p. 18.

43. "Cheering News for Union Square," *New York Times*, August 25, 1931, p. 20.

44. "Thousands View Flag Day Parade," *New York Times*, June 15, 1932, p. 3; "Celebrate Garden in Union Square," *New York Times*, June 16, 1932, p. 23; and *The WPA Guide to New York City*, p. 202.

45. The photograph (Fig. 3.16) by Marsh was probably taken in the late 1930s or early 1940s.

46. Harry Salpeter, "Kenneth Hayes Miller, Intellectual," *Esquire*, October 1937, p. 198. Salpeter described Miller's analysis of the painting, which reveals the studied classicism of his design:

Miller showed how deliberately designed and classically derived was every square inch of his *In 14th Street [Sidewalk Merchant]*. He showed, for example, how the arc of the store front, between the flanking show cases, stemmed from paintings by Watteau and Rubens which had been similarly designed, except, of course, in antique architectural settings. He showed how the leash of the Pekinese tied him into the body of the painting and how the creases in the women's dresses were plotted in order to lead the eye from and to the center, and how the dominant note was struck by the arc of the store front and the suggestion of depth beyond. Even the form of the electric light bulbs and the women's sleeves—which one might suppose to be incidental details—Miller proved to be subordinate to the main design and contributing to the impression the painter sought to convey.

This description refers to the original design for *In Fourteenth Street* of 1932; it was repainted c. 1940 and titled *Sidewalk Merchant*. A photograph of the 1932 work (in which the leash is visible) can be found in Milton W. Brown, *American Painting from the Armory Show to the Depression* (Princeton: Princeton University Press, 1955; reprint, 1972), p. 182.

47. Lloyd Morris, *Incredible New York: High Life and Low Life of the Last One Hundred Years* (New York: Random House, 1951), pp. 339–345.

48. Sloan, as quoted in David W. Scott and Edgar John Bullard, III, *John Sloan, 1871–1951* (Washington, D.C.: National Gallery of Art, 1971), p. 179.

49. The painting was one of two works Sloan executed for the Public Works of Art Project (PWAP), one of the first relief projects sponsored by the federal government.

50. It has been a commonplace (at least since the eighteenth century) that many artist-illustrators—working in graphic media as well as in painting—are more openly honest and descriptive about political and sexual matters in their graphic works than in their paintings. This is particularly true for Sloan and Marsh. It is not my intent, however, to explore the important relationship between Marsh's painting and his graphic oeuvre.

51. Helen Farr Sloan, ed., *John Sloan: New York Etchings (1905–1949)* (New York: Dover, 1978), no. 57.

52. Jean McPherson Kitchen, "Surging Fourteenth Street," *New York Times*, June 9, 1929, sec. 5, p. 23.

53. According to *New York Panorama*, American Guide Series (New York: Random House, the Guilds' Committee for Federal Writers' Publications, 1938), pp. 90–130, the Lower East Side was made up of dozens of ethnic groups, with people of Eastern European, Mediterranean, and Jewish heritage predominant.

54. "Fourteenth Street Salesmen Are Bold and High-Powered," *New York Times*, July 18, 1926, sec. 7, p. 14.

55. Nils Hogner and Guy Scott, *Cartoon Guide of New York City* (New York: Augustin, 1938), p. 55.

56. Halper, *Union Square*, p. 50.

57. *The WPA Guide to New York City*, p. 198.

58. "Fourteenth Street Salesmen."

59. *The WPA Guide to New York City*, p. 198.

60. Halper, *Union Square*, p. 48.

61. Halper, *Union Square*, pp. 47–48.

62. Halper, *Union Square*, pp. 47–48; and *The WPA Guide to New York City*, p. 198.

63. Kitchen, "Surging Fourteenth Street."

64. Edward Laning, "Reginald Marsh," *Demcourier* 13 (June 1943), p. 4.

65. Warren I. Susman, "The Culture of the Thirties," in *Culture as History: The Transformation of American Society in the Twentieth Century* (New York: Pantheon Books, 1984), pp. 156–157, distinguishes between civilization and culture, which is concerned with the quality of living an American life. Culture, according to Susman, became the central preoccupation of the 1930s.

66. John Kwiat, "John Reed Club Art Exhibition," *New Masses* 8 (February 1933), p. 23; Reginald Marsh Papers, Roll NRM-2, Archives of American Art, Washington, D.C.

67. "Congress Seceders," *Art Digest* 14 (June 1, 1940), p. 18; for a full account of events leading up to the split, see Matthew Baigell and Julia Williams, introduction to *Artists Against War and Fascism: Papers of the First American Artists' Congress* (New Brunswick, N.J.: Rutgers University Press, 1986), pp. 3–44. Baigell and Williams point out that Soyer remained with the congress through 1941, by which time it had ceased to play a major role, concentrating on the fascist threat in America rather than abroad, and on the economic crisis for artists. Helen Yglesias notes that Bishop wanted to maintain a position as politically neutral as possible during these years and was angered at Stuart Davis's pressuring her to "sign something or join some protest to do with the Artists' Union." Unable to remember the details, Bishop may well have been referring to requests by Davis and other organizers to sign the first "call." Yglesias, *Isabel Bishop*, p. 18.

68. To locate the various radical organizations in Union Square throughout the Depression, refer to Map 2 and the following sources: caption information for photograph 1003-A4, August 30, 1930, "Photographic Views of New York," Microfiche Collection, New York Public Library; "Communists Move Headquarters Here," *New York Times*, September 25, 1930, p. 29; Helen A. Harrison, "John Reed Club Artists and the New Deal: Radical Responses to Roosevelt's 'Peaceful Revolution,'" *Prospects* 5 (1980), pp. 241–243, 249–250; "Patriotic Parade Marks May Day," *New York Times*, May 2, 1938, p. 3; and *The WPA Guide to New York City*, p. 200. From 1928 to 1930, the block of buildings at 24–30 Union Square East housed the offices of the Communist party; the *Daily Worker*; the Polish, Jewish, and Hungarian dailies; the Workers' Bookstore and School; the Young Communist League of America; and the Cooperative Cafeteria, where Communist organizers gathered. The *New Masses* was located across the square at 39 Union Square West; the John Reed Club made frequent moves throughout the decade: from 65 West Fifteenth Street in the early 1930s to 131 West Fourteenth Street by the mid-1930s. The Debs Auditorium, site of frequent Socialist party meetings, lay just off the square at 5 East Fourteenth Street.

69. "May Day Rallies Pass Quietly Here" and "May Day Finds Labor Well Off in America," *New York Times*, May 2, 1926, p. 3; "May Day Passes Peacefully Here—Police Have Listless Time," *New York Times*, May 2, 1927, p. 3.

70. *The WPA Guide to New York City*, p. 199; and "City Crowds Silent on News of Death," *New York Times*, August 23, 1927, p. 1.

71. *Daily Worker*, May 2, 1929; and "Eight Slain, Seventy-three Wounded as Five Hundred Police Fight Reds in Berlin Riots," *New York Times*, May 2, 1929, p. 2.

72. "Tammany Police Paraders Tear Down Sign on Workers' Center. Children Assaulted," *Daily Worker*, May 20, 1929; *The WPA Guide to New York City*, p. 199; and *New York Times*, May 29, 1929, sec. 1, pp. 1–2.

73. For accounts of the largest and most disruptive demonstrations against unemployment, staged on March 6, 1930, see my discussion in the text and refer to the *Daily Worker*, March 3, 1930, p. 1; March 6, 1930; and March 7, 1930. See also, "All Police on Duty to Avert Violence at Red Rally Today," *New York Times*, March 6, 1930, pp. 1, 10; "Reds Battle Police in Union Square," *New York Times*, March 7, 1930, pp. 6–8; and "Veterans to Hold Union Square Parade," *New York Times*, March 8, 1930, p. 2.

74. "May Day Peaceful Here As Thousands March in a Gay Mood," *New York Times*, May 2, 1935, p. 1; "Forty Thousand March Here in May Day Parade—Quietest in Years," *New York Times*, May 2, 1936, p. 1; "Seventy Thousand Mark Orderly May Day," *New York Times*, May 2, 1937, p. 1.

75. "Veterans Rally in Union Square," *New York Times*, May 1, 1931, p. 23.

76. *New York Times*, January 21, 1932, p. 5. The Washington's birthday celebration never occurred, in part because the square was not physically ready for such an event.

77. "Mayor Walker Proclaims Union Square Fete," *New York Times*, April 4, 1932, p. 19; "Hoover Aids Union Square Fete," *New York Times*, April 21, 1932, p. 17. President Hoover pleased local business leaders with his official letter on the fete, which he said was of particular interest to him

> because of my firm belief in the value of preserving historical traditions as a stimulus to local pride in community progress. The historical interest of the park . . . and its evolution through residential and retail business to its present importance as a centre of industry, finance and commerce, give it a distinctive quality deserving commemoration. I congratulate your committee and the business interests which it represents, upon this successful celebration of a significant occasion.

78. *New York Times*, April 17, 1932, sec. 2, p. 1; and "Union Square Marks Its Centenary Gaily," *New York Times*, April 24, 1932, p. 17.

79. In addition to these works, Laning exhibited two others in John Reed Club exhibitions in 1933 and 1934. In The World Crisis Expressed in Art show beginning in December 1933, Laning exhibited *Relief*; in the Revolutionary Front show beginning in November 1934 he exhibited *Riders*. Both works are now lost.

80. In May–June 1931 Marsh attended weekly meetings, which he recorded in his diaries with entries like "workers communism class," "workers school," and "red class." Reginald Marsh Papers, Roll NRM-2, Archives of American Art.

81. Lloyd Goodrich, *Raphael Soyer* (New York: Abrams, 1972), p. 84.

82. See Raphael Soyer, "An Artist's Experiences in the 1930s," in Patricia Hills, *Social Concern and Urban Realism: American Painting of the 1930s* (Boston: Boston University Art Gallery, 1983), pp. 27–31.

83. Kantor's *Union Square* was exhibited in the Museum of Modern Art's May 1932 exhibition; see the catalog *Murals by American Painters and Photographers* (New York: Museum of Modern Art, 1932), p. 5. For the show, the museum asked each artist to make a three-part horizontal composition measuring 21 by 48 inches and to enlarge one panel to measure 7 by 4 feet. Kantor's work was the large panel.

Kantor was a Russian-born painter and lithographer who had a Fourteenth Street studio until about 1931. At that time he painted his lyrical *Farewell to Union Square* to commemorate his stay and his nostalgia at leaving. Brown, *American Painting from the Armory Show to the Depression*, p. 186.

84. Permits were required for any demonstrations or speeches in Union Square. For major gatherings like the annual May Day rallies, bandstands with microphones were erected. "All Police on Duty," pp. 1, 10.

85. At the 1931 May Day rally, veterans, Socialists, and Communists all carried American flags at the head of their processions. "Violence Avoided on May Day Here," *New York Times*, May 2, 1931, p. 4.

86. Interview with Raphael Soyer, December 28, 1982. The other painting was *Workers Armed* (Fig. 6.25).

87. For a discussion of the social meaning of the crayon style see Rebecca Zurier, *Art for the Masses: A Radical Magazine and Its Graphics, 1911–1917* (Philadelphia: Temple University Press, 1988), pp. 129–132.

88. For a discussion of these doctrines, promulgated by the American Communist party early in the 1930s, see the chapter "Propaganda in Print," in Cécile Whiting, *Antifascism in American Art* (New Haven: Yale University Press, 1989), pp. 8–33.

89. Richard N. Masteller, *"We, the People?" Satiric Prints of the 1930s*, (Walla Walla, Wash.: Donald H. Sheehan Gallery, Whitman College, 1989), pp. 7, 49.

90. Fourth Avenue, the extension of Union Square East, was on a direct line with the Bowery, whose missions and flophouses had always provided food, clothing, and shelter for the destitute. When the number of these poor increased dramatically with the massive unemployment of the 1930s, their plight became more visible.

91. Joseph Lederer, *All Around the Town* (New York: Scribner, 1975). The most prominent of these monuments, in the park and subsequently in all the works of art, was the large equestrian monument of George Washington. Its pendant was a bronze statue of Lincoln, also by Brown. There was also a bronze statue of Lafayette, by Frédéric-Auguste Bartholdi, given by the French to New Yorkers in 1876 to commemorate their support of France during the Franco-Prussian War. A bronze fountain sculpture of a woman and child by the German artist Adolf von Donndorf was located at the west side of the park. Finally, an 80-foot flagpole resting on a drum at the center of the square was a memorial to the Tammany Hall leader Charles Francis Murphy, who had died in 1924.

92. Goodrich, *Raphael Soyer*, p. 84.

93. Philip Evergood, "There Is a Difference in Bums," unpublished draft of an undated essay, American Contemporary Artists Gallery Paper, Roll D-304, frame 315, Archives of American Art, Washington, D.C., as cited in Kendall Taylor, *Philip Evergood: Selections from the Hirshhorn Museum and Sculpture Garden* (Washington, D.C.: Smithsonian Institution Press, 1978), n. 17. For a fuller discussion of Bishop's attitude toward these men, see Chapter 5.

94. William E. Leuchtenburg, *Franklin D. Roosevelt and the New Deal* (New York: Harper and Row, 1963), pp. 194–196.

CHAPTER FOUR

1. Miller's preference for Titianesque prototypes was well known and can also be studied in relation to the nudes he continued to paint throughout his career. This particular Titian image was illustrated in Oskar Fischel, *Tizian, des Meisters Gemälde*, 5th ed. (Stuttgart: Deutsche Verlags-Anstalt, 1924 [?]), p. 77.

2. Betsy Fahlman, *Guy Pène du Bois, Artist about Town* (Washington, D.C.: Corcoran Gallery of Art, 1980). Du Bois (1884–1958) was a student of Miller's only briefly, when Miller taught at William Merritt Chase's New York School for Art during the first decade of the century. Ultimately du Bois was more of a realist. His work and artistic philosophy emerged from his studies with Robert Henri and Henri's art-for-life's-sake philosophy rather than from his brief encounter with Miller's Renaissance prototypes and formalist aesthetic concerns. Isabel Bishop reported to me (interview, December 16, 1982) that Miller had little use for du Bois.

3. Du Bois was cosmopolitan in his outlook, in part from the years he spent living outside Paris (1924–30). His paintings of glamorous well-to-do figures like those in *Americans in Paris* were typical. He also took the mannequin-like flapper as his subject, portraying her as an aspiring sophisticate.

4. Held, along with his friend F. Scott Fitzgerald, did much to create the popular flapper image. Jack Shuttleworth, "John Held, Jr., and His World," *American Heritage: The Twenties*, special issue 16 (August 1965), pp. 29–32.

5. *Ladies Home Journal*, October 22, 1921, as quoted in Lois Banner, *Women in Modern America: A Brief History* (New York: Harcourt Brace Jovanovich, 1974), p. 129.

6. William E. Leuchtenberg, *The Perils of Prosperity, 1914–1932* (Chicago: University of Chicago Press, 1958), p. 172; and Alice Almond Shrock, "Feminists, Flappers, and the

Maternal Mystique: Changing Conceptions of Women and Their Roles in the 1920s," Ph.D. diss., University of North Carolina at Chapel Hill, 1974, p. 123.

7. Malcolm Cowley, *Exile's Return* (New York: Viking Press, 1951), p. 64. My characterization of the flapper is derived from Shrock, "Feminists, Flappers, and the Maternal Mystique," pp. 130–133; and Pamela Neal Warford, "The Social Origins of Female Iconography: Selected Images of Women in American Popular Culture, 1890–1945," Ph.D. diss., Washington University, St. Louis, 1979, p. 43.

8. Frederick Lewis Allen, *Only Yesterday: An Informal History of the Nineteen-Twenties*, First Perennial Library edition (New York: Harper and Row, 1931; reprint, 1964), pp. 79–81.

9. Miller grew up in and retained close ties with the Oneida community, where the silver was made; in several letters to his mother he mentions shares of Oneida stock. Because images are so closely related, it is tempting to think he might have seen this advertisement.

10. In May 1929, after Miller's show at the Rehn Gallery, Marsh bought *Party Dress* for his own collection; according to Miller's letter to his mother, May 2, 1929, he paid full price. This Miller work is the closest in iconography to Marsh's paintings of women at leisure. Kenneth Hayes Miller correspondence, Roll N-583, Archives of American Art, Washington, D.C.

11. Shrock, "Feminists, Flappers, and the Maternal Mystique," pp. 150–170; for specific examples, p. 158.

12. Allen, *Only Yesterday*, pp. 73–85. Allen attributed the revolution largely to the disillusionment of the postwar era, to woman's liberation, prohibition, the automobile, sex, magazines, and the movies. More recently, James R. McGovern has demonstrated that the revolution was under way well before the war, in part because of urbanization and industrialization. "The American Woman's Pre–World War I Freedom in Manners and Morals," *Journal of American History* 55 (September 1968), pp. 315–333.

13. Allen, *Only Yesterday*, pp. 74–76. In *Current History*'s symposium on the New Woman, the Catholic rector Hugh L. McMenamin wrote: "We may call [the flapper's] boldness greater self-reliance, brazenness greater self-assertion, license greater freedom and try to pardon immodesty in dress by calling it style and fashion, but the fact remains that deep down in our hearts we feel a sense of shame and pity." "Evils of the Woman's Revolt against the Old Standards," *Current History* 27 (October 1927), p. 31. Among those also dismayed by flapper behavior were older feminists whose sobriety and hard work for social causes were scorned by younger women. See Lillian Symes, "Still a Man's Game: Reflections of a Slightly Tired Feminist," *Harper's Monthly Magazine* 158 (May 1929), pp. 678–686.

14. Warford, "The Social Origins of Female Iconography," p. 50, suggests that some saw the flapper's realism and lack of repression as antidotes to Wilsonian idealism.

15. Banner, *Women in Modern America*, pp. 150–151, argues that the real extent of the sexual revolution of the 1920s is debatable. Surveys from the period, like Katherine P. Davis's sample of two thousand middle-class women, showed that only 7 percent of those who were married and 14 percent of those who were single had engaged in premarital sex. Among the unmarried women, 80 percent said they found little justification for engaging in sex. Birth control was difficult to obtain and remained illegal in all states. Although the number of divorces rose in the 1920s, the number of marriages remained high. In Middletown (Robert S. Lynd and Helen Merrell Lynd, *Middletown: A Study in Contemporary American Culture* [New York: Harcourt, Brace, 1929], pp. 114–117), more people were marrying by the end of the decade.

16. Lynd and Lynd, *Middletown*, p. 144.

17. Allen, *Only Yesterday*, p. 79.

18. William L. O'Neill, "The End of Feminism," in *Twentieth-Century America: Recent Interpretations*, ed. Barton J. Bernstein and Allen J. Matusow, 2d edition (New York: Harcourt Brace Jovanovich, 1972), p. 191.

19. J. Stanley Lemons, *The Woman Citizen: Social Feminism in the 1920s* (Urbana: University of Illinois Press, 1973), introduction.

20. Shrock, "Feminists, Flappers, and the Maternal Mystique," pp. 147–148.

21. In the introduction to her dissertation on three images of womanhood in the 1920s, Alice Shrock argues that the maternal mystique was a "resolution of a brief fling at Flapperdom" and that it represented a "strong, ever-present set of attitudes rooted in the [nineteenth-century] cult of true womanhood, reaffirming woman's traditional role in nurturing, conserving and protecting the home, husband and offspring." Lois Banner (*Women in Modern America*, p. 153) argues that little had been done to change sex-role conditioning in the 1920s and that once freedom had played itself out, women returned to culturally expected roles. She quoted the well-known psychologist Floyd Allport, who wrote in 1929 that a woman "not through nature but by early training . . . becomes a reflection of a feminine image which men carry around in their heads."

22. A number of recent historians have discussed the back-to-the-home movement: Banner, *Women in Modern America*; Barbara Ehrenreich and Deirdre English, *For Her Own Good: One Hundred Fifty Years of the Experts' Advice to Women* (Garden City, N.Y.: Anchor Press, 1978); and Gaye Tuchman, *Hearth and Home: Images of Women in the Mass Media* (New York: Oxford University Press, 1978). Particularly useful is Stuart Ewen, *Captains of Consciousness: Advertising and the Social Roots of the Consumer Culture* (New York: McGraw-Hill, 1978), chapter 6, "Consumption and the Ideal of the New Woman."

23. William F. Ogburn, "The Family and Its Functions," in *Recent Social Trends in the United States: Report of the President's Research Committee on Social Trends* (New York: McGraw-Hill, 1934), p. 661. Ogburn observed that such changes, continuous for one hundred years, had had a singular impact in the postwar decades.

24. The electric washing machine, invented in 1905, and the mechanical refrigerator, invented in 1917, were but two of numerous aids to household work. William F. Ogburn, "The Influence of Invention and Discovery," in *Recent Social Trends*, p. 148.

25. Lawrence K. Frank, "Social Change and the Family," *Annals of the American Academy of Political and Social Science* 160 (March 1932), p. 98. For statistics on the decrease in the number of children, see Frank, "Childhood and Youth," *Recent Social Trends*, pp. 754–755.

26. Frank, "Social Change and the Family," pp. 96–97.

27. Shrock, "Feminists, Flappers, and the Maternal Mystique," pp. 194–195. In 1922 the Better Homes Movement was inaugurated, with Herbert Hoover and Calvin Coolidge as its officers. Efforts focused on home building and furnishing, for the home environment was equated with a strong family. The back-to-the-home movement was also proclaimed in women's magazines. In "Nineteen-Twenty: An Editorial" in the *Ladies Home Journal*, January 1, 1920, p. 3, published on the heels of the franchise, M. D. Davis wrote:

> Since the beginning of time the housekeeper's job has been looked down upon; she has been considered a drudge; even the Federal census calls her a woman of "no occupation." Let us elevate the homemaker's task to the dignity of a profession. For her job is as important as that of her husband, whatever he may do. . . . she is the most important woman in the world.

28. Shrock, in "Feminists, Flappers, and the Maternal Mystique," p. 196, uses the term *hearthbound* to describe the woman desired by those who covertly reprogrammed the move-

ment, making consumption a major occupation.

29. Shrock, p. 196.

30. Ehrenreich and English, *For Her Own Good*, pp. 131, 135. A number of home economics institutions flourished in the 1920s to encourage women to acquire home management skills, among them the Pratt Institute in New York and the Garland and Fanny Farmer schools in Boston. General Electric in 1932 and Westinghouse in 1934 opened cooking institutes for women. See also Stuart Ewen, *Captains of Consciousness*, p. 172; and Glenna Matthews, *"Just a Housewife": The Rise and Fall of Domesticity in America* (New York: Oxford University Press, 1987), pp. 145–171.

31. Amey E. Watson, "The Reorganization of Household Work," *Annals of the American Academy of Political and Social Science* 160 (March 1932), p. 168.

32. Allen, *Only Yesterday*, pp. 79–80; and Lillian G. Genn, "The Bachelor Girl: Is She a Menace?" *Independent Woman* 7 (December 1928), p. 538.

33. Ehrenreich and English, *For Her Own Good*, pp. 145–148, have demonstrated that all the new inventions made more work since women had to clean more frequently.

34. On the heterosexual revolution and feminism, see Rayna Rapp and Ellen Ross, "The Twenties' Backlash: Compulsory Heterosexuality, the Consumer Family, and the Waning of Feminism," in *Class, Race, and Sex: The Dynamics of Control*, ed. Amy Swerdlow and Hanna Lessinger (New York: Barnard College Women's Center; Boston: G. K. Hall, 1983), pp. 100–101. Clifford Kirkpatrick, a sociology professor, defined the pros and cons of three marital roles in "Techniques of Marital Adjustment," *Annals of the American Academy of Political and Social Science* 160 (March 1932), pp. 178–183. As a "wife-mother," the woman assumed domestic and child-rearing responsibilities, subordinating herself economically to her husband in exchange for the "security, respect, domestic authority, economic support and loyalty of her husband." In the role of "companion," she shared pleasures, enjoyed "a more ardent emotional response" as an "object" of admiration, and received funds for dress and recreation but had to preserve her beauty to maintain her marital security, provide her husband with "ego satisfaction," cultivate advantageous social contacts, and be responsible for alleviating her husband's domestic responsibility. In the role of "partner," created by the new "cultural situation," the woman would accept certain obligations—to contribute economically to the household, to undertake equal responsibility for child support, "to dispense with any appeal to chivalry," to bear an equal responsibility for the family status through her own career success, and to renounce alimony (except for dependent children)—in exchange for certain privileges: economic independence, equal authority in family finances, and acceptance as an equal. Kirkpatrick advocated a balance of privileges and obligations to achieve domestic accord. The spokespersons for the professionalized homemaker found ways to make her wife-mother role seem more economically and socially advantageous, equal in privilege rather than overbalanced toward obligation.

35. Amey Watson, "The Reorganization of Household Work."

36. Watson, all quotations p. 171.

37. Watson, p. 172.

38. Watson, p. 171.

39. Since the complex issues of child rearing in the 1920s apply indirectly to a discussion of the matronly shopper as consumer, I will only mention them. Like "professionalized" homemaking, child rearing became both important and difficult. In his influential book *The Psychological Care of Infant and Child*, published in 1928, the behavioral psychologist John B. Watson argued that environment and psychological nurturing were as important as physiological care. Watson also worked for advertisers, and many 1920s advertisements played on women's escalating guilt about being unable to devote all the necessary care to child

rearing. Food products would mold children into particular kinds of adults, and women needed to educate children in correct consumption habits to ensure them a healthy, happy adulthood. Psychologists and advertisers created tension between a "continued ideal of motherhood and the inadequacies of that role" by unifying the tasks of motherhood and consumption. Shrock, "Feminists, Flappers, and the Maternal Mystique," pp. 203–204; and Stuart Ewen, *Captains of Consciousness*, pp. 173–175.

40. Phyllis Palmer, *Domesticity and Dirt: Housewives and Domestic Servants in the United States, 1920–1945*, Women in the Political Economy Series (Philadelphia: Temple University Press, 1990).

41. For full statistics on the time devoted to rural and urban household work, see Ogburn, "The Family and Its Functions," pp. 669–672.

42. Abraham Myerson, *The Nervous Housewife* (Boston: Little, Brown, 1920), p. 77, as quoted in Matthews, *"Just a Housewife": The Rise and Fall of Domesticity in America*, p. 194.

43. Shrock, "Feminists, Flappers, and the Maternal Mystique," p. 201; Amey Watson, "The Reorganization of Household Work," pp. 170–171. Together, wife and husband would form family policy on income, standard of living, choice of home, planning of budget, division of responsibility, number and spacing of children, vacation planning, etc.

44. Benjamin R. Andrews, *Economics of the Household, Its Administration and Finance* (New York: Macmillan, 1927), p. 3, as cited in Watson, "The Reorganization of Household Work," p. 170.

45. Andrews as quoted in Watson, p. 169.

46. William Baldwin, *The Shopping Book* (New York: Macmillan, 1929), pp. 1–2. As Stuart Ewen suggests, women's "power" was actually "circumscribed . . . by the ideology of the consumer market"—the real repository of power—and the industrial culture necessarily required a separation of the world of women (consumption) from that of men (production). *Captains of Consciousness*, pp. 169–173.

47. Kenneth Hayes Miller to Rhoda Dunn, January 19, 1920; July 20, 1920; and November 16, 1920. Kenneth Hayes Miller Papers, Roll 583, Archives of American Art.

48. "Of all the great streets in the world, there is none which possesses such splendid variety of interest, none that so consistently proclaims throughout its whole length the joys of material life in their most alluring forms, as Fifth Avenue." International Commercial Service, "Fifth Avenue: The World's Golden Highway of Wealth, Fashion, and Beauty," *Gazette des Dames*, Album of Fashion with Shopping Guide (London and New York, 1921).

49. For a good general overview of artists' activities and themes, see Patricia Hills, *Social Concern and Urban Realism: American Painting of the 1930s* (Boston: Boston University Art Gallery, 1983). See also Chapter 3.

50. Jean McPherson Kitchen, "Surging Fourteenth Street," *New York Times*, June 9, 1929, sec. 5, p. 23. Though the description does not correspond to one specific Miller image, it captures the general qualities of several Fourteenth Street works. "Middle-aged women of the district may be seen shopping, garbed for the street in knitted caps of gray hues, pulled well down over the ears, and with tweed topcoats of somewhat masculine design that suggest wear by husband or son. A frequent accessory is a bulging brown paper shopping bag."

51. Like *Fitting Room*, which conflates practices from bargain and finer department stores, other works of the early 1930s still resemble images of the early 1920s. In *Woman with an Umbrella* (Fig. 4.8) and *The Little Coat and Fur Shop* (Fig. 4.33) the women are both more attractive physically and more fashionably dressed than those of *Afternoon on the Avenue* and *The Bargain Counter* (Figs. 3.10 and 3.13).

52. This is a major theme of the essay by T. J. Jackson Lears, "From Salvation to Self-

Realization: Advertising and the Therapeutic Roots of the Consumer Culture, 1880–1920," in *The Culture of Consumption*, ed. Richard Wightman Fox and T. J. Jackson Lears (New York: Pantheon Books, 1983), pp. 3–38.

53. My interpretation of Laning's and Bishop's mural-like paintings of the early 1930s here and in Chapter 1 is supported by Karal Ann Marling, "A Note on New Deal Iconography: Futurology and the Historical Myth," *Prospects* 4 (1979), pp. 421–440.

54. The policeman's relaxed posture in this image was not that typical of the works of artists engaged in social protest. Social realists regularly saw the police as brutal perpetrators of an unfair system of justice, as cartoons and drawings in the *New Masses* demonstrate (see, for example, William Gropper's "Free Speech" [Fig. 3.38]).

55. See Matthews, "Just a Housewife," p. 193. Matthews argues that the devaluation of domesticity by the 1920s—thanks to mass-produced consumer goods—meant that women could no longer use "women's sphere" as a rationale for political activism.

56. Thorstein Veblen, as quoted in John Wilmerding, Linda Ayres, and Earl A. Powell, *An American Perspective: Nineteenth-Century Art from the Collection of Jo Ann and Julian Ganz, Jr.* (Washington, D.C.: National Gallery of Art, 1981), p. 70 n. 82.

57. I am grateful to Kathy Peiss for suggesting this reading of "middle-classness" in relation to Miller's shoppers.

58. John Kwiat, "John Reed Club Art Exhibition," *New Masses* 8 (February 1933), p. 23.

59. This painting was one of several New York City images Orozco did for a show at the Art Students League and the Downtown Gallery in 1929.

60. Lloyd Goodrich, "Exhibitions in New York," *The Arts* 15 (May 1929), pp. 328–329.

61. Hearn's also contributed to the Fireman's Honor Emergency Fund and the Police Relief Fund, and to unemployed actors through Stage Relief Day. *New York Times*, August 6, 1932, p. 23; January 8, 1933, p. 31; January 11, 1933, p. 6; February 2, 1933, p. 6; March 1, 1933, p. 14; and March 21, 1933, p.15.

62. *New York Times*, January 22, 1933, sec. 2, p. 1.

63. *New York Times*, January 22, 1933, sec. 2, p. 1. Klein made his appeal to the professionalized homemaker through Mrs. Grace Morrison Poole, president of a middle-class women's organization, the General Federation of Women's Clubs.

64. Kitchen, "Surging Fourteenth Street," p. 23.

65. "Kenneth Hayes Miller," *Art News* 30 (November 28, 1931), p. 10.

66. Photographers like Dorothea Lange in her pictures of migrant farm workers, painters working on mural commissions for the government, and novelists like John Steinbeck in *The Grapes of Wrath* took this theme as their project.

67. Lloyd Goodrich, *Kenneth Hayes Miller* (New York: Arts Publishing Corporation, 1930), pp. 1–2, 12.

68. Walter K. Gutman, "Kenneth Hayes Miller," *Art in America* 18 (February 1930), p. 92.

69. Paul Rosenfeld, *Port of New York: Essays on Fourteen American Moderns* (New York: Harcourt, Brace, 1924; reprint, Urbana: University of Illinois Press, 1961), p. 143.

70. *Art News* 28 (December 27, 1929), p. 13.

71. Lois W. Banner, *American Beauty* (Chicago and London: University of Chicago Press, 1983), pp. 275–276. Barbara Melosh, in *Engendering Culture: Manhood and Womanhood in New Deal Public Art and Theater*, discusses local criticism of monumental female figures in Section murals as part of the response to the new cult of slimness (Washington, D.C.: Smithsonian Institution Press, 1991), p. 211.

72. Quoted in Harry Salpeter, "Kenneth Hayes Miller, Intellectual," *Esquire*, October 1937, p. 197.

73. Undated correspondence between Louis Lozowick and Kenneth Hayes Miller (I assign it a date of 1932 because that was the year intellectuals endorsed the presidential candidate William Foster). Kenneth Hayes Miller Papers, Roll 583, Archives of American Art.

74. In a letter to his mother dated March 1, 1912, Miller reported that he and Nell (his wife Helen) were reading Key. Kenneth Hayes Miller Papers, Roll 583.

75. Key wrote in *Love and Ethics* (New York: Hubbsch, 1911), p. 69: "Either we believe that the sensual instincts are pitfalls and obstacles or we regard them as guides in the upward movement of life on a par with reason and conscience." Ellen Key, *Love and Marriage*, trans. Arthur G. Chater (New York: Putnam, 1911).

76. Key was not alone in her arguments. In his 1915 book *The Marriage Revolt* William Carsons reprinted an earlier *New York Times* article by the psychologist Carl Jung, who stated that Americans were more "tragic" and "neurotic" than any of the world's peoples, largely from trying to control themselves too rigidly; if American prudery were eliminated, America would become "the greatest country the world had ever known." Nathan G. Hale, Jr., *Freud and the Americans* (New York: Oxford University Press, 1971), pp. 268–269.

77. "Ellen Key's Startling Views on Love and Marriage," *Current Literature* 50 (April 1911), pp. 403–405; and "Ellen Key's Revaluation of Woman's Chastity," *Current Literature* 52 (February 1912), pp. 200–201.

78. "The New Erotic Ethics," *The Nation* 94 (March 14, 1912), p. 261.

79. "The New Erotic Ethics." Sigmund Freud, in works like *Totem and Taboo* (translated and published in the United States in 1918) similarly argued that "repression should exist for social rather than individual goals." Hale, *Freud and the Americans*, p. 347.

80. Ellen Key, "Motherliness," *Atlantic* 110 (October 1912), pp. 562–570.

81. Key, *Love and Marriage*, p. 175.

82. Key, "Motherliness," pp. 567–568.

83. Key, "Motherliness," p. 566.

84. "Ellen Key's Startling Views on Love and Marriage," p. 405.

85. Lincoln Rothschild, *To Keep Art Alive: The Effort of Kenneth Hayes Miller, American Painter (1876–1952)* (Philadelphia: Art Alliance Press, 1974), p. 32.

86. The major debate occurred in *Current Opinion*: "Ellen Key's Attack on 'Amaternal' Feminism," 54 (February 1913), pp. 138–139; "Charlotte Gilman's Reply to Ellen Key," 54 (March 1913), pp. 220–221; and "The Conflict between 'Human' and 'Female' Feminism," 56 (April 1914), pp. 291–292.

87. "The Conflict between 'Human' and 'Female' Feminism," p. 291.

88. Key, "Motherliness," p. 566.

89. William H. Chafe, *The American Woman: Her Changing Social, Economic, and Political Roles, 1920–1970* (New York: Oxford University Press, 1972), pp. 12–14.

90. Gilman, as quoted in Warford, "The Social Origins of Female Iconography," p. 41. In its focus, if not its substance, Gilman's statement represents a change from her Progressive Era vision as outlined in her arguments with Ellen Key.

91. Letter from Miller to Rhoda Dunn, dated September 21, 1909. Kenneth Hayes Miller Papers, Roll 583, Archives of American Art. In this letter Miller alluded both to his feelings for Helen and to opening a discussion with Irma about separation. He concluded by asking Rhoda to destroy the letter.

92. Miller's fascination with Freud can be traced in his letters to Rhoda, beginning in about 1915. In the teens, Miller met frequently with psychiatrists, trying to discover ties

between Freud's theories of the unconscious and the creative process. He was also interested, at a somewhat irksome level if his onetime student Rockwell Kent is to be believed, in trying to "ferret out what he alleged to be erotic symbolism in the work of the greater masters of the past," symbolism to which he attached great significance.

93.   Letter from Edward Laning to Isabel Bishop, dated August 9, 1974. Edward Laning Papers, Archives of American Art, Washington, D.C.

94.   Miller was reading *Twilight of the Gods* in October 1915 and expressed "fascination" with Nietzsche's ideas in letters to Rhoda Dunn, dated October 19 and December 13, 1915. Kenneth Hayes Miller Papers, Roll 583, Archives of American Art.

95.   For a fuller discussion of sexuality and sex roles in the Oneida Community, see Chapter 2 and John D'Emilio and Estelle B. Freedman, *Intimate Matters: A History of Sexuality in America* (New York: Harper and Row, 1988); Lawrence Foster, *Religion and Sexuality: Three American Communal Experiments of the Nineteenth Century* (New York: Oxford University Press, 1981), pp. 72–120; and Louis J. Kern, *An Ordered Love: Sex Roles and Sexuality in Victorian Utopias—the Shakers, the Mormons, and the Oneida Community* (Chapel Hill: University of North Carolina Press, 1981), pp. 207–257.

96.   In a 1976 letter to Isabel Bishop (Isabel Bishop papers, Archives of American Art, Washington, D.C.), Edward Laning described Miller's philosophy as a "primitive 19th-century form of Darwinism, the Doctrine of the 'survival of the fittest.'" Laning said that Miller and the writer Theodore Dreiser, Miller's close friend, shared this "naive" view as it applied to human behavior.

97.   Madison Grant, *The Passing of the Great Race* (New York: Scribner, 1916; reprint, New York: Arno Press, 1970), p. 263.

98.   Henry Fairfield Osborn, preface to *The Passing of the Great Race*, p. ix.

99.   Leuchtenberg, *The Perils of Prosperity*, pp. 204–205. From June 1920 to June 1921 more than 800,000 people entered the country. In February, Congress passed the Emergency Immigration Act. By 1924, the National Origins Act had been passed.

100.   Leuchtenberg, *The Perils of Prosperity*, pp. 66–83. See also Cynthia Jaffee McCabe and Daniel J. Boorstin, *The Golden Door: Artist Immigrants of America, 1876–1976* (Washington, D.C.: Smithsonian Institution Press for the Hirshhorn Museum and Sculpture Garden, 1976), pp. 17–19.

101.   In a letter to his cousin Rhoda, dated October 15, 1919, Miller speculated about the effects of various national traits on his close literary friends: "Paul Rosenfeld is a Jew—not Dreiser. That degree of creative force would be extraordinary in a Jew. And when they have intellect it is so subtle, consciously subtle. Dreiser of course is not subtle." Kenneth Hayes Miller Papers, Roll 583, Archives of American Art.

102.   Alice Shrock ("Feminists, Flappers, and the Maternal Mystique," p. 171) has observed that the stories celebrating the values of American motherhood appeared in a range of mainstream magazines: *Ladies Home Journal, Harper's, Smart Set, Cosmopolitan, Woman's Home Companion,* and *The Saturday Evening Post.*

103.   There are a few exceptions to Miller's general exclusion of other racial types. In *Women in the Store* (1937), for example, Miller depicts a black woman shopper. Besides the obvious precedent for fair women—in paintings by Titian and Rubens, Miller's favorite prototypes—there was that of Renoir's late nudes, who were often red haired. Furthermore, there was in the immediate pre- and postwar period in America a vogue for red hair. Mary Pickford was fair, and Held's flappers were usually redheads or blonds. Clearly Miller's choice of a type was governed by a variety of cultural and art-historical prototypes. Lois Banner, *American Beauty*, p. 176.

104.   Interview with Lloyd Goodrich, December 30, 1982.

1. Erica L. Doss, "Images of American Women in the 1930s: Reginald Marsh and *Paramount Picture*," *Woman's Art Journal* 4 (Fall 1983–Winter 1984), p. 3.

2. Richard N. Masteller, in his recent study of Marsh's graphic work (*"We, the People?" Satiric Prints of the 1930s* [Walla Walla, Wash.: Donald H. Sheehan Gallery, Whitman College, 1989]), has noted the contradictory critical responses to the artist:

> Marsh has been variously seen as an artist given to "lyricism and unabashed romantic abandon," a realist presenting an "accurate picture" and "bold record" of contemporary life, a "traditional painter" whose knowledge of the Old Masters informs his work, and a satirist whose caricatures "comment on social vulgarities." Lloyd Goodrich has asserted, . . . "he was not primarily or exclusively a satirist" because "fundamentally the affirmative elements in his art outweighed the negative." (pp. 49, 67 n. 53)

3. The "failing grip of categories" is Leo Steinberg's phrase, in "The Polemical Part," *Art in America* 67 (March/April 1979), p. 119.

4. Edward Laning, *The Sketchbooks of Reginald Marsh* (Greenwich, Conn.: New York Graphic Society, 1973), p. 12; and Marilyn Cohen, "Reginald Marsh: An Interpretation of His Art," Ph.D. diss., New York University, Institute of Fine Arts, pp. 95–96.

5. To follow the controversy, see "Art, U.S. Scene," *Time*, December 24, 1934, pp. 24–25; Stuart Davis, "The New York American Scene in Art," *Art Front* 1 (February 1935), p. 6; and Reginald Marsh, "A Short Autobiography," *Art and Artists of Today* 1 (March 1937), p. 8. Lloyd Goodrich analyzes the interchange and reasserts the apolitical nature of Marsh's paintings in his *Reginald Marsh* (New York: Abrams, 1972), p. 44.

6. In his interview with me, December 30, 1982, Goodrich claimed that Marsh never believed an artist could make art that was both comprehensible to the working classes and instrumental in the class struggle without sacrificing the demands of art.

7. For the discussion of "cultural satire," see Chapter 3 and Masteller, *"We, the People?"* pp. 45–65.

8. Cohen, "Reginald Marsh: An Interpretation," p. 170.

9. Cohen, "Reginald Marsh: An Interpretation," pp. 176, 179–193.

10. Rosemary Betterton, "How Do Women Look? The Female Nude in the Work of Suzanne Valadon," in *Looking On: Images of Femininity in the Visual Arts and Media*, ed. Rosemary Betterton (London and New York: Pandora Press, 1987), p. 218.

11. Laura Mulvey, "Visual Pleasure and Narrative Cinema," in Brian Wallis, ed., *Art After Modernism: Rethinking Representation* (New York and Boston: New Museum of Contemporary Art, in association with Godine, 1984), pp. 361–373. Mulvey's work as well as that of Rosalind Coward, *Female Desire: Women's Sexuality Today* (London: Paladin, 1974), p. 78, is discussed in Betterton, "How Do Women Look?" pp. 219–222.

12. Laura Mulvey, "Afterthoughts on 'Visual Pleasure and Narrative Cinema' Inspired by *Duel in the Sun*" in *Feminism and Film Theory*, ed. Constance Penley (London and New York: Routledge, 1988), pp. 69–79; Betterton, "How Do Women Look?" p. 222.

13. Teresa de Lauretis, *Technologies of Gender: Essays on Theory, Film, and Fiction* (Bloomington: Indiana University Press, 1987), pp. 4–5.

14. De Lauretis, *Technologies of Gender*, p. 2. In this introduction to the book, de Lauretis explores the limits of gender as "sexual difference." For an excellent discussion of why it is important to retain the idea of sexual difference, why gender (a social difference imposed on a sexed body) is a different kind of difference, and what results from the psychic

construction of sexual difference, see Constance Penley, *The Future of an Illusion: Film, Feminism, and Psychoanalysis* (Minneapolis: University of Minnesota Press, 1989), pp. xi–xx.

15. See Chapter 6 for a discussion of the Siren's image in the role of working girl.

16. Edward Laning, *East Side, West Side, All Around the Town* (Tucson: University of Arizona Museum of Art, 1969), pp. 96–97. Laning believes that Marsh found this woman at the burlesque. Marsh did not create the Siren stereotype (as Charles Dana Gibson created the Gibson girl), but the Marsh girl is a distinctive type, fueled by the contemporaneous Siren stereotype.

17. In January 1931, there were 22,731 motion picture theaters in America, seating an audience of 11 million. The industry developed rapidly following the introduction of sound in 1926. J. F. Steiner, "Recreation and Leisure Time Activities," in *Recent Social Trends in the United States: Report of the President's Research Committee on Social Trends* (New York: McGraw-Hill, 1934), pp. 940–941.

18. Cover page slogans from *Modern Screen*, all months, 1933.

19. European traits of the Siren are discussed in Mildred Adams, "Now the Siren Eclipses the Flapper," *New York Times*, July 28, 1929, sec. 5, pp. 4–5, and in Alexander Walker, *The Celluloid Sacrifice: Aspects of Sex in the Movies* (New York: Hawthorn Books, 1966), chapter 5, "The Fugitive Kind: Garbo," pp. 93–112.

20. Forbes Watson, a major critic of the 1930s, felt that Marsh's paintings were like photographically seen bits, pasted together without an overriding compositional order. Forbes Watson, "Innocent Bystander," *American Magazine of Art* 28 (January 1935), p. 62.

21. Although I have not located either Antoine's at 20 East Fourteenth Street or the Modern Beauty School, at 7 East Fourteenth Street (see Fig. 3.19; Plate 3), it was Marsh's practice to be documentary.

22. Edward Laning, "Reginald Marsh," *Demcourier* 13 (June 1943), p. 7; and Watson, "Innocent Bystander," p. 62. Marilyn Cohen, *Reginald Marsh's New York: Paintings, Drawings, Prints, and Photographs* (New York: Whitney Museum of American Art in association with Dover, 1983), p. 2; and Thomas H. Garver, *Reginald Marsh: A Retrospective Exhibition* (Newport Beach, Ca.: Newport Harbor Art Museum, 1972), refer to the Marsh girl as a fantasy.

23. Matthew Baigell, *The American Scene: American Painting of the 1930s* (New York: Praeger, 1974), p. 146. According to Edward Laning ("Reginald Marsh," p. 7), Kenneth Hayes Miller observed that Marsh's work looked best when viewed as a sequence. Marilyn Cohen, *Reginald Marsh's New York*, p. 12, has observed that Marsh's working process was cinematic: he liked to paste contacts of photographs into his album in long rows and also worked on several paintings at once.

24. Malcolm M. Willey, " 'Identification' and the Inculcation of Social Values," *Annals of the American Academy of Political and Social Science* 160 (March 1932), pp. 103–109.

25. Marsh's 1912 diary, entries dated January 26, October 22, November 19 and 26, and December 25. Reginald Marsh Papers, Archives of American Art, Washington, D.C.

26. Lloyd Goodrich, *Reginald Marsh*, p. 295. Between 1926 and 1930 both movie attendance and the rate of capital investment doubled, in part because of the installation of sound equipment in three-fourths of the new theaters. See J. F. Steiner, "Recreation and Leisure Time Activities," in *Recent Social Trends*, pp. 940–941.

27. Lloyd Goodrich suggested Marsh's fondness for both German films and newsreels in our interview, December 30, 1982. With Felicia, Marsh attended several operas; he also began to record his attendance at symphonies and plays in his diaries. He participated more often in museum and gallery openings and went to more parties. In 1932, Marsh accepted

new institutional responsibilities with the vice-presidency of the Art Students League's Board of Control. By 1935 he was teaching regularly in the summer. With the commencement of the Treasury Section's program for decorating public buildings, Marsh received two commissions for murals. Beginning in May 1935 he spent most of his time preparing his murals for the Post Office Department Building in Washington, D.C., and in 1937 he executed his murals for the Customs House in New York. The summary of movies and events in Marsh's life is culled from his diaries at the Archives of American Art.

28. Laning, "Reginald Marsh," p. 7.

29. Goodrich, *Reginald Marsh*, p. 6. Many of the letters from performers and viewers in the burlesque shows that Marsh reviewed can be found in the Marsh papers at the Archives of American Art.

30. Benton initially paid Marsh $100 per month and then increased the payment to $150. Cohen, "Reginald Marsh: An Interpretation," p. 83 n. 6.

31. Roland Marchand, *Advertising the American Dream: Making Way for Modernity, 1920–1940* (Berkeley and Los Angeles: University of California Press, 1985), p. 310; and Studs Terkel, *Hard Times: An Oral History of the Great Depression* (New York: Washington Square Press, 1970), p. 80.

32. Terkel, *Hard Times*, p. 81.

33. Kenneth Brooks Haas, *Adventures in Buysmanship* (Ann Arbor, Mich.: Edwards Brothers, 1937), p.13.

34. Mildred Adams, "Now the Siren Eclipses the Flapper." I do not know whether Marsh read the *New York Times* or if he would have seen this particular piece, a feature article in the Sunday supplement.

35. All quotations here from Adams, p. 4. Greta Garbo and Theda Bara are two Sirens often cited. For additional discussions of the Siren, see Lois Banner, *American Beauty* (Chicago and London: University of Chicago Press, 1983), p. 280.

36. Adams, "Now the Siren Eclipses the Flapper," p. 5.

37. Adams, p. 5.

38. Dorothy Dunbar Bromley, "Feminist—New Style," *Harper's Monthly Magazine* 155 (October 1927), pp. 552–560; Lillian Symes, "The New Masculinism," *Harper's Monthly Magazine* 161 (June 1930), pp. 98–107; and Symes, "Still a Man's Game: Reflections of a Slightly Tired Feminist," *Harper's Monthly Magazine* 158 (May 1929), pp. 678–686.

39. Cohen, *Reginald Marsh's New York*, p. 27.

40. Pamela Neal Warford, "The Social Origins of Female Iconography: Selected Images of Women in American Popular Culture, 1890–1945," Ph.D. diss., Washington University, St. Louis, 1979, pp. 78–80.

41. Adams, "Now the Siren Eclipses the Flapper," pp. 4–5.

42. *Modern Screen*, December 1933, pp. 14–16.

43. *Modern Screen*, June 1933, p. 52. Following a brief postwar baby boom, the birth rate had been in decline since about 1926, and there was some concern about the ultimate long-range effects of the decline. P. K. Whelpton, "The Population of the Nation," in *Recent Social Trends in the United States: Report of the President's Research Committee on Social Trends* (New York: McGraw-Hill, 1934), p. 39. See also *Recent Social Trends* for statistics on marriage and childbearing in the Depression. In the early 1980s *Time* magazine's cover story "The New Baby Bloom" featured "Charlie's Angels" star Jaclyn Smith as its prime example of a successful woman in her thirties turning away from a career to home and motherhood. The cover featured a radiantly pregnant Smith surrounded, like a Madonna,

by a glow of light. The article failed to mention the reality for mothers who continued to work from economic need. *Time*, February 22, 1982, pp. 52–58.

44. *Modern Screen*, April 1933, p. 4 for all quotations.

45. Occasionally, magazines and stories documented the darker side of Hollywood. One article in *Modern Screen* (ironically placed near a regular feature entitled "You Can Be Anything You Want"), citing statistics to show the near impossibility of Hollywood hopefuls' finding jobs, urged parents to keep their boys and girls at home. Jack Jamison, "Hollywood's Lost Children," *Modern Screen*, September 1934, pp. 62–63. In *The Day of the Locust*, published in 1939, Nathanael West painted a grim picture of Hollywood's failures, one of them an aspiring Siren.

46. Robert Sklar, *Movie-Made America: A Social History of American Movies* (New York: Random House, 1975), writes of three movies, all from 1932, in which this type appears—*Blonde Venus* (Marlene Dietrich), *Red Dust* (Jean Harlow), and *Back Street* (Irene Dunn). He observes that although Hollywood used this type to cater to prurient interests, these films also implied "that there was no room in the marketplace for women other than on stage or in bed" (p. 178). See also, Warford, "The Social Origins of Female Iconography," pp. 73–75.

47. Adams, "Now the Siren Eclipses the Flapper," p. 5; and Warford, p. 79.

48. Andrew Bergman, *We're in the Money: Depression American and Its Films* (New York: New York University Press, 1971), p. 51. See also Warford, p. 24 n. 11.

49. Doss, "Images of American Women in the 1930s," pp. 2–3. Much of Doss's analysis is based on Marjorie Rosen, *Popcorn Venus: Women, Movies, and the American Dream* (New York: Coward, McCann and Geoghegan, 1973).

50. Lois W. Banner, *American Beauty*, pp. 280–282.

51. A 1920s Listerine mouthwash advertisement that pictured a woman looking at a photograph of her husband read,

> Why had he changed so in his attentions? The thing was simply beyond her. She couldn't puzzle it out. And every moment it preyed on her mind and was almost breaking her heart.
>
> He had been the most attentive lover and husband imaginable. But of late some strange something seemed to have come between them. Now he was so changed.
>
> Was it some other woman? No, she told herself—it *couldn't* be! Yet *why* wasn't he the way he used to be toward her?

The ad then went on to assure the anxious reader that halitosis could indeed be cured with frequent use of Listerine.

52. *Modern Screen*, September 1933, p. 89.

53. *Modern Screen*, April 1933, p. 91.

54. My historical analysis is based on Lois Banner's argument in *American Beauty*, pp. 202–208, 218.

55. In 1920 there were 5,000 beauty parlors in the United States; by 1925 the number had grown to 25,000, and by 1930, to 40,000. In 1930, cosmetic sales reached $180 million, more than was allocated nationally to either education or social services. Banner, *American Beauty*, pp. 271–272.

56. Banner, *American Beauty*, p. 208.

57. Marchand, *Advertising the American Dream*, pp. 52–60.

58. Marchand, p. 62. Much of Marchand's material on advertisers' feelings about audi-

ence is drawn from the discussions in trade publications like *Printers' Ink* and agencies' in-house newsletters. Marchand demonstrates how in the 1920s advertising men were brought up short by the popularity of the tabloids and *True Story* magazine. Although they initially resisted the lower standards of the confessional advertisement, by the end of the decade it had become a popular form, even in magazines targeting a middle- to upper-middle-class audience.

59. Marchand, pp. 66–69.

60. Marchand, pp. 300–301.

61. *Advertising Age*, March 22, 1937, p. 50, as quoted in Marchand, p. 68.

62. "Cynic's Progress," newspaper clipping of an undated review of Marsh's one-man exhibition at the Rehn Gallery when he was thirty-four; from scrapbook no. 4, frontispiece to Cohen, *Reginald Marsh's New York*.

63. Marchand, *Advertising the American Dream*, pp. 48–50, 86–87.

64. Adolph Dehn, "My Friend, Reggie," *Demcourier* 13 (June 1943), p. 11.

65. Marsh's explanation of why his pictures didn't sell in the 1930s, in William Benton, "Reginald Marsh As I Remember Him," mimeographed essay, quoted in Cohen, "Reginald Marsh: An Interpretation," p. 27.

66. My discussion of the Siren stereotype's function is based on Pamela Warford's analysis in "The Social Origins of Female Iconography." Warford (p. viii) suggests that women have been instructed in numerous roles, often through a stereotypical model of womanhood like the Gibson girl, the flapper, and the Siren. She argues further that people in the media have recognized that a particular image at a given time was "culturally functional or economically advantageous," even if it was disadvantageous to the American woman. She assumes that the media generate and control "needs" in a given era.

67. Sumiko Higashi, "Cinderella vs. Statistics: The Silent Movie Heroine as Jazz-Age Working Girl," in Mary Kelly, ed., *Woman's Being, Woman's Place: Female Identity and Vocation in American History* (Boston: G. K. Hall, 1979).

68. Stuart Ewen and Elizabeth Ewen, *Channels of Desire: Mass Images and the Shaping of American Consciousness* (New York: McGraw-Hill, 1982).

69. Laning, *East Side, West Side*, p. 97.

70. Cohen, *Reginald Marsh's New York*, p. 21.

71. Haas, *Adventures in Buysmanship*, pp. 12–13. Haas observed that advertisers used slogans and stereotypes because we symbolize in precisely the same way. For a discussion of the way stereotypes work—and the way they are both simple and complex like ideology—see T. E. Perkins, "Rethinking Stereotypes," in Michèle Barrett et al., *Ideology and Cultural Production* (New York: St. Martin's Press, 1979), pp. 135–139.

72. T. J. Jackson Lears, "From Salvation to Self-Realization: Advertising and the Therapeutic Roots of the Consumer Culture, 1880–1930," in *The Culture of Consumption*, ed. Richard Wightman Fox and T. J. Jackson Lears (New York: Pantheon Books, 1983), pp. 3–5. Lears argues that advertising became effective as middle-class people became increasingly preoccupied with finding health and well-being (selfhood and autonomy) in secular rather than in religious or moral frameworks. This "modern therapeutic ethos," with its central goal of regenerating selfhood and autonomy, became a central modern preoccupation and fueled advertising strategies throughout the first third of the century. I borrow the terms *autonomy* and *selfhood* from Lears's discussions throughout my analysis since they apply to the Siren and the shopping crowd as Marsh depicts them.

73. Edward Laning, *The Sketchbooks of Reginald Marsh* (Greenwich, Conn.: New York Graphic Society, 1973), p. 136.

74. Sklar, *Movie-Made America*, pp. 173–174, 176. Sklar observes that between 1930

and 1934 Hollywood films were preoccupied with sex, violence, and political melodrama. Although such themes tied into social realism in general, Sklar suggests that subjects were chosen for reasons of "crassest expediency." Producers deliberately sought exaggerated forms of stimulation, appealing to prurient interest to lure audiences and reverse plummeting theater revenues in the early years of the Depression (one-third of the nation's movie theaters had shut down by 1933).

75. Erica Doss identifies this woman as a working women in "Images of American Women in the 1930s," p. 3.

76. I would like to thank Rebecca Zurier for her helpful suggestions on Marsh's "sketchiness" and his use of tempera. In fact, as Lloyd Goodrich has argued, Marsh had problems learning to handle the oil painting medium; tempera came closer to his natural way of working as a draftsman. Goodrich, *Reginald Marsh*, pp. 162–163.

77. One of the most fruitful of these studies is Herbert Blumer, *Movies and Conduct* (New York: Macmillan, 1933), part of a twelve-book series on motion pictures and youth that gives some indication of the concern about film's role in shaping values. Sponsored by the Committee on Educational Research of the Payne Fund as requested by the National Committee for the Study of Social Values in Motion Pictures—by 1933 renamed The Motion Picture Research Council—the series included the following titles: *Getting Ideas from the Movies; Motion Pictures and the Social Attitudes of Children; The Social Conduct and Attitudes of Movie Fans; Motion Pictures and Standards of Morality; Movies, Delinquency, and Crime;* and *Boys, Movies, and City Streets.*

78. This is discussed below, and documented in Ewen and Ewen, *Channels of Desire*, pp. 52–55.

79. Haas, *Adventures in Buysmanship*. The sociologist David Park at the University of Chicago was one of the major scholars to discuss individual behavior in the crowd during this period.

80. Willey, " 'Identification' and the Inculcation of Social Values," p. 108.

81. Willey, p. 109.

82. Willey, pp. 109–110.

83. Blumer, *Movies and Conduct*, p. 34.

84. Blumer, pp. 41–42. In *Advertising the American Dream*, p. 96, Marchand illustrates an advertisement featuring a testimonial by Nazimova for Lucky Strike cigarettes. European stars who were undaunted by America's prohibitions against "lady" smokers were frequently employed by the tobacco industry to promote its products.

85. Blumer, *Movies and Conduct*, p. 48.

86. These other models include Eleanor Roosevelt, Amelia Earhart, and Marian Anderson.

87. Blumer, *Movies and Conduct*, pp. 194–195.

88. Ewen and Ewen, *Channels of Desire*; Elizabeth Ewen, *Immigrant Women in the Land of Dollars* (New York: Monthly Review Press, 1985); Richard Wightman Fox and T. J. Jackson Lears, eds., *The Culture of Consumption* (New York: Pantheon Books, 1983, introduction; Joanne Meyerowitz, "Sexual Geography and Gender Economy: The Furnished Room Districts of Chicago, 1890–1930," *Gender and History* 2 (Autumn 1990), pp. 274–296; and Kathy Peiss, *Cheap Amusements: Working Women and Leisure in Turn-of-the-Century New York* (Philadelphia: Temple University Press, 1986).

89. Robert S. Lynd, "The People as Consumers," in *Recent Social Trends in the United States: Report of the President's Research Committee on Social Trends* (New York: McGraw-Hill, 1934), pp. 877–878; Sally Stein, "The Graphic Ordering of Desire: Modernization of a Middle-Class Woman's Magazine," *Heresies* 5 (1985), pp. 7–16. Lynd observed,

Fifteen years ago a manufacturer was safe in preparing for volume sale models that were fashionable in Fifth Avenue shops the year before. Today it is frequently less than a week after a model has been shown in the window of one of the exclusive couturiers of 57th street or Fifth Avenue that it appears at $6.95 or $3.95 in the 14th-Street serve-yourself stores. (p. 878)

90.   *Modern Screen*, January 1934, pp. 70–71.

91.   Willey, " 'Identification' and the Inculcation of Social Values," p. 108.

92.   Blumer, *Movies and Conduct*, pp. 197–198.

93.   Ewen and Ewen, *Channels of Desire*. The Ewens write from a Marxist perspective and assume that working-class Americans are exploited and directed by institutions of culture run by the ruling class. Their assumption that "it is the agencies of communication that provide the mechanisms for social order" rests on a belief that the individual has no will or choice. Their analyses of immigrant women's acceptance of movies and advertising as models for a way of life help to interpret Marsh's *image* of the voluptuous shopper as a consumer automaton on Fourteenth Street. For a more extensive analysis of immigrant women in the New World, see Elizabeth Ewen, *Immigrant Women in the Land of Dollars*.

94.   Louis Palmer, "The World in Motion," *Survey* 11 (1909), p. 357, as quoted in Ewen and Ewen, *Channels of Desire*, p. 88.

95.   Ewen and Ewen, p. 87.

96.   All quotations are from Ewen and Ewen, p. 87.

97.   Caroline F. Ware, *Greenwich Village, 1920–1930: A Comment on American Civilization in the Post-War Years* (Boston: Houghton Mifflin, 1935), pp. 129, 167. Ware detected these patterns among immigrant women in Greenwich Village.

98.   The Immigration Act of 1917 included a literacy requirement and excluded peoples from much of Asia and the Pacific Islands. The Quota Act of 1921 (following the height of the Red scare and the Palmer raids of 1920) added numerical limitations to U.S. immigration laws. The Immigration Act of 1924 (the Johnson-Reed Act) reduced the annual quota for each nationality to 2 percent of the number of persons of the national origin in the United States in 1890. This reduced the number of immigrants from eastern and southern Europe. Cynthia Jaffee McCabe and Daniel J. Boorstin, *The Golden Door: Artist Immigrants of America, 1876–1976* (Washington, D.C.: Smithsonian Institution Press for the Hirshhorn Museum and Sculpture Garden, 1976), pp. 66–72; Ewen and Ewen, *Channels of Desire*, pp. 43–44; 98–101; and Higashi, "Cinderella vs. Statistics," pp. 112–113.

99.   Edgar D. Furniss, *Labor Problems* (Boston, 1925), p. 176, as quoted in Ewen and Ewen, p. 52.

100.   Ewen and Ewen, pp. 53–54.

101.   For an excellent discussion of assimilation and new mass-culture amusements, see John Kasson, *Amusing the Million: Coney Island at the Turn of the Century* (New York: Hill and Wang, 1978).

102.   Lears, "From Salvation to Self-Realization," pp. 19–20.

103.   Lynd, "The People as Consumers," especially the section on consumer literacy, pp. 881–889.

104.   Marchand, *Advertising the American Dream*, pp. 312–318.

105.   Kay Austin, *What Do You Want for $1.98? A Guide to Intelligent Shopping* (New York: Carrick and Evans, 1938); Ruth Brindze, *How to Spend Money: Everybody's Practical Guide to Buying* (New York: Vanguard Press, 1935); Jessie Vee Coles, *The Consumer-Buyer and the Market* (New York: Wiley, 1938); and Haas, *Adventures in Buysmanship*.

106.   Stuart Chase and F. J. Schlink, *Your Money's Worth: A Study in the Waste of the*

Consumer's Dollar (New York: Macmillan, 1927), p. 2.

107. Lynd discussed "puffing," the practice of distorting claims about products, in "The People as Consumers," p. 873. See also Peter E. Samson, "The Emergence of a Consumer Interest in America, 1870–1930," Ph.D. diss., University of Chicago, 1980. Haas, *Adventures in Buysmanship*, pp. 12–21.

108. Richard Wightman Fox, "Epitaph for Middletown," in *The Culture of Consumption*, ed. Richard Wightman Fox and T. J. Jackson Lears (New York: Pantheon Books, 1983), p. 123. Fox traces a historical shift from a belief in the individual's power to resist the consumer environment to an acceptance of the consumer's inherent irrationality. He locates this shift in the thinking and underlying value system of the social scientist Robert Lynd.

109. Fox, "Epitaph for Middletown," pp. 125–128. Lynd's early thinking was founded in John Dewey's Progressive Era belief in the common man. Like Dewey, Lynd believed that re-education in the processes of a new culture occurred with the agency of the individual. Community change also originated with the individual. Lynd's thinking in his earlier works represented a conscious challenge to the influential Chicago school of sociologists headed by David Park, who argued that urbanization was an impersonal, natural process with a life of its own, and that individuals played no determining role.

110. Lynd, "The People as Consumers," p. 866. In a roughly contemporary piece, "Family Members as Consumers," *Annals of the American Academy of Political and Social Science* 160 (March 1932), Lynd voiced similar concerns but placed even greater emphasis on tensions in consumer culture and demonstrated his mistrust of big business.

> Living as a husband or wife or boy or girl in these 1930s is a nerve-racking affair under the most favorable circumstances. Impelled from within by the need for security in the most emotionally insecure culture in which any recent generation of Americans has lived, beset on every hand by a public philosophy that puts not the quality of family living but the health of business first, untrained in the backward art of spending to live, buttressed by his government only against a few of the grossest abuses of his efforts to buy an effective living, the consumer faces a trying dilemma. (p. 92)

111. Haas, *Adventures in Buysmanship*, p. 21.

112. Fox, "Epitaph for Middletown," p. 139.

113. See Rockwell Kent's autobiography, *It's Me, O Lord* (New York: Dodd, Mead, 1955), as quoted in Lincoln Rothschild, *To Keep Art Alive: The Effort of Kenneth Hayes Miller, American Painter (1876–1952)* (Philadelphia: Art Alliance Press, 1974), p. 34. See Chapter 2, n. 57, for a discussion of Marsh's analysis.

114. T. J. Jackson Lears, a historian of consumer culture, has demonstrated that Marsh's anxieties were widely felt among members of the middle to upper-middle class. Lears shows that by the last decades of the nineteenth century middle-class individuals began to lose their sense of autonomy in the face of an economic system based increasingly on consumption rather than individual production. This loss of autonomy resulted in a demand for more vigorous behavior, a new "quest for real life"—the cult of the strenuous life, with its emphasis on athletic achievement, preached throughout Marsh's boyhood by President Theodore Roosevelt. Lears summarizes the causes of the dilemma:

> In all, the modern sense of unreality stemmed from extraordinarily various sources and generated complex effects. Technological change isolated the urban bourgeoisie from the hardness of life on the land; an interdependent and increasingly corporate economy

circumscribed autonomous will and choice; a softening Protestant theology undermined commitments and blurred ethical distinctions. Yet a production ethos persisted; self-control became merely a tool for secular achievement; success began to occur in a moral and spiritual void.

In his work on advertising and the therapeutic roots of consumer culture, Lears traces the mutual relationship between what he calls the feeling of unreality, which "helped to generate longings for bodily vigor, emotional intensity and a revitalized sense of selfhood," and advertising strategies that helped satisfy these longings and ultimately advanced the culture of consumption. Lears, "From Salvation to Self-Realization," pp. 7–10, and Lears, *No Place of Grace: Antimodernism and the Transformation of American Culture, 1880–1920* (New York: Pantheon Books, 1981), p. 222.

CHAPTER SIX

1. Patricia Hills and Roberta K. Tarbell, *The Figurative Tradition and the Whitney Museum of American Art: Paintings and Sculpture from the Permanent Collection* (New York and Newark, Del.: Whitney Museum of American Art in association with University of Delaware Press, 1980), p. 71.

2. Susan Porter Benson, "The Cinderella of Occupations: Managing the Work of Department Store Saleswomen, 1900–1940," *Business History Review* 55 (Spring 1981); Benson, "The Clerking Sisterhood: Rationalization and the Work Culture of Saleswomen in American Department Stores, 1890–1960," *Radical America* 12 (March–April 1978), pp. 41–55; and Benson, *Counter Cultures: Saleswomen, Managers, and Customers in American Department Stores, 1890–1940* (Urbana: University of Illinois Press, 1986).

3. Benson, *Counter Cultures*, chapter 6, " 'The Clerking Sisterhood': Saleswomen's Work Culture," pp. 227–271.

4. Critics throughout the 1930s placed Soyer squarely within the movement away from landscape toward a "commercial and industrial" subject matter that focused on "human beings affected by social conditions." Soyer's art, often referred to as "social commentary," was also praised for its frank realism and its often penetrating psychological observation. Far from suggesting that Soyer's art might be a propagandistic vehicle for social change, most critics praised the artist's craftsmanship, his subtle palette, and his direct, strong brush-work and marked him as one of the most promising painters of his generation. See, for example, "Social Commentaries Mark the Pennsylvania Academy's Annual," *Art Digest* 8 (February 15, 1934), quotations pp. 5–7; Lloyd Goodrich, "In the New York Galleries," *The Arts* 15 (May 1929), p. 334; "Around the Galleries," *Art News* 30 (February 27, 1932), p. 10; "Exhibitions in New York," *Art News* 31 (February 18, 1933), p. 5; and "New Exhibitions of the Week: Human Studies by Raphael Soyer," *Art News* 37 (April 15, 1939), p. 14.

5. Interview with the artist, March 13, 1987. The relationship of horizontal and vertical hand gestures at the center of *Shop Girls* is loosely based on that of the gestures of Christ, Peter, and the disciple between them in Masaccio's *Tribute Money* (Fig. 6.7).

6. James Lane, "The Passing Shows," *Art News* 40 (April 1–15, 1941), p. 29.

7. Patricia Hills, with an essay by Raphael Soyer, *Social Concern and Urban Realism: American Painting of the 1930s* (Boston: Boston University Art Gallery, 1983), p. 39. Davis spent most of his life in Arizona. During the 1930s, however, he was a student at the National Academy of Design and exhibited widely on the East Coast. He was also active in the WPA.

8. Hills, *Social Concern and Urban Realism*, p. 91. Born in Vienna, Vavak immigrated

to New York in 1904. He settled in Chicago and studied at the Art Institute. During the 1930s, he was in the WPA and was a member of the Chicago Artists' Union. His goal was to create a contemporary history painting.

9. Margaret Breuning, "Art in New York," *Parnassus* 10 (March 1938), p. 20 (review of Soyer's 1938 show at the Valentine Gallery); Helen Buchalter, "Carnegie International, 1939," *Magazine of Art* 32 (November 1939), p. 630; "New Exhibitions of the Week."

10. Soyer told me that Degas was always on his mind when he worked. His early interest in the French painter began when his twin brother, Moses, sent him a large volume of plates of Degas's work from France in 1926. As early as the 1930s, critics began to recognize the affinities between the Soyers and the French painter. Interview with the artist, December 27, 1982; Milton W. Brown, *American Painting from the Armory Show to the Depression* (Princeton: Princeton University Press, 1955; reprint, 1972), p. 185; and Harry Salpeter, "Raphael Soyer: East Side Degas," *Esquire*, May 1938.

11. Hills and Tarbell, *The Figurative Tradition*, p. 71. My discussion of the studio-picture tradition is taken from Brown, *American Painting from the Armory Show to the Depression*, pp. 154–155. For the interpretation of Degas's bather images see Eunice Lipton, *Looking into Degas: Uneasy Images of Women and Modern Life* (Berkeley and Los Angeles: University of California Press, 1986), pp. 165–186; and (for the monotypes), Hollis Clayson, "*Avant-Garde* and *Pompier* Images of the Nineteenth Century French Prostitution: The Matter of Modernism, Modernity, and Social Ideology," in *Modernism and Modernity*, ed. Benjamin H. D. Buchloh, et al., Vancouver Conference Papers (Halifax: Press of the Nova Scotia College of Art and Design, 1983), pp. 43–64. For a discussion of the female nude in early twentieth-century modernist painting see Carol Duncan, "Virility and Domination in Early Twentieth-Century Vanguard Painting," in *Feminism and Art History: Questioning the Litany*, ed. Norma Broude and Mary D. Garrard (New York: Harper and Row, 1982), pp. 293–314.

12. Brown, *American Painting from the Armory Show to the Depression*, p. 154.

13. Interview with Isabel Bishop, December 16, 1982.

14. Frank Gettings, *Raphael Soyer: Sixty-five Years of Printmaking* (Washington, D.C.: Smithsonian Institution Press, 1982), p. 11; and interviews with Raphael Soyer, December 27, 1982, and March 13, 1987. Soyer rarely used professional models. In my last interview with him, he said he knew many of his models intimately, and they in turn would know him better than almost anyone else. Many of his last models had worked for him for ten to twenty years; some in their forties he had known since their early twenties. Soyer remarked that their late twentieth-century dilemmas—principally failed relationships with men reluctant to make commitments or to have the children many of the women were desperate for—were markedly different from those of the Depression era. One sensed in Soyer's commentary on his models long-standing relationships of mutual respect. It may have been the care Soyer took in these relationships beginning in the 1930s that prompted the *New York Post* reviewer Jerome Klein's comment that Soyer "reaches the greatest freedom under the most intimate conditions in the quiet of the studio where the distinction between model and person breaks down." Quoted in "Raphael Soyer, Realist, Captures That 'Haunted Look of the Unemployed,'" *Art Digest* 12 (March 15, 1938), p. 12.

15. Frances Fisher Dubuc, "Women Wanted by Department Stores," *Saturday Evening Post*, June 23, 1928, p. 134.

16. *New York Times*, May 9, 1926, sec. 2, p. 17.

17. As I've indicated elsewhere, polls in the 1920s showed that the white middle-class working woman preferred marriage over a career and usually dropped out of the work force with marriage or the birth of a child. Consequently, the proportion of working women

between twenty-five and forty-four years old rose from only 3.3 to 7.3 percent between 1900 and 1920. Furthermore, the occupational distribution of married women showed that of those who worked following marriage the largest group held low-level factory or domestic positions. By 1940 only 15 percent of all married women were employed, and only one-third of these women held professional, mercantile, or clerical positions. Lois Scharf, *To Work and to Wed: Female Employment, Feminism, and the Great Depression*, Contributions to Women's Studies no. 15 (Westport, Conn.: Greenwood Press, 1980), pp. 41, 16.

18. Alice Calvin, "The Shop Girl," *Outlook* 88 (February 15, 1908), pp. 383–384; Mary Rankin Cranston, "The Girl behind the Counter," *World Today* 10 (March 1906), pp. 270–274; Mary Alden Hopkins, "The Girls behind the Counter," *Collier's*, March 16, 1912; Mary Maule, "What Is a Shop Girl's Life?" *World's Work* 14 (September 1907); Anne O'Hagan, "The Shop-Girl and Her Wages," *Munsey's Magazine* 50 (November 1913), pp. 252–259; Mary Van Kleek, "Working Conditions in New York Department Stores," *Survey*, October 11, 1913, pp. 50–51. Van Kleek was writing as secretary of the Russell Sage Foundation's Committee on Women's Work. In New York and other major cities, there was a phenomenal growth in the number of department stores from the mid–nineteenth century until World War I. Older New York stores, like Arnold Constable, Lord & Taylor, and A. T. Stewart, had moved uptown and were joined by numerous others. Stores were clustered in districts between Sixth Avenue and Broadway and from just below Fourteenth Street to Forty-second Street. Within this small geographical area by 1910 between twenty and thirty thousand "girls and women" were employed in dry goods and department stores, as many as three thousand in some of the largest emporiums. John William Ferry, *A History of the Department Store* (New York: Macmillan, 1960), pp. 35–39; and Mary Maule, "What Is a Shop Girl's Life?" p. 9311.

19. Cranston, "The Girl behind the Counter," p. 270; Calvin, "The Shop Girl," p. 383; O'Hagan, "The Shop-Girl and Her Wages," pp. 253–254, 256; and Alice Kessler-Harris, *Women Have Always Worked: A Historical Overview* (Old Westbury, N.Y.: Feminist Press, 1981), p. 99. In 1900, less than 10 percent of the female working population held jobs in sales; about 33 percent were domestic servants; 25 percent worked in factories or mills; and about 10 percent worked in agriculture. Most of these jobs paid more than sales work, but sales work had a higher status because the environment was cleaner and, though minimal, opportunities for advancement were comparatively greater (p. 80).

20. Benson, "The Cinderella of Occupations," p. 6, and *Counter Cultures*, p. 132. One indignant writer observed in 1913 that although social workers had estimated nine dollars per week as the lowest reasonable wage on which a working girl could be self-sufficient, ten thousand New York shopgirls received less than eight dollars. Van Kleek, "Working Conditions," p. 50. The belief that the shopgirl was prey to the "social evil" was the primary motive for some of the writers who investigated her job and life. Many feared that a young girl receiving low wages would succumb to advances by unscrupulous male superiors and store patrons who might, with money or goods, make her life easier. Even when a federal report showed that 75 percent of female crimes were committed by women in domestic and personal service and only 2 percent by saleswomen, the belief that a shopgirl was likely to compromise her virtue persisted. According to one author, both the staff and customers of one of the better New York stores believed "many of its saleswomen were subsidized by private illicit relations." O'Hagan, "The Shop-Girl," p. 256.

21. Helen Stuart Campbell, "Among the Shop-Girls," in *Victorian Women: A Documentary Account of Women's Lives in Nineteenth-Century England, France, and the United States*, ed. Erna Olaf Hellerstein, Leslie Parker Hume, and Karen M. Offen (Stanford: Stanford University Press, 1981), p. 374.

22. Helen Stuart Campbell, "Among the Shop-Girls," p. 374.

23. Benson, *Counter Cultures*, p. 178. "At the suggestion of a minimum wage for women and children, employers variously invoked the Constitution, grieved over the inefficient, whom they would be forced to dismiss to utter poverty in the event of any governmental interference with wages, and recited their ancient creed that woman works for 'pin-money.'" O'Hagan, "The Shop-Girl," p. 252. O'Hagan also observed (p. 253) that employers always tried to hire women who lived at home with male wage earners so as not to threaten their belief that she worked for spending money.

24. Mrs. John Van Vorst, "*Grisettes* and *Midinettes*," *Lipincott's Magazine* 80 (July 1907), quotations from pp. 101, 103.

25. Van Vorst, "*Grisettes* and *Midinettes*," pp. 104, 107.

26. Many of the observations here are based on an extended discussion with Soyer about his relationship to his models, March 13, 1987.

27. Frances Donovan, *The Saleslady* (Chicago: University of Chicago Press, 1929; reprint New York: Arno Press, 1974). In the introduction, Donovan's fellow sociologist David Park observed, "the little shopgirl whose fortunes have been touchingly described by O'Henry, has been very largely superseded; the saleslady is likely to be a mature woman. Many of them are married or widowed, and in any case they hold their jobs by their competence rather than by their charm" (p. ix).

28. Frederick Lewis Allen, *Only Yesterday: An Informal History of the Nineteen-Twenties*, First Perennial Library edition (New York: Harper and Row, 1931; reprint, 1964), p. 80.

29. Changes in labor laws, thanks in part to lobbying efforts by organizations like the Consumers' League of New York, altered some of the worst conditions. In 1913, for example, a law was passed prohibiting women from working more than 54 hours per week, children between fourteen and sixteen from working over 48 hours (previous limits had been 60 and 54 hours). Mary Dewhurst Blankenhorn, "Behind the Counter," *Outlook*, 144 (December 22, 1926), p. 531. Frances Donovan, *The Saleslady*, p. 83. Donovan, a sociologist who worked in the dress department of a New York store as a participant-observer, suggested that commissions for a good saleswoman could average ten to fifteen dollars per week. Blankenhorn, "Behind the Counter," p. 532, pointed out that the hiring of a nurse and provision for mutual-aid societies, uncommon in the prewar period, were by the 1920s established practice. See also Dubuc, "Women Wanted by Department Stores," pp. 130–134.

30. Donovan was quoting from an article in *Woman's Wear*, dated August 21, 1926, called "A Shop Girl by Any Other Name." *The Saleslady*, pp. 160–161.

31. "Where the Schools Fail," *Dry Goods Economist* 67 (May 10, 1913), p. 27, as quoted in Benson, "The Cinderella of Occupations," p. 12. There were also strong prescriptions on race: black women were almost never saleswomen but served as elevator operators or backstage personnel. Benson, *Counter Cultures*, p. 209.

32. Benson, "The Cinderella of Occupations," pp. 13–14, and *Counter Cultures*, pp. 142–146; Paul Brown, "Shopgirls: 1930 Model," *Commonweal* 12 (October 8, 1930), p. 577; and Donovan, *The Saleslady*, p. 83.

33. In *The Saleslady*, Frances Donovan expressed surprise at the difficulty of her training class. The teacher

scores us, calls our attention to errors, has us make out more checks, tells us in detail how to handle "C.O.D.s," when it is necessary to have the section-manager sign slips, when to send the money to the cashier in a gray carrier, when in a red or a blue one, which form to put into the carrier, which with the merchandise, which to keep and how. She explains the intricacies . . . detail after detail until we are exhausted and dizzy. (p. 21)

Helen Rich Norton, *Department-Store Education: An Account of the Training Methods Developed at the Boston School of Salesmanship, under the Direction of Lucinda Wyman Prince*, Department of the Interior, Bureau of Education Bulletin, 1917, no. 9 (Washington, D.C.), p. 12, as quoted in Benson, "The Cinderella of Occupations," p. 15.

34. Benson, "The Cinderella of Occupations," p. 9.

35. Donovan, *The Saleslady*, introduction by David Park, p. ix; and Dubuc, "Women Wanted by Department Stores," p. 130. The manager of the book department in one store said that the store preferred college women, "although we will train high-school graduates if their home background is good" (p. 133).

36. Among these schools were the Prince School of Store Service Education (a graduate school of Simmons College in Boston); the Research Bureau for Retail Training, the University of Pittsburgh; and the School of Retailing at New York University. Helen Law, "A New Job for the College Girl," *Review of Reviews* 81 (June 1930), pp. 74–75.

37. Benson, *Counter Cultures*, p. 160.

38. Law, "A New Job," p. 74. Three years earlier, Reyburn, a key figure in training store managers, in a speech before the Store Managers' Division, National Dry Goods Association, spoke about the greater effects the middle- to upper-class store environment would have on the lower-class girl.

Constant contact with the woman who is in charge of her department will have an influence on her. Daily contact with other girls who have been subjected to influences in business will have an influence on her. Daily observations of customers in the building will influence her, and slowly she will change because of these influences. She will lower the tone of her voice, grow quiet in her manner, exhibit better taste in the selection of her clothes, become more considerate of others.

Quoted in Benson, "The Cinderella of Occupations," p. 13.

39. Donovan, *The Saleslady*, p. 9.

40. "We go our separate ways. . . . During the business week we are like a family with the close bond of a common interest. We know each other's outside life only through what we tell each other. We are not interested in the husbands, children, friends, except as they affect the attitudes of the girls in the store. Later I was to learn that there were outside contacts, carefully safeguarded, not at all general." Donovan, *The Saleslady*, p. 41.

41. "There are two girls who hold themselves aloof. They do not chatter but they take pains to tell us that they belong to the Training Squad, which is composed of college graduates who are given an intensive training in department-store procedure for a period of two years. One of the girls says, 'And when we get through, we are going to be store superintendents.' " Donovan, *The Saleslady*, p. 20.

42. John Wanamaker, as quoted in Benson, *Counter Cultures*, p. 155. Donovan recorded a conversation she had with Alice, a store model hired for her looks who was an unsuccessful saleswoman because she had left school early and used poor grammar when she spoke. Alice assured Donovan that she (Donovan) would get ahead because of her education (*The Saleslady*, pp. 66–67). Helen Law, in "A New Job," p. 74, observed the passage of what she called the chewing-gum era among shopgirls in department stores, and Paul Brown, in "Shopgirls: 1930 Model," p. 576, noted how the O'Henry shopgirl became the

modern salesgirl with the elimination of the " 'dese, dem and dose' school of pronunciation."

43. Dubuc, "Women Wanted for Department Stores," p. 134; and Benson, *Counter Cultures*, pp. 153–159.

44. Scharf, *To Work and to Wed*, p. 37.

45. At the turn of the century, saleswomen (shopgirls) were required to wear black so they would not detract from the store displays. Cranston, "The Girl behind the Counter," p. 270. A writer in the 1920s suggested that the practice continued, to avoid the "danger of display of poor taste and lack of background on the part of employees." "Employees' Dress Regulations," *Bulletin of the National Retail Dry Goods Association* 10 (October 1928), p. 457, as quoted in Benson, "The Cinderella of Occupations," p. 20. Donovan suggests that dark dresses remained appropriate and observed that salesladies changed into lighter-colored dresses to go out for lunch or to leave at the end of the day. Donovan, *The Saleslady*, p. 101. Miller's saleswomen conform to the practice by wearing monochromatic dresses with simple collars.

46. Richard R. Brettell and Suzanne Folds McCullagh, *Degas in the Art Institute of Chicago* (New York: Art Institute of Chicago and Abrams, 1984), p. 131. For a further discussion of Degas's milliners see Lipton, *Looking into Degas*, pp. 161–164.

47. Lorine Pruette, ed., *Women Workers through the Depression: A Study of White Collar Employment Made by the American Woman's Association* (New York: Macmillan, 1934), pp. 20, 66–74; and Scharf, *To Work and to Wed*, p. 120.

48. Although the WPA brought some relief, three-fourths of the women on WPA rolls were former factory workers or domestics, who found creative art or sewing projects more easily than sales or clerical workers could have done. This occurred even though the proportion of white-collar women was higher and they were generally out of work longer. Scharf, *To Work and to Wed*, pp. 121–122; and Meridel Le Sueur, "Women on the Breadlines," *New Masses* 7 (January 1932), pp. 5–7.

49. The only image that alludes to women's unemployment is Isabel Bishop's painting *Waiting* (1935–37). It shows a plainly dressed mother leaning back with her child resting in her lap. Although the Depression era viewer might have interpreted this woman, very different from Bishop's other females, as one waiting for work, Bishop said that she was trying to portray the dependence that exists between mother and child.

50. Grace Hutchins, *Women Who Work* (New York: International Publishers, 1934), pp. 83–84. Since the turn of the century, stools had been placed behind counters so that women could rest their feet when not waiting on customers. Managers believed, however, that seated workers undermined a store's reputation for prompt and energetic service, and girls caught using the stools received reprimands for laziness. The unwritten rule that stools were never to be used persisted and a shopgirl, particularly in the Depression, would endure aching feet rather than risk losing her job or the chance for a much-needed raise or promotion. O'Hagan, "The Shop-Girl," p. 253.

51. Lauren Gilfillan, "Weary Feet," *Forum and Century* 90 (October 1933), p. 202.

52. The NRA was established to enforce the wage and hour regulations resulting from the 1933 NIRA (National Industrial Recovery Act), designed to pump new life into the economy. The act resulted from long discussions among businessmen, labor leaders, and government officials and also involved a massive public-relations program to stimulate consumer support (and purchasing). Businesses conforming to NRA practices could display the NRA sticker—a blue eagle with the slogan We Do Our Part emblazoned beneath. Klein's annex proudly displays it in a 1936 Berenice Abbott photograph (Fig. 3.5).

53. *New York Times*, September 5, 1933, p. 5; and "S. Klein: 'On the Square' Store Plays Santa to Its Employees," *Newsweek*, December 29, 1934, pp. 28–30.

54. "S. Klein Loses Wage Plea," *New York Times*, November 30, 1933, p. 10; and "S. Klein: 'On the Square,' " p. 29.

55. Stella Ormsby, "The Other Side of the Profile," *New Republic* 72 (August 17, 1932), p. 21. Although wages had improved by the time Soyer painted *Shop Girls* in 1936, the piece approximates the working conditions at Klein's.

56. Stella Ormsby, "The Other Side of the Profile," p. 21. Ormsby's letter was submitted to Klein by the *New Republic* editorial staff, who invited him to reply for simultaneous publication. After waiting three weeks, they published the letter, promising to print his reply. Apparently one was never forthcoming.

57. "NRA Violation Laid to Klein's Store," *New York Times*, December 18, 1934, p. 14; and *New York Times*, February 3, 1935, p. 12.

58. On February 10 an audience at the Civic Repertory Theater on Fourteenth Street was left waiting when five actors in the radical play *Sailors of Cattero* were arrested for picketing Ohrbach's. On February 7 a warrant had been issued for the arrest of the author Nathaneal West, also for picketing. For details on the strike, see *New York Times*, January 3, 1935, p. 8; January 4, 1935, p. 14; January 6, 1935, p. 28; January 11, 1935, p. 27; February 7, 1935, p. 40; February 10, 1935, p. 17; February 12, 1935, p. 6; February 13, 1935, p. 22; February 17, 1935, p. 17; February 21, 1935, p. 6; February 24, 1935, p. 23; February 27, 1935, p. 10; March 3, 1935, p. 30; March 9, 1935, p. 8.

59. The signs in Marsh's painting read, Locked Out for Joining Union, Don't Buy at Ohrbachs, and Young Men and Young Women Jailed for Picketing, Don't Buy at Ohrbachs.

60. Department stores continued their practice of seeking out mature women and in the 1930s hired and rehired working wives more than any other white-collar employer. Scharf, *To Work and to Wed*, p. 103. Whether or not Miller intended his matronly saleswomen to represent married women, the paintings corroborate the social fact. Although he believed in women's traditional roles, moreover, Miller was sympathetic to their doing other work as children grew older. Kenneth Hayes Miller Papers, Roll 583, Archives of American Art, Washington, D.C.

61. Scharf, *To Work and to Wed*, chapter 2, "Marriage and Careers: Feminism in the 1920s," pp. 21–38. Against historians who argue that feminism died in the 1920s (see William H. Chafe, *The American Woman: Her Changing Social, Economic, and Political Roles, 1920–1970* [New York: Oxford University Press, 1972], and William L. O'Neill, "The End of Feminism," in *Twentieth-Century America: Recent Interpretations*, ed. Barton J. Bernstein and Allen J. Matusow, 2d edition [New York: Harcourt Brace Jovanovich, 1972], pp. 186–196), Scharf exposes this feminist "voice" that advocated the right of married women to work, one which, though never as strong as that advocating suffrage, should nonetheless be considered in evaluating the feminist movement and its relation to working women. The arguments of this small group of feminists, however, never altered the dominant image of the womanly homemaker or the womanly worker.

62. I would like to thank Peter Boswell for his thoughtful contribution to this analysis.

63. New York State Assemblyman Arthur Schwartz, for example, claimed in 1931 that the employment of married women was "reprehensible," and he admonished both federal and local governments to "cooperate and remove these undeserving parasites." George Gallup, after seeing the results of a 1936 poll on whether to permit married women to work, stated that he had never seen respondents "so solidly united in opposition as on any subject imaginable including sin and hay fever." Scharf, *To Work and to Wed*, pp. 47, 50.

The most telling example of strong public opposition to working wives appeared in the controversy over Section 213 of the 1932 Economy Act, which stated that whenever personnel reductions had to be made in government jobs, married persons (meaning married women) must be discharged if their spouses were also government employees. Since this discriminatory clause applied only to a narrow group of government employees, President Hoover initially opposed it for the economic hardship it would cause as it made only an inconsequential contribution to economic recovery. With the growing sentiment against working wives, however, the section received widespread public attention and enjoyed strong public support. Women's groups who found the act economically and socially repugnant campaigned for its repeal. Yet Congress, recognizing a "politically advantageous symbol," debated for two years before repealing it, in July 1937. Scharf, *To Work and to Wed*, pp. 46–47, 50.

Scharf assumes some public familiarity with Section 213, to judge from her citation of newspaper references to it. Artists might have noticed the controversy. The journalist Adela Rogers St. John published case-study articles in the *Washington Herald* on the hardships of women who lost jobs because of the federal legislation. The novelist Rupert Hughes wrote a six-part serial in the winter of 1936 for the *New York Herald Tribune* entitled "Section 213—a Story behind the Headlines." A year before, in the same paper, the humorist Franklin Pierce Adams published the following ditty:

Oh for a play by Bernard Shaw
On the Federal Marital Status Law

Finally, an official history of the civil service, written in the early 1940s, noted that Section 213 was "the best known of the [Economy Act's] provisions." Scharf, *To Work and to Wed*, p. 51.

64. Scharf, *To Work and to Wed*, pp. 100–102.

65. For descriptions of the humanity, honesty, and sincerity of Soyer's women see "Around the Galleries," *Art News* 30 (February 27, 1932), p. 10; Robert Coates, "Latter Day Impressionist," *New Yorker* (March 13, 1948), pp. 61–62; and Carl Zigrosser, *The Artist in America: Twenty-four Close-ups of Contemporary Printmakers* (New York: Knopf, 1942), pp. 60–61.

66. The critic Emily Genauer was quoted on Soyer's drab women in the anonymous review "Raphael Soyer Paints Twenty-three Artists and Some Hungering Shop Girls," *Art Digest* 15 (April 1, 1941), p. 17. A reviewer of Soyer's 1929 show at the Daniel Gallery spoke of the grotesque stupidity of his model Susan in "Raphael Soyer: Daniel Galleries," *Art News* 27 (April 27, 1929), p. 10. Reviewing the same show, Walter Gutman spoke of Soyer's "unconscious way of deforming which makes his subjects ludicrous" ("Raphael Soyer," *Creative Art* 6 [April 1930], pp. 258–260); "Reviews and Previews," *Art News* 48 (April 1948), p. 51.

67. For the classic discussion of this phenomenon in the Western European tradition of oil painting, of which Soyer was a part, see John Berger, *Ways of Seeing* (London and New York: Penguin Books, 1972), pp. 45–64.

68. Alfred Kazin, *Starting Out in the Thirties* (Boston: Little, Brown, 1962), as quoted in Dore Ashton, *The New York School: A Cultural Reckoning* (New York: Penguin Books, 1972), p. 54.

69. According to Frances Donovan, a store's management typically chose the prettiest saleswomen as models (*The Saleslady*, p. 66).

70. "Exhibitions in New York," *Art News* 31 (February 18, 1933), p. 5.

71. Reviews, in the order quoted, are "Raphael Soyer Paints Twenty-three Artists," p. 17; "New York Criticism," *Art Digest* 9 (March 1, 1935), p. 18; Soyer quoted from Gettings, *Raphael Soyer*, p. 30; "Social Commentaries Mark the Pennsylvania Academy's Annual,"

Art Digest 8 (February 15, 1934), pp. 5–7; and Laurie Eglington, "Exhibitions in New York," *Art News* 33 (February 23, 1935), p. 10.

72. Interview with the artist, December 27, 1982.

73. Hills, *Social Concern and Urban Realism*, p.27.

74. Moses Soyer, "Three Brothers," *Magazine of Art* 32 (April 1939), p. 207. In *Self-Revealment: A Memoir* (New York: Maecenas Press, 1969), Raphael Soyer also recalled feeling lonely and disenchanted with France, in part because he knew no French and had few friends there, in part because Parisian museums had not yet been renovated (p. 22). My discussion of Soyer's relation to the aesthetic policies and politics of the Popular Front is indebted here and below to Cécile Whiting, *Antifascism in American Art* (New Haven: Yale University Press, 1989).

75. Soyer, *Self-Revealment*, p. 23. Soyer saw Grosz's works in Munich at an exhibit called Von neue Sachlichkeit zu kein Sachlichkeit (From new objectivism to non-objectivism).

76. Lloyd Goodrich, *Raphael Soyer* (New York: Abrams, 1972), p. 66; and statement of purpose from the Artists' Congress, as quoted in Hills, *Social Concern and Urban Realism*, p. 29.

77. Soyer did several paintings of dancers, often at rest in the studio rather than in performance. His brother Moses had married a dancer, and perhaps through him Raphael became interested in the theme. In mid-decade he painted dancers from the studios of Fé Alf and Jane Dudley, relatively unknown figures at that time who were interested in presenting revolutionary themes in dance. The determined pose of Fé Alf in Figure 6.24 suggests this purpose. John Martin, "Fé Alf Seen Here in Dance Recital," *New York Times*, February 25, 1935, p. 12; *New York Times*, April 21, 1935, sec. 9, p. 4; and Harry Salpeter, "Raphael Soyer: East Side Degas," p. 158.

78. Whiting, *Antifascism in American Art*, pp. 38–39, 165.

79. Pruette, *Women Workers through the Depression*, p. 155.

80. For a discussion of *Art Front*, its role in the Artists' Union and its changing editorial policy, see Gerald M. Monroe, "Art Front," *Archives of American Art Journal* 13 (1973), pp. 13–19.

81. The argument here is based on my understanding of the content of *Art Front* from Monroe; from selections from articles quoted in Hills, *Social Concern and Urban Realism*, pp. 16–17; and from Whiting, *Antifascism in American Art*, chapters 2, 5.

82. Harold Rosenberg, "The Wit of William Gropper," *Art Front* 2 (March 1936), pp. 7–8, as quoted in Hills, *Social Concern and Urban Realism*, p. 17.

83. Louis Lozowick, "Towards a Revolutionary Art," *Art Front* 2 (July–August 1936), pp. 12–13, as quoted in Hills, *Social Concern and Urban Realism*, p. 17. Lozowick's statement reads:

> Nor does partisanship narrow the horizon of revolutionary art. Quite the contrary, the challenge of a new cause leads to the discovery of a new storehouse of experience and the exploration of a new world of actuality. Even a tentative summary will show the vast possibilities, ideologic and plastic; relations between the classes; relations within each class; a clear characterization in historic perspective, of the capitalist as employer, as philanthropist, as statesman, as art patron; the worker as victim, as striker, as hero, as comrade, as fighter for a better world; the unattached liberal, the unctuous priest, the labor racketeer; all the ills capitalist flesh is heir to—persons and events treated not as chance snapshot episodes but correlated among themselves shown in their dramatic antagonisms, made convincing by the living language of fact and made meaningful from the standpoint of a world philosophy. The very newness of the theme will forbid a conformity in technique.

1. See, for example, "Isabel Bishop Finds Critics Receptive," *Art Digest* 13 (February 1, 1939), p. 21; "New York Criticism: A Miller Pupil's Shackles Loosen," *Art Digest* 10 (March 1, 1936), p. 16; and Bernard Myers, ed., "*Sleeping Child*, by Isabel Bishop," Scribner's American Painters Series, no. 9, *Scribner's* 122 (November 1937), p. 32; and "New Paintings Shown by Isabel Bishop," *New York World-Telegram*, January 21, 1939, p. 16.

2. One notable exception to this type is the 1937 painting *Young Woman* (Fig. 7.10), a three-quarter-length portrait of a self-assured, business-like woman standing against a column with a hazy urban backdrop behind her. She assumes a relaxed contrapposto pose, her coat and purse over one arm, her gloves in the other hand.

3. See, for example, Grace L. Coyle, "Women in the Clerical Occupations," *Annals of the American Academy of Political and Social Science: Women in the Modern World* 143 (May 1929),p. 184; Orlie Pell, "Two Million in Offices," *Woman's Press* 33 (June 1939), p. 256; and U.S. Department of Labor, Women's Bureau Bulletin no. 120, *The Employment of Women in Offices*, by Ethel Erickson, 1934, pp. 3, 7. For important historical overviews see Lorine Pruette, ed., *Women Workers through the Depression: A Study of White Collar Employment Made by the American Woman's Association* (New York: Macmillan, 1934); Margery Davies, "Woman's Place Is at the Typewriter: The Feminization of the Clerical Labor Force," *Radical America* 8 (July–August 1974), pp. 1–28, and her *Woman's Place Is at the Typewriter: Office Work and Office Workers, 1870–1930* (Philadelphia: Temple University Press, 1982); and Lois Scharf, *To Work and to Wed: Female Employment, Feminism, and the Great Depression*, Contributions to Women's Studies no. 15 (Westport, Conn.: Greenwood Press, 1980).

4. See, for example, Loire Brophy, *If Women Must Work* (New York: Appleton-Century, 1936); Hazel Rawson Cades, *Jobs for Girls* (New York: Harcourt, Brace, 1928); Dorothy Dayton, "Personality Plus—or Minus," *Independent Woman* 15 (November 1936), pp. 343, 362; Frances Maule, *She Strives to Conquer: Business Behavior, Opportunities, and Job Requirements for Women* (New York: Funk and Wagnalls, 1937); Elizabeth Gregg MacGibbon, *Manners in Business* (New York: Macmillan, 1936); and Ruth Wanger, *What Girls Can Do* (New York: Henry Holt, 1926).

5. Griselda Pollock, "Modernity and the Spaces of Femininity," in *Vision and Difference: Femininity, Feminism, and the Histories of Art* (London and New York: Routledge, 1988), p. 56.

6. The fifty-story Metropolitan Life Insurance Company at Twenty-third Street also employed seven thousand women in a total staff of nine thousand. *New York in Pictures*, vol. 2 (New York: Sun Printing and Publishing Association, 1928), p. 7. Information on the tasks for each institution is in U.S. Department of Labor, *The Employment of Women in Offices*, p. 5.

7. Bishop recalled that many of her models were from the block of buildings, which included the Bank of Manhattan Building, the Decker Building, The Union Building, and the Hartford Building, ranging from 31 to 41 Union Square West, between Sixteenth and Seventeenth streets, just adjacent to Bishop's studio (see Fig. 3.1 and Maps 1, 2). Interview with the artist, December 16, 1982.

8. In the work force in general, between 1890 and 1920 the percentage of native-born white women grew while the proportion of working women who were foreign-born declined. Among clerical workers the percentage remained high—80 percent by 1940. Scharf, *To Work and to Wed*, pp. 11–12. According to a report on women's occupational progress, for the years 1910 to 1920 the increase among women in the clerical occupations was "seven and a half times as great as the increase among women in manufacturing and mechanical

pursuits, and almost three times as great as that among women in professional service." U.S. Department of Labor, Women's Bureau, *The Occupational Progress of Women*, p. 17, as quoted in Coyle, "Women in the Clerical Occupations," p. 180.

9. Between 1900 and 1920 the participation in the work force of women aged 16 to 24 increased from 39 to 50 percent while the proportion of working women aged 25 to 44 rose from 3.3 to 7.3 percent. Scharf, *To Work and to Wed*, pp. 13, 41.

10. Over half of all women surveyed were under twenty-five. For hiring policies, see MacGibbon, *Manners in Business*, p. 26; U.S. Department of Labor, *The Employment of Women in Offices*, pp. 14, 27.

11. U.S. Department of Labor, *The Employment of Women in Offices*, p. 30.

12. Married women made up 35.3 percent of all the women in trade, 35 percent of those in domestic service, and 32.4 percent of those in manufacturing and mechanical industries. In the 1934 New York survey of 14,025 clerical workers, only 10.1 percent reported that they were married. U.S. Department of Labor, *The Employment of Women in Offices*, pp. 12–13, 29.

13. Coyle, "Women in the Clerical Occupations," p. 183.

14. Coyle, p. 183; and U.S. Department of Labor, *The Employment of Women in Offices*, p. 13.

15. *The Employment of Women in Offices*, pp. 5–8; and Wanger, *What Girls Can Do*, p. 112.

16. U.S. Department of Labor Women's Bureau, *The Employment of Women in Offices*, pp. 5–7; and Wanger, *What Girls Can Do*, p. 113.

17. Unpublished interviews with Isabel Bishop conducted in September 1957 by Louis M. Starr of the Oral History Research Office, Columbia University, New York. Quoted in Helen Yglesias, *Isabel Bishop* (New York: Rizzoli, 1989), p. 66.

18. See John Berger, *Ways of Seeing* (London and New York: Penguin Books, 1972); and Rosemary Betterton, ed., *Looking On: Images of Femininity in the Visual Arts and Media* (London and New York: Pandora Press, 1987), introduction, pp. 10–14.

19. Emily Genauer, "Miss Bishop Rates High as Painter," *New York World-Telegram*, February 15, 1936, p. 15; Edward Alden Jewell, as quoted in *Art Digest* 13 (February 1, 1939), p. 21; James W. Lane, "Bishop," *Art News* 41 (June 1942), p. 42, and Lane, "Canvases by Isabel Bishop, Painter of Subtle Tonalities," *Art News* 37 (January 21, 1939), p. 12; and Forbes Watson, "Isabel Bishop," *Magazine of Art* 32 (January 1939), p. 52.

20. Bishop's technique was complicated, and she took many months to complete a single painting. She worked either in oil or tempera, building up meticulously crafted layers of paint. The pencil strokes, which she added toward the end of the process, often to a surface still wet, suggest where a contour might appear without really defining it. As a result, the pencil strokes seem to hover above the surface, implying motion.

21. In most New York offices women worked a thirty-nine-hour week, seven hours a day with four hours on Saturday mornings, except during the summer. In large offices there were good benefit packages that included two weeks of paid vacation, one week of paid sick leave, some group insurance, and small bonuses, either for Christmas or with continued service. Some offices made provision for additional education, and in banks there were often lunchrooms where employees could have inexpensive midday meals. U.S. Department of Labor, *The Employment of Women in Offices*, pp. 29–33.

Clerical wages seem to have been considerably better than those of domestic, industrial, and sales workers. In the early 1930s a beginning file clerk in a large institution seems to have made about a dollar a week more (or around $17) than a beginning saleswoman in a major department store, and a secretary two to five dollars a week more than an upper-level saleswoman (or around $42.50). According to Lorine Pruette, in *Women Workers through the Depression* (pp. 66–74), saleswomen were always at the low end of the white-collar pay scale. My own estimate is based on an evaluation of several median wage charts in *The Employment of Women in Offices* (pp. 20–23), modified by reports of somewhat lower salary ranges in "Women in Business II," *Fortune* 12 (August 1935), p. 85.

22. Wanger, *What Girls Can Do*, p. 111.

23. Coyle, "Women in the Clerical Occupations," p. 181.

24. U.S. Department of Labor, *The Employment of Women in Offices*, p. 1.

25. Bishop believed a painter had to maintain an awareness of the painted surface even while creating the illusion of forms existing or moving in space. She argued that representational painters had two basic historical "forms" of painting by which they could simultaneously maintain an awareness of surface and of depth. Renaissance artists like Raphael retained planar integrity by arranging forms parallel to the surface, even though those forms were so solidly demarcated from the surrounding space that they could be removed from it, leaving the setting undisturbed. Other artists, like Rubens, Watteau, and Renoir, destroyed the compositional integrity of the picture plane by animating their figures and by creating diagonal recessions into the picture plane. But they reinforced the plane again by minimizing contour and by creating such a strong painterly continuity between figure and ground that figures could no longer be detached from their settings.

In her own work, Bishop chose the second method. In "Concerning Edges," *Magazine of Art* 32 (January 1939), pp. 57–58, she explained her theories. She summarized some of the problems she and like-minded representational painters faced:

> And if the painter wants to make the thing painted on look different from what it is, he has to keep several balls in the air at once—that is, he has to create several sets of suggestions—one set always keeping you aware of what the thing painted on is like, while other suggestions are persuading you of depth, movement, weight, and what not. Jean Helion has defined painting as ". . . combining opposed purposes so that they develop instead of annihilate each other."

26. Sheldon Reich, *Isabel Bishop*, introduction by Martin H. Bush (Tucson: University of Arizona Museum of Art, 1974), p. 24.

27. In "Isabel Bishop, the Grand Manner, and the Working Girl," *Art in America* 63 (September 1975), p. 63, the art critic Lawrence Alloway identified this technique as a metaphor.

28. Reich, *Isabel Bishop*, p. 23.

29. Reich, *Isabel Bishop*, p. 24.

30. Cindy Nemser, "A Conversation with Isabel Bishop," *Feminist Art Journal* 5 (Spring 1976), p. 15.

31. "Isabel Bishop," *Current Biography Yearbook* (New York: Wilson, 1977), p. 63; and Karl Lunde, *Isabel Bishop* (New York: Abrams, 1975), p. 169.

32. "American Painting Bought by the Metropolitan," *New York Herald-Tribune*, February 20, 1936, p. 15.

33. Nemser, "A Conversation with Isabel Bishop," p. 15; and interview with the artist, December 16, 1982.

34. William Engle, "Portrait of Two Girls Bought by Metropolitan Reunites Two Ex-Waitresses Who Posed for It," *New York World-Telegram*, February 27, 1936, p. 3.

35. William Engle, "Portrait of Two Girls."

36. Interview with the artist, December 16, 1982. Quotations from Cindy Nemser, "A Conversation with Isabel Bishop," p. 18; and Reich, *Isabel Bishop*, pp. 14, 25.

37. Alloway, "Isabel Bishop, the Grand Manner, and the Working Girl," p. 63. Alloway also argued that Bishop's fully articulated theories about mobility were a way for her to assuage her conscience for her remarks about the social limitations of these figures, a judgment that may have been unfair given Bishop's values and her position in particular social and political discourses in the 1930s.

38. Positive attributes of clerical conditions, like the ones I have cited, served as preliminary comments to the studies of the rapid disappearance of occupational advantages once attributed to office work. Economic, technological, and institutional change had made them largely fictional by the 1930s.

39. Grace Hutchins, *Women Who Work* (New York: International Publishers, 1934), p. 84. Hutchins, a writer with a Marxist perspective, quoted a 1926 National Industrial Conference Board report that showed 39 percent of all clerks received less than twenty dollars per week. Her study is an excellent foil for Lorine Pruette's study of white-collar workers on large salaries. Every woman in Pruette's sample, however, is forty-five or older. That these women earned so little after twenty to twenty-five years of working experience is the astonishing statistic.

40. "Women in Business II," p. 55.

41. In New York, where employers generally paid the highest wages, secretaries, who in 1931 had earned $30–$60 per week, received $25–$35 in 1935; stenographers dropped from $20–$40 per week to $15–$25; typists, who earned $18–$30 in 1935, received $16–$18 after three years' experience. "Women in Business II," p. 55; Grace Hutchins quotes a different, still lower, scale and looks to some of the lower clerical occupations. In 1929, clerks earned $10–$22 per week; in 1931 their wages dropped to $8–$18 per week.

42. Hutchins, *Women Who Work*, p. 84; "Women in Business II," p. 50; and Elizabeth Gregg MacGibbon, "Exit—the Private Secretary," *Occupations* 15 (January 1937), p. 300.

43. A bookkeeper might absorb the jobs of a saleswoman, stenographer, and general clerical worker and work six days, eleven to fourteen hours each, for half her former wage. She dared not complain for fear of losing her job. Hutchins, *Women Who Work*, p. 84. According to a New York Emergency Relief Committee report from 1932, stenographers were hardest hit by unemployment, followed by seamstresses and general clerical workers. Once stenographers had lost their jobs, they were often out of work longer than women in other occupations, and many were forced to move down the occupational scale and take domestic positions. Furthermore, 50 percent of clerical workers, like saleswomen, reported substantially decreased earnings. Pruette, *Women Workers through the Depression*, pp. 64–74; and Scharf, *To Work and to Wed*, pp. 160–162.

44. MacGibbon, *Manners in Business*, p. 165. Eunice Fuller Barnard, in "Girl Graduate, 1936," *Independent Woman* 15 (July 1936), assessed prospects for graduates:

The main trouble seems to be that even today's college graduate, and more extensively and tragically the high school graduate, has had too little informed guidance as to which occupation offers her a really promising field. She has had access to no accurate charts to show her long-time occupational trends. She has had as a rule no adviser with the requisite combination of patience, insight and scientific data to aid her in discovering her own best capabilities. With all her haunting worry about landing a job, with all the experience of her predecessors as a warning, the girl graduate still too often follows sheeplike, in the crowded paths of certain standardized occupations, such as office work and teaching. (p. 203)

45. Barnard, p. 203.

46. Caroline Ware, "The 1939 Job of the White Collar Girl," *Woman's Press* 33 (June 1939), pp. 254–255; and Coyle, "Women in the Clerical Occupations," p. 184.

47. MacGibbon, "Exit—the Private Secretary," p. 296, reported that in one enormous New York office, seventy-seven private secretaries, each of whom had served an executive, were replaced by twenty-two workers. One private secretary served the corporation president, while seven stenographers and fourteen voice-machine transcribers turned out the rest of the work. See also, Coyle, "Women in the Clerical Occupations," pp. 185–186; and Ware, "The 1939 Job," pp. 254–255.

48. The male figure here is Walter Broe, an unemployed man who modeled for all the artists. When I questioned Soyer about the conjunction of male unemployment with female labor, he said that given the opportunity to redo the work, he would eliminate the man, who added too strong a "storytelling" element.

49. For a discussion of how the cartoon or crayon drawing came to be used and understood as a medium of social protest in earlier radical publications see Rebecca Zurier, *Art for the Masses: A Radical Magazine and Its Graphics, 1911–1917* (Philadelphia: Temple University Press, 1988). pp. 126–132.

50. Rembrandt was by no means Bishop's only old master model, and she also painted the female nude. As I suggested in looking at her early mural-like paintings, she was inspired by Renaissance art. She also admired Rubens's drawing style and his ability to convey movement in his art. Many of her "favorite" works were also models for Miller and Marsh, but she used her models to different ends.

51. Lawrence Alloway, "Isabel Bishop, the Grand Manner, and the Working Girl," p. 64.

52. In "Danaë: Virtuous, Voluptuous, Venal Woman," *Art Bulletin* 60 (March 1978), pp. 43–55, Madlyn Millner Kahr described Rembrandt's humanizing depiction of women, particularly nudes, as a new image of woman.

53. Scharf, *To Work and to Wed*, pp. 100–101.

54. MacGibbon, *Manners in Business*, pp. 12, 28. Some of these job advice manuals were scientific in their approach, with many categories of investigation; others were impressionistic; and still others took the form of letters between mothers and daughters, providing highly personalized advice. As the number of working women increased, advice literature helped to establish better lines of communication between high school guidance counselors, professional employment counselors, and businesses.

55. Cades, *Jobs for Girls*, p. 16.

56. MacGibbon, *Manners in Business*, pp. 16–17. MacGibbon also reported that heads of women's colleges said that those women with the best scholastic averages were usually the last hired for office positions because they spent so much time at their studies that they failed to take care of themselves.

57. In "Women in Business II" it was estimated that more than a fifth of an office girl's salary was spent on clothing. The most expensive items were silk stockings, at the rate of a pair a week (p. 85). See also MacGibbon, *Manners in Business*, p. 29; and Maule, *She Strives to Conquer*, p. 125.

58. Interview with the artist, December 16, 1982. "New York Types at the Midtown Galleries, New York," *Art Digest* 10 (February 15, 1936), p. 19. Another critic identified *Head No. 2* as a shopgirl. "Colorado Springs Buys," *Art Digest* 16 (March 15, 1942), p. 15; and "Museumized: *Noon Hour* by I. Bishop Bought by Springfield," *Art Digest* 13 (May 1, 1939), p. 5.

59. Maule, *She Strives to Conquer*, p. 6; and MacGibbon, *Manners in Business*, p. vii.

60. Cades, *Jobs for Girls*, p. 16; Dayton, "Personality Plus—or Minus," p. 343. Dayton

wrote that personality was about 75 percent of getting a job, brains and technical training, less than 25 percent. Her article discusses the increasing reliance on experts to help a girl change her voice and improve her personality, first by testing, then through a series of classes.

61. Brophy, *If Women Must Work*, pp. 35–41.

62. Scharf, *To Work and to Wed*, p. 97.

63. Maule, *She Strives to Conquer*, p. 6; MacGibbon, *Manners in Business*, pp. 66–72; and "Women in Business II," p. 55.

64. "Women in Business II," p. 55. As the historian Lois Scharf described this new woman, she was "nothing less than the office mate of the harried male executive [who] dutifully fulfilled the emotional and business needs of her boss. In direct imitation of marriage, in which the wife derives her social status from her husband, the private secretary achieved her exalted position through the man to whom her services were indispensable" (*To Work and to Wed*, p. 98). See also Eugenia Wallace, "Office Work and the Ladder of Success," *Independent Woman* 6 (October 1927), pp. 16–18.

65. "Women in Business II," p. 86.

66. For an extended discussion of this painting, see Ellen Wiley Todd, "Will [S]he Stoop to Conquer? Preliminaries Toward a Reading of Edward Hopper's *Office at Night*" in Norman Bryson et al., eds., *Visual Theory: Method and Interpretation in Art History and the Visual Arts* (New York: HarperCollins, 1990); Victor Burgin, *Between* (Oxford: Basil Blackwell in association with the Institute of Contemporary Arts, 1986), p. 184; Gail Levin, "Edward Hopper's *Office at Night*," *Arts Magazine* (January 1978), pp. 134–137; and Linda Nochlin, "Edward Hopper and the Imagery of Alienation," *Art Journal* 41 (Summer 1981), pp. 136–141.

67. "Women in Business II," p. 55. The persistent belief that these jobs were temporary was buttressed by the departure of four out of five women who entered clerical occupations when they married.

68. MacGibbon, *Manners in Business*, pp. 61, 116–127.

69. MacGibbon, *Manners in Business*, p. 127.

70. Margaret Culkin Banning, *Letters to Susan* (New York: Harper and Brothers, 1936), pp. 92, 94. To support her argument, Susan's mother offered the case study of a married woman who owned her own bookstore. Her husband had to go to his club every afternoon to wait for her while she finished her "unimportant" work. They lived in an apartment and ate many of their meals in restaurants so that she did not have to cook, a practice Susan's mother deplored as an avoidance of wifely responsibility. She concluded, "Martha won't give up her bookshop though dozens of girls could step into her place. She should be building him up. And bearing a child would do more for Martha than any number of sales slips." The feminist argument that women continued to work and needed to work after marriage for personal satisfaction was completely at odds with the demands, responsibilities, and obligations of traditional marriage.

71. Banning, *Letters to Susan*, p. 7.

72. Wanger, *What Girls Can Do*, p. 4.

73. Unlike her nineteenth-century predecessors Mary Cassatt and Berthe Morisot, who would never have thought of entering the cafés, nightclubs, and brothels that emblematized modern life for their fellow Impressionists, Isabel Bishop accompanied Marsh to the burlesque and to striptease joints on occasion. But as a proper upper-middle-class female viewer and producer of representations of women, she could not "properly" or "publicly" (through paintings) enter those spaces or envision female sexuality in that way for herself or her female viewers.

74. By the 1930s there were a few small local unions that combined bookkeepers, ste-

nographers, accountants, and occasionally saleswomen. In May 1934 the legislative body of the Y.W.C.A., along with representatives of business and professional clubs, adopted resolutions identifying the welfare of office workers with that of other workers and proposing study and educational groups to help office workers prepare for unionization. Neither the movement nor the organization was widespread in the 1930s. Marion H. Barbour, "The Business Girl Looks at Her Job," *Woman's Press* 30 (January 1936), pp. 18–19; Clyde Beals, Pearl Wiesen, Albion A. Hartwell, and Theresa Wolfson, "Should White Collar Workers Organize?" *Independent Woman* 15 (November 1936): pp. 340–342; and Ware, "The 1939 Job," p. 255.

75. "Women in Business II," p. 85.

76. Interview with the artist, December 16, 1982.

77. Henry McBride, "Some Others Who Arouse Interest," *New York Sun*, February 15, 1936, p. 28; Bernard Myers, "*Sleeping Child* by Isabel Bishop," p. 32.

CONCLUSION

1. Cecelia F. Klein, Editor's Statement, "Depictions of the Dispossessed," *Art Journal* 49 (Summer 1990), p. 108.

2. Virgil Barker, "The Search for Americanism," *American Magazine of Art* 27 (February 1934), p. 52.

3. Editor's Statement, "The New Woman," *Current History* 27 (October 1927), p. 1.

4. The phrase "regime of representation" is Griselda Pollock's, used to describe "visual codes and their institutionalized circulation," in *Vision and Difference: Femininity, Feminism, and the Histories of Art* (London and New York: Routledge, 1988), p. 14.

5. The points here about the aesthetic and social agenda in the Popular Front period are discussed in Cécile Whiting, *Antifascism in American Art* (New Haven: Yale University Press, 1989).

BIBLIOGRAPHY

BOOKS AND ARTICLES

Abbott, Harriet. "What the Newest New Woman Is." *Ladies Home Journal,* August 1920, 154.

Adams, Henry. *Thomas Hart Benton: An American Original.* New York: Knopf, 1989.

Adams, Mildred. "Now the Siren Eclipses the Flapper." *New York Times,* July 28, 1929, sec. 5, pp. 4–5.

Albright, Thomas. "Street Artist of the Depression" (Reginald Marsh). *San Francisco Chronicle,* November 27, 1983, 14–15.

Alcoff, Linda. "Cultural Feminism vs. Post-Structuralism: The Identity Crisis in Feminist Theory." *Signs* 13, no. 3 (Spring 1988): 399–436.

Allen, Frederick Lewis. *Only Yesterday: An Informal History of the Nineteen-Twenties,* First Perennial Library edition. New York: Harper and Row, 1931; reprint, 1964.

Alloway, Lawrence. "Isabel Bishop, the Grand Manner, and the Working Girl." *Art in America* 63 (September 1975): 61–65.

"American Painting Bought by the Metropolitan" (Isabel Bishop's *Two Girls*). *New York Herald-Tribune,* February 20, 1936, p. 15.

Andrews, Benjamin R. *Economics of the Household, Its Administration and Finance.* New York: Macmillan, 1927.

———. "The Home Woman as Buyer and Controller of Consumption." *Annals of the American Academy of Political and Social Science: Women in the Modern World* 143 (May 1929): 41–48.

Andrist, Ralph K., ed. *The American Heritage History of the 1920s and 1930s.* New York: American Heritage, n.d.

"Around the Galleries" (Raphael Soyer). *Art News* 30 (February 27, 1932): 10.

"Art, U.S. Scene." *Time* (December 24, 1934): 24–27.

Ashton, Dore. *The New York School: A Cultural Reckoning.* New York: Penguin Books, 1972.

Austin, Kay. *What Do You Want for $1.98? A Guide to Intelligent Shopping.* New York: Carrick and Evans, 1938.

Baigell, Matthew. *The American Scene: American Painting of the 1930s.* New York: Praeger, 1974.

Baigell, Matthew, and Julia Williams. Introduction to *Artists Against War and Fascism: Papers of the First American Artists' Congress.* New Brunswick, N.J.: Rutgers University Press, 1986.

Baldwin, William. *The Shopping Book.* New York: Macmillan, 1929.

Banner, Lois W. *American Beauty.* Chicago and London: University of Chicago Press, 1983.

―――. *Women in Modern America: A Brief History.* New York: Harcourt Brace Jovanovich, 1974.

Banning, Margaret Culkin. *Letters to Susan.* New York: Harper and Brothers, 1936.

Banta, Martha. *Imaging American Women: Ideas and Ideals in Cultural History.* New York: Columbia University Press, 1987.

Barbour, Marion H. "The Business Girl Looks at Her Job." *Woman's Press* 30 (January 1936): 18–19.

Barker, Virgil. "The Search for Americanism." *American Magazine of Art* 27 (February 1934): 51–52.

Barnard, Eunice Fuller. "Girl Graduate, 1936." *Independent Woman* 15 (July 1936): 203, 222.

Barthes, Roland. "From Work to Text." In *Image-Music-Text,* edited and translated by Stephen Heath, 155–164. New York: Hill and Wang, 1977.

Baur, John I. H. *Revolution and Tradition in Modern American Art.* Cambridge: Harvard University Press, 1951.

Beals, Clyde, Pearl Wiesen, Albion A. Hartwell, and Theresa Wolfson. "Should White Collar Workers Organize?" *Independent Woman* 15 (November 1936): 340–342.

Beckman, Frank. "I Remember When . . . " *New Yorker News* (Spring 1964): 24.

Beers, Richard. "As They Are at Thirty-Four" (Raphael Soyer). *Art News* 32 (January 13, 1934): 13.

Belsey, Catherine. "Constructing the Subject: Deconstructing the Text." In *Feminist Criticism and Social Change: Sex, Class, and Race in Literature and Culture,* edited by Judith Newton and Deborah Rosenfelt, 45–64. New York: Methuen, 1985.

Benson, Susan Porter. "The Cinderella of Occupations: Managing the Work of Department Store Saleswomen, 1900–1940." *Business History Review* 55 (Spring 1981): 1–25.

―――. " 'The Clerking Sisterhood:' Rationalization and the Work Culture of Saleswomen in American Department Stores, 1890–1960." *Radical America* 12 (March–April 1978): 41–55.

―――. *Counter Cultures: Saleswomen, Managers, and Customers in American Department Stores, 1890–1940.* Urbana: University of Illinois Press, 1986.

Berger, John. *Ways of Seeing.* London and New York: Penguin Books, 1972.

Bergman, Andrew. *We're in the Money: Depression America and Its Films.* New

York: New York University Press, 1971.

Betterton, Rosemary. "How Do Women Look? The Female Nude in the Work of Suzanne Valadon." In *Looking On: Images of Femininity in the Visual Arts and Media,* edited by Rosemary Betterton, 217–234. London and New York: Pandora Press, 1987.

Bishop, Isabel. "Concerning Edges." *Magazine of Art* 32 (January 1939): 53–58.

Blankenhorn, Mary Dewhurst. "Behind the Counter." *Outlook* 144 (December 22, 1926): 531–532.

Blossom, Frederick A. "Reginald Marsh as a Painter." *Creative Art* 12 (April 1933): 256–265.

Blumer, Herbert. *Movies and Conduct.* New York: Macmillan, 1933.

Bolin, Winifred D. Wandersee. "American Women in the Twentieth-Century Work Force: The Depression Experience." In *Woman's Being, Woman's Place: Female Identity and Vocation in American History,* edited by Mary Kelley, 296–312. Boston: G. K. Hall, 1979.

Brettell, Richard R., and Suzanne Folds McCullagh. *Degas in the Art Institute of Chicago.* New York: Abrams, 1984.

Breuning, Margaret. "Art in New York" (Raphael Soyer). *Parnassus* 10 (March 1938): 20.

———. "Little Touched by a Changing World" (Kenneth Hayes Miller). *Art Digest* 28 (October 1, 1953): 19, 31.

Brindze, Ruth. *How to Spend Money: Everybody's Practical Guide to Buying.* New York: Vanguard Press, 1935.

Bromley, Dorothy Dunbar. "Feminist—New Style." *Harper's Monthly Magazine* 155 (October 1927): 552–560.

"Brook and Soyer Enter the Metropolitan." *Art Digest* 7 (September 1, 1933): 7.

Brophy, Loire. *If Women Must Work.* New York: Appleton-Century, 1936.

Brown, Milton W. *American Painting from the Armory Show to the Depression.* Princeton: Princeton University Press, 1955; reprint, 1972.

Brown, Paul. "Shopgirls: 1930 Model." *Commonweal* 12 (October 8, 1930): 576–578.

Buchalter, Helen. "Carnegie International, 1939." *Magazine of Art* 32 (November 1939): 630.

Buhle, Mari Jo. *Women and the American Left: A Guide to Sources.* Boston: G. K. Hall, 1983.

Burgin, Victor. *Between.* Oxford: Basil Blackwell in association with the Institute of Contemporary Arts, 1986.

Burroughs, Alan. "Kenneth Hayes Miller." *The Arts* 14 (December 1928): 301–306.

———. *Kenneth Hayes Miller.* American Artists Series. New York: Whitney Museum of American Art, 1931.

———. "Young America—Reginald Marsh." *The Arts* 3 (February 1923): 138.

Cades, Hazel Rawson. *Jobs for Girls.* New York: Harcourt, Brace, 1928.

Caffin, Charles. *The Story of American Painting.* New York: Frederick A. Stokes, 1907.

Calvin, Alice. "The Shop Girl." *Outlook* 88 (February 15, 1908): 383–384.

Campbell, Helen Stuart. "Among the Shop-Girls." In *Victorian Women: A Documentary Account of Women's Lives in Nineteenth-Century England, France, and the United States,* edited by Erna Olaf Hellerstein, Leslie Parker Hume, and Karen M. Offen, p. 374. Stanford: Stanford University Press, 1981.

Carey, Henry R. "This Two-Headed Monster—the Family." *Harper's Monthly Magazine* 156 (January 1928): 162–171.

Chafe, William H. *The American Woman: Her Changing Social, Economic, and Political Roles, 1920–1970.* New York: Oxford University Press, 1972.

"Charlotte Gilman's Reply to Ellen Key." *Current Opinion* 54 (March 1913): 220–221.

Chase, Stuart, and J. F. Schlink. *Your Money's Worth: A Study in the Waste of the Consumer's Dollar.* New York: Macmillan, 1927.

Clayson, Hollis. "*Avant-Garde* and *Pompier* Images of Nineteenth-Century French Prostitution: The Matter of Modernism, Modernity, and Social Ideology." In *Modernism and Modernity,* Vancouver Conference Papers, edited by Benjamin H. D. Buchloh, et al., 43–64. Halifax: Press of the Nova Scotia College of Art and Design, 1983.

Coates, Robert. "Latter Day Impressionist" (Raphael Soyer). *New Yorker,* March 13, 1948, pp. 61–62.

Cohen, Marilyn. *Reginald Marsh's New York: Paintings, Drawings, Prints, and Photographs.* New York: Whitney Museum of American Art in association with Dover, 1983.

Coles, Jessie Vee. *The Consumer-Buyer and the Market.* New York: Wiley, 1938.

"Colorado Springs Buys" (Bishop's *Head*). *Art Digest* 16 (March 15, 1942): 15.

"The Conflict between 'Human' and 'Female' Feminism." *Current Opinion* 56 (April 1914): 291–292.

"Congress Seceders." *Art Digest* 14 (June 1, 1940): 18.

Connoly, Louise. "The New Woman." *Harper's Weekly* 57 (June 7, 1913): 6.

Contemporary American Painting and Sculpture. Urbana: University of Illinois Press, 1963.

Cott, Nancy. *The Grounding of Modern Feminism.* New Haven: Yale University Press, 1987.

Cowley, Malcolm. *Exile's Return.* New York: Viking Press, 1951.

Coyle, Grace L. "Women in the Clerical Occupations." *Annals of the American Academy of Political and Social Science: Women in the Modern World* 143 (May 1929): 180–187.

Cranston, Mary Rankin. "The Girl behind the Counter." *World Today* 10 (March 1906): 270–274.

Craven, Thomas. "A Paean for Marsh." *Art Digest* 11 (December 1, 1936): 10.

"Critics Lose Some Enthusiasm for Miller." *Art Digest* 9 (February 15, 1935): 8.

"Critics Unanimously Condemn Modern Museum's Mural Show." *Art Digest* 6 (May 15, 1932): 7.

Davies, Margery. *Woman's Place Is at the Typewriter: Office Work and Office Workers, 1870–1930.* Philadelphia: Temple University Press, 1982.

———. "Woman's Place Is at the Typewriter: The Feminization of the Clerical Labor Force." *Radical America* 8 (July–August 1974): 1–28.

Davis, M. D. "Nineteen-Twenty: An Editorial." *Ladies Home Journal*, January 1, 1920, p. 3.

Davis, Stuart. "The New York American Scene in Art." *Art Front* 1 (February 1935): 6.

Dayton, Dorothy. "Personality Plus—or Minus." *Independent Woman* 15 (November 1936): 343, 362.

Dehn, Adolph. "My Friend, Reggie." *Demcourier* 13 (June 1943): 11.

de Lauretis, Teresa. *Alice Doesn't: Feminism, Semiotics, Cinema.* Bloomington: Indiana University Press, 1984.

———. *Technologies of Gender: Essays on Theory, Film, and Fiction.* Bloomington: Indiana University Press, 1987.

D'Emilio, John, and Estelle B. Freedman. *Intimate Matters: A History of Sexuality in America.* New York: Harper and Row, 1988.

Dijkstra, Bram. *Idols of Perversity: Fantasies of Feminine Evil in Fin-de-Siècle Culture.* New York: Oxford University Press, 1986.

Donovan, Frances. *The Saleslady.* Introduction by David Park. Chicago: University of Chicago Press, 1929. Reprint. New York: Arno Press, 1974.

Doss, Erica L. "Images of American Women in the 1930s: Reginald Marsh and Paramount Picture." *Woman's Art Journal* 4 (Fall 1983–Winter 1984): 1–4.

Downey, Fairfax. *Portrait of an Era As Drawn by C. D. Gibson.* New York: Scribner, 1936.

Dubuc, Frances Fisher. "Women Wanted by Department Stores." *Saturday Evening Post*, June 23, 1928, 130–134.

Duncan, Carol. "Virility and Domination in Early Twentieth-Century Vanguard Painting." In *Feminism and Art History: Questioning the Litany*, edited by Norma Broude and Mary D. Garrard, 293–314. New York: Harper and Row, 1982.

Editor's statement. "The New Woman." *Current History* 27 (October 1927): 1.

Eglington, Laurie. "Exhibitions in New York" (Raphael Soyer). *Art News* 33 (February 23, 1935): 10.

Ehrenreich, Barbara. *The Hearts of Men: American Dreams and the Flight from Commitment.* Garden City, N.Y.: Anchor Books, 1984.

Ehrenreich, Barbara, and Deirdre English. *For Her Own Good: One Hundred Fifty Years of the Experts' Advice to Women.* Garden City, N.Y.: Anchor Press, 1978.

"Ellen Key's Attack on 'Amaternal' Feminism." *Current Opinion* 54 (February 1913): 138–139.

"Ellen Key's Revaluation of Woman's Chastity." *Current Literature* 52 (February 1912): 200–201.

"Ellen Key's Startling Views on Love and Marriage." *Current Literature* 50 (April 1911): 403–405.

Elzea, Rowland, and Elizabeth Hawkes. *John Sloan, Spectator of Life.* Wilmington: Delaware Art Museum, 1988.

Engle, William. "Portrait of Two Girls Bought by Metropolitan Reunites Two Ex-Waitresses Who Posed for It." *New York World-Telegram,* February 27, 1936, p. 3.

Ewen, Elizabeth. *Immigrant Women in the Land of Dollars.* New York: Monthly Review Press, 1985.

Ewen, Stuart. *Captains of Consciousness: Advertising and the Social Roots of the Consumer Culture.* New York: McGraw-Hill, 1978.

Ewen, Stuart, and Elizabeth Ewen. *Channels of Desire: Mass Images and the Shaping of American Consciousness.* New York: McGraw-Hill, 1982.

Exhibition of Contemporary American Painting. Urbana: University of Illinois Press, 1951.

"Exhibitions in New York" (Raphael Soyer). *Art News* 31 (February 18, 1933): 5.

Fahlman, Betsy. *Guy Pène du Bois, Artist about Town.* Washington, D.C.: Corcoran Gallery of Art, 1980.

Fairbrother, Trevor J. *The Bostonians: Painters of an Elegant Age, 1870–1930.* Boston: Museum of Fine Arts, 1986.

Ferry, John William. *A History of the Department Store.* New York: Macmillan, 1960.

Filene, Peter. *Him/Herself: Sex Roles in Modern America.* New York: Harcourt Brace Jovanovich, 1975.

Fish, Stanley. *Is There a Text in This Class? The Authority of Interpretive Communities.* Cambridge: Harvard University Press, 1980.

Ford, Donna. "Other Women's Lives." *Worcester Telegram,* May 20, 1941, n.p.

Foster, Lawrence. *Religion and Sexuality: Three American Communal Experiments of the Nineteenth Century.* New York: Oxford University Press, 1981.

Fox, Richard Wightman. "Epitaph for Middletown." In *The Culture of Consumption,* edited by Richard Wightman Fox and T. J. Jackson Lears, 103–141. New York: Pantheon Books, 1983.

Frank, Lawrence K. "Childhood and Youth." In *Recent Social Trends in the United States: Report of the President's Research Committee on Social Trends,* 751–800. New York: McGraw-Hill, 1934.

———. "Social Change and the Family." *Annals of the American Academy of Political and Social Science* 160 (March 1932): 94–102.

Freedman, Estelle B. "The New Woman: Changing Views of Women in the 1920s."

Journal of American History 61 (September 1974): 372–393.

Garver, Thomas H. *Reginald Marsh: A Retrospective Exhibition.* Newport Beach, Ca.: Newport Harbor Art Museum, 1972.

Genauer, Emily. "Miss Bishop Rates High as Painter." *New York World-Telegram,* February 15, 1936, p. 15.

Genn, Lillian G. "The Bachelor Girl: Is She a Menace?" *Independent Woman* 7 (December 1928): 538, 563–564.

Gettings, Frank. *Raphael Soyer: Sixty-five Years of Printmaking.* Washington, D.C.: Smithsonian Institution Press, for the Hirshhorn Museum and Sculpture Garden, 1982.

Gilfillan, Lauren. "Weary Feet." *Forum and Century* 90 (October 1933): 201–208.

Goodrich, Lloyd. "*The Arts* Magazine: 1920–1931." *American Art Journal* 5 (May 1973): 79–85.

———. "Exhibitions in New York." *The Arts* 15 (May 1929): 322–342.

———. "In the New York Galleries" (Raphael Soyer). *The Arts* 15 (May 1929): 334.

———. *Kenneth Hayes Miller.* New York: Arts Publishing Corporation, 1930.

———. *Raphael Soyer.* New York: Abrams, 1972.

———. *Reginald Marsh.* New York: Abrams, 1972.

Gordon, Linda. *Woman's Body, Woman's Right: A Social History of Birth Control in America.* New York: Penguin Books, 1977. Reprint, 1986.

Graham, Julie. "American Women Artists' Groups: 1867–1930." *Woman's Art Journal* 1 (Spring–Summer 1980): 7–12.

Grant, Madison, *The Passing of the Great Race.* New York: Scribner, 1916. Reprint. New York: Arno Press, 1970.

Gutman, Walter K. "Kenneth Hayes Miller." *Art in America* 18 (February 1930): 86–92.

———. "Raphael Soyer." *Creative Art* 6 (April 1930): 258–260.

Gutman, Walter K., Jerome Klein, and Raphael Soyer. *Raphael Soyer: Paintings and Drawings.* New York: Shorewood, 1961.

Haas, Kenneth Brooks. *Adventures in Buysmanship.* Ann Arbor, Mich.: Edwards Brothers, 1937.

Hale, Nathan G., Jr. *Freud and the Americans.* New York: Oxford University Press, 1971.

Halper, Albert. "Behind the Scenes of *Union Square*." *Wings* 7 (March 1933): 5–8.

———. *Union Square.* New York: Viking Press, 1933.

Hapgood, Norman. "What Women Are After." *Harper's Weekly* 58 (August 16, 1913): 28–29.

Hargreaves, Mary. "Darkness before the Dawn: The Status of Working Women in the Depression Years." In *Clio Was a Woman,* edited by Mabel E. Deutrich and

Virginia Purdy, 178–189. Washington, D.C.: Howard University Press, 1980.

Harrison, Helen A. "John Reed Club Artists and the New Deal: Radical Responses to Roosevelt's 'Peaceful Revolution.' " *Prospects* 5 (1980): 241–268.

Hart, John. *Albert Halper.* Boston: Twayne, 1980.

Hawkes, Elizabeth H. *American Painting and Sculpture.* Wilmington: Delaware Art Museum, 1975.

Haywood, Robert. "George Bellows's *Stag at Sharkey's*: Boxing, Violence, and Male Identity." *Smithsonian Studies in American Art* 2 (Spring 1988): 3–15.

Higashi, Sumiko. "Cinderella vs. Statistics: The Silent Movie Heroine as Jazz-Age Working Girl." In *Woman's Being, Woman's Place: Female Identity and Vocation in American History,* edited by Mary Kelley, 109–126. Boston: G. K. Hall, 1979.

Hills, Patricia. "John Sloan's Images of Working-Class Women: A Case Study of the Roles and Interrelationships of Politics, Personality, and Patrons in the Development of Sloan's Art, 1905–1916." *Prospects* 5 (1980): 157–196.

———. *Social Concern and Urban Realism: American Painting of the 1930s.* With an essay by Raphael Soyer. Boston: Boston University Art Gallery, 1983.

Hills, Patricia, and Roberta K. Tarbell. *The Figurative Tradition and the Whitney Museum of American Art: Paintings and Sculpture from the Permanent Collection.* Foreword by Tom Armstrong. New York and Newark, Del.: Whitney Museum of American Art in association with the University of Delaware Press, 1980.

Hogner, Nils, and Guy Scott. *Cartoon Guide of New York City.* New York: Augustin, 1938.

Hopkins, Mary Alden. "The Girls behind the Counter." *Collier's,* March 16, 1912, 16–17, 30.

———. "Women March." *Collier's,* May 18, 1912, 13, 31.

Hoppin, Martha J. *Marie Danforth Page: Back Bay Portraitist.* Springfield, Mass.: George Walter Vincent Smith Art Museum, 1979.

Howells, William Dean. *Criticism and Fiction.* 1891. Reprint. New York: Hill and Wang, 1967.

Hutchins, Grace. *Women Who Work.* New York: International Publishers, 1934.

International Commercial Service. *Gazette des Dames.* Album of Fashion with Shopping Guide. London and New York, 1921.

"Isabel Bishop." *Current Biography Yearbook.* New York: Wilson, 1977.

"Isabel Bishop Finds the Critics Receptive." *Art Digest* 13 (February 1, 1939): 21.

"Isabel Bishop Shows Her New York Types." *Art Digest* 10 (February 15, 1936): 19.

"Is Feminism Really So Dreadful? Listen to Charlotte Perkins Gilman." *Delineator* (August 1914): 6.

Jamison, Jack. "Hollywood's Lost Children." *Modern Screen,* September 1934, 62–63.

Jones, Alfred Haworth. "The Search for a Usable American Past in the New Deal Era." *American Quarterly* 23 (December 1981): 710–724.

Kahr, Madlyn Millner. "Danaë: Virtuous, Voluptuous, Venal Woman." *Art Bulletin* 60 (March 1978): 43–55.

Kasson, John. *Amusing the Million: Coney Island at the Turn of the Century.* New York: Hill and Wang, 1978.

"Kenneth Hayes Miller." *Art News* 28 (December 7, 1929): 13.

"Kenneth Hayes Miller." *Art News* 30 (November 28, 1931): 10.

Kenneth Hayes Miller: A Memorial Exhibition. New York: Art Students League of New York, 1953.

"The Kenneth Hayes Miller Papers." *Archives of American Art Journal* 13 (1973): 19–24.

Kent, Rockwell. *It's Me O Lord: The Autobiography of Rockwell Kent.* New York: Dodd, Mead, 1955.

Kern, Louis J. *An Ordered Love: Sex Roles and Sexuality in Victorian Utopias—the Shakers, the Mormons, and the Oneida Community.* Chapel Hill: University of North Carolina Press, 1981.

Kessler-Harris, Alice. *Out to Work: A History of Wage-Earning Women in the United States.* New York: Oxford University Press, 1982.

———. *Women Have Always Worked: A Historical Overview.* Old Westbury, N.Y.: Feminist Press, 1981.

Key, Ellen. *Love and Ethics.* New York: Huebsch, 1911.

———. *Love and Marriage.* Translated by Arthur G. Chater. New York: Putnam, 1911.

———. "Motherliness." *Atlantic* 110 (October 1912): 562–570.

Kinser, Suzanne L. "Prostitutes in the Art of John Sloan." *Prospects* 9 (1984): 231–254.

Kirkpatrick, Clifford. "Techniques of Marital Adjustment." *Annals of the American Academy of Political and Social Science* 160 (March 1932): 178–183.

Klein, Cecelia F. Editor's Statement, "Depictions of the Dispossessed." *Art Journal* 49 (Summer 1990): 106–109.

Kleinbauer, W. Eugene. *Modern Perspectives in Western Art History.* New York: Holt, Rinehart and Winston, 1971.

Koch, Robert. "Gibson Girl Revisited." *Art in America* 1 (1965): 70–73.

Kouwenhoven, John A. *The Columbia Historical Portrait of New York.* Garden City, N.Y.: Doubleday, 1953.

Kramer, Hilton. "Marsh's Search for a Style." *New York Times,* June 24, 1979, sec. 2, p. 31.

———. "Miller's Art: City in a Dimmed Light." *New York Times,* January 17, 1970, p. 25.

———. "Reginald Marsh, New York Romantic." Undated clipping from *New York Times* News Service.

————. "The Unhappy Fate of Kenneth Hayes Miller." *New York Times*, March 11, 1979, sec. D, p. 31.

Kwiat, John. "John Reed Club Art Exhibition." *New Masses* 8 (February 1933): 23.

Lane, James W. "Bishop." *Art News* 41 (June 1942): 42.

————. "Canvases by Isabel Bishop, Painter of Subtle Tonalities." *Art News* 37 (January 21, 1939): 12.

————. "The Passing Shows" (Raphael Soyer). *Art News* 40 (April 1–15, 1941): 29.

Laning, Edward. *East Side, West Side, All Around the Town*. Tucson: University of Arizona Museum of Art, 1969.

————. "The New Deal Mural Projects." In *The New Deal Art Projects: An Anthology of Memoirs*, edited by Francis V. O'Connor, 79–113. Washington, D.C.: Smithsonian Institution Press, 1972.

————. "Reginald Marsh." *Demcourier* 13 (June 1943): 3–7; 16.

————. *The Sketchbooks of Reginald Marsh*. Greenwich, Conn.: New York Graphic Society, 1973.

Law, Helen. "A New Job for the College Girl." *Review of Reviews* 81 (June 1930): 74–76.

Leader, Bernice Kramer. "Antifeminism in the Paintings of the Boston School." *Arts Magazine* 56 (January 1982): 112–119.

Lears, T. J. Jackson. "From Salvation to Self-Realization: Advertising and the Therapeutic Roots of the Consumer Culture, 1880–1920." In *The Culture of Consumption*, edited by Richard Wightman Fox and T. J. Jackson Lears, 3–38. New York: Pantheon Books, 1983.

————. *No Place of Grace: Antimodernism and the Transformation of American Culture, 1880–1920*. New York: Pantheon Books, 1981.

Lederer, Joseph. *All Around the Town*. New York: Scribner, 1975.

Lemons, J. Stanley. *The Woman Citizen: Social Feminism in the 1920s*. Urbana: University of Illinois Press, 1973.

Le Sueur, Meridel. "Women on the Breadlines." *New Masses* 7 (January 1932): 5–7.

Leuchtenberg, William E. *Franklin D. Roosevelt and the New Deal*. New York: Harper and Row, 1963.

————. *The Perils of Prosperity, 1914–1932*. Chicago: University of Chicago Press, 1958.

Levin, Gail. "Edward Hopper's *Office at Night*." *Arts Magazine* (January 1978): 134–137.

Lipton, Eunice. *Looking into Degas: Uneasy Images of Women and Modern Life*. Berkeley and Los Angeles: University of California Press, 1986.

Lunde, Karl. *Isabel Bishop*. New York: Abrams, 1975.

Lurie, Alison. *The Truth about Lorin Jones*. Boston: Little, Brown, 1988.

Lynd, Robert S. "Family Members as Consumers." *Annals of the American Academy of Political and Social Science* 160 (March 1932): 86–93.

———. "The People as Consumers." In *Recent Social Trends in the United States: Report of the President's Research Committee on Social Trends*, 857–911. New York: McGraw-Hill, 1934.

Lynd, Robert S., and Helen Merrell Lynd. *Middletown: A Study in Contemporary American Culture*. New York: Harcourt, Brace, 1929.

McBride, Henry. "Some Others Who Arouse Interest." *New York Sun*, February 15, 1936, p. 28.

McCabe, Cynthia Jaffee, and Daniel J. Boorstin. *The Golden Door: Artist Immigrants of America, 1876–1976*. Washington, D.C.: Smithsonian Institution Press for the Hirshhorn Museum and Sculpture Garden, 1976.

McCausland, Elizabeth. "The Daniel Gallery and Modern American Art." *Magazine of Art* 44 (November 1951): 280–285.

MacGibbon, Elizabeth Gregg. "Exit—the Private Secretary." *Occupations* 15 (January 1937): 295–300.

———. *Manners in Business*. New York: Macmillan, 1936.

McGovern, James R. "The American Woman's Pre–World War I Freedom in Manners and Morals." *Journal of American History* 55 (September 1968): 315–333.

McMenamin, Hugh L. "Evils of the Woman's Revolt against the Old Standards." *Current History* 27 (October 1927): 30–33.

Marchand, Roland. *Advertising the American Dream: Making Way for Modernity, 1920–1940*. Berkeley and Los Angeles: University of California Press, 1985.

Marling, Karal Ann. "A Note on New Deal Iconography: Futurology and the Historical Myth." *Prospects* 4 (1979): 421–440.

Marsh, Reginald. "Kenneth Hayes Miller." *Magazine of Art* 45 (April 1952): 170–171.

———. "Let's Get Back to Painting." *Magazine of Art* 37 (December 1944): 292–296.

———. "A Short Autobiography." *Art and Artists of Today* 1 (March 1937): 8.

———. "What I See in Laning's Art." *Creative Art* 12 (March 1933): 186–188.

Masteller, Richard N. *"We, the People?" Satiric Prints of the 1930s*. Walla Walla, Wash.: Donald H. Sheehan Gallery, Whitman College, 1989.

Matthews, Glenna. *"Just a Housewife": The Rise and Fall of Domesticity in America*. New York: Oxford University Press, 1987.

Maule, Frances. *She Strives to Conquer: Business Behavior, Opportunities, and Job Requirements for Women*. New York: Funk and Wagnalls, 1937.

Maule, Mary K. "What Is a Shop-Girl's Life?" *World's Work* 14 (September 1907): 9311–9316.

Melosh, Barbara. *Engendering Culture: Manhood and Womanhood in New Deal Public Art and Theater*. Washington, D.C.: Smithsonian Institution Press, 1991.

Meyerowitz, Joanne. "Sexual Geography and Gender Economy: The Furnished

Room Districts of Chicago, 1890–1930." *Gender and History* 2 (Autumn 1990): 274–296.

Milkman, Ruth, ed. *Women, Work, and Protest: A Century of U.S. Women's Labor History.* Boston: Routledge, 1985.

Millier, A. "Murals and Men." *Art Digest* 9 (September 1, 1935): 6.

Moi, Toril. *Sexual/Textual Politics: Feminist Literary Theory.* London and New York: Methuen, 1985.

Monroe, Gerald M. "Art Front." *Archives of American Art Journal* 13 (1973): 13–19.

Moore, Sally. "Isabel Bishop: Half a Century of Painting the Flotsam of Union Square." *People,* May 26, 1975.

Morris, Lloyd. *Incredible New York: High Life and Low Life of the Last One Hundred Years.* New York: Random House, 1951.

Moses Soyer. Introduction by Alfred Werner. Memoir by David Soyer. South Brunswick, N.J., and New York: A. L. Barnes, 1970.

Mulvey, Laura. "Afterthoughts on 'Visual Pleasure and Narrative Cinema' Inspired by *Duel in the Sun.*" In *Feminism and Film Theory,* edited by Constance Penley, 69–79. London and New York: Routledge, 1988.

———. "Visual Pleasure and Narrative Cinema." In *Art after Modernism: Rethinking Representation,* edited by Brian Wallis, 361–373. New York and Boston: New Museum of Contemporary Art in association with Godine, 1984.

Murals by American Painters and Photographers. New York: Museum of Modern Art, 1932.

"Museumized: *Noon Hour* by I. Bishop Bought by Springfield." *Art Digest* 13 (May 1, 1939): 5.

Myers, Bernard, ed. "*Sleeping Child* by Isabel Bishop." Scribner's American Painters Series, no. 9. *Scribner's* 122 (November 1937): 32.

Myerson, Abraham. *The Nervous Housewife.* Boston: Little, Brown, 1920.

Nead, Lynda. "Representation, Sexuality, and the Female Nude." *Art History* 6 (June 1983): 227–236.

Nemser, Cindy. "A Conversation with Isabel Bishop." *Feminist Art Journal* 5 (Spring 1976): 14–20.

"The New Baby Bloom." *Time,* February 22, 1982, 52–58.

"The New Erotic Ethics." *The Nation* 94 (March 14, 1912): 261.

"New Exhibitions of the Week: Human Studies by Raphael Soyer." *Art News* 37 (April 15, 1939): 14.

"New Instructors at the Art Students League." *Art Digest* 8 (October 1, 1933): 25.

"New Paintings Shown by Isabel Bishop." *New York World-Telegram,* January 21, 1939, p. 16.

Newton, Judith, and Deborah Rosenfelt. "Introduction: Toward a Materialist-Feminist Criticism." In *Feminist Criticism and Social Change: Sex, Class, and Race in Literature and Culture,* edited by Judith Newton and Deborah Rosenfelt, xv–xxxix. New York: Methuen, 1985.

"New York Criticism" (Raphael Soyer). *Art Digest* 9 (March 1, 1935): 18.

"New York Criticism: A Miller Pupil's Shackles Loosen" (Isabel Bishop). *Art Digest* 10 (March 1, 1936): 16.

New York in Pictures, vol. 2. New York: Sun Printing and Publishing Association, 1928.

New York Panorama. American Guide Series. New York: Random House, Guilds' Committee for Federal Writers' Publications, 1938.

New York Times, 1920–1940, articles on Union Square, Fourteenth Street.

"New York Types at the Midtown Galleries, New York" (Isabel Bishop). *Art Digest* 10 (February 15, 1936): 19.

Nochlin, Linda. "Edward Hopper and the Imagery of Alienation," *Art Journal* 41 (Summer 1981): 136–141.

Noyes, Velma. "Conflicts in the Business Girl's Mind." *Woman's Press* 32 (October 1938): 451, 456.

"Office Workers Analyze Themselves." *Woman's Press* 29 (November 1935): 506.

Ogburn, William F. "The Family and Its Functions." In *Recent Social Trends in the United States: Report of the President's Research Committee on Social Trends*, 661–708. New York: McGraw-Hill, 1934.

———. "The Influence of Invention and Discovery." In *Recent Social Trends in the United States: Report of the President's Research Committee on Social Trends*, 122–166. New York: McGraw-Hill, 1934.

O'Hagen, Anne. "The Shop-Girl and Her Wages." *Munsey's Magazine* 50 (November 1913): 252–259.

Olson, Stanley. *John Singer Sargent: His Portrait.* New York: St. Martin's Press, 1986.

Onativia, Elizabeth. "Give Us Our Privileges." *Scribner's* 87 (June 1930): 593–598.

O'Neill, William L. "The End of Feminism." In *Twentieth-Century America: Recent Interpretations*, edited by Barton J. Bernstein and Allen J. Matusow, 186–196. 2d edition. New York: Harcourt Brace Jovanovich, 1972.

Ormsby, Stella. "The Other Side of the Profile." *New Republic* 72 (August 17, 1932): 21.

Owens, Gwendolyn. "Pioneers in American Museums: Bryson Burroughs." *Museum News* 57 (May 1979): 46–53; 84.

Paintings by Nineteen Living Americans. Exhibition catalog. Foreword by Alfred H. Barr, Jr. New York: Museum of Modern Art, 1930.

Palmer, Gretta. *A Shopping Guide to New York.* New York: McBride, 1930.

Palmer, Phyllis. *Domesticity and Dirt: Housewives and Domestic Servants in the United States, 1920–1945.* Women in the Political Economy Series. Philadelphia: Temple University Press, 1990.

Peiss, Kathy. *Cheap Amusements: Working Women and Leisure in Turn-of-the-Century New York.* Philadelphia: Temple University Press, 1986.

Pell, Orlie. "Two Million in Offices." *Woman's Press* 33 (June 1939): 256.

Pells, Richard H. *Radical Visions and American Dreams: Culture and Social Thought in the Depression Years.* New York: Harper and Row, 1973.

Penley, Constance. *The Future of an Illusion: Film, Feminism, and Psychoanalysis.* Minneapolis: University of Minnesota Press, 1989.

Perkins, T. E. "Rethinking Stereotypes." In *Ideology and Cultural Production,* edited by Michèle Barrett, Philip Corrigan, Annette Kuhn, and Janet Wolff, 135–159. New York: St. Martin's Press, 1979.

Perlman, Bennard B. *The Immortal Eight: American Painting from Eakins to the Armory Show, 1870–1913.* Introduction by Mrs. John Sloan. Cincinnati, Ohio: North Light, 1979.

Petruck, Peninah R. Y. *American Art Criticism, 1910–1939.* New York: Garland, 1981.

Phillips, Sandra S. "The Art Criticism of Walter Pach." *Art Bulletin* 65 (March 1983): 106–121.

Pitz, Henry C. "Charles Dana Gibson: Creator of a Mode." *American Artist* 20 (December 1956): 50–55.

Pollock, Griselda. "Van Gogh and the Poor Slaves: Images of Rural Labour as Modern Art." *Art History* 11 (September 1988): 406–432.

————. *Vision and Difference: Femininity, Feminism, and the Histories of Art.* London and New York: Routledge, 1988.

Poovey, Mary. "Feminism and Deconstruction." *Feminist Studies* 14 (Spring 1988): 51–65.

Pruette, Lorine, ed. *Women Workers through the Depression: A Study of White Collar Employment Made by the American Women's Association.* New York: Macmillan, 1934.

"Raphael Soyer: Daniel Galleries." *Art News* 27 (April 27, 1929): 10.

"Raphael Soyer Paints Twenty-three Artists and Some Hungering Shop Girls." *Art Digest* 15 (April 1, 1941): 17.

"Raphael Soyer, Realist, Captures That 'Haunted Look of the Unemployed.' " *Art Digest* 12 (March 15, 1938): 12.

Rapp, Rayna, and Ellen Ross. "The Twenties' Backlash: Compulsory Heterosexuality, the Consumer Family, and the Waning of Feminism." In *Class, Race, and Sex: The Dynamics of Control,* edited by Amy Swerdlow and Hanna Lessinger, 93–107. New York: Barnard College Women's Center; Boston: G. K. Hall, 1983.

Ratcliff, Carter. *John Singer Sargent.* New York: Abbeville Press, 1982.

Reich, Sheldon. *Isabel Bishop.* Introduction by Martin H. Bush. Tucson: University of Arizona Museum of Art, 1974.

"Reviews and Previews" (Raphael Soyer). *Art News* 48 (April 1948): 51.

Rosen, Marjorie. *Popcorn Venus: Women, Movies, and the American Dream.* New York: Coward, McCann and Geoghegan, 1973.

Rosen, Randy, and Catherine C. Brawer. *Making Their Mark: Women Artists Move into the Mainstream, 1970–1985.* New York: Abbeville Press, 1989.

Rosenberg, Rosalind. *Beyond Separate Spheres: Intellectual Roots of Modern Feminism.* New Haven: Yale University Press, 1982.

Rosenfeld, Paul. *Port of New York: Essays on Fourteen American Moderns.* New York: Harcourt, Brace, 1924. Reprint. Urbana: University of Illinois Press, 1961.

Rothschild, Lincoln. *To Keep Art Alive: The Effort of Kenneth Hayes Miller, American Painter (1876–1952).* Philadelphia: Art Alliance Press, 1974.

Rupp, Leila J. "Feminism and the Sexual Revolution in the Early Twentieth Century: The Case of Doris Stevens." *Feminist Studies* 15 (1989): 289–309.

Ryan, Mary P. *Womanhood in America: From Colonial Times to the Present.* 3d Edition. New York: F. Watts, 1983.

Salpeter, Harry. "Kenneth Hayes Miller, Intellectual." *Esquire,* October 1937, 89, 197–203.

———. "Raphael Soyer: East Side Degas." *Esquire,* May 1938, 59, 155–158.

———. "The Roar of the City" (Reginald Marsh). *Esquire,* June 1935, 46–49, 126, 128.

Santayana, George. "The Genteel Tradition in American Philosophy." In *Winds of Doctrine: Studies in Contemporary Opinion.* New York: Scribner, 1926.

Sasowsky, Norman. *The Prints of Reginald Marsh.* New York: Clarkson N. Potter, 1976.

Schapiro, Meyer. *Modern Art, Nineteenth and Twentieth Centuries: Selected Papers.* New York: George Braziller, 1978.

Scharf, Lois. *To Work and to Wed: Female Employment, Feminism, and the Great Depression.* Contributions to Women's Studies no. 15. Westport, Conn.: Greenwood Press, 1980.

Scharf, Lois, and Joan M. Jenson, eds. *Decades of Discontent: The Women's Movement, 1920–1940.* Contributions to Women's Studies no. 28. Westport, Conn.: Greenwood Press, 1983.

Scott, David W., and Edgar John Bullard, III. *John Sloan, 1871–1951.* Exhibition catalog. Washington, D.C.: National Gallery of Art, 1971.

Scott, Joan. "Deconstructing Equality-versus-Difference: Or, the Uses of Poststructuralist Theory for Feminism." *Feminist Studies* 14 (Spring 1988): 33–49.

Shapiro, David, ed. *Social Realism: Art as a Weapon.* New York: Ungar, 1973.

Shuttleworth, Jack. "John Held, Jr., and His World." *American Heritage: The Twenties,* special issue 16 (August 1965): 29–32.

Sklar, Robert. *Movie-Made America: A Social History of American Movies.* New York: Random House, 1975.

"S. Klein: 'On the Square' Store Plays Santa to Its Employees." *Newsweek,* December 29, 1934, 28–30.

Sloan, Helen Farr, ed. *John Sloan: New York Etchings (1905–1949).* New York: Dover, 1978.

Smith-Rosenberg, Carroll. "Bourgeois Discourse and the Progressive Era." In *Dis-*

orderly Conduct: Visions of Gender in Victorian America. New York: Oxford University Press, 1986.

———. "The New Woman as Androgyne: Social Disorder and Gender Crisis, 1870–1936." In *Disorderly Conduct: Visions of Gender in Victorian America.* New York: Oxford University Press, 1986.

"Social Commentaries Mark the Pennsylvania Academy's Annual." *Art Digest* 8 (February 15, 1934): 5–7.

Soyer, Moses. "Three Brothers." *Magazine of Art* 32 (April 1939): 201–207.

Soyer, Raphael. "An Artist's Experiences in the 1930s." In Patricia Hills, *Social Concern and Urban Realism: American Painting of the 1930s.* Exhibition catalog. Boston: Boston University Art Gallery, 1983.

———. *Diary of an Artist.* Washington, D.C.: New Republic Books, 1977.

———. *Homage to Thomas Eakins.* Edited by Rebecca L. Soyer. South Brunswick, N.J.: T. Yoseloff, 1966.

———. "The Lesson: The Academy, the League, the Classroom." *Arts Magazine* 42 (September 1967): 34–36.

———. *A Painter's Pilgrimage.* New York: Crown, 1962.

———. "Reginald Marsh." *Reality: A Journal of Artists' Opinions* 3 (Summer 1955): 5–6.

———. *Self-Revealment: A Memoir.* New York: Maecenas Press, 1969.

Stein, Sally. "The Graphic Ordering of Desire: Modernization of a Middle-Class Women's Magazine, 1914–1939." *Heresies* 5 (1985): 7–16.

Steinberg, Leo. "The Polemical Part." *Art in America* 67 (March/April 1979): 114–127.

Steiner, J. F. "Recreation and Leisure Time Activities." In *Recent Social Trends in the United States: Report of the President's Research Committee on Social Trends,* 912–957. New York: McGraw-Hill, 1934.

Susman, Warren I. *Culture as History: The Transformation of American Society in the Twentieth Century.* New York: Pantheon Books, 1984.

Symes, Lillian. "The New Masculinism." *Harper's Monthly Magazine* 161 (June 1930): 98–107.

———. "Still a Man's Game: Reflections of a Slightly Tired Feminist." *Harper's Monthly Magazine* 158 (May 1929): 678–686.

Taylor, Kendall. *Philip Evergood: Selections from the Hirshhorn Museum and Sculpture Garden.* Washington, D.C.: Smithsonian Institution Press, 1978.

Teller, Susan, ed. *Isabel Bishop: Etchings and Aquatints, A Catalogue Raisonné.* New York: Associated American Artists, 1981.

Terkel, Studs. *Hard Times: An Oral History of the Great Depression.* New York: Washington Square Press, 1970.

Tickner, Lisa. "Feminism, Art History, and Sexual Difference." *Genders* no. 3 (Fall 1988): 92–128.

Ticknor, Caroline. "The Steel-Engraving Lady and the Gibson Girl." *Atlantic*

Monthly 88 (July 1901): 105–108.

Todd, Ellen Wiley. "Will [S]he Stoop to Conquer? Preliminaries Toward a Reading of Edward Hopper's *Office at Night.*" In *Visual Theory: Method and Interpretation in Art History and the Visual Arts,* edited by Norman Bryson, Michael Holly, and Keith Moxey, 47–53. New York: HarperCollins, 1990.

Trimberger, Ellen Kay. "Feminism, Men, and Modern Love: Greenwich Village, 1900–1925." In *Powers of Desire: The Politics of Sexuality,* edited by Ann Snitow, Christine Stansell, and Sharon Tompson, 131–152. New York: Monthly Review Press, 1983.

Tuchman, Gaye. *Hearth and Home: Images of Women in the Mass Media.* New York: Oxford University Press, 1978.

Tufts, Eleanor. *American Women Artists, 1830–1930.* Washington, D.C.: International Exhibitions Foundation for the National Museum of Women in the Arts, 1987.

U.S. Department of Labor, Women's Bureau Bulletin no. 120. *The Employment of Women in Offices,* pp. 1–17. By Ethel Erickson, 1934.

Van Hook, Bailey. "Decorative Images of American Women: The Aristocratic Aesthetic of the Late Nineteenth Century." *Smithsonian Studies in American Art* 4 (Winter 1990): 45–70.

Van Kleek, Mary. "Working Conditions in New York Department Stores." *Survey,* October 11, 1913, 50–51.

Van Vorst, Mrs. John. "*Grisettes* and *Midinettes.*" *Lippincott's Magazine* 80 (July, 1907): 101–107.

Wald, Carol. *Myth America: Picturing Women, 1865–1945.* New York: Pantheon Books, 1975.

Walker, Alexander. *The Celluloid Sacrifice: Aspects of Sex in the Movies.* New York: Hawthorn Books, 1966.

Wallace, Eugenia. "Office Work and the Ladder of Success." *Independent Woman* 6 (October 1927): 16–18.

Wanger, Ruth. *What Girls Can Do.* New York: Henry Holt, 1926.

Ware, Caroline F. *Greenwich Village, 1920–1930; A Comment on American Civilization in the Post-War Years.* Boston: Houghton Mifflin, 1935.

———. "The 1939 Job of the White Collar Girl." *Woman's Press* 33 (June 1939): 254–255.

Ware, Susan. *Holding Their Own: American Women in the 1930s.* Boston: Twayne, 1982.

Watson, Amey E. "The Reorganization of Household Work." *Annals of the American Academy of Political and Social Science* 160 (March 1932): 165–177.

Watson, Forbes. Editorial. *The Arts* 3 (January 1923): 1.

———. "Innocent Bystander" (Reginald Marsh). *American Magazine of Art* 28 (January 1935): 62.

———. "Isabel Bishop." *Magazine of Art* 32 (January 1939): 52.

———. "Opening Studio." *The Arts* 10 (October 1927): 220.

———. "A Perspective on American Murals." In *Art in Federal Buildings I: Mural Designs 1934–1936*, edited by Edward Bruce and Forbes Watson. Washington, D.C.: Art in Federal Buildings, Inc., 1936.

Wertheim, Arthur Frank. *The New York Little Renaissance: Iconoclasm, Modernism, and Nationalism in American Culture, 1908–1917*. New York: New York University Press, 1976.

Whelpton, P. K. "The Population of the Nation." In *Recent Social Trends in the United States: Report of the President's Research Committee on Social Trends.* New York: McGraw-Hill, 1934.

Whiting, Cécile. *Antifascism in American Art.* New Haven: Yale University Press, 1989.

Wilcox, Susanne. "The Unrest of Modern Woman." *Independent* 67 (July 8, 1909): 62–63.

Willey, Malcolm M. " 'Identification' and the Inculcation of Social Values." *Annals of the American Academy of Political and Social Science* 160 (March 1932): 103–109.

Wilmerding, John, Linda Ayres, and Earl A. Powell. *An American Perspective: Nineteenth-Century Art from the Collection of Jo Ann and Julian Ganz, Jr.* Washington, D.C.: National Gallery of Art, 1981.

Wolfe, Gerald R. *New York: A Guide to the Metropolis.* New York: New York University Press, 1975.

"Women Art Critics Attack Organization of Modernist Women." *Art Digest* 3 (March 1, 1929): 9.

"Women in Business I." *Fortune* 12 (July 1935): 50–55, 90–96.

"Women in Business II." *Fortune* 12 (August 1935): 50–55, 85–86.

Wooden, Howard E. *Edward Laning, American Realist, 1906–1981: A Retrospective Exhibition.* Wichita, Kans.: Wichita Art Museum, 1982.

The WPA Guide to New York City: The Federal Writers' Project Guide to 1930s New York. Originally published as *New York City Guide.* New York: Random House, 1939. Reprint. New York: Pantheon Books, 1982.

Yglesias, Helen. *Isabel Bishop.* Foreword by John Russell. New York: Rizzoli, 1989.

Zigrosser, Carl. *The Artist in America: Twenty-four Close-ups of Contemporary Printmakers.* New York: Knopf, 1942.

Zurier, Rebecca. *Art for the Masses: A Radical Magazine and Its Graphics, 1911–1917.* Philadelphia: Temple University Press, 1988.

———. "Real Men, Real Life, Real Art: Gendering Realism at the Turn of the Century." Paper delivered at the American Studies Association annual meeting, Baltimore, Md., November 1, 1991.

UNPUBLISHED SOURCES

Archives of American Art, Smithsonian Institution, Washington, D.C.:
Artists' Papers

Associated American Artists, Inc.
Isabel Bishop
Edward Laning
Seymour Lipton
Macbeth Gallery
Reginald Marsh
Midtown Galleries
Kenneth Hayes Miller
Rehn Gallery
Raphael Soyer
Whitney Museum of American Art

Museum of the City of New York

Reginald Marsh Photographic Archives
Union Square/Fourteenth Street Archives

The New York Public Library

"Photographic Views of New York" Microfiche Collection

Interviews on Tape

Isabel Bishop, December 16, 1982
Minna Citron (friend of Bishop, Miller, and Marsh), December 22, 1982
Lloyd Goodrich, December 30, 1982
Jack Henderson (friend of Edward Laning), November 22, 1982
Raphael Soyer, December 27, 1982; June 18, 1983; April 26, 1984; and March 13, 1987

Dissertations

Cohen, Marilyn. "Reginald Marsh: An Interpretation of His Art." New York University, Institute of Fine Arts, 1986.
Doss, Erica L. "Regionalists in Hollywood: Painting, Film, and Patronage, 1925–1945." University of Minnesota, 1983.
Leader, Bernice. "The Boston Lady as a Work of Art: Paintings by the Boston School at the Turn of the Century." Columbia University, 1980.

Peeler, David. "American Depression Culture: Social Art and Literature of the 1930s." University of Wisconsin, 1980.

Samson, Peter E. "The Emergence of a Consumer Interest in America, 1870–1930." University of Chicago, 1980.

Shrock, Alice Almond. "Feminists, Flappers, and the Maternal Mystique: Changing Conceptions of Women and Their Roles in the 1920s." University of North Carolina at Chapel Hill, 1974.

Warford, Pamela Neal. "The Social Origins of Female Iconography: Selected Images of Women in American Popular Culture, 1890–1945." Washington University, St. Louis, 1979.

INDEX

PAGE REFERENCES TO ILLUSTRATIONS
ARE IN BOLD TYPE

Feminism *(continued)*
Greenwich Village, 3, 24; and homemaking roles, 154, 158; and individualism, 4; and National Woman's Party, 38, 313; and protective labor legislation debates, 37–38; and right-to-work claims, 252, 262, 313; and sexuality, 4; and socialism, 3, 38; and spectatorship, 182; and suffrage campaign, 4, 12, 27–31

Feminist: stereotypes of, 32–34

Ferrar Art Club: and Robert Henri, 65

Ferry, Irma (Miller's first wife), 44–45, 173

Field, Hamilton Easter: as founder, editor of *The Arts,* 73

Fife, Mary: *Klein's Dressing Room,* 100, 102

Fifth Avenue, xxv; contrasted to Fourteenth Street, 117–118

Film. *See* Movies

Flapper, 24, 36; attributes of, 33–34, 110, 147–150; and feminism, 151–152; and Gibson girl, 33–34; and Miller matron, 148–149, 151, 175; and sexual liberation, 33–34; and Siren, 178, 196, 197

Fleming, Tom: "Home or Street Corner for Woman? Vote No on Woman Suffrage," 27–28

Force, Juliana: and Whitney Studio Club, 67, 72

Ford, James Bishop: as Bishop's financial support, 56–57, 61

Fortune magazine, 50; on office workers, 296–297, 302, 305, 308

Foster, William (Communist party presidential candidate, 1932), 170

Foucault, Michel: on discourse, xxix–xxx

Fourteenth Street, 126; and Bishop's studios, 58–59, 97; and Marsh's studios, 51, 53, 330n.48, 336n.132; as Marsh subject, 223; and mass

commercial entertainment, 112–120, 123; and Miller's studios, 47; as shopping center, xxv, 87, 96, 105; and Soyer's studios, 67, 336n.132. *See also* Fourteenth Street–Union Square district; Union Square; *individual artists*

Fourteenth Street Association, 87, 88, 96

Fourteenth Street realism: artistic strategies, 75–81; and Ashcan school realism, 75, 79–81; and Miller's contemporary classical realism, 75, 76–79. *See also* Fourteenth Street School

Fourteenth Street School: and American Scene painting, 70–71, 72–74; artists, xxv, 36, 38; audience of, 314, 315; historiography of, 40–41, 327n.5; images of Depression, 122–131; images of womanhood, xxvii, 316–317; and old masters, 63, 71–72; and pictorial strategies, 85, 90, 108, 123–124, 135–136, 313, 314, 317; and politics of 1930s, 120–121, 124, 315–316; social gatherings of, 73–74; and unemployed, 131, 133–134

Fourteenth Street–Union Square district: as center for mass culture, 108–120; as center for radical politics, 120–131; as commercial district, 86–96; early history, 85–86; effects of Depression on, 105–108; growth of, 92–96; and retail women's wear, 96–105. *See also* Fourteenth Street; Union Square

Fox, Richard (historian): on consumer culture, 217, 222

Freedman, Estelle (historian): and historiography of feminism, 31–32

Freud, Sigmund, 151, 154; and Miller, 46–47, 222

Fry, Roger: and early formalist

Shopgirl: attributes of, 229, 244; as
    fictional type, 246–247; and social
    class, 364n.38, 364–365n.42;
    working conditions of, 245, 247,
    258–262, 362n.20, 363n.29,
    365n.50. *See also* Saleslady; Soyer,
    Raphael
Shreiner, Olive: on sexual equality, 4,
    34
Siegel, William: "Office Worker's
    Lunch Hour," 298, **299**
Sinclair, Upton: and naturalism, 18
Siren, 189; and advertising, 202; and
    anti-feminism, 197, 199; attributes
    of, 196–202; and consumer culture,
    208–214; in movies, 200–202; and
    sexuality, 208. *See also* Marsh,
    Reginald; Voluptuous shopper
Sloan, John, 50, 51; as Art Students
    League instructor, 72; and Ashcan
    school realism, 79, 81; critical
    reception of, 21, 23; early influence
    on Soyer brothers, 65; and female
    sexuality, 19; humor of, 24; and
    National Academy of Design, 71;
    and prostitution in his art, 21–22;
    and representation of working-class
    new women, 19–24, 108, 110; on
    socialism, 19, 130; and
    spectatorship, 22–24, 324–
    325n.51; and technique, 214. *See
    also* Ashcan school. *Works:*
    "Hooray, Hooray for Mother," 30;
    illustration for Mary Alden
    Hopkins, "Women March," **29;**
    Return from Toil, 108–110, 111,
    232–233, 255; *Subway Stairs*, 108–
    110, 111; *Sunday Afternoon in
    Union Square*, 20–22; *Sunday,
    Women Drying Their Hair*, 23–24,
    255; *The Wigwam, Old Tammany
    Hall*, 81, 82, 108
Smith-Rosenberg, Carroll (historian):
    on New Woman, xxvii, 2
Socialist party: and Ashcan school, 18;

and feminism, 3, 38; and Popular
    Front, 135; and Sloan, 19; and
    Union Square demonstrations, 122
Social realism: and American Scene,
    xxxii; and Fourteenth Street School,
    xxxii, 131, 134; and Morris
    Kantor, 125; and Miller, 161, 167;
    and Soyer, 230
Society for Modern Artists, 121, 295
Soyer, Abraham (Soyer's father): and
    immigration, 64; as scholar-teacher,
    63, 333n.88
Soyer, Bella (Soyer's mother): and
    immigration, 64, 333n.88
Soyer, Fannie (Soyer's sister), 63, 67,
    68, 334n.101
Soyer, Isaac (Soyer's brother), 63;
    Office Girls, **307,** 308
Soyer, Moses (Soyer's twin brother),
    63–66
Soyer, Raphael, 1, 40, 47, 62–70;
    artistic education of, 63–66, 72,
    333n.90; and *The Arts*, 73;
    biographical evidence, 41–42; and
    Alexander Brook, 74; critical
    reception of, 235, 262–263, 264–
    266, 360n.4, 367n.66; early life,
    63–65; exhibitions and galleries,
    67, 69–70; and family, 63–64, 68;
    and Fourteenth Street realism, 75,
    79–81, 83; and Fourteenth Street
    School artists, 74; and immigrant
    experience, 63–66, 68–69; and
    influence of Degas, 71, 80, 235,
    236, 237, 361n.10; and influence of
    twin, Moses, 65–66; and John Reed
    Club activities, 67–69, 74, 120,
    127; and Rebecca Letz, 67–68, 70;
    on Marsh, 54–55; and Miller, 66,
    334n.94; and models, 69, 240, 247,
    361n.14; and new womanhood,
    67–68; personality of, 64–66,
    334n.95; pictorial strategies, 182,
    224–228, 230, 240–241, 263–264,
    271–272, 287; and politics, 121,